Electronic Data Processing
An Introduction

ELECTRONIC DATA PROCESSING

An Introduction

by **E. WAINRIGHT MARTIN, JR.**
Professor of Business Administration
School of Business, Indiana University

1961

RICHARD D. IRWIN, INC.
HOMEWOOD, ILLINOIS

First Printing, April, 1961
Second Printing, November, 1961
Third Printing, September, 1962
Fourth Printing, January, 1963

Library of Congress Catalogue Card No. 61–8832

PRINTED IN THE UNITED STATES OF AMERICA

To my "book widow,"
CHARLENE

Preface

THIS book is based upon the fundamental premise that an organization's data-processing system is of crucial importance to the attainment of effective management control. The electronic computer potentially has a revolutionary impact upon data-processing systems, and thus upon management control, but the full realization of this potential cannot be attained without widespread management understanding of the opportunities and problems associated with the use of this equipment.

Written specifically as a textbook for an introductory course in electronic data processing, this book was designed for the mature student (advanced undergraduate or MBA), but it does not presuppose any prior background in mechanized data processing or any mathematics beyond an ability to manipulate positive and negative decimal numbers. These materials were developed and tested through five years' experience in teaching courses with the following basic objectives:

1. To provide the general manager, who does not expect to specialize in computer technology, with an understanding of the capabilities and limitations of the electronic computer and of the management considerations involved in its use.
2. To provide an introduction to this subject to those who aspire to specialize in the design of data-processing systems.

In the attainment of the above objectives, I have attempted to provide a reasonable compromise between technical material and discussions of general implications, with major emphasis upon the concepts involved, but with enough specific material included to make the concepts meaningful. This compromise has been motivated by my feeling that general management typically suffers from too superficial a knowledge of the characteristics of electronic data-processing equipment, while on the other hand data-processing specialists are frequently handicapped by lack of understanding of the basic objectives of data processing and of the management problems involved in the use of computers. Since the field of electronic data processing is in its infancy, I do not pretend to provide answers to all of the problems, but instead attempt to bring up the pertinent questions.

Although the answers appear to change from time to time, the problems, like death and taxes, will always be with us.

This book is organized as follows: The over-all impact of the computer upon our society is presented in Chapter 1. Chapter 2 is devoted to the basic objectives of data processing, to an introduction to the systems approach, and to a breakdown of data processing into its elementary components. Chapters 3 and 4 present a concise introduction to the functions of punched card machines, the principles upon which they operate, and their use in data processing. The development of mechanized procedures are introduced, and the data recording and processing rigor required for mechanized data processing are illustrated.

It is my belief that even the general manager, although he may never have to write a program for a computer, needs to have a brief experience with computer programming in order to understand what computers can and cannot do, and (more importantly) what is involved in using them. Thus, Chapters 5–7 are devoted to the characteristics of the stored program and to basic programming techniques.

The preparation of a workable computer program involves much more than the mere writing of a series of program steps. This over-all process, starting with the definition of the problem and concluding with conversion of processing from the previous system to the computer, is discussed in Chapter 8. The interrelationships between the steps in this process, and their consequences, are emphasized. Chapter 9 provides some illustrations of uses of intermediate computers, with emphasis upon the creative aspects of using such equipment for data processing.

Chapters 10–12 discuss magnetic tape and random access files and their use, and Chapter 13 provides a summary of the general characteristics of the various types of equipment.

Systems analysis and design, which has been introduced in Chapters 2 and 8, is the subject of more concentrated discussion in Chapter 14, where basic techniques are explored and the systems approach is again emphasized.

Chapters 15–17 are concerned with the management considerations associated with electronic data processing. Chapter 15 discusses the human relations, organizational, administrative, and economic problems involved in installing electronic data-processing machines. Chapter 16 is concerned with the organization and staffing of a centralized data-processing facility. The final chapter explores the reasons for failure in the use of electronic data-processing equipment and the relationships between computers, management science, and data processing. Chapter 17 concludes with a discussion of the impact of the computer and associated information technology upon the individual manager.

To provide student motivation and realistic complexity, an actual machine is used as an illustration in Chapters 6 and 7. Since the basic ideas are common to most machines, many different ones could have been used for this purpose. The IBM 650 was chosen because of its widespread availability, with over 1,500 in use and with over 70 machines on college and university campuses. Thus, a 650 is likely to be available for class demonstrations and laboratory exercises. In my classes I have included a demonstration of the computer and punched card equipment at the beginning of Chapter 6. My students are also divided into small groups and encouraged to write a program for Exercise 7.13, punch loading cards, debug, and run the program under supervision of a graduate assistant. Although helpful, a 650 is by no means essential in this course, for 650 simulators are available for many other machines, and short programming exercises can easily be checked by the instructor or an assistant.

I am deeply indebted to so many for help in preparing this book that it is impossible to mention everyone here. However, I would like to express special appreciation to the IBM Corporation in whose employment I received my first training and experience with computers. So much of the philosophy expressed herein and so many of the illustrations included are derived from my IBM background and experience, as well as from IBM publications, that it is impossible for me to give detailed credit for this material. However, I am particularly indebted to IBM for Exercise 7.13, and the illustrations in Chapters 4, 8, 9, 11, and 12. I am also indebted to the Data Processing Department of the U.S. Army Adjutant General's School, Fort Benjamin Harrison and to RCA for materials on the grid chart and associated techniques in Chapter 14, to Robert L. Johnson for the illustration on page 318–19, and to the editor of *Business Horizons* for permission to reproduce material used in Chapters 1, 15, and 17. I would also like to express my appreciation to R. L. Ackoff as the source of some of the ideas concerning operations research and information flows expressed in Chapters 2 and 17.

Among the many others who read, used, and commented upon the various versions of the manuscript the following were especially helpful: D. R. Mason (especially Chapter 16), Van B. Thompson (especially Chapters 3 and 4), Loren E. Waltz (Chapter 14), Max H. Fitz (Chapter 14), Jack R. Smith (Chapter 12), Norman F. Kallaus, Robert B. Fetter, and my father, E. W. Martin, Sr. Untold classes of students also contributed significantly by comments, criticisms, questions, and suggestions that have served to improve these materials. My gratitude must be expressed to Mrs. Margaret A. Price and Mrs. Helen Gonce who typed and retyped these materials with competence and good humor.

Research that contributed significantly to the development of this book was supported by the Indiana University School of Business, its Alumni and friends, and the Ford Foundation. Finally, I would like to express my appreciation to the Indiana University School of Business for encouragement and for cheerfully providing the secretarial and duplicating services that enabled me to test the various versions of these materials in my classes.

E. W. MARTIN, JR.

Bloomington, Indiana
February, 1961

Table of Contents

CHAPTER   PAGE

1. THE IMPACT OF THE ELECTRONIC COMPUTER   1

History. Computers and Office Automation. Computers in Science. Computers in Engineering. Computers and Automatic Control. Computers and Management Science. Speculations Concerning the Future. Conclusion.

2. FUNDAMENTALS OF DATA PROCESSING   16

Why Data Processing? Servomechanism Concept of Control. The Systems Approach. Patterns of Information Flow. Basic Terminology. Recording. Data Transmission. Manipulation. Report Preparation. Summary.

3. PUNCHED CARD DATA PROCESSING   32

The Punched Card. Information Representation. What the Punched Card Does. Card Format. Fields. Card Design. Recording Methods. Key Punching. Prepunching. Mark Sensing. Other Punching Methods. Verification. Key Verification. Visual Verification. Batch Totals. Self-Checking Numbers. Sorting. Auxiliary Equipment. Reproducing. Gang Punching. Interpreting. The Collator. Merging. Matching. Match-Merging. The Accounting Machine. Group Control. Detail Printing and Group Printing. Counters. Summary Punching. Selectors. Forms Control. The Calculator. Example. The Punched Card Installation. Summary.

4. A PUNCHED CARD APPLICATION   67

Payroll Application. Card Forms. Flow Charting. Payroll Procedure. Time and Cost Determination. Scheduling. Exercise.

5. BASIC CONCEPTS OF ELECTRONIC COMPUTERS   85

Input. Memory. Files. Arithmetic. Output. Control. The Stored Program. Yes-or-No Decisions. Instruction Modification. Universality. Summary.

6. AN INTERMEDIATE COMPUTER—PART I   99

Memory Drum. Input-Output. Representation of Information. Instruction Format. Internal Information Flow. Programming. Add, Subtract, and Store Operations. Input and Output Instructions. Multiplication and Shifting. Division.

7. AN INTERMEDIATE COMPUTER—PART II 136

Branching. Programming Group Control. Overflow Detection. Control Words. Instruction Modification. Looping. Instruction Synthesis. Table Look-up. Index Registers. Switches. Loading the Program.

8. DEVELOPMENT OF A COMPUTER PROCESSING SYSTEM 166

Defining the Problem. Devise Procedure. Block Diagrams. Coding. Automatic Programming. Library Subroutines. Interpretive Routines. Compilers. Efficiency of Automatic Programming. Debugging. Conversion. Relation-

xi

CHAPTER   PAGE

ships between the Steps. Organization and Personnel. Cost Estimation. Control of Accuracy. Summary.

9. APPLICATIONS OF MAGNETIC DRUM MACHINES 199

Parts Requirement Planning. Automobile Insurance Rate Checking and Coding. Public Utility Billing. Overhead Cost Distribution. Summary.

10. LARGE ELECTRONIC DATA-PROCESSING MACHINES 221

Alpha-Numeric. Various Representations of Information. Magnetic Core Memory. Variable Word Length. Order Structure. Magnetic Tapes. Magnetic Tape Instructions. End-of-File Procedures. Error Detection. Tape Handling and Control. Overlapping Operations. Other Input-Output Equipment. On-Line and Off-Line Operation. Summary.

11. PROCESSING MAGNETIC TAPE FILES 246

Sorting Magnetic Tape. A Hypothetical Machine. Costs and Time for Sorting. Generalized Sort Routines. Inventory Control, Accounts Receivable, and Billing Application. Procedure. Time Estimation. Electronic Data Processing in Life Insurance Companies. Activity Ratio. Multiprogramming. Some Characteristics of Batch Processing. Summary.

12. RANDOM ACCESS FILES 276

Large Magnetic Drums. Remington Rand File Computer. Channel Search. Cost versus Access Speed. Movable Read-Write Heads. Magnetic Disk Memory. RAMAC. Magnetic Disk Storage for the IBM 650. Removable Magnetic Disks. Magnetic Tape Bins. Wholesale Grocery Application. Consolidated Manufacturing Control Operations. The Addressing Problem. Control of Accuracy. Summary.

13. CLASSIFICATION OF COMPUTERS 300

Scientific Computers versus Electronic Data-Processing Machines. Binary Notation. Automatic Floating Decimal Point. Index Registers. Special Purpose versus General Purpose. Airline Reservations. Processing Checks. Classification of Computers. Desk-Size Computers. Small Data-Processing Machines. Magnetic Tape File Processors. Random Access File Processors. Large-Scale Data-Processing Machines. High-Speed Computers. Summary.

14. SYSTEMS ANALYSIS AND DESIGN 312

Defining the Present System. The Total Systems Concept. The Grid Chart. Flow Charting. Obtaining the Information. Improving the Results of the System. Design of an Improved System. Relationships between Systems Objectives, Systems Design, and Data-Processing Equipment. Equipment Selection. Summary.

15. PROBLEMS INVOLVED IN INTRODUCING A COMPUTER 334

Human Problems. Effect on Individuals. Morale Problems. Organizational Problems. Location of Computer. Effects on Decentralized Management. Installation and Conversion Problems. The Decision to Buy. Physical Problems. Conversion Problems. Pattern of Costs. Summary.

16. THE DATA-PROCESSING ORGANIZATION 362

Organization of the Data-Processing Function. Manager of Data Processing. The Data-Processing Policy Committee. Systems and Procedures. Manager

CHAPTER   PAGE

of Centralized Data Processing. Systems Development and Programming. Organization of Systems Development and Programming. Program Maintenance. Machine Procedures. Data-Processing Operations. Data Origination and Control. Input Preparation. Punched Card Operations. Computer Operations. Tape Librarian. Cost Accounting. Salary Ranges.

17. MANAGEMENT RESPONSIBILITY TOWARD INFORMATION TECHNOLOGY 377

Piecemeal Approach. Lack of Objectives. Quality of People Required. Management Participation. Operations Research. Decision Problems. Mathematical Models. Simulation. Monte Carlo Technique. Advantages of Quantitative Approach. Limitations of Operations Research. The Computer's Contributions to Operations Research. Contributions of Operations Research to Data Processing. Effect on Management.

APPENDIX

A. OPERATING THE 650 402

B. TRACING ROUTINES 408

C. BINARY NOTATION AND ARITHMETIC 411

D. FLOATING DECIMAL REPRESENTATION 416

INDEX 419

CHAPTER **1** ▪ The Impact of the Electronic
Computer

FEW DEVELOPMENTS of our age have captured the imagination of the public as has the electronic computer. Almost everyone has marveled at the exploits of these so-called "giant brains" which have been reported in the newspapers and magazines and on our television screens. Much of this publicity is inaccurate and misleading, but behind the publicity is a series of accomplishments and promises of future accomplishment which indicate that the electronic computer is one of the most important developments of this century.

In testimony before a congressional subcommittee on automation, Ralph J. Cordiner, then president of the General Electric Company, expressed his faith in the future of the electronic computer in the following words:

When the history of our age is written, I think it will record three profoundly important technological developments:

Nuclear energy, which tremendously increases the amount of *energy* available to do the world's work;

Automation, which greatly increases man's ability to use *tools;*

And *computers,* which multiply man's ability to do *mental* work.

Some of our engineers believe that of these three, the computer will bring the greatest benefit to man.[1]

Although the major emphasis of this book lies in the area of the use of the electronic computer for business data processing, this is but one of the areas in which the impact of the computer is being felt upon our society. Since there is a tendency among businessmen to emphasize the application of the computers in the office, to the virtual exclusion of the other areas to which they have significantly contributed, this chapter will be devoted to an attempt to present

---

[1] Quoted from testimony of Ralph J. Cordiner before the Subcommittee on Economic Stabilization of the Joint Committee on the Economic Report, October 26, 1955, p. 444 of the printed record.

an over-all view of the influence which the computer is exerting upon our society.

History

The first large-scale electronic computer was the Eniac, which was completed in 1946 by the Moore School of Electrical Engineering at the University of Pennsylvania. This machine was designed primarily to perform the calculations required in the preparation of ballistics tables. Although composed of some 18,000 tubes, by modern standards the Eniac had very little flexibility, was slow, and was quite unreliable, but it was a significant step forward in computing ability and demonstrated conclusively that the electron could be harnessed to compute.

During the next few years, computers were built at various government laboratories and universities. These computers were usually "one-of-a-kind" machines, because once they had been built, the designers learned so much from their experience that they would never build another one exactly the same. However, around 1953, the Remington Rand Univac and the IBM 701 became available on a production-line basis, and dependable large-scale computers were a commercial reality. Starting from the few machines in existence in 1953, the use of computers has grown by leaps and bounds. Late in 1957, there were around 200 large-scale electronic computers and around 600 small- and intermediate-sized machines in use in the United States. By late 1959, this had grown to an estimated 400 large-scale computer systems and over 2,000 small- and intermediate-sized machines.

Although they started slower than the United States, other countries have also made rapid strides in the use of computers. In mid-1959, it was reported that about 100 electronic computers were in use in Britain alone, and the Russians were known to be utilizing some of the most powerful computing machines in existence.[2]

This rapid growth is not explained by any single use of computers —they have been widely used in both scientific computation and business data processing, they show great future promise in the area of automatic control, and they are practically indispensable to our national defense and in space technology.

Computers and Office Automation

One of the major objectives of office automation is the reduction of clerical costs. Although attempts at cost reduction have often fallen

---

[2] Reported in *Datamation*, March–April, 1959, p. 30.

short of the goal, there have been some successes, mainly in situations involving extremely large volume. For example, the Ford Motor Company is using a large electronic computer to save several hundred thousand dollars a year in the cost of preparing their 100,000-man payroll in the Detroit area.

Among the largest "paper-work" industries is life insurance, where large amounts of information must be maintained on each policy in force. Franklin Life, John Hancock, Prudential, National Life, Metropolitan Life, and Pacific Mutual are among the life insurance companies that have installed large electronic computers for such functions as premium billing, commission accounting, dividend calculations, actuarial calculations, calculations of reserves, and so on. It is reported that one insurance company replaced 113 people and punched-card equipment costing around $216,000 per year with a large-scale computer.[3] Although they probably have over $2 million invested in the computer and the various costs of getting started, they should be saving several hundred thousand dollars per year above the cost of amortizing this initial investment.

However, the possible increase in the operative efficiency of an organization made possible by the use of "higher-quality" information provides an even larger potential savings than that of increased clerical productivity. For optimal control of a complex industrial organization, management should have current information. If an electronic computer can be used to predict accurately the total electoral vote in an election on the basis of a few early returns, why cannot similar computers and techniques be used to predict the "votes" of customers for certain products?[4]

Of course, it is much easier to talk abstractly about the need for "higher-quality" information than it is to provide it, even if an electronic data-processing machine is available. Perhaps the most consistently valuable application of computers in the manufacturing industries has been in the area of material control. In a typical situation, the production schedule in terms of end items is broken down to obtain a schedule (taking into account lead time) of parts and materials required. By maintaining up-to-date inventory infor-

[3] K. G. Van Auken, Jr., "The Introduction of an Electronic Computer in a Large Insurance Company," *Automation and Technological Change* (Hearings before the Subcommittee on the Economic Stabilization of the Joint Committee on the Economic Report, 84th Cong., 1st sess.) (Washington, D.C.: 1955), pp. 290–300.

[4] On November 4, 1952, a Univac was used by CBS-TV to predict the outcome of the presidential election. At 8:30 P.M., on the basis of early returns from only 27 states (3.4 million votes out of an expected 60.0 million votes), the machine predicted the outcome within four electoral votes. See John Lear, "Can a Mechanical Brain Replace You?" *Colliers,* April 4, 1953, p. 59.

mation available to the machine, it is possible to detect future shortages and even to write shop orders or vendor releases for the required parts and materials. The speed with which a computer can
determine the effects of a schedule change can provide a monetary
saving by permitting lower inventory levels; expediting and general
confusion have often been spectacularly reduced. Many of the organizations that have the material-control situation well in hand are
considering the use of the machines in production control, an area of
vast and virtually untouched potential.

Incidentally, it seems inevitable that as these machines become
used more widely, and as many of the clerical functions of the controller's department are mechanized, the accountant will have an
opportunity (or even a responsibility) to produce all of the internal information necessary for management to control the organization—rather than only the necessary financial information. The
accountant of the future should be capable of determining what
information is required and should be able to design the data-
processing system to produce this information in the desired form
at the proper time.

Computers in Science

Computers were originally developed by scientists and engineers
to aid in the solution of problems involving large amounts of computation. The classic scientific method consists of:

1. Observation of a situation under study.
2. Formation of a hypothesis to explain what was observed.
3. Further observation and experimentation to check the hypothesis.
4. Modification of the hypothesis.
5. Further observation and experimentation—and so on ad infinitum.

The hypotheses frequently are mathematical statements expressing relationships between observable variables. These mathematical
statements are used for prediction, and the predictions are compared with the results of the hypothesis. This process of using mathematical statements for prediction often involves a tremendous
amount of calculation.

For example, let us consider astronomy. In astronomy, you cannot experiment; you can only observe. The motions of the various
planets, comets, and stars can be represented by mathematical
equations. The validity of the equations can be determined only by
calculating future positions of these bodies based upon these equations, and verifying (or failing to verify) these predictions on the

basis of observations. Before the development of the electronic computer, many astronomers spent the major portion of their working years slaving away over hand calculators making these computations. Today, they can concern themselves with formulating better equations, devising equipment for obtaining more precise observations, and developing more efficient methods for solution of the equations.

Similar types of problems occur in nuclear physics, and in chemistry in the area of molecular structure. In the study of our atmosphere and its weather, extremely complicated equations involving large numbers of variables arise; great strides have been made in the understanding of weather since the development of the electronic computer. As a matter of fact, the late John von Neumann predicted that within our lifetimes we may learn enough about weather to actually control our climate.[5]

In many areas of scientific research, the availability of an electronic computer is an absolute necessity if a scientist wishes to pursue his interests with the most promising techniques. In certain areas of physical chemistry, for example, progress in techniques of computing eigenvalues of matrices immediately produces significant progress in the size of molecule that can be investigated. Thus, major universities are providing computers for the use of their faculty and graduate students, just as they provide laboratory equipment, so that scientists can effectively pursue their research.

Computers in Engineering

One approach to the design of a product to meet certain specifications is for the engineer to "guess" a first design of the product (based on his past experience), build it, and test the result. If this design is not satisfactory (and the first try usually isn't), he can make some changes, build a new model, and test it. This process then continues until a satisfactory product is obtained. Such an approach is extremely costly in terms of both time and money, and for complex systems (aircraft, guided missiles, and atomic reactors), it is too slow and costly to be practical.

The aircraft industry provides numerous illustrations of the value of the electronic computer in design work. Indeed, it is safe to say that intercontinental ballistic missiles and space rockets could not be designed without the aid of these machines. It is simply not possible to build a multistage rocket without some assurance that it will

---

[5] J. von Neumann, "Can We Survive Technology?" *Fortune,* June, 1955, p. 108.

perform properly. You must know before you build it not only whether or not it will get off the launching pad, but also the thrust it will produce, the path it will follow, the speed it will attain, the fuel consumption it will require, and a host of other factors concerning its performance. Likewise, in the design of a nuclear reactor, you must know before you build it whether it will remain under control or explode.

It is not surprising that computers are desirable or necessary in the design of the fantastically complex mechanisms discussed above. But it may not be so readily apparent that the electronic computer is becoming increasingly important to the engineers who design our automobiles, dishwashers, cameras, air conditioners, and the myriad other products which we use every day. The computer has had such an important influence upon engineering that the better engineering schools have radically altered their curriculums to prepare their graduates to take advantage of the computer's abilities.

Rather than build a physical model of their first design, modern engineers develop sets of equations (mathematical models) that represent the performance of the product. For example, for an electric motor, these equations would involve the shape of the stator, the length of the rotor and the number of poles on it, the number of turns in the winding, the type of iron used and the shape of the magnetic circuit, and similar design parameters. To design a motor with given power and speed characteristics, an engineer would choose a combination of these design parameters. Then, using the equations, he would calculate the power and speed output given by his design. As before, if these characteristics did not meet his requirements, he would vary some of the design parameters and repeat this process. For an electric motor, the calculations involved for one set of parameters would take about two days of the engineer's time using a slide rule. On an electronic computer, these calculations would require but a few seconds.

With an electronic computer available, the engineer might take a slightly different approach. Rather than choosing a set of parameters for just one design and evaluating this design, the engineer would choose parameters for many designs and, finally, compute several hundred designs in one batch. Then he would be in a position to choose the best of these many designs to put into production. Thus, rather than merely obtaining a workable design, there is a good chance that the best possible design would be obtained.

A method for designing transformers has been devised that

eliminates the engineer completely.[6] In this scheme, the computer is given the performance figures that the design must meet, and the computer simulates the method that the engineer might use as follows: The electronic computer chooses a set of design parameters, goes through the calculations to evaluate that design, and compares it with the specifications. If it does not meet these specifications, the machine decides which parameters to change and how much to change them. Then it repeats the process over and over until it achieves a satisfactory design.

In order to use a computer in this way, it was necessary to analyze the thinking process followed by an engineer when designing transformers so that a computational procedure could be devised to: (1) choose the starting design on the basis of the performance specifications required; and (2) decide which design parameter to change and how much to change it when the trial design does not meet specifications.

With a moderately fast electronic computer, the process of designing a transformer requires about 20 seconds. Not only does this release the engineer for more creative work, but it also results in more efficient transformer designs from the viewpoint of economics. The computer can be forced to consider cost whenever it must make a design decision, and thus produce a design that is likely to be less costly than that produced by an engineer, who only considers costs when he feels like it. For example, the computer can be programmed to devise its designs from standardized parts so that production economies can be realized, while the engineer is often tempted to design something new just to feel creative.

Computers and Automatic Control

The basic concept of automatic control (or the servomechanism) is that of the feedback loop (see Figure 2–1, p. 19), in which the results of the operations under control are observed and compared with the standard or planned results. If the results deviate from plans, the proper controls must be changed by the correct amount in order to bring the operations back to standard. Today, most such control loops involve one or more humans making the decisions; but, in the future, the computer may take over the control of entire factories in this manner, especially in the processing industries such as petroleum and chemicals.

_____
[6] Marshall Middleton, Jr., "Product Design by Digital Computers," *Westinghouse Engineer*, March, 1956, pp. 39–43.

Among the first computer-controlled factories was the Texaco Polymerization Plant at Port Arthur, Texas, where a Thompson Ramo Wooldridge Corporation R/W 300 special-purpose computer receives information from about 110 sources and controls 16 flows, pressures, and temperatures.[7] The advantage of automatic control is not derived from manpower savings, since this plant was already instrumented so that it could be operated by a three-man crew. However, because of the complexity of the process being controlled, humans are able to achieve only about 85 to 87% efficiency, while the computer should improve on this by about 6%, in addition to significantly reducing the amount of catalyst required.

Among the problems that must be solved in order to use a digital computer for control purposes is that of converting continuous physical quantities (such as voltage, length, rotation of a shaft, and so on) into discrete numbers that the machine can use. This "digitizing" problem has been solved, and there are several installations of computers in wind tunnels where data from several hundred gauges (indicating temperature, wind velocities, pressures, and so on) are read directly into a computer, and this information is analyzed and converted to obtain the performance of the aircraft or engine under test. This information is presented to the test engineer while the test is in progress so that he can control the future course of the test on the basis of these results.

The reverse of this problem occurs at the other end of the control loop, where we must convert numbers into physical characteristics (voltage, motion of a shaft, and so on) that will control the operations involved. Examples of the solution of this phase of the problem are the several "numerically controlled milling machines" which produce complex parts, without human intervention, from a series of numbers representing the mathematical co-ordinates of the surfaces involved.[8]

Of course, the major difficulties in the control loop lie in the area of decision: After determining that the operations are deviating from the standard, what action must be taken in order to correct the observed deviations? The more complex the system being controlled, the more difficult this question becomes, and the more desirable a powerful computer appears.

By far the most ambitious automatic control system in existence

---

[7] Reported in "Computer Runs Refinery Unit for Texaco," *Business Week,* April 4, 1959, pp. 44–54.

[8] "Making a Machine Run Itself," *Business Week,* March 9, 1957, pp. 183–87.

is the SAGE air defense system.[9] The heart of this system is an extremely large electronic computer into which is fed flight plan information, reports from the ground observer corps, and weather data. By means of a giant communication network, warning radar is tied directly into the computer. When an aircraft is detected, its position is screened against the stored flight plans to determine whether or not it is a potential enemy. If it is not accounted for as friendly, the machine presents its position, direction, and speed pictorially on a cathode-ray tube map in front of the sector commander. In addition, the computer suggests a distribution of available forces to meet all of the threats. However, the human commander decides on the allocation of forces (he may accept the computer's recommendations or may modify them in any way that he sees fit) and indicates this distribution to the computer. At this point, the computer again takes over and guides the interceptors or anticraft missiles to their designated targets.

This entire system is essentially an automatic control loop in which a human being has a veto power. However, it should be noted that the subprocess of guiding the interceptors to their targets involves a closed feedback loop, since deviations in the course of the interceptors must be detected and corrected, and the interceptor must react to evasive action by the enemy. Furthermore, it is obvious that if an attack comes, the situation facing the sector commander may be so complex and the time pressure so intense that he will be unable to do anything but accept the computer's suggestion.

Unfortunately, the SAGE system was obsolete before it was fully installed, for it was designed to cope with manned aircraft flying at about the speed of sound, while it is likely to be faced with intercontinental ballistic missiles for which there are no adequate warning radar or defense weapons. However, without the experience in the problems of automatic control gained through SAGE, we would have scant hope of developing defense systems to cope with missiles, so what we have learned has probably been worth the cost.

There has been considerable discussion in the press of the growing hazards of air travel due to our lack of an adequate air-traffic control system. Our already-inadequate system is faced with growing congestion and faster and faster airplanes. It seems inevitable that an electronic air-traffic control system similar to SAGE will be re-

---

[9] H. T. Rowe, "The IBM Computer AN/FSQ-7 and the Electronic Air Defense System SAGE," *Computers and Automation*, September, 1956, p. 6.

quired long before such a system can be designed and installed. Although electronic computers are being used to assist in the data processing involved in air-traffic control, an adequate and integrated system is still far from a reality.

Likewise, it is apparent that our present planes are approaching the speed at which human reactions are too slow to control them. And, as we explore space in rockets, it is likely that the direct guidance will be in the hands of computers, with the humans along to make policy decisions and maintain the equipment.

Computers and Management Science

During the past few years, a great deal of effort has been applied in the area of "operations research" or "management science" in order to develop a more satisfactory understanding of some of the complex decision problems facing management. The simultaneous development of computers has interacted quite fortuitously with these efforts, for the mathematicians and scientists involved have developed some powerful quantitative techniques that often require computers for their application, while, at the same time, the computers have been used with some success in the process of the research itself. Although the purpose of this research is to understand and solve problems rather than to find uses for computers, some of the most significant applications of computers have been developed in organizations with active operations research programs.

Some of the mathematical models that have been developed involve tremendous amounts of computation to obtain a solution. In this respect, the solution of these problems resembles the solution of scientific and engineering problems much more than it does clerical data-processing operations. One of the best known of these techniques is linear programming, which has been used to decide where to locate new plants, how to ship a product from plants to warehouses, and which bid to accept in a complex situation. Linear programming has also been used in scheduling refinery production in order to obtain the most profitable mixture of output products, given the cost of the input materials, the characteristics of the refinery involved, and the prices to be obtained from the various output products.

At least one company has developed a mathematical and logical model to represent the internal cost structure of a major division. By using an electronic computer, the company can manipulate this model to forecast a complete operating budget based upon product mix, price, and marketing program. By examining several alternative combinations of these variables, management is able to reduce the area of uncertainty involved in making these extremely important and complicated decisions.

Along similar lines, many universities are utilizing a "war games" approach in the training of executives to become more efficient decision makers.[10] In this approach, teams of executives compete with each other in the operation of a hypothetical business by making such decisions as determining production levels, price, product research effort, and marketing expenditures for the coming quarter. On the basis of these decisions, a resulting balance sheet and income statement for each team is produced on an electronic computer (or by hand calculation). Then the same decisions must be made again for the next quarter of operations, and the computer produces the results for these decisions. Thus, in a few hours, the men are able to gain experience representing several years of actual operation of a business, and the results of the decisions are available while the decision itself is still fresh in the minds of the decision makers.

The relationships between computers and management science will be discussed at greater length in Chapter 17.

Speculations Concerning the Future

During the past few years, development work has been done by scientists toward the use of the electronic computer in quite revolutionary areas. Although these things are not practical at the present, there are strong indications that most of them will be realities within our lifetimes.

One of the most challenging of these problems is that of language translation. Although there are many details that remain to be solved, the feasibility of the use of an electronic computer to translate from one language to another was demonstrated in January, 1954, when an IBM 701 was used to translate several paragraphs from Russian into English. Although this demonstration involved a vocabulary of only around 250 words, and employed only about 8 of the estimated 90 necessary grammatical rules, it did produce a sensible output that was in proper word order and that chose between the meaning of words on the basis of context. Incidentally, shortly after this, the Russians demonstrated on one of their large-scale computers the practicality of translating from English into Russian. Needless to

---

[10] E. W. Martin, "Teaching Executives via Simulation," *Business Horizons,* Vol. 2. No. 2, pp. 100–109.

say, language scientists are devoting a lot of work to the theoretical developments that will make automatic translation of languages feasible.

The problem of retrieval of information from libraries is also receiving extensive study. Who knows how much unnecessary research work is being done today because the worker is not familiar with the results that have been obtained by others? Searching a library is a difficult problem because of the lack of an adequate abstracting system with which to extract the meaningful content from the written material and classify it for reference purposes. Also, it is extremely difficult to specify exactly the information for which you are searching. If the question asked is too specific, the answer may not include all of the available information; if the question is too general, a large percentage of the references in the entire library may completely snow you under. However, as an understanding of these problems is obtained, it may be possible in the future to construct machines that will automatically classify the material in the best libraries in the world and automatically search for the information pertinent to specified problems.

A large-scale scientific computer has been programmed to play an amazingly good game of checkers.[11] To decide on its next move, the machine examines each possible move, evaluates it (looking five moves into the future) and, on the basis of a formula that has been developed, chooses the best of the possible moves. Is this of any practical importance? No. But it does raise an intriguing possibility. Suppose a computer plays 10,000 games of checkers against human opponents. On the basis of this large amount of experience, could it be programmed to change the rules under which it chooses its next move? In other words, can a computer learn?

In answer to this question, a computer program called the "Logic Theorist" has been written that is designed to prove theorems in mathematical logic by simulating the processes that are used by humans in approaching similar problems.[12] Using the Logic Theorist program, a computer was able to discover proofs for 38 of the first 52 theorems in *Principia Mathematica,* which is perhaps the most influential mathematical book of this century.[13] Incidentally, this was

---

[11] "Putting Ideas to Work—Research at IBM," advertisement in *Computers and Automation,* January, 1957, p. 39.

[12] Allen Newell, J. C. Shaw, and Herbert A. Simon, "Elements of a Theory of Human Problem Solving," *Psychological Review,* Vol. 65, No. 3, 1958, pp. 151–66.

[13] A. N. Whitehead and B. Russell, *Principia Mathematica* (2d ed.; Cambridge: Cambridge University Press, 1925) , Vol. I.

no mean performance, since the average, beginning graduate student in mathematics would have some difficulty proving these theorems. It is interesting to note that the Logic Theorist found a proof for one of the theorems that was more elegant and concise than the proof included in the book.

The use of a computer as discussed above, to solve poorly structured problems, is called "heuristic" problem solving, and much research is currently being devoted to this area. Sufficient success is being made in this endeavor to lead to the predictions that within ten years:

1. A digital computer will be the world's chess champion, unless the rules bar it from competition.
2. A digital computer will discover and prove an important new mathematical theorem.
3. A digital computer will write music that will be accepted by critics as possessing considerable aesthetic value.
4. Most theories in psychology will take the form of computer programs or of qualitative statements about the characteristics of computer programs.[14]

The use of a computer for heuristic problem solving depends upon the development of a theory of learning and problem solving. If we reach an understanding of how a human being learns, it may be feasible to develop a machine that can learn. Conversely, as we develop theories concerning how a human learns, we may be able to test these theories by means of a computer, and observe whether or not the theory actually works. Thus, the machines, though they are not themselves in any way brains, may lead us to a more satisfactory understanding of the human brain, and consequently to the development of new machines or new techniques that more closely approach the capabilities of the human brain.

Conclusion

Ignoring the research area of heuristic problem solving, it should be noted that computers do not by themselves solve problems—they only compute. If you know what your problem is, and if you can devise a method by which the problem can be solved by computation, then the electronic computer can be used as a very powerful tool to obtain a solution. But if you do not understand the problem, or if you cannot devise a method to solve it using arithmetic, then any

[14] H. A. Simon and A. Newell, "Heuristic Problem Solving: The Next Advance in Operations Research," *Operations Research Journal*, January–February, 1958.

electronic computer is just so much excess baggage. Remember that each achievement of a so-called "giant brain" is actually the product of some man or group of men who devised the method that was utilized.

Thus, we can see that the future impact of the electronic computer is restricted primarily by the limitations of our knowledge of ourselves and our environment. Surely if we can gain an understanding of problems of the complexity of language translation and of the processes of learning, then we can begin to gain an understanding of the difficult problems that face the executive. But none of these problems will solve themselves—someone must solve each of them!

Most large manufacturing firms have found that money spent on product research and development pays off manyfold. Some leading executives are beginning to realize that research on management problems can pay off in the same way. First we must have understanding, and then we can begin to utilize efficiently the capabilities of the electronic computer.

Assuming that we can learn to use it efficiently, what is the impact of the electronic computer? The major impact is on productivity: productivity of the scientist, the engineer, the production worker, the office worker, and the manager.

The future course of our material progress depends to a considerable extent on the productivity of our scientists and engineers. Any increase in the amount of effective work that a creative scientist or engineer can accomplish in a lifetime causes a corresponding increase in the productivity of our production-line workers, for many such productivity increases are the result of the design of better products or of more efficient machinery for production.

During recent times, the productivity of the office worker, and consequently his standard of living, has lagged significantly behind that of the production worker. The advent of the electronic computer, however, should give the clerical worker the tools with which to compete effectively with the production worker who has had the benefit of increasingly powerful machinery over a period of years.

Among the most important productivity gains are those of management, for the productivity of management determines the efficiency with which a business organization operates. This efficiency is often measured in dollars of profit or in return on investment, but it may also result in a better quality product for the same price or in the same product at a reduced price. Thus, the productivity of management has a profound influence upon the course of our economy.

The operation of a modern business organization is extremely complex, and no one knows how efficiently we are presently operating as compared with the possible optimum. However, many authorities agree that, over a period of time, management productivity will be increased significantly through the use of computers to obtain more effective information for management control, and through the use of advanced mathematical techniques for decision making.

We are presently engaged in a political struggle that will in all probability be decided on the basis of the productivity of capitalism as opposed to that of communism. Thus, the development of the electronic computer may not only influence our future standard of living, but it may help determine the future political situation under which we will live, or (in the extreme case) whether or not our civilization, as we know it, can continue to exist. It is apparent that the electronic computer may be one of the most significant developments of our time.

The remainder of this book is devoted primarily to computers and their use in data processing. However, it is impossible to divorce data processing from science, engineering, automatic control, management science, and the use of the computer in simulating human thinking processes. For, whenever we replace a lowly clerk with a machine, we are attempting to simulate human thought processes, and when we consider providing information for improved management control, we are likely to get involved in the areas of engineering and management science. The potential of the computer is much greater than routine, paperwork mechanization, but its potential will only be attained through better understanding of our problems and the creation of new techniques which use the capabilities of the computer for the solution of these problems.

CHAPTER 2 · Fundamentals of Data Processing

THE AREA of business data processing forms the major subject matter of this book. Although we will not attempt a precise definition of data processing, the term essentially refers to gathering, recording, and manipulation of numbers and alphabetical symbols that are necessary for the proper functioning of a modern business organization. During the past few years, we have witnessed an astounding growth in the size and complexity of business and government organizations which has been accompanied by an even more fantastic growth in the amount of "paper work" processing that has been required. This seemingly ever-growing burden of nonproductive paper work has caused grave concern, and has led management to a growing awareness of the importance of data processing.

Under these circumstances, it is not surprising that the development of the electronic computer was hailed with enthusiasm by those who could envision its potential in the area of data processing. After several years of experience, it is apparent that much of this potential still exists, for, as yet, the computer has not stemmed the tide of paper work except in isolated instances. One of the major reasons for the lack of spectacular results is our lack of understanding of data processing itself.

It is widely accepted that the computers have progressed far beyond our ability to effectively utilize them. This is not intended to imply that the machines are by any means perfect or that they are even suitable to be used in all circumstances or that there will not be fantastic improvements in the machines themselves during the next few years. This statement is merely a reflection of our appalling lack of knowledge concerning the problems of data processing and of the fact that our knowledge of the capabilities of the computers and the techniques necessary for their use has grown rather slowly. Thus,

16

it is important that we consider data processing itself, and attempt to analyze why it is necessary to perform data processing.

Why Data Processing?

Although it should be unnecessary to say it, perhaps the most important fundamental is that data processing is not an end in itself. Data processing is a means to an end, and unless the results of the processing are used to obtain something of value, the data processing itself is valueless. *We should not process data just to process data.*

Why, then, do we process data? Consider the following characteristics of an organization:

a) An organization is a social group, which implies that it consists of people and that there is potential intercommunication.
b) There is a collective objective of this group.
c) There is a functional division of the labor involved in attaining the objective.

The concept of a functional division of labor (or specialization) to achieve a group objective implies that there must be co-ordination or control of these individual efforts in order to attain the group objective. This co-ordination is one of the major functions of management. Co-ordination also implies communication, for the co-ordinator must be aware of the activity of the individuals involved.

Granting that communication is necessary to control an organization, the question arises: Is communication sufficient? Communication is the transmission of information (facts) from one place to another. Although, in our American civilization, we tend to glorify facts, we must always remember that, without a frame of reference, "facts" are merely random noise. For example, it is a fact that you are reading this piece of paper. However, depending on your frame of reference, this fact has many different meanings. To a savage who has no knowledge of reading, this fact is pure foolishness or profound magic, while to the physicist, this fact is related to the reflection and transmission properties of light. To the physiologist, this fact is associated with the transmission of impulses along nerve pathways and the "thought" processes which translate these impulses. To the author, this fact means that, perhaps, someone is gaining an understanding of an interesting subject.

It may at first appear to be obvious that the more information everyone has and the more freely various individuals in an organization can communicate with one another, the more effectively they can work together to achieve their common goal. Thus, we might obtain the best results by using an intercom system (like that used in World War II bombers) to tie everyone in the organization together and make all information available to everyone. Upon reflection, however, it becomes apparent that, as the organization grows larger, this unlimited communication becomes unwieldy and individuals begin to interfere with each other. Furthermore, experiments have shown that even small groups can operate more effectively when their communication channels are limited and, therefore, structured.[1]

Moreover, in the complex situation presented by most modern organizations, it is often necessary to take a "macroscopic" rather than a "microscopic" attitude toward facts. For example, although it may be of little significance that among the thousands of sales during a given day one of them is for a blue dress, the fact that we have sold 1,000 blue dresses as opposed to 150 pink dresses during a given period of time may be of great significance. The thousands and thousands of individual occurences are often quite meaningless until they are classified and summarized.

Thus, it is apparent that effective co-ordination of an organization involving functional division of labor requires data-processing functions other than pure communication in order to: (1) provide a frame of reference, (2) select the information to be presented to different individuals, and (3) present information in summarized form. Incidentally, the above represent only a few of the reasons why data processing is required.

Servomechanism Concept of Control

Coincident with the development of the electronic computer a theory of control has been created. Since one of the major purposes of management is to provide the control that enables an organization to achieve its goals, and since data processing and control are closely related, we will consider a simple representation of this servomechanism concept of control.

In the first place, the basic concept of control is applicable whether we are considering control of a living organism, a group of organisms, man-machine systems (such as a car and driver), or automatically controlled machines. In the diagram of Figure 2–1, the block labeled "operations" represents that thing (or things) which is to be

---

[1] For example, see Harold Guetekow and Herbert Simon, "The Impact of Certain Communication Nets in Task Oriented Groups," *Management Science*, Vol. 1, No. 3–4 (April–July, 1955) , pp. 233–50.

controlled. The basis for control is information concerning the operations that is introduced into the control loop itself.

Control depends fundamentally upon a comparison between the results attained and the goals (or objectives) sought. There can be no concept of control without goals, objectives, expectations, or plans concerning the outcome that the operations should produce. Incidentally, these objectives must come from outside the control sys-

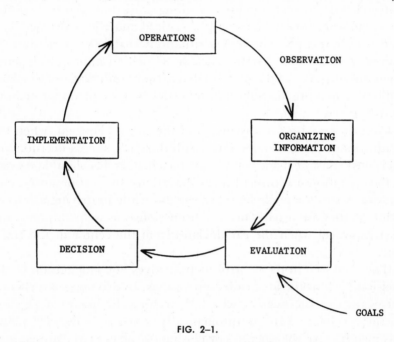

FIG. 2–1.

tem itself. If the desired results are of any complexity, it is usually necessary to organize the raw information obtained from operations and to put it into a form that can conveniently be compared with the desired goals. For example, if specified profits are the goals desired, a considerable amount of manipulation is required to determine the profit obtained based upon income and expense figures. In the usual case, the measurements of the results of operations that can conveniently be obtained are not in a form in which it is convenient to express the goals.

When the results are compared with the goals, there are two possible results; either they are in agreement or they differ. If the results attained meet the goals, then the remainder of the control system is not activated, but when there is a difference, the control process involves further steps. The above discussion provides an introduction to the well-known concept of "management by exception," which involves the gathering and processing of information into a form where it can easily be compared with plans so that only the deviation from plans need be brought to the attention of management. Since a large proportion of the information does not require management consideration, the implementation of the management by the exception concept in the design of data-processing systems not only relieves management of much tedious screening work but also makes sure that significant observations will be noticed and allows management to concentrate upon correcting situations that require action. Of course, it is obvious that the success of such an approach depends upon the adequacy of the plans to detect significant deviations, which implies that more thought must be devoted to planning than is usually given.

Continuing with our discussion of the control concept, when the results of operations do not agree with the goals, then a decision (or decisions) must be made concerning the changes that should be made in the operations to correct for the deviations. In most organizations, these decisions are made by management, while in driving a car, for example, they are usually made subconsciously as we manipulate the steering wheel when the car deviates from the center of the traffic lane.

The final step in the control loop involves implementation of the decision back in the area called operations. In driving a car, this involves turning the steering wheel, depressing the brake, or pressing on the accelerator. In an automatically controlled chemical plant, this may involve the opening or closing of valves or the adjustment of temperatures. In the business organization, this usually involves a process of "order issuance" which instructs everyone concerned what he is to do to implement the decision. For example, to increase production, schedules must be established, materials must be procured, labor must be obtained—literally hundreds of individually small but co-ordinated tasks must be performed.

In the control of a business organization, it is apparent that the functions involved in organizing the information and implementation are almost exclusively data processing. As the use of the management by exception approach becomes increasingly popular and the computer is more widely used, the area of evaluation becomes a part of data processing. And, as mathematically derived decision rules are devised, the decision block reduces to a matter of data processing. In any case, it is difficult, if not impossible, to separate the feedback concept of control from data processing, for data processing is inevitably involved in some or all parts of the loop.

It should be noted that in the business organization, another loop is involved at the planning level where some of the information on operations is processed to evaluate the plans in the preceding loop, so that better plans can be formulated for the control of the organization. Thus, we obtain Figure 2–2 as a more realistic representation of the control mechanism in an organization.

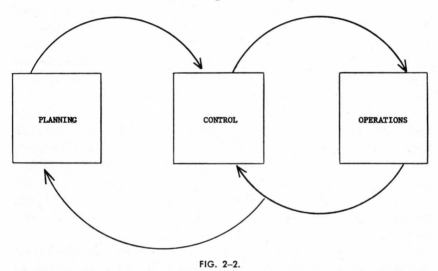

FIG. 2–2.

Of course, even Figure 2–2 is much too simple to represent the over-all situation in the actual business organization. In the modern organization with its various levels of management, literally thousands of such loops are intertwined with each other and piled on top of one another in confusing profusion, with the decision maker in one loop being the operations block of another loop, and so on.

However, much can be gained from an analysis of this concept of control. For example, the common thermostat on a furnace is an example of a simple feedback loop of control. The thermostat, of course, involves very little data processing and quite simple rules of decision. These rules are as follows: (1) When the temperature exceeds a certain level (say 73 degrees) the furnace is to be turned off; (2) when the temperature falls below a certain level (say 71 degrees) the furnace is to be turned on. Thus, the temperature in the house is maintained between the limits of 71 and 73 degrees. However, consider the effect of a two-hour time lag in the operation of the thermostat. In this case, when the temperature reaches 73 degrees the furnace would continue to run full blast for two hours and then shut off, then the house would gradually cool down to 71 degrees, and two hours later the furnace would again turn on. Thus, the temperature in the house would oscillate back and forth in a quite uncomfortable manner. We can see that the speed with which the feedback loop operates can be extremely important; therefore, if satisfactory control is to be maintained, the speed with which information can be processed may be quite important.

It is also important to notice that the information being processed in a feedback loop of control must provide the basis for detection of deviations and for the decisions necessary to correct these deviations. Here, of course, is the crucial problem involved in the design of data-processing systems: What information is required for effective control of an organization? This question is most difficult to answer, and we do not have adequate techniques for determining answers to this question. However, it is frequently possible to show that the information being processed in a specific organization is not adequate for control purposes. This will be discussed further in Chapter 14.

It should be noted that at least three interrelated questions are involved in the design of a data-processing system for control purposes: (1) What information should be gathered; (2) how should it be processed; and (3) how much time delay can be allowed without destroying the effectiveness of the system? In a substantial proportion of situations, the time question is *not* the only controlling factor. In other words, merely speeding up the processing in an existing system may produce an insignificant improvement in the effectiveness of control, and it is theoretically possible that reducing the processing delay may actually decrease the effectiveness of the system.[2]

The preceding discussion has expounded the viewpoint that one of the major functions of management is that of controlling the organization so that the goals can be attained. By a brief examination of the theory of control, we have demonstrated that an adequate control system depends upon data processing as well as upon management planning and decision making. Thus, we cannot escape the conclusion that the design and functioning of the data-processing system itself is of vital concern to management, and is not merely the domain of the lowly clerk or of a machine. Management must decide what information is necessary to control the operations of a business

---

[2] For an excellent illustration, see Jay W. Forrester, "Industrial Dynamics–A Major Breakthrough for Decision Makers," *Harvard Business Review,* July–August, 1958, 37–66.

organization. This does not imply that management cannot (or should not) use technical assistance in designing data-processing systems, but still it is the responsibility of management to set the objectives for these specialists and to make sure that the objectives are properly attained.

Two basic classifications of specialists are utilized by management in designing the data-processing systems: operations research groups and systems and procedures specialists. Operations research is frequently utilized when management requires research designed to provide a more basic understanding of the organization and to decide what and when information is required for proper control. The systems and procedures analysts can then design an efficient data-processing system to provide the needed information at the proper time.

Again, let us emphasize that the attitude of management toward the use of the information and the participation of management in the establishment of the objectives of the data-processing system are vital ingredients which are necessary for effective data processing, and, thus, for effective management control.

In much of the remainder of this book, the tools and means for efficiently accomplishing data processing will be discussed. We will become involved in a study of powerful and glamorous machines and the techniques that are required for their use. However, we must diligently guard against the temptation to ignore the basic objectives to which data processing must contribute.

The Systems Approach

Basically, the systems approach consists of designing a data-processing system as an integrated system to satisfy the information needs of the entire organization. The complex of data processing of a typical organization has grown haphazardly over the years in response to the needs and desires of hundreds of individuals and in response to the requirements of a multitude of emergencies and conditions which no longer exist. Managers typically institute recurring reports, but they seldom terminate them. Managers are promoted, fired, and die, but their pet reports often become eternal. Similar reports, used for different purposes, are often prepared in separate parts of the organization. Files are created and maintained, but seldom referred to, while the information that is actually needed is not obtainable.

The above diatribe is intended to suggest that most data-processing systems were not designed—they just grew. They are not systems except by accident. Thus, tremendous improvement can usually be obtained by actually designing a data-processing system to suit the needs of the organization. In the first place, it is usually possible to eliminate a substantial amount of effort and expense devoted to duplication of processing or to processing information that is not being used. But even more important is the potential improvement in the efficiency of operation of the organization that may be obtained by providing the proper information for adequate management control.

The systems approach is not an easy solution to the problem however, for it is much easier to talk about designing a data-processing system than it is to actually produce an adequate system. It is not too difficult for reasonably intelligent people to examine a data-processing system and detect duplication and unused reports. Every organization should have someone (or some group) charged with this responsibility. On the other hand, as was pointed out in our discussion of the feedback control loop, the design of a control system is a difficult task—so difficult that it has seldom been applied to the complex control systems associated with organizations.

When changing from a manual to a mechanized data-processing system, there is an obvious opportunity to approach data processing from a system-wide viewpoint. It is highly desirable, for instance, to capture information in machine-processable form as early as possible in the processing system so that from this point all manipulation and communication can be accomplished through the use of machines. This concept, which has been popularized under the name of *integrated data processing,* implies that a single machine does all of the processing of information, a group of machines utilizes a common media for the transmission of information and its entry into the various machines, or devices are used which can translate from one media to another. Originally this "common language" concept was applied to machines which processed paper tape, but the concept does not depend upon any particular common language media.

Patterns of Information Flow

In order to better understand what is involved in the systems approach and to understand the difficulties which must be overcome in its use, let us consider for a moment the patterns of information flow within an organization. How does information flow? And how may we discover where the basic information originates and how it affects each of the reports and documents produced?

Our first impulse is to look at the organization chart of the company involved. However, although an organization chart sometimes gives a picture of the lines of authority and responsibility of an organization, it almost never gives any indication of the basic information flow within the organization. Most of the information flow is across organizational lines rather than along them.

As a matter of fact, it is almost impossible to generalize concerning the detailed flow of information within organizations. We must consider an individual organization, and, in order to determine the flows of information, it is usually necessary to spend a considerable effort (usually involving several man-months or even man-years) actually following pieces of paper in their flow throughout the organization.

A simplified representation of some of the basic information flows within a manufacturing organization is presented in Figure 2–3. As

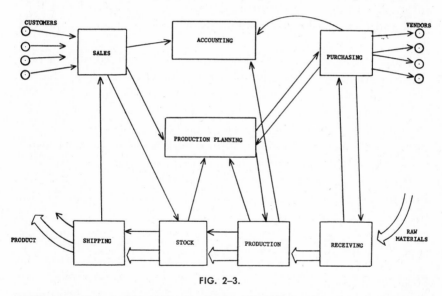

FIG. 2–3.

can be seen from this diagram, the basic information comes in from the customers in the form of orders. When these orders reach the sales department, the information is transcribed into a document that is sent to the stock room for filling the order, from there to the shipping room where the material is packed, and from there a copy goes to the customer and back to the sales department to indicate that the order has actually been shipped. In addition, copies of this document go to the accounting department, and summarized information goes to the production-planning department. The production-planning department utilizes this sales information to determine when to manufacture the various products and in what quantities. Then, it sends information to the production department in the form of production orders, and the production department notifies production planning when production has been completed and sends the product to the stock room along with a transmittal document, a copy of which goes back to production planning to inform them that the material is now in stock. Likewise, the production planning department sends information to the purchasing department, which writes orders to the vendors and sends copies of these orders to the receiving department so that when the materials are received they can be identified. When the material arrives, the receiving department sends back a copy of this document to purchasing, which then notifies production planning that the material has been received. In addition, of course, production planning, production, and purchasing all send information into the accounting department, and information flows back and forth between the organization and its customers and vendors.

Thus, it can be seen that there is a considerable volume of common information in the areas of production scheduling, production control, timekeeping, payroll, inventory control, order writing, billing, accounts receivable, and accounting. Likewise, there are many common aspects to product development, engineering specifications, parts requirements, machine loading, material control, purchasing, stores inventory accounting, and accounts payable.

It can be readily seen that the integration of these various areas into an efficient data-processing system is a difficult proposition, but the accomplishment of this integration not only can cut data-processing costs but also can provide the information necessary for proper control of the organization at the time when it is needed.

Basic Terminology

The previous discussion has been concerned primarily with the establishment of a frame of reference in which to consider data processing. Now let us discuss some of the basic terms used when describing data processing.

The fundamental unit of raw material of data processing is the transaction, which is a complete unit of information concerning some occurrence. For example, the sale of an item to a customer, the removal of an item from inventory, the payment of an account, the work of one man on one particular job, and the ordering of a quantity of a specific raw material all give rise to transactions.

Two basic types of information are necessary to describe a complete transaction. Of course, there must be *quantitative* information telling how much or how many. But the majority of the information contained in a transaction is usually included for the purpose of *identification*. This type of information denotes the type of transaction, tells who or what was involved, and describes the pertinent characteristics of the transaction for the data processing which is to follow. For example, in the sale of a single item, the quantitative information in the transaction consists of the quantity sold and the total dollar amount of the sale, while the identifying information may include the item number, the date, the salesman who made the sale, the customer who bought the item, and the terms of the sale.

Thus, data processing starts with transactions, any one of which may affect many of the end products of the data-processing system. It is imperative, then, that the transaction include the information necessary to associate the quantitative information in the proper relationship with other transactions in order to produce all of the required end products.

Data processing may be roughly divided into four major functions: data recording, data transmission, data manipulation, and report or document preparation. Let us consider further subdivisions of these major functions of data processing.

Recording

The importance and the complexity of the data-recording function is frequently overlooked. In order to properly record a given transaction, it is usually necessary to perform each of the following: *Identify* the particular transaction so that it can be distinguished from other transactions; *audit* the information contained in the transaction to determine that it is consistent and accurately represents the occurrence itself; *edit* the information to eliminate that which is extraneous in relation to the further processing necessary; *assign codes* to the transaction which will be used to control some of the further processing of the information; *record* the information in a form where a human or a machine can process the transaction during the data-manipulation phase; and, finally, *verify* that this entire procedure has been accomplished without error.

It may be desirable to elaborate upon the subject of coding. Basically, coding accomplishes two purposes: classification and condensation. For example, John Robert Smith, Jr. may be referred to as J. R. Smith, Jr., J. Robert Smith, Jr., John R. Smith, Jr., Bob Smith, Jack Smith, and so on ad infinitum. Even humans, and especially machines, have a difficult time recognizing that all of these variations refer to the same person. However, if we assign this man the employee number 97621, then we have classified all of these representations into a specific and concise way of referring to this employee in our data processing.

Incidentally, the advantage of conciseness associated with coding introduces a corresponding disadvantage of lack of redundancy which makes errors much more serious. For example, John R. Smrth, Jr. would probably be interpreted properly by anyone reading it, while the man-number 97261 (instead of 97621) not only fails to signal that a mistake has occurred, but also gives no clue as to the correct information. Thus, the step of verification assumes greater importance when coding is involved.

The design of a coding system is inextricably related to the data manipulation that is to be performed to produce the results desired from the data-processing system. It is desirable that two transactions that are identical with respect to subsequent processing be assigned the same code, yet it is impossible for manipulation in the data-processing system to provide an analysis with a finer breakdown than that which is provided by the coding system.

Data Transmission

The difficulty and complexity of data transmission can vary from the simple case where it consists only of moving a piece of paper from one desk to another to the complexity involved in instantaneous electronic communication from one continent to another. The method of data transmission chosen will depend upon the time requirements imposed by the system, the accuracy which must be maintained, and the economics of the communications' facilities themselves.

Engineering developments in the transmission of information in machine-processable form have come thick and fast in recent years. It is now possible to connect together a wide variety of devices by means of telephone or telegraph circuits, with the only major considerations involved being the cost of the facilities used. Punched cards, punched paper tape, and magnetic tape may be transmitted from one location and reproduced in another, and, if desirable, the information thus transmitted may be entered directly into a computer for immediate processing and the results automatically returned to the remote location. The above discussion does not imply, however, that the design of a data-processing system involving such transmission is a simple task, or that such spectacular communications facilities are always required (or even desirable) in a data-processing system.

Manipulation

Data manipulation can be quite complex and difficult to categorize but can be roughly classified into the following subfunctions: *Arrangement* of the information into the proper sequence so that it can be associated with file information and/or conveniently processed; *reference* to file information, which must be associated with the current information; a *logical* function, which consists of a precise determination of the procedure or subprocedure to be followed in the processing of a particular transaction or group of transactions; the *arithmetic* functions of addition, subtraction, multiplication, and division; and the *updating* of the file information to reflect the effect of the transaction being processed.

As an example of the influence of arrangement, suppose we are concerned with reflecting the result of 1,000 transactions upon 200 accounts. Several approaches might be used. The straightforward approach would be to place the transactions in a stack, pick up the first one, find the record for the account which it affects, post the transaction, and then repeat this process with each succeeding transaction. Another approach involves the preliminary step of arranging the transactions in sequence according to account number. Then all the transactions affecting a given account are together so that the account record must be located but once. A third approach would be to sort the transactions as in the previous approach and then total the transactions for each account, thus posting only this summarized total rather than the individual transactions.

When most of us think of sorting (or arrangement), the first thing that comes to mind is arranging a hand of cards. One usual way to do this is to look at the whole group of cards, pick out the first, then the second, then the third, and so forth. Another approach is to build the hand up by successively looking at cards and inserting each card in its proper place when it occurs. Both of these techniques are quite satisfactory when only a few cards are involved, but, when there are thousands of cards, neither approach is practical. In succeeding portions of this book, we will discuss methods of sorting that are practical when large numbers of transactions are involved and which lend themselves to mechanization.

Much to the surprise of most people who have experience in

manual data processing, the logical function mentioned above is of considerable complexity and requires a great proportion of the effort when data processing is mechanized. Seemingly, in most cases, humans perform these logical functions without conscious effort, while machines require that a special effort be expended in this area. Humans find these logical choices much less difficult than performing arithmetic, while for machines arithmetic is easy and choices are difficult. Thus, when a computer is performing data processing, it may be spending 75 per cent of its time performing logical functions while to perform the same job a human would spend 75 per cent of his time calculating.

Report Preparation

In addition to the arrangement of the information and the physical printing necessary in report or document preparation, other important characteristics must be considered. In the first place, the reports or documents must be available when they are needed; they must contain all the information necessary for the use to which they are to be put; and, finally, they must be presented in a form that is understandable and convenient to use with a minimum of further analysis. Of course, the above considerations actually influence the entire process of data processing, including the recording, transmission, and manipulation of the data, as well as the actual preparation of the reports.

Summary

The achievement of adequate management control so that the objectives of the organization may be most efficiently attained is the basic motivation for data processing. This implies that data processing is an important management consideration, for efficient control is impossible without suitable data processing.

The data-processing complex of an organization must be considered as a system, and this system should be designed to eliminate duplication and waste while providing the information needed for control purposes at the required place and time and in a usable form.

The raw materials for data processing consist of transactions. The basic functions of data processing are recording, transmission, manipulation, and report preparation. Each of these functions involves several subfunctions and many considerations.

The motivation discussed above and the functions described apply to data processing without regard to the tools used for its accomplishment. The objective is the important thing—the tools are secondary. If we lose sight of these objectives and have a data-processing system that cannot contribute to adequate control, then the most elaborate and powerful tools are useless.

EXERCISES

2.1 Describe the feedback concept of control. Discuss its implications for data processing.

2.2 What are the objectives of data processing?

2.3 Discuss the advantages of the systems approach to data processing.

2.4 How can you determine the data flows within a specific organization?

2.5 What is a transaction, and what two basic types of information must be included?

2.6 Describe each of the four major data-processing functions.

2.7 Why do we code information for data processing?

2.8 Describe the logical function in data manipulation. Why is this function of importance?

2.9 How does your instructor determine your grade? Relate this process to the major functions of data processing described in question 2.6.

SUPPLEMENTAL READINGS

CANNING, RICHARD G. *Electronic Data Processing for Business and Industry*, New York: John Wiley & Sons, Inc., 1956.
    Chapter 2 includes a good discussion of the motivation for data processing and information flows within an organization.

CHAPIN, NED. *An Introduction to Automatic Computers*. New York: D. Van Nostrand Co., Inc., 1955.
    Chapters 3 and 4 contain a discussion of feedback control systems and their relationship to data processing.

CHURCHMAN, C. W.; ACKOFF, R. L., and ARNOFF, E. L. *Introduction to Operations Research*. New York: John Wiley & Sons, Inc., 1957.
    Chapter 2 presents an excellent analysis of information flows in a manufacturing organization.

Introduction to Data Processing. Haskins & Sells, 1957.
    The first 59 pages of this little book present an excellent introduction to the basic operations involved in data processing.

KOZMETSKY, G., and KIRCHER, P. *Electronic Computers and Management Control*, New York: McGraw-Hill Book Co., Inc., 1956.
    Chapter 8 includes a discussion of feedback and its importance in management control. Chapter 9 discusses the systems approach to data processing.

CHAPTER 3 · Punched Card Data Processing

ALTHOUGH we must never lose sight of the basic motivation for data processing presented in Chapter 2, this book is primarily concerned with the *mechanization* of data processing. Before studying the use of electronic computers for data processing, it is desirable to discuss the use of punched card machines. Punched cards are of great importance in their own right, for they are powerful data-processing tools and have achieved widespread popularity. Also, most of the computers now in use have been installed in organizations in which data processing has become highly mechanized through the use of punched card machines, and the computers have been combined with punched card systems so that both types of machines are usually utilized together within the same organization. Many of the problems that must be solved to use computers are the same problems that must be solved when data processing is mechanized by any method, so a study of punched card data processing provides a valuable background for the study of electronic data processing. Furthermore, the various data-processing functions discussed in Chapter 2 are performed by separate punched card machines, while the same computer equipment may be used for everything; thus, a study of punched cards allows us to become more familiar with the individual data-processing functions.

The Punched Card

Basic to the punched card method, of course, is the ubiquitous punched card itself. Few among us have not had contact with punched cards in some way, for they are in general use as government checks, defense bonds, soap coupons, gasoline credit slips, student registration cards, Christmas Club coupons, utility bills, and insurance renewal notices, while business employees handle them in the form of internal documents such as time cards, labor tickets, requisitions, inventory-picking tickets, and so on.

Basically, the punched card is a piece of high-quality paper $7\frac{3}{8}$ inches long and $2\frac{3}{4}$ inches wide (the size of the old style United States dollar bill) on which information is recorded by means of holes punched in specified positions on the card. One corner of the card is usually clipped at an odd angle so that the cards can be easily replaced in the proper orientation if they are accidentally dropped.

Information Representation

There are two major manufacturers of punched card equipment in the United States: the International Business Machines Corporation and the Remington Rand Division of the Sperry Rand Corporation. Although they are the same size and shape, the cards used by the two companies may be distinguished from one another by the fact that the IBM cards are punched with rectangular holes, while the holes in the Remington Rand cards are round. As can be seen in Figure 3–1 and Figure 3–2, the digits zero through 9, the letters A through Z, and several special characters may be represented in each system by means of vertical combinations of holes. Each character requires one "column" of the card, so the amount of information that may be recorded on any single card is limited by the standard number of columns available.

The IBM card includes 12 horizontal rows and 80 vertical columns. Each row of the card has a specific designation. Reading from the top to the bottom, the top row is called the 12 (or Y) row; the next row is the 11 (or X) row. These two rows are used primarily for recording

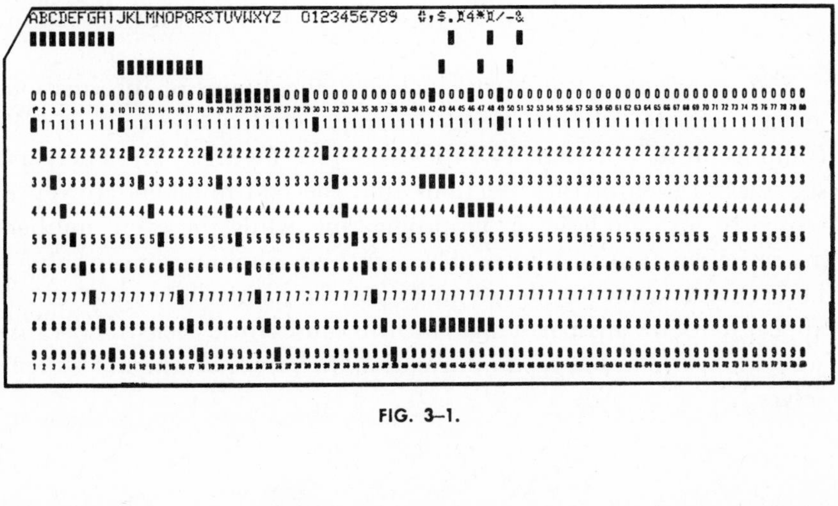

FIG. 3–1.

holes which control the operation of the machines or as *zone* punches when recording alphabetic information. Proceeding toward the bottom of the card, the third row represents the number zero, the fourth represents the number 1, and so on till we reach the bottom row which represents the number 9. As can be seen from Figure 3–1, each numeric digit can be represented in any column by a single punch in the row associated with that digit. Alphabetic information is repre-

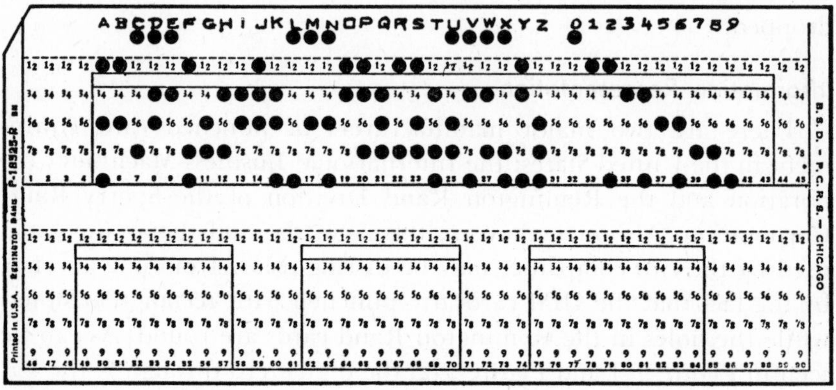

FIG. 3–2.

sented by means of a zone punch (X, Y, or zero) combined with a numeric punch (1 through 9) in a simple code in which the first nine letters of the alphabet (A through I) are each represented by a combination of a Y punch and one of the numbers 1 through 9; the next nine letters (J through R) are represented by a combination of an X punch and one of the numbers 1 through 9; and the last eight letters (S through Z) are represented by a combination of a zero punch and one of the numbers 2 through 9. The special symbols are represented by various combinations of one, two, or three punches within one column.

The Remington Rand card includes 90 columns of information, arranged in 45 columns along the upper half of the card and 45 columns on the lower half of the card. (See Figure 3–2.) There are six rows in each of these sections, and the odd numbers are represented by a single hole in the proper row, while the even numbers are represented by two holes. The punching combinations for alphabetic characters are as shown in Figure 3–2, and while they do not appear to follow any particular rule this causes little difficulty because we seldom attempt to read information directly from the holes themselves.

What the Punched Card Does

The punched card serves a variety of uses in a punched card data-processing system. First, it is an input media which enters information into the machines (which cannot read ordinary written material) in a form in which they can accept information. The card also provides an output from these machines. In other words, the punched card is the principal media through which men communicate with the machines. Secondly, the punched card is a common communication media between the various specialized machines which are used in punched card processing. It is the connecting link that ties together a long series of processing steps which culminate in the production of the desired results. Thirdly, the punched card performs the function of storing information in the form of machine-processable files, so this information will be available for use when it is required. And lastly, the punched card may in certain cases be a document (such as a check, time card, and so forth) which has a use in the organization that does not depend upon the fact that holes are punched in the piece of paper.

The punched card is frequently referred to as a *mobile unit record*. The word *unit* implies that the information concerning a single transaction is usually recorded on a single card—one and only one transaction per card. The word *mobile* implies that these unit records may be rearranged and reprocessed at will to allow the transaction to be incorporated into the various reports which it affects. Thus, by recording the information once on a punched card, it may be posted to different accounts, ledgers, or reports by a mechanized process without additional human effort and without the transcription errors that are so prevalent in manual data processing. This concept of mobility is of such great importance that a rule of thumb is frequently applied which states that the information should be used in at least three different postings in order to qualify as a good punched card application.

Card Format

One of the basic requirements associated with mechanized data processing is that information to be entered into the machines be recorded in a rigid format. The information is identified to the machine as a man number or a dollar amount by means of its position alone. That is to say (in terms of punched cards) that the column or columns in which a number is recorded is the only means by which the machine can identify the information; hence, this location becomes the key to meaningful processing. Thus, each type of transaction is recorded on cards of a specific format so that each unit of information occupies the same position on all cards for a particular type of transaction.

Fields

A group of card columns (usually adjacent) that is assigned to a particular unit of information (such as a name, hourly rate, description, unit cost, or tax class) is called a field. In designing the format of the punched card, the eighty or ninety columns may be grouped together to form fields in any way that seems desirable, subject to the restriction that the total number of columns in all the fields may not exceed the number of columns available on the card.

Enough columns must be allowed in each field to permit recording of the largest number or the longest group of alphabetic characters that may occur among the units of information that are to be recorded in that field. For example, if price may range from 25¢ to $850.00, a five-digit field must be assigned to price; whereas, if the price could go as high as $1,000.00, a six-digit field would be required. Numeric fields are customarily justified to the right, and zeros are inserted to the left of small numbers to completely fill the columns allocated. Thus, in a five-digit field, 745 would be recorded as 00745. Alphabetic fields are customarily justified to the left, and unused columns to the right are left blank.

Card Design

One of the important preliminary steps in utilizing punched card equipment for data processing is that of designing the cards that are involved. Several considerations are involved in allocating the card columns among the various pieces of information, such as the total amount of information to be recorded, the sequence in which the fields should appear on the cards, and the relationship of the location of a specific field on one card form to the location of the same field on another card form. As we will see when we discuss the accounting machine, it is not necessary that there be any relationship between the sequence of fields on the cards and the location of the information on the reports that are printed.

As can be seen from Figure 3–3, once the allocation of the fields is made, special forms may be printed designating the uses to which each field is put. The different cards that enter into the processing usually have different formats, and may be made of different colors of paper or be identified by different corner cuts or horizontal stripes of various colors. The machines do not detect color nor do they read the information printed on the surface of the card. A blank card would suffice as far as the machines are concerned, but the different colors and the different printed formats are used to reduce the

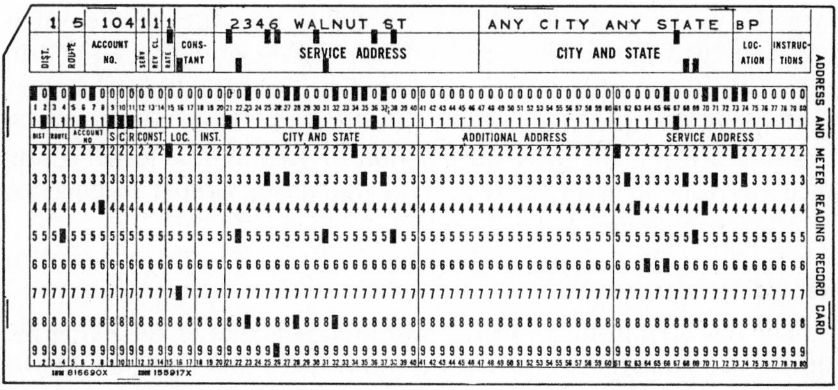

FIG. 3–3.

chance of confusing the people who may be working with the cards.

The machines are able to distinguish between card formats on the basis of control punches. For example, if the card has an X punch in column 70 it may be designated as a payroll master-name card, while a card with an X punch in column 78 is identified as a year-to-date earnings card.[1] These control punches do not require an extra card column, for they may be over numeric fields. In such cases, the combination of a zone and numeric punch is not interpreted by the machines as an alphabetic character because no letter can appear in a numeric field. How these control punches are used to enable the machine to handle cards with different formats in different ways will be discussed later in the section on selectors.

Good card design is of great importance to the successful use of punched card machines. In the first place, all of the information that will be needed (even sometime in the future) should be included in the original design, for the card form is difficult to change, and it is costly and inconvenient to add information to cards that have already been punched. Secondly, poor card design may significantly

---

[1] As discussed above, an X punch is a punch in the second from the top row of the card. This is not to be confused with the letter X, which is a zero punch combined with a seven punch.

increase the complexity of the processing procedures and may even cause the capabilities of the machines to be exceeded.

Due to the limitations in space and time that we can devote to the subject of punched card data processing, the following discussion will be based upon the equipment of but one manufacturer. We have chosen to discuss the IBM equipment because about 90 per cent of the punched card equipment in use in the United States is of this type. However, even though the individual machines of the different manufacturers differ considerably in details of operation and in the combination of functions that they perform, the basic functions performed are, fortunately, almost identical. Thus, the capabilities that are present in an installation of Remington Rand equipment are roughly equivalent to those found in a similar installation of IBM equipment.

Recording Methods

The first step in the punched card process is that of recording the information in a form which can be processed—that is, punching the information into cards. There are a variety of methods by which cards may be punched, and, in many situations, several different methods are used within the same punched card procedure or even to record information on the same card.

Key Punching

The most commonly used punching method, called key punching, involves the use of a manually operated machine with a keyboard resembling that of an electric typewriter both in appearance and in operation. Since no distinction is made between the upper case and lower case characters on punched card equipment, it is possible to superimpose a ten-key numeric keyboard upon the normal alphabetic keyboard, distinguishing one from the other by means of the shift key (see Figure 3–4). Cards are automatically fed into this machine one at a time, and are punched column by column as the keys are depressed. By means of a previously prepared program card, which moves in synchronization with the cards being punched, skipping between fields, ejection of the card, assignment of the keyboard to alphabetic or numeric status for each card field, and duplication of fields from one card into the following cards may be automatically controlled. Some models of the key punch can simultaneously print all or part of the information along the top of the card as it is being punched.

Recording by means of key strokes is basic not only to punched card data processing, but also to most other methods of mechanized data processing, including electronic data processing. This is essentially a manual step, and frequently represents a substantial per cent of the total cost of the entire data-processing procedure. Therefore,

FIG. 3–4.

it is important that key punching be accomplished as efficiently as possible. It is customary to perform the functions of editing and coding before key punching so that the key punch operator can concentrate on recording the information accurately and efficiently. Moreover, the arrangement of the form from which the information is punched should be correlated with the sequence of fields on the card form so that the information appears in the order in which it is to be punched with a minimum of skipping around. Because of the design of the keyboard on the key punch, it is desirable that the operator be right handed; and it is generally conceded that women perform this operation more efficiently than men.

The Remington Rand key punch does not punch the card column by column as does the IBM key punch. As the keys are operated, the information is stored within the machine, and after the card is completed, all the holes are punched simultaneously when a trip bar is depressed. This method of operation has two advantages, for not only can the keyboard be operated slightly faster than with the IBM key punch, but also keying errors which are detected by the operator may be corrected before the holes are actually punched, so the card itself is not destroyed. However, as will be seen in a later section, these advantages must be balanced against IBM advantages in the area of verification.

Prepunching

Another widely used method of recording information is by pre-punching the cards. A number of duplicates of a master card may be prepared by gang punching or an entire file of cards may be dupli-cated by a machine process called reproducing (see the subsequent discussion on these subjects). Then, the information so recorded may be introduced into the punched card procedure by simply choosing the proper prepunched card. Prepunching is frequently combined with key punching or some other method of recording so that the constant information is prepunched, and variable informa-tion pertaining to the transaction is entered by some other method. For example, in a payroll procedure the time cards may be pre-punched with man number, department number, shift code, hourly rate, and any other information peculiar to the man, and the total hours worked may be entered into the card by key punching.

Mark Sensing

Another useful method for entering small quantities of informa-tion into a card is by means of "mark sensing." By using a special pencil or pen, conductive marks may be made in designated spots on the punched card, and these marks may be converted into punches at a speed of 100 cards per minute by the use of the mark-sensing reproducer (available only from IBM). As can be seen from Figure 3–5, for each column to be punched there must be a column of mark-ing areas on the card, and a mark corresponding to the desired hole must be made in each such column. Since alphabetic information requires two holes per column and the alphabetic code is not easily remembered, the use of mark sensing is usually restricted to the recording of numeric information. Similar equipment, operating on a photoelectric principle, is available from Remington Rand.

Although many of the most prevelant errors involved in marking cards, such as failure to mark a digit or to make a readable mark, are detected by the machine, these errors cause the machine to stop, and the operator must isolate the card and correct the error. If these stoppages become frequent, the operation becomes inefficient, so it is apparent that the marking must be done with care. Thus, mark sensing can be effectively used only when the persons recording the

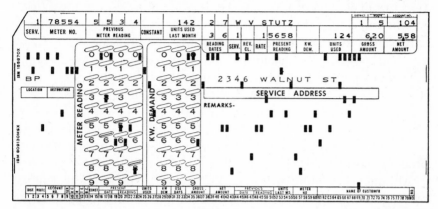

FIG. 3–5.

information can be motivated to take the care necessary to do it properly. Since the possibility of confusion increases rapidly with the number of columns to be marked, it is most effective when only a few columns must be marked on each card. Key punching from written material is much faster than placing the marks on mark-sense cards, so it is not usually efficient for someone to read from a document and mark the cards. Mark sensing is most efficient when the marking can be done at the point where the information originates by a person who can perform the marking as a by-product of his major work without adversely affecting his working efficiency. An example of an excellent mark-sensing application is that of utility meter reading, where the mark-sense cards become the meter book, and the meter reader marks the card as he is reading the meter dials.

Other Punching Methods

A widely used method of punching, that of duplicating information from one card to another when using the key punch, has already been mentioned. Occasionally, a modified conductor's punch, aligned by means of minute *finder holes,* is used for recording small amounts of information in the Remington Rand system. Also, IBM produces "Port-A-Punch" cards in which some of the punching positions are prescored and may be punched out by use of a pencil point or a special tool in a manner similar to a punchboard.

A wide variety of devices are available that produce machine-processable information as a by-product of their major function. For example, electric typewriters exist that produce standard punched cards containing selected portions of the information that is typed. Certain production-recording equipment produces information in punched card form. And toll-road equipment is in use that weighs and counts the axles of each vehicle and produces a punched card that is used as a ticket. A multitude of adding machines, typewriters, bookkeeping machines, and production recorders produce selected by-product information in the form of punched paper tape. The information in these paper tapes can then be automatically transmitted over teletype, converted, through a card machine, to punched cards or fed directly into a computer. Needless to say, the format of the paper tape must be carefully integrated into the data-processing system.

Although key punching is undoubtedly the basic method of recording information in punched card form, it should be emphasized again that in a mechanized system the recording function is of utmost importance and that ingenuity in the choice of recording techniques employed may pay handsome dividends.

Verification

Not only is recording of information important from the standpoint of costs, but it is also crucial from the standpoint of accuracy. Although the machines can and do make mistakes, their accuracy is phenomenal when compared with that of humans. On the other hand, machines do not have judgment—although they may be programmed to perform specific tests that may detect errors; they cannot sense that a number is wrong in the same way that a human might sense the presence of an error.

Errors in recording can only be rectified when the source documents are available to provide the correct information. After the mechanized processing begins, the source documents and the cards prepared from them go their separate ways and correction of these recording errors becomes much more difficult, for it also involves locating the source document. Furthermore, once the processing reaches the mechanized stage, interruption to correct errors may cause grave disruption and drastically reduce the efficiency of the over-all process. Therefore it is extremely important that the information which enters a mechanized system be as accurate as possible. It is usually worthwhile to go to considerable effort and expense to reduce the incidence of transcription and recording errors before reaching the machine-processing stage. Thus, verification is an important preliminary step in a mechanized data-processing procedure. There are several methods that may be used singly or in combination for verifying the accuracy of recording.

Key Verification

Key verification is quite similar to key punching except that a verifier is used rather than a key punch. In outward appearance, the two machines are almost identical, but in place of a punching mechanism the verifier has a sensing device that reads the holes in the card column and compares them with the key that is depressed by the operator. If the holes do not agree with the key that the verifier operator has depressed, this indicates that the card was mispunched or that the verifier operator has depressed the wrong key. In this case, the machine keyboard locks, a red light turns on, and the verifier operator then has two opportunities to depress the proper key. Since the card column being verified is covered by the mechanism and the card cannot be spaced without indicating an error, there is some assurance that the operator cannot know what is punched in the card in order to release it without indicating an error. If the card is in error, a notch is punched in the top of the card in the column in which the error occurred. If no errors are detected in the card, the machine places a notch in the right edge of the card as it is ejected from the machine so that the cards which are in error may be easily located.

After a group of cards has been key-punched, the cards, along with the documents from which they were punched, are taken to a verifier where they are verified by a different operator. Frequently, only a portion of the information that was punched must be key verified, for the accuracy of certain information (such as alphabetic descriptions) may be of little importance in the subsequent processing, or some of the information may be verified by other methods. As with the key punch, format control, skipping of fields, designation of alphabetic and numeric status, and feeding and ejection of the cards is automatically controlled by use of a program card.

Cards that are found to be in error must be returned, along with the source documents from which they were punched, to a key punch for repunching. The duplicating feature of the key punch may be used to repunch the correct portions of the cards. Since the verifier operator has a chance to correct her errors without damaging the cards involved, verification may be performed faster than key punching.

In the Remington Rand system, the key punch machine is also used as a key verifier. The card is simply displaced vertically about one sixteenth of an inch, and the card is then repunched. After this process, the correct information will be represented by oval-shaped holes. The cards are then run through a machine (called a verifier) which detects the round holes and inserts a finder card in front of each card containing an error. Then the error cards must be returned to a key punch operator, the source documents from which they were punched must be found, and the cards must be repunched. You may have noticed that in this system not only the errors arising in key punching but also those made in the process of verification require repunching of the cards.

Visual Verification

One of the least effective verification methods is visual verification. After the cards have been punched, they may be printed (one line for each card) on a punched card accounting machine; then, this printed list can be visually compared with the original source documents. This comparison is best accomplished using two persons, one reading aloud to the other. It is neither a popular nor effective method, for not only is its cost higher than that of key verification (if there is enough verifying to keep a machine busy), but it also is substantially inferior to key verification in detecting errors. Incidentally, the holes themselves are seldom visually read for verification.

Batch Totals

Batch totals obtained by running the cards through the accounting machine may be compared with totals obtained independently from the source documents to provide another effective verification method. In this method, the source documents are delivered to the key punch operator in batches accompanied by an adding machine tape totaling one or more fields of information. After the cards are punched, they may be listed on the accounting machine to provide totals to compare with the adding machine totals. If these totals agree, there is an excellent probability that this field (or fields) of the cards is correctly punched, since compensating errors are highly unlikely. If the totals do not agree, however, there is either a key punching or an adding machine error (or errors) in the batch which must be located by comparing the adding machine tape item by item with the list prepared on the accounting machine.

The number of cards that should be included in a batch is determined by the expected error rate, for if there are one or more errors in each batch, the situation reduces to sight verification. For this method to be used effectively, the batches must be small enough so that most of them will contain no punching errors.

This method of verification is frequently used because the batch totals may also be used to establish over-all controls on the entire data-processing procedure, for these totals may be accumulated again at later stages in the processing to verify that all of the proper cards have been processed at that stage. This is an extremely important technique in the over-all control of accuracy of mechanized data-processing systems.

Self-Checking Numbers

One of the most interesting methods of verification involves the use of so called *self-checking numbers* along with a special device on the IBM key punch. This method cannot be used to check the accuracy of quantitative information but is only used with identifying information because it involves the modification of the number itself by the addition of a check digit. The check digit is computed by applying some rule to the original digits of the number so that most of the usual mistakes will give numbers for which a different check digit would be computed. One method of computing a check digit involves multiplying every other digit of the original number by 2 and adding these values and the remaining digits of the number together. The units digit of the result obtained is then subtracted from 10 to obtain the check digit.[2]

To illustrate the process used, let us compute the check digit for the number 72546. The alternate digits are first multiplied by 2:

$$\begin{array}{r r r} 7 & 5 & 6 \\ & & 2 \\ \hline 15 & 1 & 2 \end{array}$$

Then the remaining digits (2 and 4) are included and the digits are added.

$$1 + 5 + 2 + 1 + 4 + 2 = 15$$

---

[2] Two other variations of self-checking numbers are explained in the booklet *Account Numbering System,* Form G1196, published by Burroughs Corporation.

The 5 is subtracted from 10 to give a check digit of 5, so the number becomes 725465.

As the digits of the self-checking number are being punched, a special device on the key punch repeats the above calculation. When the check digit is punched, it is automatically compared with the computed number to detect punching errors. Suppose the above number were punched as 752465. The check digit computation would be as follows:

$$
\begin{array}{ccc}
7 & 2 & 6 \\
 & & 2 \\
\hline
14 & 5 & 2 \\
\end{array}
$$

$$1 + 4 + 5 + 5 + 4 + 2 = 21$$

$$10 - 1 = 9 \text{ check digit}$$

Thus, when the digit 5 is punched the machine expects a 9, so an error would be indicated.

Incidentally, this method of verification also detects errors of original coding and transcription, for it makes no difference to the equipment whether the inconsistency in the number came from a key punching error or an error in assigning the number or in transcribing it onto the source document. Thus, at the expense of an extra key stroke and an extra card column, it is possible to provide an excellent verification for identifying information for which the check digits may be precomputed and treated as an integral part of the number itself.

The use of self-checking numbers is not restricted to punched card systems, for they are frequently used in assignment of account numbers in banking systems and could profitably be used by mail-order houses when assigning catalogue numbers so that transcription errors by the customer in ordering could be easily detected. They may be used in punched card systems for assigning man numbers which must be written on labor tickets, for item identification numbers in inventory control procedures, and for customer account numbers in accounts receivable procedures.

The check digits must be computed and added to the number before it is assigned to the item which it is to identify. For example, the number 725465 would be assigned to a man as a man number when he first becomes an employee, and he need not be aware that it is a self-checking number, so the last digit has no special significance to him. But whenever the number is key-punched it may automatically be checked for accuracy. The check digit may originally be computed by a punched card calculator, or it may be generated by use of the self-checking number device on the key punch.

Sorting

After the cards have been punched and verified, the next step in a typical punched card procedure is that of sorting the cards to arrange them in the proper sequence for further processing. Indeed, much of the power of the punched card method is due to the ability to rapidly and inexpensively arrange the punched cards in sequence according to any field (or group of fields) on the card. This field (or fields) is called the sorting *key*. For example, in a payroll procedure punched card labor tickets might first be sorted by man number in order to group together all of the cards for each man for pay computation purposes. Later in the procedure, the cards might be sorted to job number sequence to group them by job number so that the total cost for each job could easily be determined.

The sorter has one card-feeding mechanism and thirteen output card stackers (called pockets), twelve of which are for the twelve possible punching positions (or rows), and the reject pocket is for cards that are blank. On each pass of the cards through the machine, it examines a single column and routes each card into one of the thirteen output pockets, depending upon the punch in that column. Thus, if that column of the card is punched with a hole in the seven row, the card is placed in the seven pocket, while if that column has a punch in the three row, the card is placed in the three pocket. By depressing certain buttons, it is possible to cause any of the rows of the card to be ignored in this process. If, for example, we wished to extract all cards with a seven punch in column 20 (without disturbing the sequence of the other cards) we could depress the buttons blanking out all the rows except the seven row. Then, when sorting on column 20, those cards containing a seven would be placed in the seven pocket and the other cards would be placed in the reject pocket.

Sorting is accomplished by repeatedly passing the cards through the machine, setting it on a different column during each pass. The usual *reverse digit* method of sorting numeric information involves first setting the machine on the column corresponding to the low-order digit of the field upon which the cards are to be sorted. Upon completion of each pass, the cards are removed from the pockets and recombined so that the zeros are first, ones next, the twos next, and so on through the nines. As shown in Figure 3–6, the first pass arranges the cards according to the low-order digit of the key field. The cards are replaced in the machine, and it is set on the column correspond-ing to the next higher-order digit of the key. After the cards are properly recombined from this pass, they are arranged from 00 to 99 according to the two low-order digits of the field. This process is repeated, moving left one column for each additional digit of the key (see Figure 3–6), so that a three-column field requires three passes through the machine, while a seven-column field requires seven passes.

Random Order	End of First Pass	End of Second Pass	End of Third Pass
346	640	905	035
248	232	232	232
232	383	035	248
383	353	640	346
640	905	346	353
366	035	248	366
905	346	353	383
353	366	366	640
686	686	383	686
035	248	686	905

FIG. 3–6.

For large sorting jobs, it is sometimes convenient to split the work between several sorters by using the technique of *block sorting*. In this method, the cards are first sorted according to the high-order digit of the key field, thus separating the cards into ten separate groups, each of which can be sorted individually by the preceding method. At the conclusion of the process, the separately sorted decks must be recombined in the proper sequence.

Alphabetic sorting requires that the cards be passed through the sorter twice for each column of the key field. The first pass arranges the cards according to the numeric punch so that the A's and J's are placed in the one pocket, the B's, K's, and S's are placed in the two pocket, and so forth. The second pass then ignores the numeric punch and arranges the cards by zone, so that the A's through I's fall in the twelve pocket, the J's through R's fall in the X pocket, while the S's through Z's fall in the zero pocket.

Various models of the sorter operate at 450, 650, 1,000 and 2,000 cards per minute per pass. Since a considerable amount of card handling is involved in the sorting process, the machines actually operate substantially below their rated speed. It is not unusual for one person to operate as many as three of the 650-card-per-minute machines simultaneously. A large punched card installation is likely to have several of the high-speed sorters and to keep them operating most of the time.

Auxiliary Equipment

The basic steps involved in most punched card procedures include punching, verifying, sorting, and report preparation. Report preparation is accomplished on the accounting machine and will be discussed later. However, between the punching step and that of report preparation, there may be a number of intermediate processing steps, some of which will be discussed in the following sections.

Reproducing

The term *reproducing* refers to the process of making a duplicate of an original deck of cards, thus preparing a single copy of each old card containing some or all of the information punched in the original card. A machine called the *reproducer* performs this operation (and several others, including mark sensing) at the speed of 100 cards per minute.

Like most other IBM machines, the reproducer is controlled through the use of a removable panel (called a control panel) con-

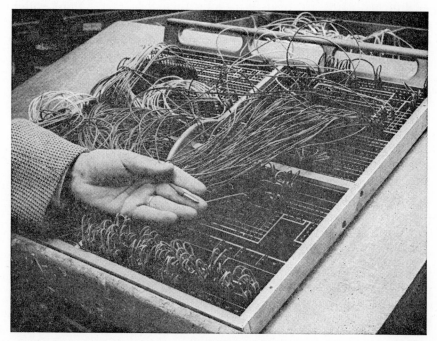

FIG. 3–7.

taining holes into which the ends of special wires may be inserted to provide paths for electrical impulses which (in this case) transfer the information from one card to another (see Figures 3–7, 3–8, and 3–9). Incidentally, the newer Remington Rand machines also utilize this method of control, but many of the others use removable *wiring*

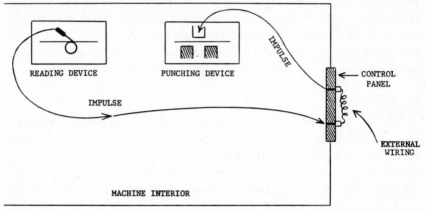

FIG. 3–8.

*unit*s by means of which physical force is applied from one part of the machine to another to perform the functions desired.

Punched cards are read by passing them between a brass roller and a set of wire brushes, one brush for each of the columns of the card. The card serves as an insulator, but where there is a hole, the brush makes contact with the roller and current is able to flow (see Figure 3–10). Everything within the machine is synchronized with the movement of the card.

Figure 3–11 shows a diagram of the reproducer. The original deck is placed in the left-hand feed and blank cards are placed in the right-hand feed.[3] The movement of both decks of cards is synchronized so that cards are passing each of the three sets of reading brushes and the punch dies simultaneously. Thus, when the ones' row of a card is under the reproducing brushes, the ones' row is also being read at both the comparing and punch brushes, and the ones' row of a card is under the punching dies at the punching station.

The control panel of the reproducer includes a set of holes for each of the reading stations, one hole for each card column for each reading station. There is also a set of holes which are connected to the punching mechanism, one hole for each of the eighty columns which may be punched. By inserting one end of a wire into the hole

---

[3] Any stack of cards is usually referred to as a deck.

FIG. 3–9.

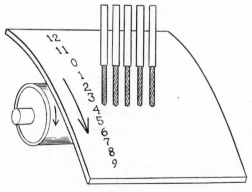

FIG. 3–10.

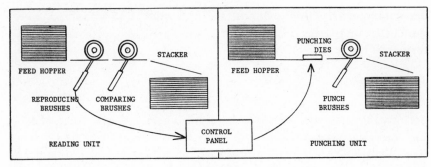

FIG. 3–11.

corresponding to a column of a card being read by the reproducing brushes, and the other end of the wire into a hole corresponding to a punching magnet, a hole that is read causes the machine to punch a corresponding hole in the card that is under the punch magnets. Thus, as each card of the original deck passes under the reproducing brushes, the information in the columns wired to punch is punched into the corresponding card under the punch mechanism.

Gang Punching

The reproducer is also used in *gang punching,* which is the process of making a large number of duplicates of a single card, frequently called a master card. This is accomplished by placing the master card to be duplicated, followed by the proper number of blank cards, into the punch feed of the machine. By wiring from the punch brushes through the control panel to the punching dies (refer to Figure 3–11), the original card is duplicated into the first blank card, and this card then moves to the punch brushes where it is duplicated into the next card, and so on. It is possible to interrupt this process for one card cycle, so master cards may be interspersed between groups of cards into which the master information is to be duplicated.

Interpreting

So that humans do not have to read the holes, whenever it is necessary for people to read directly from cards, the interpreter may be used to print information that has been punched into a card on the face of that same card. Although key-punched information may also be printed along the top of the card, sometimes this information is not located in the best place on the cards when they are to be used for documents or for reference. Furthermore, information may have been punched by some machine method such as reproducing, gang punching, or by the calculator. In these cases, the cards may be interpreted before they become part of a file or are used as documents.

The Collator

The collator is one of the most versatile punched card machines, performing such operations as sequence checking, selecting, matching, merging, and various combinations of these. As can be seen from Figure 3–12, the collator has two input feeds and four output

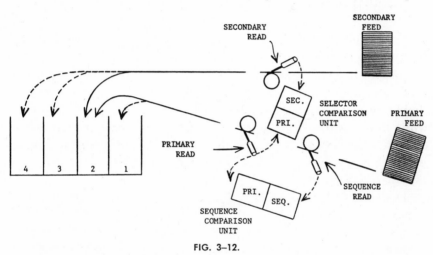

FIG. 3–12.

pockets. Its basic function is that of comparison, and it feeds cards and ejects them into the desired pocket on the basis of these comparisons. Cards from the primary feed may go into pockets number 1 and 2 while those in the secondary feed may go into pockets number 2, 3, or 4.

By storing a number A in the sequence unit and a number B in the selector comparison unit and comparing them with the card read at the primary reading brushes, it is possible to select from a file of cards those cards in which the number in a given field lies between the numbers A and B. Proceeding at a speed of 240 cards per minute, this operation might be used to select for further processing those accounts in an accounts receivable file that are between four and six weeks overdue.

Merging

The collator is frequently used to combine two files that are in the same sequence according to the numbers in some field into a single file in that same sequence. This is called *merging,* and may be used to insert transaction cards in their proper place in a file.

In the merging operation, the card read at the primary reading brushes is compared with that read at the secondary reading brushes, and the card with the smaller number is dropped into pocket number 2. Then the next card is compared with the one that was larger, and the process is repeated. By experimenting with different numbers in the collator diagram, it can readily be seen that this process works properly only when the two files are in correct sequence. This is an important characteristic of those collator operations in which two decks of cards are involved.

Matching

Another basic collator operation is that of matching, in which the cards in the primary and the secondary feeds are compared and those that are equal are dropped side by side into pockets 2 and 3, while those secondary cards for which there is no matching primary card are placed in pocket 4, and those primary cards for which there is no matching secondary card are dropped into pocket 1 (see the example in Figure 3–13).

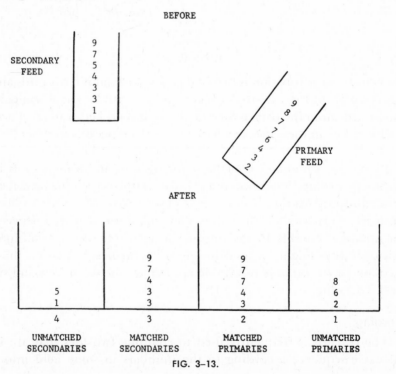

FIG. 3–13.

Match-Merging

The matching and merging operations may be combined, so that the cards that match are merged together rather than being placed side by side. In a punched card payroll procedure, a master payroll file is maintained (in man-number sequence) containing a card for each worker. When the time cards are returned from the timekeeper, they may be sorted in man-number sequence. If they are then match-merged with the payroll master file (with the payroll master cards in the primary feed), unmatched primary cards represent workers whose time cards are missing, while unmatched secondary cards represent time cards for which there is no payroll master card. Both of these situations would have to be investigated and the proper corrections made. The merged master cards and time cards would then be processed in the payroll calculation.

The Accounting Machine

The fourth basic step in the punched card method is that of report preparation which is performed with various models of the accounting machine. This type of machine adds and subtracts, takes totals, prints, controls the spacing of the forms being printed upon, and (in conjunction with the reproducer) *summary punches* into new cards for balance-forward purposes.

The accounting machine can print a line for each card at a speed of 100 or 150 lines per minute for the two most popular models. Through the wiring of the control panel, it is possible to eliminate part of the information on the card and to rearrange the sequence in which the information is printed across the page so that it need have no relationship to the sequence in which it appears on the card. However, the continuous forms which are fed through the machines can only space upward, whence the cards must be arranged in the proper sequence so that the information will print on the desired line of the form. That is to say, if card A precedes card B through the machine, then card B cannot print above card A on the form. If they both print on the same line, then all cards between the two must either not print or must also print on that line.

Most models of the accounting machines include from 80 to 120 counter positions, grouped to form counters of various sizes, which may be used for adding and subtracting fields from the cards to accumulate totals. Thus, each accounting machine may be thought of as containing several adding machines, each of which may be associated with a particular field of the cards.

Group Control

One of the most important capabilities of the accounting machine is its ability to pause between cards and take a total at the proper time. This capability, known as *group control,* depends upon the fact that the cards are in sequence before they are placed in the accounting machine. The process of sorting not only arranges the cards in sequence, but it also associates them together in groups, for all those cards which contain the same number will be together in the deck (see below).

$$
\left.\begin{matrix} 103 \\ 103 \\ 103 \end{matrix}\right\} \text{First Group}
$$

$$
117 \} \text{Second Group}
$$

$$
\left.\begin{matrix} 119 \\ 119 \end{matrix}\right\} \text{Third Group}
$$

$$
\left.\begin{matrix} 123 \\ 123 \\ 123 \end{matrix}\right\} \text{Fourth Group}
$$

As shown in Figure 3–14, the accounting machine contains two sets of reading brushes and a comparing mechanism which emits an

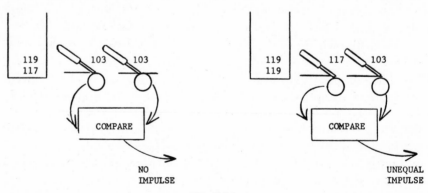

FIG. 3–14.

impulse when the two numbers being compared are unequal. By wiring from both sets of reading brushes into the comparing mechanism, it is possible to compare each card with its successor. If the two are equal, then the second card is a member of the same group as the first, but if they are not equal, the first card is the final card in its group, and the machine may be directed to print a total and clear the counter.

The accounting machine can handle three separate sets of comparisons at the same time, enabling it to handle three different classes of totals (called minor, intermediate, and major). Thus, for example, if we wish to produce a labor distribution report from a deck of cards which contain a department number, job number, hours worked, and labor costs, we would first sort the cards on the job number field and then sort them according to department number. By using the job number as the minor control and the department number as the intermediate control, a report of hours and cost by job within department can be produced (see Figure 3–15). No-

LABOR COST REPORT			
Department Number	Job Number	Hours	Cost
21	1234	20	45:23
	1234	69	147:82
	1234	5	12:70
		94*	205:75*
	1265	105	224:40
	1265	243	517:82
	1265	90	203:00
	1265	175	386:07
		613*	1331:29*
	1342	73	150:20
	1342	65	143:56
	1342	38	81:93
		176*	375:69*
		883**	1912:73**
23	1234	55	125:64

FIG. 3–15.

tice that each intermediate total (identified by **) is the sum of the minor totals (identified by *) in that department.

The relationship between sorting and the use of the accounting machine is extremely important. The minor control is associated with the finest breakdown on the report, the intermediate control gives totals of minor totals, and the major control gives totals of intermediate totals. To arrange the cards in proper sequence, we must first sort on the minor control field, then sort on the intermediate control field, and finally sort on the major control field.

Detail Printing and Group Printing

On the report in Figure 3–15, there is a line for each card and a line for each total. Such a report is called a *detail printed* or *listed* report. It is also possible to produce a report in which only identifying information and the totals are printed (see Figure 3–16). Such a report is said to be *group printed* or *tabulated*.

LABOR COST REPORT			
Department Number	Job Number	Hours	Cost
21	1234	94	205:75
	1265	613	1331:29
	1342	176	375:69
		883*	1912:73*
23	1234	182	387:50
	------	-----	-----:---

FIG. 3–16.

Counters

By means of control panel wiring, each counter must be given four basic directions: (1) what field of the card to add (or subtract); (2) which cards to add, subtract, or ignore; (3) when to take a total and/or clear; (4) where on the report to print the total. Thus, great flexibility is provided in the results that may be obtained through the use of counters.

As was mentioned previously, counters may be of several different sizes. On most machines, there are counters with two positions, others with four, six, or eight positions. It is possible to couple two (or more) counters together to form a larger counter. A six-position counter and a four-position counter may be coupled to form a single ten-position counter.

The size of counter required is related to the number of digits in the largest total that is to be accumulated in that counter. If negative totals may be produced, it is necessary to provide one more counter position than there are digits in the largest total. A separate counter must be provided for each class of total that is produced on the report. Thus, each of the reports in Figures 3–15 and 3–16 require four separate counters, two counters for hours and two for cost.

Summary Punching

By means of a cable, a reproducer may be connected to the accounting machine to summary punch new cards containing information from the accounting machine counters during accounting machine total cycles. In this process, blank cards are inserted into the punch feed of the reproducer. By control-panel wiring, it is possible to pause before the counters are cleared during a total cycle and cause the reproducer to punch a card containing information from some or all of the accounting machine counters. All information to be summary-punched, including identifying information, must be in the accounting machine counters.

Summary punching is used to carry balances forward from one processing cycle to another and to condense the size of files by punching the sum of several cards into a single card which may be used in future procedures.

Selectors

Punched card machines are both flexible and versatile. The selector, which is used in most of the machines, contributes greatly to the flexibility of this equipment. Basically, the selector enables the machines to distinguish between two kinds of cards and to handle them differently.

For example, suppose that in using the accounting machine we wish to add a field from a *sales* card and subtract that field on a *returns* card to arrive at a net sales figure. In the first place, the machine must be able to distinguish between the two types of cards, and this is accomplished by including an X punch in a specific column of all of the returns cards while specifying that an X may not appear in that column of any of the sales cards. Thus, all returns cards might be distinguished by an X punch in column 56.

A selector is a relay that acts like a switch in a railroad track—it routes electricity along one of two possible paths, a *normal* path and a *transferred* path. The path chosen when the card is at the second reading station is determined by whether the pickup of the selector has been actuated by a pulse of electricity produced when an X punch was read when that card was at the first reading station (see Figure 3–17).

To add the sales cards and subtract the returns cards we: (1) Take a wire on the control panel from the column 56 reading brush (at the first reading station) to the selector pickup; (2) take a wire from a source which produces an impulse on each card to the common hub of the selector; (3) take a wire from the normal hub of the selector to the add hub of the counter; and (4) take a wire from the transferred hub of the selector to the subtract hub of the counter. Then on the cards which do not have an X in column 56 (the sales cards), the counter is told to add, while on those cards with an X in column 56 (the returns cards), the counter is told to subtract (see Figure 3–18).

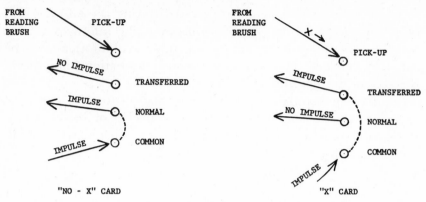

FIG. 3–17.

Selectors may also be used to route impulses so that a field will print in one column of the form for an X card and in another column on a no-X card; or so that one field on an X card will print in the same place as another field on a no-X card; or so that an X card will not print at all; or so that spacing will not take place after an X card, and so on. Multiple point selectors exist so that several columns of the card can be controlled by means of the same pickup. For example,

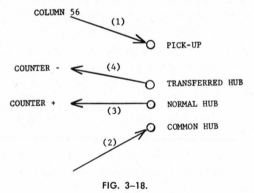

FIG. 3–18.

if we wish to print columns 1 through 5 from an X-50 card in the same area of the form as columns 76 through 80 of a card that has no X in column 50, we would wire as shown in Figure 3–19.

Obviously, the selector is an extremely useful device on a punched card machine. However, there are only a limited number of selectors on any machine, and when they are all used, this places a limitation on the ability of the machine to handle further complications.

Forms Control

To avoid the problems involved in separate feeding of forms, it is customary to use continuous forms with the accounting machines.

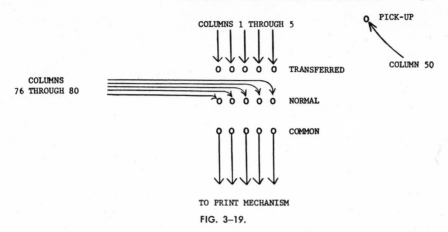

FIG. 3–19.

Of course, it is possible to produce multiple copies by using carbon paper or special chemically treated paper.

Spacing and skipping may be controlled to handle most of the types of forms that are in common use. For example, payroll checks and earnings statement may be printed on the accounting machine, and invoices can be prepared containing a heading section and a body section with the invoice total printed on the bottom line of the form. Such invoices present interesting forms control problems, for it is possible to have more lines on an invoice than can appear on a single page. In this case, the machine can be controlled so as to number the pages and skip the heading of the following form so that the remaining lines are printed in the body of the form.

The Calculator

The punched card accounting machine can add and subtract, but it does not multiply and divide. Punched card machines that can perform all four arithmetic operations are called calculators. These machines usually read several fields from a card, perform a number of calculating steps to produce answers, and punch these answers into the same card. Depending upon the model of the machine and the complexity of the problem, these machines operate at between 20 and 150 cards per minute.

Although most of these punched card calculators employ electronic circuits to perform their computations, they are not included in the category of electronic computers. The punched card calculator and the electronic computer are distinguished from one another primarily by the means through which they are controlled, and secondarily by the fact that the electronic computer frequently includes means of input and output other than the punched card. In a later section, we will discuss how the electronic computers are controlled.

The punched card calculator, like the other punched card machines, is controlled by means of a wired control panel. These control panels contain a series of rows of program hubs which emit impulses one row at a time starting with the first row and proceeding to the last one. By wiring these impulses to other sets of hubs on the control panel, it is possible to select each factor that enters into the calculation, to determine what arithmetic operation is to be performed, or to place a result in the proper position to be punched into the card. In various models of the calculators, from 12 to over 100 rows of program hubs are available, so calculations involving over 100 steps may be accomplished on one pass of the cards through the latter type of machine.

Example

Suppose we wish to use the IBM 604 calculator to: read three-digit numbers A, B, and C from a card; calculate $(A + B) \times C = D;$ and punch the result D into the card. We would first break this calculation down into simple steps by preparing a planning chart (see Figure 3–20). In the line corresponding to READ, we assign A to factor storage unit 1, B to factor storage unit 2, and C (by which we will multiply) to the multiplier-quotient unit.

This chart would then be translated into wires on two control panels, one devoted to reading and punching the card and the other to the calculations. The first will not be illustrated, but the entering of A and B into factor storage (in step R) and the punching of the result from the counter would be wired on that control panel.

In Figure 3–21 (which is not a geometrically accurate representation of the 604 control panel), the wires for each program step correspond to one line on the planning chart. On program step 1, wire A reads out factor storage 1, and wire B causes the counter to add. On

OP. NO.	OPERATION	FACTOR STORAGE				MULTI.- QUOT.	COUNTER	GENERAL STORAGE			
		1	2	3	4						
R	Read	A xxx	B xxx			C xxx					
1	Add A	R.O.					A xxx				
2	Add B		R.O.				A+B xxxx				
3	Store & Reset						Read Out & Reset	A+B xxxx			
4	Mult.(A+B)C						(A+B)C xxxxxx	R.O.			
5											

FIG. 3–20.

program step 2, wire C causes factor storage 2 to read out, and wire D causes the counter to add. On step 3, wire E reads A plus B out of the counter and resets it to zero, and wire F causes A plus B to enter general storage 2. Then, in step 4, wire G causes the machine to multiply the contents of the multiplier-quotient register by the sum of A

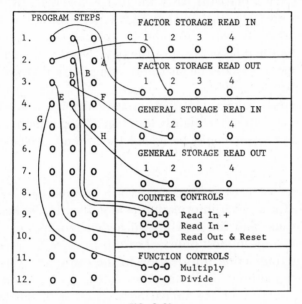

FIG. 3–21.

and B, which is designated by wire H, and the result appears in the counter.

Punched card calculators are used in payroll computations, in invoicing applications to multiply quantity times price, in computing parts and material requirements based upon a production schedule, and in any other punched card application which involves multiplication or division. In some applications, the cards are passed through the calculator several times to perform (and check) all of the calculations involved.

The Punched Card Installation

It is obvious that any single punched card machine is of little use by itself. They are designed to be used together to perform the various functions involved in data processing. However, the number and types of machines required in any given installation are determined by the type and volume of work to be done. Although the machines discussed above are considered basic, there are other punched card machines that can be included in an installation to perform specialized functions.

A typical, medium-sized, punched card installation might include five key punches, three verifiers, three 650-card-per-minute sorters, three reproducers, two accounting machines, one collator, and one interpreter. On a one-shift basis, the total rental for this type of installation would be approximately $2,000 per month. For additional hours that any piece of equipment is operated outside of the basic shift, an additional 50 per cent of the basic hourly rental is charged. The equipment may also be purchased at a price ranging from about 45 to 60 months' rental.

An electromechanical punched card calculator could be added to the above installation for slightly less than $300 per month, while an electronic calculator could be added for around $600 per month.

Summary

The punched card is used to record information in machine-processable form. Such information is identified to the machines by the card format and the field in which the information is located.

The basic steps in most punched card procedures involve: (1) recording the transaction information in the cards; (2) verifying the accuracy of recording; (3) sorting the cards according to one or more identifying fields; and (4) preparing a report with the accounting machine. In most cases, the efficiency of the use of punched cards depends upon repeating steps 3 and 4 several times so that the information is used in several sequences to prepare a number of results.

An installation of punched card equipment includes a number of different machines. The particular configuration is determined by the volume of transactions, the results to be produced, and the procedures employed.

EXERCISES

3.1 Define each of the following terms:
a) A field.
b) A self-checking number.
c) Interpreting.
d) Gang punching.
e) Reproducing.
f) Matching.
g) Merging.
h) Summary punching.
i) Listing.
j) Group printing.
k) An X punch.

3.2 Describe the functions performed by the accounting machine.

3.3 Describe group control on the accounting machine and discuss what it accomplishes.

3.4 What is a selector, and what does it do?

3.5 Describe three ways that information may be recorded in punched cards.

3.6 Which is faster, key punching or mark-sense recording?

3.7 Explain why the accuracy of recording is even more important for mechanized data processing than it is for manual systems.

3.8 Describe three methods of verification used in punched card work.

3.9 How is mark-sense information verified?

3.10 What are the basic steps involved in the typical punched card procedure?

3.11 *a*) If we wish to sort cards on a five-digit numeric field, how many passes through the sorter would be required?

b) If there are 10,000 cards in part (*a*), how many cards would be processed through the machine?

c) If the sorter operates at an effective speed of 600 cards per minute, how long would it take to complete this sort?

3.12 *a*) If no collator were available, how could two decks of cards be merged?

b) Could this same technique be used to match-merge two decks of cards? Why?

3.13 A rate master computation deck (containing rate, hours, and rate times hours), a sorter, a collator, and a gang punch can be used to multiply rate times hours to compute gross pay in a payroll procedure. Can you suggest how this might be accomplished?

3.14 Suppose we wish to add all cards except those with an X in column 75 into a counter. Draw a diagram showing how the selector would be wired to accomplish this.

3.15 Suppose we wish to add those cards into a counter that have an X in column 75 unless they also have an X in column 60, in which case, we wish to subtract the card. Cards with neither an X in 75 nor in 60 and those with an X in 60 but not in 75 are to be ignored. Draw a diagram showing selector wiring. *Hint:* Use two selectors.

SUPPLEMENTAL READINGS

Functional Wiring Principles. Form Number 224–6275–0. New York: International Business Machines Corp., 590 Madison Avenue.

An excellent general presentation of the way that the various functions of the IBM machines are accomplished with emphasis on the basic principles of the control panel wiring involved.

Functions of Remington Rand Univac Data-Automation System. Form Number U 1363. New York: Remington Rand Univac Division of Sperry Rand Corp., 315 Fourth Avenue.

A brief presentation of each of the major Remington Rand punched card machines and the functions they perform.

IBM Accounting Machine Functions. Form Number 22–8208–2. New York: International Business Machines Corp., 590 Madison Avenue.

A brief presentation of each of the major IBM punched card machines and the functions they perform.

Introduction to Data Processing. New York: Haskins and Sells, 1957.

Pages 60 through 83 present an excellent basic discussion of the punched card machines and how they are used for data processing.

IN CHAPTER 3, the basic considerations involved in punched card data processing and the capabilities of the most common punched card machines were discussed. The objectives in this chapter are: (1) to illustrate how these capabilities may be utilized in a data-processing system; and (2) to obtain an understanding of the considerations involved in designing a mechanized system.

In order to accomplish the first of these objectives, an example of a punched card payroll procedure will be presented. Unfortunately, the presentation of such a procedure does not also attain fully the second objective, for in this study of end results it is not always possible to adequately reconstruct the somewhat devious process by which these end results were created. Thus, an exercise is included which should at least raise some of the problems that must be faced in such a process.

Payroll Application

To illustrate how punched card equipment may be used for data processing, a simple payroll application will be discussed. This example will be simplified in at least two distinct ways. In the first place, the payroll will be on an hourly basis without the complications involved in job rates or incentives. Secondly, only a few of the many reports that must be produced from payroll records will be considered.

The first step in the design of a data-processing procedure is that of determining the required results. In this example, we wish to produce a payroll register, a check and earnings statement for each employee, and a labor cost report. Although the final forms of these reports are shown in Figures 4–1, 4–2, and 4–3, it should be understood that only their general information content would be known at the start, while the development of their exact formats would depend to a certain extent upon processing considerations. The first

67

FIG. 4-1

ACME MANUFACTURING CO.
Acme City, Ohio

J. P. BURDELL

to the order of

Date		
Month	Day	Year
8	7	59

Pay * * 70 58   Dollars | Cents

ACME CITY BANK

Authorized Signature

ACME MANUFACTURING CO.
Acme City, Ohio

Social Security No. 254 33 4218

J. P. BURDELL

Dept. No.	Man No.	Period Ending
23	2715	8 7 59

Statement
of
Earnings & Deductions

Hours	O.T. Prem.	Reg. Earn.	Total Earn.
43 0	1 5	86 00	89 00
10 30	2 23	89	18 42-
W.H.Tax	FICA	State	

SAVINGS BONDS	3 00-
HOSP INS	1 50-
UNITED FUND	50-

W. H. Tax Earnings	483 37
Year to date	
Net Pay	70 58
	3425 70

FIG. 4-1.

PAYROLL REGISTER

Employee		Social	Hours	Rate	Earnings			Deductions				Net	Year to Date			
Dept.	Number	Security No.	Worked		Regular	Overtime	Total	W.H. Tax	FICA	State	Other	Pay	W.H.Tax	FICA	State	Earnings
1	433	143652407	40 0	2 100	84 00		84 00	16 00	2 35	1 68	6 75	57 22	235 50	38 25	25 90	1177 50

FIG. 4-2.

			Current Week		Total	
Job Number	Work Order Number	Dept.	Hours	Amount	Hours	Amount
			LABOR COST REPORT			
143	2047	1	15	30	25	168	342	75
		5	7	15	32	78	172	98
		13	62	148	16	359	824	50
		37	22	53	43	204	475	83
			106*	247	16*	809*	1816	06*
	2881	3	19	41	12	253	540	77
		5	56	212	77	803	1836	28
		12	12	26	07	48	104	00
		13	92	198	95	241	516	26
		34	24	53	40	105	218	83
			203*	532	31*	1450*	3216	14*
	3456	10	18	39	50	63	143	23
		11	44	102	25	105	221	11
		12	7	15	16	27	56	10
		22	15	33	42	45	99	63
		29	26	61	05	63	131	17
		30	14	29	20	40	86	05
		35	31	66	88	31	74	00

FIG. 4–3.

approximations with which we start would be repeatedly modified to result in the reports shown. The card forms and procedures, which will be discussed later, are also presented in their final form.

It is worth remarking again that we are considering but a few of the reports that are desired (or required) from a payroll system. Other reports that might be involved include deduction registers, employee earnings records, analysis of overtime by department, attendance analyses, W-2 forms or each employee, social security reports, and income tax reports for federal and state governments.

The next step in designing a procedure is to determine where the information required in the output results may be obtained. In this case, the information comes from the employee's time card, from labor tickets which record the time worked on each job, and from file information concerning the employee, his deductions, and his past payment history.

Card Forms

Our next step is to consider the card forms which are required. We must determine the number of different card forms that should be involved, decide what information must be included on each card form, and assign each field to specific columns on each card form.

The size of each field is determined by the largest number that will be recorded there, while the determination of the arrangement of the fields is complicated by three considerations:

1. The Relationship of the Cards to the Source Document. Cards should be designed to correspond to the document from which they are key-punched (and vice versa) so that the key punch operator may punch from the document with a minimum of skipping around.

2. The Relationship of the Cards to Each Other. Similar fields should be located in the same columns of card forms in which they both occur.

3. The Relationship of the Cards to the Reports Required. Fields which will appear in the same column of a printed report should be located when possible in the same columns of the cards involved.

In our illustration, the time card will be a punched card in which total hours worked will be entered by means of mark sensing. The time card, shown in Figure 4–4, will be prepunched with department

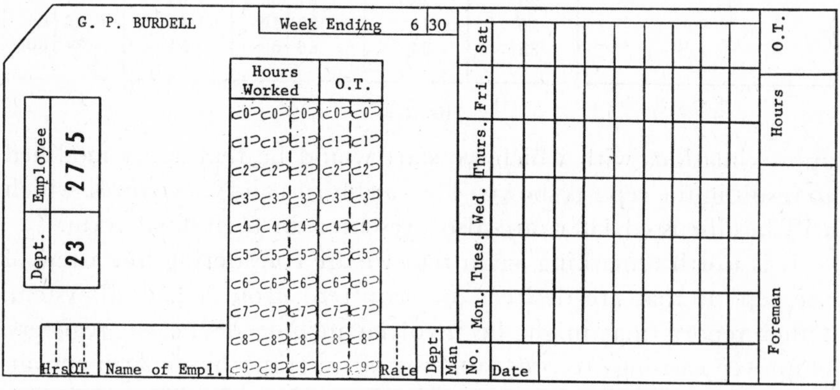

FIG. 4–4.

number, employee number, employee name, hourly rate, and date, while regular hours and overtime premium hours will be mark-sense punched. The labor ticket is a dual card, that is, a card designed so that information may be written on its face and subsequently key-punched into the same card. As can be seen in Figure 4–5, this card form provides separate locations in which to write department number, employee number, job number, work order number, operation code, hours, and date. These may then be key-punched in the same card and verified.

Four additional cards are involved in the payroll processing: the payroll master card, the current earnings card, deduction cards, and the year-to-date earnings card (see Figure 4–6). Notice that depart-

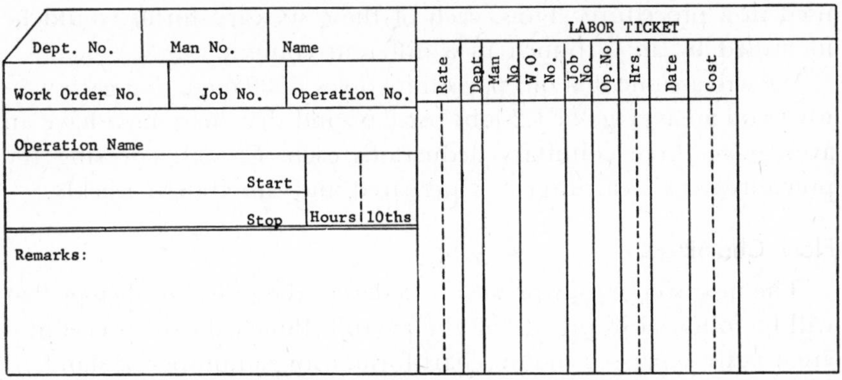

FIG. 4–5.

ment number and man number are lined up in the same columns on all six card forms. Also, by referring to the earnings statement, it is possible to observe that fields on the current earnings and year-to-date cards that print in the same columns of this report are punched in the same columns of the card, which simplifies the accounting machine control panel wiring. As was mentioned in Chapter 3, X punches are used to identify to the machines the various card forms

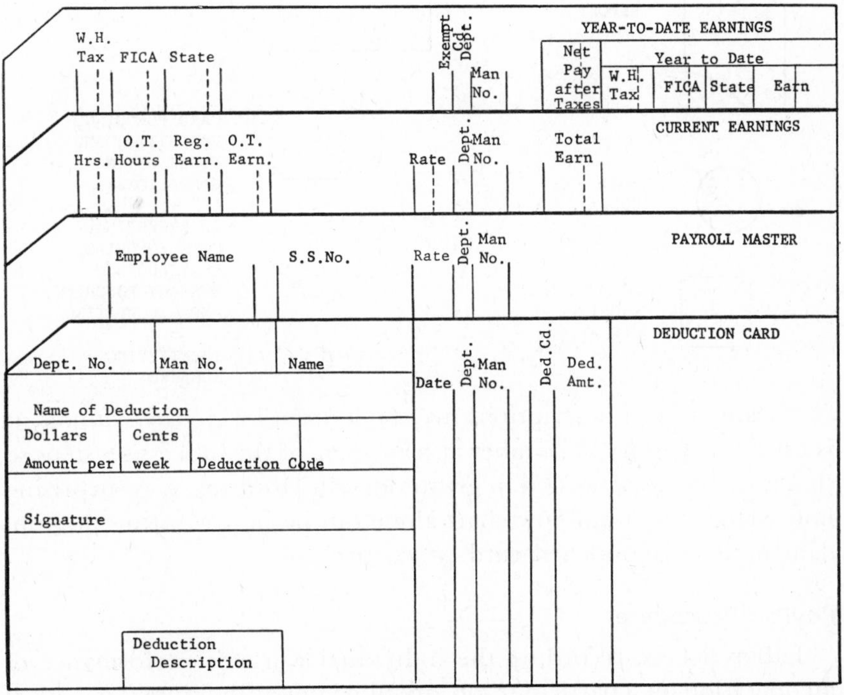

FIG. 4–6.

used in a procedure. Thus, each of these six card forms would be identified by an X punch in a different column.

We will assume that our payroll involves 1,500 men, that each man works on an average of 1.2 jobs per day, and that these men have an average of three voluntary deductions each. Checks, covering the previous week's earnings, are prepared and distributed weekly.

Flow Charting

The next step in our process is to design the procedural steps that will be followed in processing the payroll. Punched card procedures are usually expressed in flow chart form, using a number of standard symbols (which are found in the flow-charting template available from the machine manufacturers) to visually represent the various machine operations and the cards, documents, and reports. These symbols are explained below.

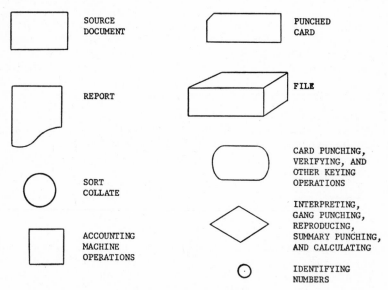

SOURCE DOCUMENT

PUNCHED CARD

REPORT

FILE

SORT COLLATE

CARD PUNCHING, VERIFYING, AND OTHER KEYING OPERATIONS

ACCOUNTING MACHINE OPERATIONS

INTERPRETING, GANG PUNCHING, REPRODUCING, SUMMARY PUNCHING, AND CALCULATING

IDENTIFYING NUMBERS

Although brief descriptions may be written inside the symbols, it is usually necessary to number at least some of the processing steps so that they can be described in greater detail. However, it is surprising how effective a visual flow chart alone can be in presenting the fundamentals of a punched card procedure.

Payroll Procedure

Labor tickets, recording the individual worker's performance of an operation on a particular job, are filled out at the time the work is performed and turned in to the machine accounting department on a daily basis. These cards may be key punched and verified as they are turned in during the week. The time cards, recording attendance time during the week, are marked by the timekeepers, and turned in to the machine accounting department at the end of the week. The payroll is then processed according to the procedure shown in Figure 4–7. The following comments refer to the numbered steps of this procedure.

1. Match-merge (on man number and department) the time cards and the labor tickets. Any unmatched cards will have to be investigated to determine the reason.

2. For each man, the accounting machine adds attendance time from the time card and substracts each of the job times from the job cards. If this total is not zero, the difference is printed (along with the department and man number) so that the differences can be investigated and corrected.

3. The employee's rate from his time card is gang-punched into the job cards which follow so that the hours can be multiplied by rate in step 8. Then, in the following step, the time cards and job cards are separated by sorting on the column containing one of the identifying X punches (while blanking out the other rows), so one type of card is placed in the X pocket and the other type in the reject pocket. The time cards are reproduced and filed (they are legal records), and the current earnings cards thus prepared are used for further processing.

4. This step calculates regular earnings, overtime earnings, and total earnings and punches them into the current earnings card. A second pass through the calculator usually is required to check these calculations. Before gross-to-net calculations can be made, it is necessary to insert the year-to-date cards by match-merging, investigating any unmatched cards.

5. This pass calculates federal and state withholding tax and Old Age, Survivors, and Disability Insurance to produce net pay before voluntary deductions. Exemption code and year-to-date earnings from the year-to-date card are used in this calculation. A second pass through the calculator is necessary to check these calculations. Before preparing the payroll register, it is necessary to merge in the payroll master cards and the voluntary deduction cards so that complete information is available on each employee.

6. Only one line is printed for each man on the payroll register. This is accomplished by accumulating totals and suppressing spacing so that all of the cards for an employee print on the same line.

7. The checks and earnings statements are printed simultaneously side by side. At the same time, new year-to-date cards are summary-punched for use next week. The new year-to-date cards must be run through the accounting machine again so that their total can be compared with the payroll register total in order to check the accuracy of the summary-punching operation.

8. This portion of the procedure is concerned with the distribution of

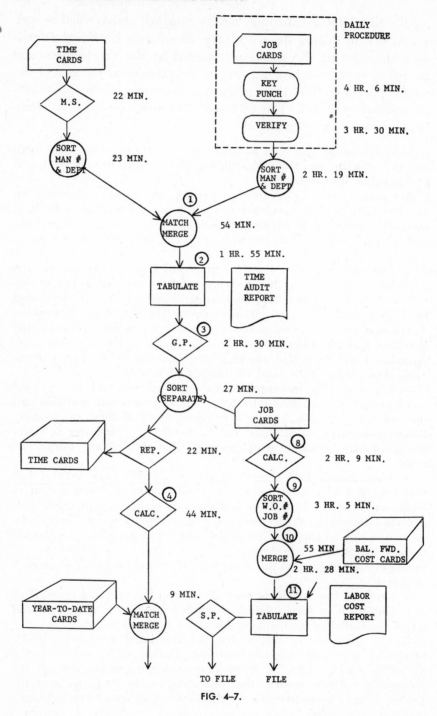

FIG. 4–7.

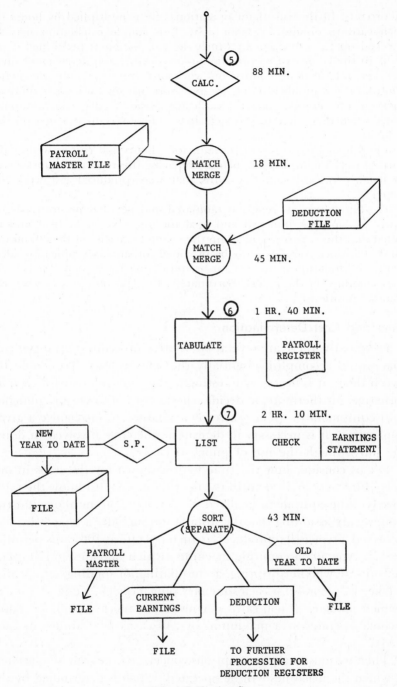

FIG. 4–7 (Continued).

labor costs. In this calculator operation, rate is multiplied by hours for each card to obtain the labor cost. This simple calculation may be checked on the same run in which the calculation is performed.

9. In the labor cost report, the minor control is on department number, the intermediate control on work order number, and the major control on job number. Thus, we must sort first on work-order number, then on job number. Since the cards are already in department-number order when they come to this step, it is unnecessary to sort first on this field.

10. The labor cost report contains total hours and cost as well as the current week's figures. Thus, before preparing this report, we must merge in balance-forward summary cards that were produced last week (in step 11).

11. The labor cost report is tabulated and new balance-forward cost cards are summary-punched and filed for use next week. It should be noted that this report would strain the counter capacity of the 80-counter IBM 402, since counters must be provided for summary punching identifying information as well as for accumulating three totals for each of four columns on the report. Fortunately, the IBM 407 has at least 120 counter positions.

Time and Cost Determination

Frequently, there are several alternative procedural arrangements that would accomplish essentially the same results. To choose between them, it is necessary to estimate the time and cost for each alternative. Furthermore, to decide whether or not to acquire punched card equipment or (if it is already available) to mechanize a given application, it is necessary to determine the costs involved in doing the job through the use of punched cards.

Let us consider how the time figures shown for the steps in our procedure were arrived at. In the first place, we must know the rated speeds of the equipment involved. For example, in the above illustration, we are assuming that the installation includes a type 604 calculator and a type 519 reproducer (which operate at 100 cards per minute), a type 407 accounting machine (which operates at 150 cycles per minute whether printing, accumulating, or totaling, except that it takes 1.2 seconds for each summary punch cycle), a type 082 sorter (which operates at 650 cards per minute), and a type 077 collator (which operates at a maximum of 240 cards per minute in each feed).

Then we must make assumptions concerning the over-all efficiency at which the machines will be operated, which is determined by the setup time, card handling time, machine error time, and so forth. In the above illustration, we have assumed that the sorter operates at

60 per cent efficiency and that the other equipment operates at 70 per cent efficiency. We have also assumed that the key punch operator will produce an average of 10,000 key strokes per hour and that the verifier will be operated at 12,000 key strokes per hour, with an additional second required to feed and eject each card on each of these two machines.

We must also determine the card volume through each machine. This is determined by the number of men on the payroll and by the average number of jobs per day per man. Since we have assumed that there are 1,500 men, and 1.2 jobs per man per day, we know that there will be 1,500 time cards per week and 1,800 job cards per day. Now, starting with the mark-sense punching of the time cards, 1,500 cards divided by 70 per cent of 100 cards per minute gives about 22 minutes. The time to sort these cards on man number and department number (six columns) is $6 \times 1,500$ divided by $.60 \times 650$, which equals slightly over 23 minutes.

Assuming that 20 columns on each job card must be key-punched and verified, the punching time in hours would be $1,800 \times 20$ divided by 10,000 plus 1,800 seconds for card feeding, which gives 4 hours and 6 minutes. Similarly, verifying will require $1,800 \times 20$ divided by 12,000 plus 1,800 seconds, or a total of 3 hours and 30 minutes. Some additional time will be required to repunch cards that are in error. The time to sort the 9,000 job cards at the end of the week is $6 \times 9,000$ divided by $.60 \times 650$, which gives about 139 minutes, or 2 hours and 19 minutes.

Timing the collator operations requires more specific knowledge of how the collator operates than has been included in the discussion in Chapter 3, for we must know when the two feeds operate simultaneously and when they operate separately. At step one, 9,000 job cards and 1,500 time cards will be involved, but the time cards will fall into a pocket simultaneously with the first job card for that man, so we need only allow time for 9,000 cards at 240 cards per minute at 70 per cent efficiency, giving approximately 54 minutes. Incidentally, IBM furnishes a plastic calculator which may be used like a slide-rule to perform the calculations involved in estimating time.

In addition to the 10,500 cards involved in step 2, a total is required for each man, giving 12,000 machine cycles for the report. Thus, the time required is 12,000 divided by $.70 \times 150$, which gives slightly less than 115 minutes. To separate the time cards from the job cards requires but one pass, so the time required is given by 10,-500 divided by $.60 \times 650$, which equals slightly less than 27 minutes.

In the payroll side of the procedure, 1,500 cards are involved in reproducing the time cards and in the calculation of item 4, but the calculation involves two passes through the machine. Then we merge in 1,500 year-to-date cards, but the cards involved feed simultaneously, so the time required is 1,500 divided by .70 × 240, which is slightly less than 9 minutes. After step 5, we merge in 1,500 payroll master cards, which would fall simultaneously with the year-to-date cards, so the time necessary is that required for a single feed operation with 3,000 cards.

The merge step preceding step 6 involves 4,500 cards in each feed. The situation here is more complex, for the only simultaneous feeding obtained would be the current-earnings card and the first deduction card for each man, so 7,500 card-feed cycles are required. Thus, the time is 7,500 divided by .70 × 240, which equals about 45 minutes.

In step 6, a total is required for each man, so 10,500 cycles would be needed, which takes 1 hour and 40 minutes. Step 7 requires the same time plus time for 1,500 summary punch cycles at 1.2 seconds each for a total of 2 hours and 10 minutes. Since the identifying X punches are in different card columns, the separation shown in the last sort operation cannot be accomplished in one pass. On the first pass, requiring 23 minutes, we would pull out the 4,500 deduction cards. Thus, the next pass to extract the payroll master cards would involve but 4,500 cards and require 12 minutes. The final pass of 3,000 cards would separate the current earnings and the old year-to-date cards, and could be accomplished in 8 minutes, for a total of 43 minutes.

Returning to the procedure for preparing the labor cost report, the 9,000 job cards are involved in steps 8 and 9. Step 9 requires sorting 9,000 cards on 8 columns. In step 10, the balance-forward cards will fall simultaneously with the first current card, so they will require no extra time except in cases where there is no activity on the work order in a department that had previously worked on it. We will assume that this occurs infrequently. Thus, the merge requires 54 minutes, and we will allow an extra minute for inactive work orders.

In order to time step 11, we must estimate the number of summary punch and total cycles. This estimate in a given situation would be based on an analysis of experience, but we will assume that there is an average of 5 departments working on each work order, 6 work orders for each job, and 50 active jobs. Thus, we would have 5 × 6 × 50 minor totals and summary cards, 6 × 50 intermediate totals, and 50 major totals. Thus, we have 10,500 cards, 1,850 totals, and 1,500 summary punch cycles, which require a total of 2 hours and 28 minutes.

Scheduling

Translating the individual machine times involved into a schedule for machine operation, it appears that Monday would be devoted to key punching and verifying (which can be partially overlapped) the job cards for Friday's work and to sorting the entire 9,000 job cards. The time necessary to mark-sense punch and sort the time cards is relatively insignificant. On Tuesday, we could overlap steps 1, 2, and 3 and perform them in around 3½ to 4 hours. However, we must leave sufficient time to reconcile any discrepancies noted in the time-audit report, so we will allow Tuesday for performing these functions and for separating the job cards from the time cards.

Considering the main payroll processing, it appears possible to complete the payroll on Wednesday. Thus, the payroll checks could be available for distribution Thursday morning. However, this does not leave any time for emergencies such as machine downtime and operator errors. Thus, we probably should not plan to distribute the checks until Thursday afternoon or on Friday (since weekly payrolls are traditionally paid on Friday).

The labor cost report should also be available sometime Thursday, especially if some block sorting were done to overlap part of the sorting with the printing of the report.

It should be noted that the above discussion on scheduling ignores machine conflicts which may arise as a result of other applications for which the machines may be used. The fitting together of schedules for several procedures is an involved process, but it must be planned and adhered to if the punched card installation is to operate efficiently and produce its reports on time. The efficiency of scheduling and the due dates of reports also influence the total amount of punched card equipment required for the installation. Since much accounting work seems to be concentrated at the end of the month, either some of the reports must be substantially delayed, or excess equipment must be provided which will be idle during slack periods of the month. This problem is sometimes handled economically by using overtime, extra shift operation, or service bureau facilities during the peak-load periods.

In order to estimate the total cost of a procedure, it is customary to estimate the cost per hour involved in operating each of the different machines. This cost must include not only the machine rental, but also the operator cost and usually an overhead cost. Then the total time involved for each machine may be multiplied by the cost per hour for that machine, and these figures accumulated to estimate the total cost of the procedure. If these costs can be favorably compared to the present costs of performing the work, or if intangible factors are involved which make mechanization desirable, it may be advantageous to convert to the use of punched cards.

If it is decided to mechanize the application, much remains to be done before the reports are actually prepared on punched card equipment. Control panels must be wired, operating procedures must be written, card and report forms must be ordered, additional punched card equipment may have to be installed, and personnel outside the machine accounting department may have to be trained in new procedures. Then, once the change-over starts, a substantial period of time is necessary to iron out the bugs that will arise and to complete the conversion. From the above discussion, it is obvious that several months is required to plan and convert to a mechanized procedure for any application of moderate complexity.

Exercise

As was mentioned at the beginning of this chapter, it is difficult to obtain an understanding of how a procedure was created by studying the end product. Thus, the primary purpose of this exercise is to raise questions and to force you to deduce answers. It may occur that you will not be able to satisfactorily answer all the questions that arise on the basis of your rather incomplete knowledge of the equipment and its use. If so, do not just give up—assume a reasonable answer and go on with the rest of the problem so that you will encounter further questions. An awareness of the type of questions that must be faced is frequently more important than the answers themselves. According to Charles Kettering, "It isn't the things you don't know that get you into trouble, it's the things you know for sure that are not so."

This illustration is in the area of sales analysis, which is usually integrated with inventory control, invoicing, and accounts receivable for efficient mechanization. But, in order to restrict the scope of the problem, not only are the output requirements specified, but also the input has been set up so as to isolate the application from others with which it would normally be associated. Thus, we may concentrate solely upon obtaining a basic understanding of how the punched card machines are used for data processing without introducing unnecessary complexity.

The General Manufacturing Company manufactures and sells casters of various sizes and shapes throughout the country. We will assume that this company has an installation of punched card machines, including all the equipment described in the previous illustration except the calculator, and that they wish to produce two daily reports and three monthly reports as shown below and in Figures 4–8 through 4–12.

Daily	*Monthly*
Invoice register	Sales by product
Product class report	Sales by location
	Sales by salesman (with year-to-date amounts)

DAILY

SALES BY CLASS
Report 2

Class	Amount
1	106601
2	98493
3	117380
4	62175
5	141918
6	110021
7	97550
8	107190
9	118083
	959411*

FIG. 4–8.

INVOICE REGISTER
Report 1

Invoice No.	Date Invoice Mo.	Date Invoice Day	Date Invoice Yr.	Quantity	Product Cl.	Product Item	Unit Price	Sales Amount		Cost Amount		Sales Br.	Sales Man	Location City	Location St.	Cust. No.
12351	10	31	60	15	1	7203	1 62	24	30	19 50		10	24	015	23	14765
12351	10	31	60	5	2	1103	1 77	8	85	6 67						
12351	10	31	60	50	3	2103	2 69	134	50	103 60						
12351	10	31	60	20	5	4107	4 98	99	60	81 68						
								267	25*							
12352	10	31	60	10	1	6102	1 53	15	30	12 25		16	30	147	38	61742
12352	10	31	60	5	3	5105	3 28	16	40	11 73						
12352	10	31	60	15	4	4104	3 51	52	65	42 20						
12352	10	31	60	50	5	3208	4 85	242	50	182 20						
								326	85*							
								9594	10							

FIG. 4–9.

				MONTHLY			
Sales by Product							
Report 3							
Product							
Cl.	Item	Description	Quantity	Amount		Cost	
1	210	Square Shank Rg 1	40000	14765	54	18437	54
	1426	Square Shank Rg 2	205	1476	31	1344	52
	2735	Square Shank Rg 3	1473	19437	24	17655	54
			41678	35679	09*	37437	60*
2	610	Caster 10/22	9	141	50	150	75
	2011	Caster 10/32	4765	9655	40	8613	42
	6314	Caster Red 14/52	451	10571	20	9544	67*
				914376	50	549176	43

FIG. 4–10.

An analysis of the source documents and reports has been made, resulting in the determination of the following average volume figures:

Invoices per day. 100	States. 40
Items per invoice. 10	Cities per state. 40
Working days per month. 22	Product classes per city. 2.5
Product classes. 9	Product classes per salesman. 4
Items. 3,000	Salesmen. 110
	Branches. 12

We will assume that the billing department types invoices from orders which have been stamped with a serial invoice number (see Figure 4–13). Note that the cost column would not appear on the copy of the invoice that is sent to the customer.

				MONTHLY			
Sales by Location							
Report 4							
Location		Pr.					
St.	City	Cl.	Quantity	Amount		Cost	
29	1	1	4007	4176	52	2075	43
		2	275	549	76	275	97
		5	7643	3919	87	2715	43
			11925*	8646	15*	5066	83*
	2	2	4310	4975	37	2197	61
		5	510	1041	00	971	67
		6	204	465	87	401	19
		7	120	305	40	255	20
	40	1	21	47	50	29	75
		2	470	397	50	298	40
			491*	445	00*	328	15*
	State	Totals	74343**	40419	75**	29547	53**

FIG. 4–11.

MONTHLY
Sales by Salesman
Report 5

Sales		PR.	Current Month				Year to Date			
Br.	Man	Cl.	Amount		Cost		Amount		Cost	
1	1	1	143	27	98	00	4133	33	3142	20
		2	2100	00	1000	05	19742	76	9176	50
		6	3201	20	2107	62	21734	12	10147	61
			5444	47 *	3205	67 *	45610	21 *	22466	31 *
	2	1	104	37	89	42				
2	3		24845	97 **	15486	27 **	14476	10 **	97239	10 **
			-----	--	-----	--	-----	--	-----	--

FIG. 4–12.

At the end of each day an adding machine tape of the invoice totals
is run. Then the invoices, in consecutive number sequence, are sent
to the machine accounting department accompanied by the adding
machine tapes.

GENERAL MANUFACTURING CO.
Podunk, Indiana

Invoice No.   12351   Date: 10/31/60
Branch 10   Salesman 24

To: Local Furniture Co.
        2314 S. Ferry Street
        Crawfordsville, Mo.

City	State	Customer
15	23	14765

Quantity	Item	Description	Unit Price	Amount	Cost
15	17203	Caster Rnd	$1.62	$ 24.30	$ 19.50
5	21103	Caster Ball Brng	1.77	8.85	6.67
50	32103	Caster S.S 10/22	2.69	134.50	103.60
20	54107	Caster Brass 14/52	4.98	99.60	81.68
			Total	$267.25	

FIG. 4–13.

EXERCISES

4.1   Design the card form (or forms) for this application. What fields are required and how large should they be?

4.2   Devise a daily procedure to produce the cards, invoice register, and product class report.

4.3   Devise a monthly procedure to produce the monthly reports.

4.4   Making the same timing assumptions as in the previous illustration, estimate the time required for each machine operation in the two procedures. About how many working days would be required for the production of the monthly reports?

4.5   Which of the monthly reports would be prepared first? Why?

4.6   The foregoing has assumed that the cost amount on the invoice is entered manually by cost clerks before the invoice is sent to the machine accounting department. If this cost figure were not entered on this invoice and a punched card calculator were available, what modification in the daily procedure could be used to enter costs automatically into the sales analysis reports and to check price and the extended amount?

4.7   How many counter positions will be required to produce the sales-by-salesman report? What information will be contained in the summary cards produced with this report? How many summary cards will be produced each month?

4.8   What would happen if several cards were lost during the monthly procedure? How could this loss be detected? How could the error be corrected?

CHAPTER 5 · Basic Concepts of Electronic Computers

IN PREVIOUS chapters, data processing itself and the use of punched card equipment for data processing were discussed. All of this has been preliminary to the major purpose of this book—obtaining an understanding of the electronic computer and its use in data processing. This chapter introduces the basic ideas associated with the electronic computers themselves and is concerned with the question: What is an electronic computer, and what are its capabilities?

In the first place, the term *electronic computer* has been applied to two basically different types of machines—digital computers and analog computers. The digital computer operates on numbers just as humans do—adding, subtracting, multiplying, and dividing the numbers as does a hand calculator or an adding machine, or just as we learned to do in grade school. On the other hand, the analog computer does not compute directly with numbers, but manipulates some physical quantity such as voltage or length or shaft rotation which (to a certain degree of accuracy) represents the numbers that are being computed. In other words, the analog computer utilizes an analogous physical situation for the purpose of computing, while the digital computer computes with numbers themselves. Although for certain engineering and scientific problems the analog computer is simpler and more convenient to use than the digital computer, the accuracy of these machines is limited by physical considerations to approximately one tenth of 1 per cent. Thus, they are not satisfactory for most data-processing purposes, and we will confine our discussion to the digital type machines.

Many different types of digital computers have been built, ranging in cost from a few thousand to several million dollars. Though they vary greatly in size, speed, and details of their operations, fortunately, most of them have the same basic logical structure. Thus, the block diagram in Figure 5–1 is representative of the entire class of machines that we will be considering. In Figure 5–1, the heavy arrows represent flows of data, and the single arrows indicate im-

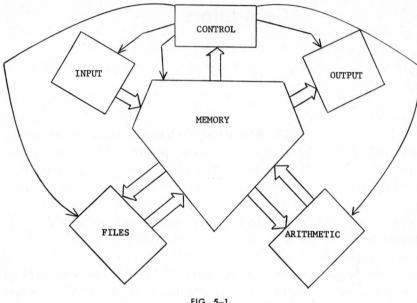

FIG. 5–1.

plementation of control functions. Let us consider each block of this diagram.

Input

. If a machine is to process information, that information must be made available to the machine in a form that it can utilize. In a computer, information is not directly usable in the form of written symbols like those on this page. As was seen in the discussion of punched card equipment, in a machine, information is represented in the form of electrical pulses, where different combinations of pulses represent different characters, in a manner similar to the familiar Morse code, which uses combinations of dots and dashes (short and long pulses).

Although great progress has been made in the development of devices that will read printed material and translate each character into the corresponding pulse code, most computer inputs are presented in a form that directly produces the pulse code itself. Many such devices are available to be used as inputs to electronic computers. Among them are punched cards, punched paper tape, magnetic tape, and ordinary adding machine type keyboards. One or more of the above devices may be used to enter information into a computer, and the speed with which the information is entered can range (depending on the devices used) from a manual speed of a few characters per second up to around 100,000 characters per second on magnetic tape.

In Chapter 3, it was shown that information may be recorded in punched cards in many ways, including key punching, prepunching, mark sensing, and as the output of various information-recording and -processing devices. Likewise, punched paper tape and magnetic tape may be generated by the use of key-driven equipment (similar in operation to the key punch) or by other information-recording and -processing devices. Thus, the function of recording information for entry into an electronic computer is similar to that of recording for punched card data processing, and the same basic considerations are involved.

Memory

From the input device or devices, the information is entered into the heart of the machine, which is the information storage section (or *memory*). Although the memory of an electronic computer serves many purposes, it is sufficient at this point to note that the complexity of the problems that can easily be handled by a machine and the speed with which they can be handled are basically determined by the size and the speed of the memory of the machine.

The memory of a machine serves many of the same purposes as the memory of a human, but the machine memory is more analogous to the memory of a reference book than it is to the memory of the human brain. For a machine to be able to recall information, it is necessary that it be told the location (or page) in the memory where the information is stored. For this reason, the memory of a machine is usually divided into cells called *words*. Each word consists of a certain number of digits or characters, and each of these cells is identified by a number called the *address* of that word, usually starting with zero and continuing sequentially to the highest number required. For example, if the memory of the machine contains 4,000 ten-digit words (or storage for 40,000 digits of information), they will be numbered from 0000 to 3999.

The average time necessary for a machine to recall information from a single memory cell is termed the *average access time* of the memory. Currently two major types of memory are in use—magnetic drum memory and magnetic core memory. Although they differ greatly in the engineering details of their method of operation, the major difference between these two methods of memory from the standpoint of the user of the machine is their speed. The magnetic drum memory has an average access time of from approximately 1 millisecond (1 millisecond represents 1/1,000 of a second) to around 20 milliseconds, while magnetic core memory will have an average access time of from 2 to 50 microseconds (a microsecond is 1/1,000,000 of a second). Thus, magnetic core memory is several hundred times as fast as magnetic drum memory, but magnetic core memory is also more expensive than magnetic drum memory. The size of the memory for most machines will range from 10,000 characters (1,000 ten-digit words) to around 320,000 characters (32,000 ten-digit words).

Files

As was mentioned in Chapter 2, one of the functions of data processing is reference to files of information, and this is accomplished within machines (as shown by the block diagram in Figure 5–1, page 86) by having machine processable files available for many (but not all) of the machines.

There are two basic types of files that can be referred to by computers—*sequential* and *random* access files. The sequential type file usually consists of reels of magnetic tape, which have the property that the first record in the file must be read before the second, which must be read before the third, etc. Magnetic tape has the advantages of low cost and almost unlimited capacity. One reel of tape may hold millions of characters of information, and as many reels may be used as is required.

The random access files are characterized by an ability to skip around within the file and to extract information with no particular regard to the sequence in which the extraction is performed. Large, slow magnetic drums, magnetic tape bins, and magnetic disc memories are among the devices used for random access memory. They will range in capacity from around 100,000 characters for the magnetic drums to 20,000,000 characters for the tape bins, and their access times will range from around 15 milliseconds for the drums up to around 10 seconds for the tape bins.

Machine files are actually a type of memory, and are distinguished from the *working memory,* discussed in the previous section, by several characteristics. In the first place, file memory is usually larger than working memory, and access to file memory is much slower than to working memory. Secondly, information in the file memory cannot be processed without first bringing it into the working memory. In this respect, file memory resembles an input device. It should be noted at this point that magnetic tapes, for example, can be used either for input or file memory, and for output as well.

Arithmetic

With the transaction information entered into the memory from the input devices, and the file information entered from the files, the computer is in a position to manipulate the information and perform its arithmetic and logical operations. These operations are performed in the arithmetic section of the machine, one operation at a time, with intermediate results being stored in the memory, which, in this case, is used as scratch paper. Thus, the arithmetic section will perform the operations of addition, subtraction, multiplication, division, and certain simple logical operations, such as comparing two numbers for equality. Depending upon the size and cost of the machine, the speed of arithmetic will range from an average of around 100 operations per second up to around 500,000 operations per second, where each operation is typically performed on a machine *word*.

Output

Finally, when the processing is completed, it is again necessary for the machine to communicate with the outside world and produce information in a form that humans can use. This is accomplished through various output devices, such as electric typewriters, line printers, punched cards, magnetic tapes, and punched paper tapes. The latter three of these can be processed further on auxiliary equipment to produce printed copy or can be re-entered into the machine for further processing. These output devices will range in speed from about ten characters per second for the electric typewriter to several thousand 120-character lines per minute for direct printed output, or around 100,000 characters per second on magnetic tape (which can be printed on a line printer in a separate operation).

Control

To recapitulate, variable information is read from the input devices into memory, where it is combined with file information and manipulated in the arithmetic section to produce intermediate results, and, eventually, the final results, which are then produced by output devices. All of these processes can take place with amazing speed. Still, we have not yet seen the true power of the electronic computer, for although it is amazing that a machine can perform thousands of calculations in a second, the truly amazing aspect is that they can perform the particular operations in the specified sequence to produce the results that are required. The outstanding capability of the electronic computer is best explained in terms of the remaining block—the block labeled *control*.

As can be seen from Figure 5–1, p. 86, information is taken from the memory section of the machine into the control section, and, on the basis of this information, all of the functions of the machine are controlled. The control section tells the input devices when and what information to enter into the memory; it tells the memory where to place this information; it tells the arithmetic section what operations to perform, where in memory to find the information and where to store the results; it locates the file information and stores it in the memory; and, finally, it controls the output section and determines what information is printed or written. All of this is accomplished by means of a concept called the *stored program*, which is the fundamental idea associated with the electronic computer.

The Stored Program

The words *stored program* refer to the concept of storing within the memory of the machine the procedure which the machine is to follow to accomplish the desired processing. Thus, the memory not only collects the information to be processed, associates it with other information, and serves as scratch paper, but it also is used to tell the machine what to do. The procedure to be followed must be broken down into a series of elementary machine operations that can be performed by the machine being used, and each of these basic operations is represented by a single instruction. These instructions are stored in the memory of the machine, and when the machine is in operation, the first instruction is taken to the control section, interpreted, and the operation called for is carried out. Then the next instruction is taken to the control section, interpreted, and executed; the third instruction is taken to the control section, interpreted, and executed; and so on through the procedure. When the last instruction has been completed, the machine automatically returns to the first instruction, and the process is again repeated with new information to process another transaction.

Each instruction includes two basic types of information. The first type of information is embodied in the *operation code*, which tells the machine what function it is to perform. For example, the code 70 may tell the machine to read a card, the code 60 may tell the machine to add, the code 19 may tell the machine to multiply, and so forth. The other type of information required (called the *address*) designates the location (or locations) in memory where the data to be manipulated can be found, or where the results that have been produced are to be stored in memory. A particular machine will have from 20 to over 100 different operation codes available for use, depending upon the design of the logic of the machine and the variety of input and output units which are used. The address section of the instruction can refer to any of the locations available in memory. Of course, each of the instructions is also stored in a memory location, and, therefore, each instruction has associated with it the address at which it itself is located.

At this point, it would be desirable to present an illustration of a typical computer program, but, unfortunately, this is not feasible for two reasons. In the first place, a computer program merely consists of a list of numbers which tell the machine in code what operation to perform. The reader is probably not yet familiar with any of these codes. Secondly, a typical computer program is long and complex, involving hundreds or even thousands of individual instructions. Without descriptive material (such as written descriptions and/or flow charts) a typical computer program is very difficult for a human (as opposed to the computer) to understand; even the man who wrote it may later find it difficult to read.

However, at this point, a simple illustration of a small portion of a program can be presented, using words rather than codes to describe the operations. Incidentally, most machine programs are initially written in a form similar to this.

Suppose that we have computed gross pay and the total of the voluntary and mandatory deductions for an employee and have them stored in memory. We would like to subtract the deductions total from gross pay to obtain and store net pay in memory. First, we must be more specific; we must specify exactly where in memory each of these numbers is to be found, and where net pay is to be stored. Suppose that gross pay is in location 1450, the sum of the deductions is in 1451, and we wish to store net pay in 1452.

This portion of the program would involve three steps:

1. Insert into the accumulator the number in location 1450.
2. Subtract the number in location 1451 from the contents of the accumulator.
3. Store the contents of the accumulator in location 1452.

Also, each of these instructions must be located in memory, say in locations 1000, 1001, and 1002. Then the program might appear as follows:

Location of Instruction	Operation Code	Address
1000	65	1450
1001	16	1451
1002	20	1452

The above program would accomplish the following:

	Memory		Accumulator
1450	Gross Pay	→	Gross Pay
1451	Deductions	→	− Deductions
1452	Net Pay	←	Net Pay

This is a good place to introduce some terminology. With each memory word there are associated two numbers: (1) the address of the word; and (2) the contents of the word. In the above example, 1450 is the address of gross pay, and the contents of location 1450 is gross pay. Likewise, the contents of location 1000 is the instruction 65 1450, while the location of the instruction 65 1450 is 1000. This is further complicated by the fact that the address 1450 is a part of this instruction, since the instruction performs an operation involving gross pay (the contents of 1450).

Yes-or-No Decisions

One of the most powerful capabilities of the electronic computer is its ability to make simple "yes-or-no" decisions. This is accomplished by the use of so-called *branching* instructions, which decide where in memory to go for the next instruction on the basis of the answer to a specific question that can be answered by either a yes or a no (see the following illustration).

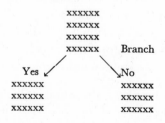

Typical branching questions are: Are these two numbers equal? Did the card have an X in column 75? Have we reached the end of this magnetic tape? Each of the preceding can be answered by yes or no, and on the basis of the answer, the machine can determine which set of instructions to execute next.

This branching ability enables the computer to handle data-processing situations in which exceptions occur, for the exceptions can be isolated by means of these questions, and the proper procedures for handling the exceptions can be executed. Thus, the normal data-processing program appears as in Figure 5–2. On the basis of the particular transaction being processed, the proper path through this maze of instructions is chosen. The first transaction may follow the

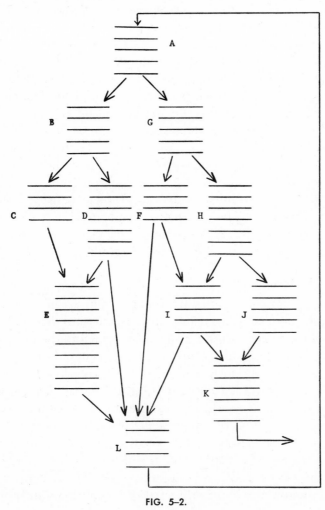

FIG. 5–2.

path from A to B to C to E to L; the second transaction, from A to G to F to I to K; the third, from A to B to D to L; the fourth, from A to G to H to J to K; the fifth, from A to G to F to I to L; and so forth. It should be noted that the machines are able to make these yes-or-no decisions at the same speed at which they compute.

Let us examine further this decision-making ability of the electronic computer. Notice that the machines are not actually making decisions in the normal sense of the word; they are following decisions that have been made when the program was designed. In other words, someone must decide what exceptions can arise, someone must devise a set of yes-or-no questions adequate to distinguish one exception from another, and someone must also determine the exact procedure that can be used to process each exception. Then the machine can follow through this maze of decisions and procedures quite rapidly and accurately. But if an exception arises that was not planned for in the program, the computer is completely helpless—it must either stop or process the transaction incorrectly.

In Chapter 2, we discussed the logical function in data manipulation which involves the precise determination of the procedural steps to be followed in the processing of a transaction. In the use of computers for data processing, this logical function is performed through the use of branching instructions. From the standpoint of the person who must devise the computer program, the establishment of the logical framework of the problem is usually the most important part of the job—so much so that he tends to view the entire program in terms of its branch points rather than in terms of the program steps that perform the actual manipulation.

Instruction Modification

The late John von Neumann (a famous and versatile mathematician's mathematician who created the mathematical theory of games) was one of the pioneer thinkers who contributed to the logical development of the electronic computer. He is generally credited with having originated the idea that since the instructions are numbers, and since the electronic computer is quite talented at manipulating numbers, perhaps it would be possible for the computer to apply this manipulating power to the instructions in its program, and thus produce new instructions to be executed by the machine.

This is a simple concept, yet it is difficult for the uninitiated to visualize how it might be put to practical use. To the contrary, however, instruction modification is used quite routinely in both scientific calculation and in data-processing applications. Instruction modification is of such importance in the use of computers that special instructions and machine components (such as indirect addressing and index registers) have been devised to accomplish the same results with less arithmetic and manipulation.

Although instruction modification is used in many other ways, so that the following example does not do justice to its capabilities, let us consider a situation in which we have 100 numbers stored in memory which we would like to add together in order to obtain their total. This could be accomplished by using 101 instructions, one to add each of the numbers into the accumulator and one more to store the results. However, if the numbers were stored in sequential memory locations, we might write an instruction which would add the first number into the accumulator, then a set of instructions that would add one to the address in this instruction, thus making it refer to the next number, and go back and repeat this process of instruction execution and modification until the entire 100 numbers have been totaled.[1] This program, using instruction modification, involves only about 10 instructions rather than the 101 required with the direct approach.

In the process of instruction modification, does the computer exhibit any creativity? Is the machine actually creating its own instructions? Probably not, for again a human is performing all of the creative work in this process. The person who designs the program must write the instructions that determine how the machine will manipulate the instructions that are being modified, and the human must plan each possible outcome of this modification so that the machine will perform the operations that will produce the desired results. Thus, again, the computer only follows through (at a rapid pace) a procedure based upon the thinking of the human who developed it.

Universality

Theoretically, any electronic computer can solve any problem that can be solved by computation—hence, they are called universal automatic computers. Thus, a small, inexpensive computer can theoretically be used to solve any problem that the largest, most expensive computer can solve, since both of them have the same general structure and capabilities. However, the amount of time required

---

[1] As will be seen in Chapter 7, the main problem in this process is how to stop after the last number has been added.

with the small machine may make its use impractical for some problems, just as many problems that are routinely solved by computers are impractical to solve by hand.

Thus, the economic question involved in the use of computers is not "How much does the machine cost?" or even "How fast is it?" The fundamental question is "How much does it cost to solve a specific set of problems using a particular machine?" There are many different computing machines, varying in reliability and cost, from which to choose, and each has a different mixture of input and output devices and speeds, memory size and speed, order structure and arithmetic speed, and file storage devices. For any particular set of problems, one of these different computers will be best, yet no single machine is best for all types of problems.

Summary

The basic components of an electronic computer are input devices, memory devices, an arithmetic and logical unit, output devices, and the control section. Many computers also include storage devices which make file information available for machine reference and processing.

The characteristic of the electronic computer that distinguishes it from the punched card calculator and other calculating machines is the manner in which they are controlled. Thus, the stored program, which provides a powerful method of automatic control, is the most important concept associated with the computer, and an understanding of the stored program and its use provides an understanding of the capabilities and limitations of the electronic computer.

As an illustration of the importance of the stored program, suppose we had a desk calculator that would do an addition, subtraction, multiplication, or division in one millionth of a second. This super desk calculator would still operate at about the same speed as an ordinary machine, for, without the stored program, it would still be tied to the speed at which a human operator could push the buttons telling it what to do.

The stored program, through its capability of branching and instruction modification, also allows elementary decisions to be incorporated into an automatic procedure. And the stored program gives these machines great flexibility, for a computer can be changed from one job to another by simply entering a new program into its memory. For example, to change from computing the solution of a set of simultaneous linear equations to the processing of inventory records, it is only necessary to feed the inventory program into the memory through the input device and place inventory information in the input mechanism.

The electronic computer has the following important capabilities:

1. It can follow long and complicated procedures involving large numbers of exceptions.
2. Through the use of its memory and its access to files, it can organize all the information necessary for processing.
3. It can perform arithmetic.
4. It can do all of the above with amazing speed and heretofore unobtainable accuracy.

On the other hand, in order to use a computer, we must completely prethink the procedure and express it in great detail. It is not possible in a data-processing situation to tell the computer to "use your own judgement," or even to "come and ask me if something comes up that you do not know how to handle." Not only must we figure out how to answer all the questions beforehand—we must also know what the questions are going to be before they actually arise.

Thus, the machines are utterly dependent upon humans—rather than being giant brains, they are large, fast morons, for they do just what they are told without question. Computers can provide the quickest and most efficient method yet devised for turning out wrong answers, for if they are fed incorrect information or an inadequate program, they will obligingly produce wrong answers at the same fantastic speed with which they can produce correct results.

Furthermore, in addition to a volume of processing sufficient to justify its use, a computer can only be used to solve problems that involve a lot of repetition, for writing a computer program is many times as hard as computing the answer once. The necessary repetition usually arises in data processing because many transactions must be processed. But in scientific computation, a single problem, such as solving a set of simultaneous linear equations, may involve performing the same elementary sequences of operations over and over with the coefficients of the unknowns. Thus, a computer may be efficiently used to solve one (or a small number) of problems.

EXERCISES

5.1   What is the typical basic structure of an electronic computer?

5.2   What are the various functions performed by the memory of a computer?

5.3   How are computers controlled?

5.4   What is a word? Distinguish between the address and the contents of a memory location.

5.5   Distinguish between the working memory and file memory of a computer.

5.6   What is branching? Why is branching important?

5.7   Is there any "best" computer? Explain your answer.

5.8   What are the capabilities of the computer?

5.9   What are the limitations of the computer?

5.10   Can a computer think? Defend your answer? In Chapter 1, it is reported that a computer can prove mathematical theorems. Is this thinking? What do we mean by the word *think?*

5.11   All computers have basically the same capabilities—they can add, subtract, multiply, divide, and branch. Can they all be used to solve the same problems? How do computers differ?

SUPPLEMENTAL READINGS

BELL, WILLIAM D.   *A Management Guide to Electronic Computers.* New York: McGraw-Hill Book Co., Inc.

Chapter 2 introduces the basic concepts associated with electronic computers.

CHAPIN, NED.   *An Introduction to Automatic Computers.* Princeton, N.J.: D. Van Nostrand Co., Inc., 1957.

Chapter 2 poses the question "What is an Electronic Computer?"

Introduction to Data Processing.   New York: Haskins & Sells, 1957.

Pages 86 through 94 present an introduction to the electronic computer.

CHAPTER 6 · An Intermediate Computer— Part I

IN ORDER to obtain a realistic understanding of the capabilities and limitations of the electronic computer, as well as the management problems involved in the use of a computer for data processing, it is necessary to progress beyond the stage of vague generalities and to study in some detail how the computer is programmed. This is not to imply that the major objective of this book is to develop programmers—it is simply an expression of the conviction that anyone who makes decisions concerning computers, or works with computers in any way, needs to understand what is involved in programming.

In order to obtain this important understanding of computer programming, we will study an actual machine, the IBM Type 650 Magnetic Drum Electronic Data-Processing Machine (hereafter referred to as the 650). The 650 is widely used—more than 1,500 such machines have been installed—therefore, such a machine is frequently available for demonstrations or for running the exercises included at the end of this and the next chapter. It should be noted that many other machines would have served well for this purpose, for the detailed study of any computer provides an excellent background for understanding the entire class of electronic computers.

The 650 is an illustration of an "intermediate" electronic data-processing machine—it is intermediate in size, speed, and cost. The basic 650 rents for around $4,000 per month on a single-shift basis, and it performs an average of 200 to 500 operations per second. Designed to be integrated into a normal punched card installation and provide it with the capabilities of stored program machines at a relatively moderate cost, the 650 is an illustration of a host of small and intermediate computers with magnetic drum memory. Although the 650 and several of the other machines of this group can be augmented to include magnetic-tape input and output, we will only consider the basic configuration for which the input and output is limited to punched cards. Thus, additional considerations involved in the use of magnetic tapes will be deferred to Chapter 10.

Memory Drum

As can be readily deduced from its name, the memory of the 650 is provided by a magnetic drum, a cylinder of metal about 16 inches long and 4 inches in diameter that is spinning on its axis at a speed of approximately 12,500 revolutions per minute. On the surface of this drum, room is available to record 2,000 words of information, each word consisting of a 10-digit number and its sign. The addresses of these 2,000 words run consecutively from 0000 to 1999.

The surface of this drum is plated with a magnetizable cobalt-nickel alloy, and the information is written on the drum by magnetizing small areas (or spots) on this surface.[1] These magnetic spots are written and read by means of devices called *read-write heads,* which are basically electromagnets with an extremely small gap between the poles. These read-write heads are placed a few thousandths of an inch from the revolving surface of the drum, and when a short (a few microseconds) pulse of electricity is sent through the coil from A to B, the reading head is magnetized and some of the magnetic flux leaks down to pass through the surface of the magnetic drum (see Figure 6–1), thus magnetizing a small area of the drum

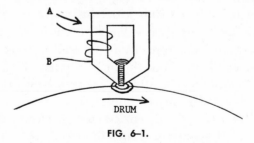

FIG. 6–1.

surface. As the drum rotates and the magnetic spot comes under the reading head again, the flux from the small magnet on the surface of the drum passes through the iron of the electromagnet and a pulse of electricity is generated in the coil of wire. Thus, the pulse can be read.

In all digital computers, information is recorded in coded form by

---

[1] Much of the information concerning how the machine operates is a simplification of material presented in the *IBM Type 650 Technical Information Manual* published by IBM and dated January 26, 1955.

some combination of elements (called bits) which have but two possible states, usually designated by 0 and 1. For example, in the punched card, we use a ten-bit code for numeric information in which the absence of a hole (in a row) corresponds to a "zero" bit, and the presence of a hole represents a "one" bit. In this code, each digit is represented by a combination of nine zero bits and a single one bit.

On the 650 drum, the zero and one bits are distinguished from each other by the direction of magnetization of the spot on the surface—either north-south or south-north, depending upon the direction of flow of the current in the coil of the read-write head. When these magnetized spots are read, they give rise to electrical pulses of different shapes which can be readily interpreted by the machine circuits as a zero bit or a one bit (see Figure 6–2).

"ONE" BIT   "ZERO" BIT

FIG. 6–2.

These magnetic spots are recorded at a density that allows 600 of them to be included in the path traced by each read-write head. Naturally, it requires more than one bit for the code used to record a digit, so several read-write heads are grouped together to form a band in which the bits required to represent a digit are simultaneously recorded (or read) in parallel. The 600 positions available in each band are grouped to form 50 ten-digit words, with a sign position for each word and a blank position between each word. Thus, on the drum, the word 0 1 2 3 4 5 6 7 8 9 + would be recorded digit by digit in serial fashion as shown in Figure 6–3. To obtain the 2,000 words of memory, there are 40 of these bands on the

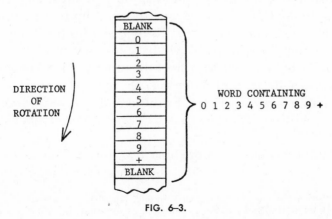

DIRECTION
OF
ROTATION

WORD CONTAINING
0 1 2 3 4 5 6 7 8 9 +

FIG. 6–3.

drum, with the first band containing words 0000 through 0049, the second band containing words 0050 through 0099, the third band containing words 0100 through 0149, and so forth, to the last band containing words 1950 through 1999. As the drum revolves, corresponding words on each band are under the read-write heads at the same instant.

Considering the speed at which the drum revolves, it is obvious that exceptionally good timing is required to record a word digit by digit in the area on the surface of the drum corresponding to the memory address involved. Likewise, split-second timing is required to select the proper area from which to retrieve a specified word from memory. In order to select the desired area, there exist several timing tracks on the drum. On one of these is recorded a pulse for each of the 600 digit positions around the drum, and on another is recorded a pulse corresponding to the beginning of each of the 50 words around the drum. During each drum revolution, the machine continually counts these pulses and thus keeps track of the position of the drum at each instant so that when the desired word comes under the read-write heads, the reading or writing circuitry may be activated.

At a speed of 12,500 revolutions per minute, it requires 4.8 milliseconds for this drum to make a complete revolution.[2] Thus, after a word has been written on the drum, it is 4.8 milliseconds before that word can be read. On the other hand, if at any instant a given word is required, that word may be just ready to pass under the reading heads, or it may be on the opposite side of the drum, or it may have just passed under the reading heads. Therefore, the time necessary to recall a word is variable—it depends upon the position of the drum at the time the information is desired, and the time may vary from as little as a few microseconds up to a maximum of 4.8 milliseconds. Since it is just as likely that a word will be close to the reading head as it is that it will have just been read, the average word will be on the opposite side of the drum from where you start, so the average delay (called the *average random access time*) will be one half a revolution or 2.4 milliseconds.

Input-Output

The input and output of the basic 650 consists of punched cards. The 650 has a read feed in which the information on punched cards

---

[2] A millisecond is one thousandth of a second. Sound travels about one foot in a millisecond. Thus, if a friend speaks to you from 24 feet away, the 650 drum will have made approximately five revolutions before the sound reaches you.

may be read (transferred into the magnetic drum memory) at a maximum rate of 200 cards per minute. It also has a separate punch feed which allows the machine to punch information from the drum into blank cards at a maximum rate of 100 cards per minute. Notice that the machine configuration with which we are concerned cannot punch into the cards which are read nor can it read from the cards which are punched without manually moving the cards from one feed to the other.[3]

Both the input and the output of this machine are "buffered," which means that the operations of reading, computing, and punching can be overlapped. In other words, the machine can be punching the results of one calculation, calculating on a card that has just been read, and, at the same time, physically reading a third card. The 650 has a wired control panel which is used to rearrange the format of the input cards as they are read and the output cards as they are punched in order to allow the most efficient processing within the machine.

Representation of Information

Within the 650 and on its console lights, numbers are presented in biquinary notation.[4] This representation requires seven bits— two binary bits, and five quinary bits. Figure 6–4 gives a representation of each of the digits zero through nine as they appear on the console lights. The two upper lights represent the binary portion, and the five vertical lights represent the quinary portion of the digit.

The use of this biquinary notation allows the 650 to be virtually 100 per cent self-checking without extensive additional circuitry, for most conceivable errors will result in a violation of the rule (which is checked on each operation) that one and only one bit be present in each of the two sections of the biquinary representation. For example, transfers within the machine are accomplished by sending pulses of electricity along seven parallel paths, one pulse for each of the bits present. If one of these pulses does not get through, that bit is not recorded, and this gives an "invalid" representation of the resulting

---

[3] The usual 650 configuration includes the 533-card read-punch unit which is described herein. However, a type 537-card read-punch unit may be obtained that reads from and punches into the same card.

[4] Actually, biquinary notation is used everywhere in the machine except on the magnetic drum, where a "two-out-of-five" bit code (described in Chapter 10) is used to conserve read-write heads. The machine automatically translates between these codes whenever information is stored or retrieved from the drum. This hybrid system was probably devised because it was less expensive to include the translating circuitry than either to add 80 read-write heads to the drum or to build the calculating circuitry utilizing the five-bit code.

number. Likewise, if there are gremlins in the machine, and an extra bit appears during a transfer, again we obtain an invalid representation. Only if we simultaneously lose a bit and gain a bit can a transfer error go undetected.[5]

Although the mechanism is not as obvious as that of checking transfers of information, the biquinary notation also provides a

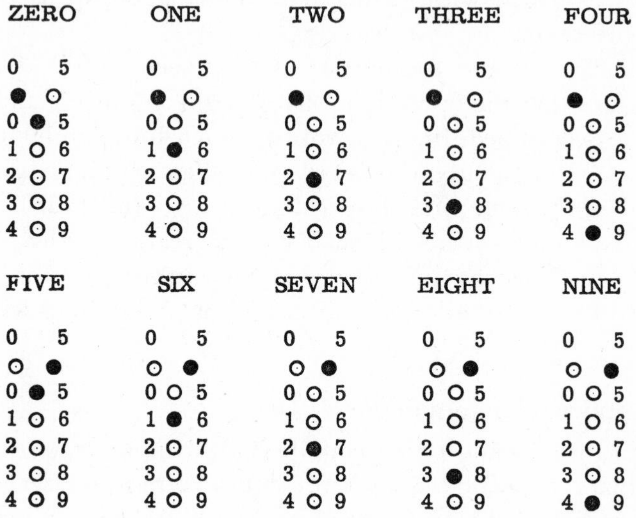

```
    ZERO        ONE         TWO        THREE        FOUR

   0   5       0   5       0   5       0   5       0   5
   ●   ○       ●   ○       ●   ○       ●   ○       ●   ○
  0  ●  5     0  ○  5     0  ○  5     0  ○  5     0  ○  5
  1  ○  6     1  ●  6     1  ○  6     1  ○  6     1  ○  6
  2  ○  7     2  ○  7     2  ●  7     2  ○  7     2  ○  7
  3  ○  8     3  ○  8     3  ○  8     3  ●  8     3  ○  8
  4  ○  9     4  ○  9     4  ○  9     4  ○  9     4  ●  9


    FIVE        SIX        SEVEN       EIGHT        NINE

   0   5       0   5       0   5       0   5       0   5
   ○   ●       ○   ●       ○   ●       ○   ●       ○   ●
  0  ●  5     0  ○  5     0  ○  5     0  ○  5     0  ○  5
  1  ○  6     1  ●  6     1  ○  6     1  ○  6     1  ○  6
  2  ○  7     2  ○  7     2  ●  7     2  ○  7     2  ○  7
  3  ○  8     3  ○  8     3  ○  8     3  ●  8     3  ○  8
  4  ○  9     4  ○  9     4  ○  9     4  ○  9     4  ●  9
```

FIG. 6–4.

check on the arithmetic within the 650. Arithmetic is performed through the use of a *single-digit adder,* which is an electronic "black box" that adds two digits. Essentially, this black box has two sets of seven input wires and a single set of seven output wires. When, for example, the number three is entered through one set of input wires and the number four is entered through the other, the black box emits the proper bits to represent a seven. The black box is designed so that if something goes wrong, and the correct bits for a seven are not emitted, it will usually produce an invalid representation. In other words, the 650 is so stupid that if it does not get the correct answer, it produces gibberish rather than a number.

Like many other similar machines, the IBM 650 is basically numeric, since the only characters that can be directly recorded in memory are the ten decimal digits. However, a special device may be obtained which automatically translates alphabetic information to and from a two-digit code when reading or punching cards, so

---

[5] The five-bit code used on the drum is also self-checking in a similar manner, and errors in that code are translated into invalid biquinary combinations.

that a ten-digit word can store five alphabetic characters. For example, in this code JONES would be represented as 71 76 75 65 82. Thus, alphabetic information can be conveniently processed by machines which are basically numeric.

Instruction Format

Each 650 instruction requires 10 digits and, therefore, fits quite snugly into a single 650 word (see Figure 6–5). Since each instruc-

Address of Instruction	Operation Code	Data Address	Instruction Address
X X X X	X X	X X X X	X X X X

FIG. 6–5.

tion must be stored in the machine memory, it must be stored in some location, and that location is given by the address of the instruction. In the instruction itself, the first two digits give the operation code, which tells the machine what operation to perform— addition, subtraction, multiplication, division, storing, reading a card, punching a card, shifting a number left, etc. The data address tells the machine where to find the information that is to be manipulated in this operation (or where to store the result of an operation). Finally, the instruction address tells the machine where to go to find the next instruction—it gives the address of the next instruction. If the instructions are stored sequentially on the drum, the instruction address will be one larger than the address of the instruction itself. At any rate, the instruction address of the first instruction *is the same as* the address of the second instruction, and the instruction address of the second instruction gives the address of the third instruction, and so on. The machine operates by finding the first instruction, interpreting the operation code to see what it is to do, finding the data in memory and performing the operation, and then finding the next instruction and repeating this process again.

It is not immediately obvious why the instruction-address portion of the instruction is necessary, for if the instructions were stored sequentially the machine could merely look in the next memory location to find the next instruction. As a matter of fact, most machines do store their instructions sequentially, and thus require no instruction address. Why then does the 650 have this extra address in its instruction? The answer is associated with speed as related to the use of the magnetic drum memory. At the instant when the machine completes an operation and is ready to execute the next instruction, the delay involved in obtaining this instruction depends upon the position of the drum at that instant in relation to the location of the next instruction. Thus, if we can place the next instruction so that it is in a position that will be close to the reading heads when it is required, this waiting time can be greatly reduced (see Figure 6–6). This process of locating the instructions to obtain maxi-

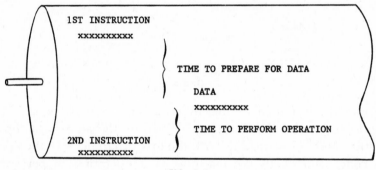

FIG. 6–6.

mum speed, called *optimum programming*, can double or triple the operating speed of the machine. It should be noted that automatic programming aids (such as SOAP) can be employed to utilize the machine itself to locate the instructions for increased speed.

Many magnetic drum machines utilize some such technique to minimize the effective access time associated with the magnetic drum. For example, the Univac Solid-State 90 computer utilizes an instruction address similar to the 650 for optimum programming. This machine also provides a large block of memory for which there are four sets of read-write heads on each band so that a maximum of one fourth of a drum revolution is required to reach any of these locations (see Figure 6–7).

The Datatron 205 is equipped with four "quick-access loops" which provide a total of 80 words of memory for which an access requires only one tenth the time required to refer to the main drum. All four quick-access loops are obtained from one drum band upon which are mounted four sets of read heads and four sets of write heads. These are associated together in pairs located 20 words apart on the drum (see Figure 6–8), and as each word is read by the read heads, it is written back on the drum by the write heads, and will again be read 20 word-times later. Thus, each word in a quick-access loop is accessible in a maximum of 20 word-times or 1.7 milliseconds.

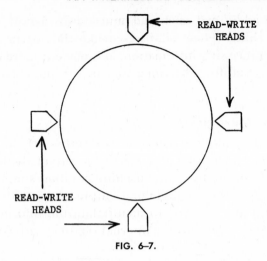

FIG. 6–7.

By placing data in a quick-access loop and transferring 20 instructions from main memory into another quick-access loop and then executing these 20 instructions, then transferring 20 more words to the quick-access loop and executing them, and so forth, the Datatron 205 achieves speeds comparable to the optimally programmed 650.

Like several of the other intermediate machines, the basic 650

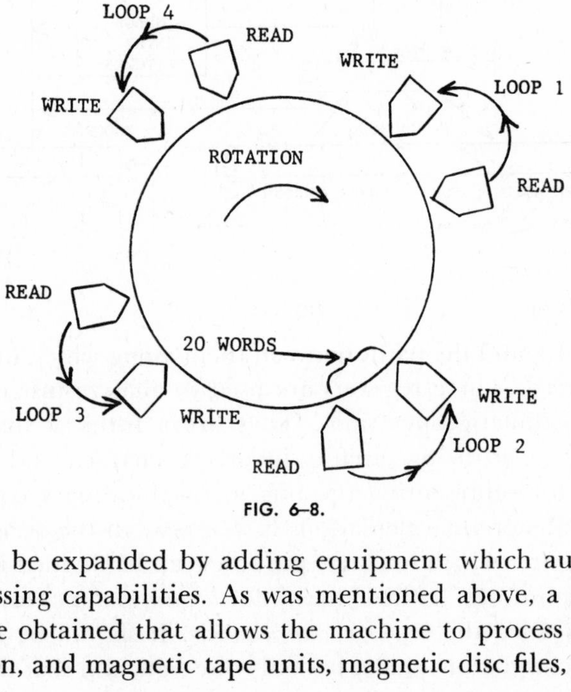

FIG. 6–8.

system can be expanded by adding equipment which augments its data-processing capabilities. As was mentioned above, a special device can be obtained that allows the machine to process alphabetic information, and magnetic tape units, magnetic disc files, direct line printers, and additional card read-punch units may be attached to the basic machine. These additions make the system much more powerful for processing information, and make it more expensive— the monthly rental for a maximal system is in the neighborhood of $17,000.

Internal Information Flow

Although physically the 650 consists of miles of wire, over 1,000 vacuum tubes, and several thousand germanium diodes, resistors, and capacitors, to the user, the machine is rather simple. The user is concerned only with the input and output, the memory, and a few registers which are required to manipulate the information being processed. Figure 6–9 shows the internal registers with which we will

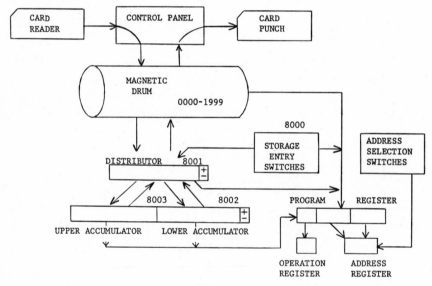

FIG. 6–9.

be concerned, and the paths between them along which numbers can be transferred. These registers are used to analyze instructions and perform arithmetic operations. They are a form of instantaneous access storage, utilizing circuits involving charged and discharged capacitors for representing the bits in the biquinary code.

The results of any calculations first appear in the accumulator, a 20-digit register which for some purposes can be divided into a high-order ten positions (called the *upper accumulator*), low-order ten positions (called the *lower accumulator*). It should be emphasized that the accumulator usually has only one sign, and that the machine considers the contents of the entire accumulator to be a single 20-digit number.

All numbers that are transferred from the drum into the accumulator or from the accumulator to the drum must pass through and appear in the distributor, a register that holds a ten-digit number with its sign. Since the drum is always in motion, a number stored on the drum is available for only a few microseconds during each revolution. The 650 performs all its arithmetic a single digit at a time, so it can be readily seen that the word from the drum must be remembered while the entire arithmetic operation is being performed. The distributor performs this function of storage of the word from memory while it is being acted upon by the arithmetic unit.

The accumulator does not calculate but only stores the results of calculations. The calculation is accomplished by means of a one-digit adder (see Figure 6–10) which takes one factor from the dis-

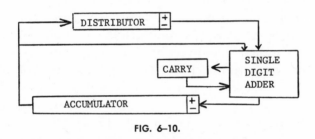

FIG. 6–10.

tributor and the other from the accumulator and places the result in the accumulator. The one-digit adder is not available to the programmer of the machine—knowing about it simply explains how the machine operates as it does.

As each instruction is executed, it is transferred from the drum into the program register, where it is broken down into the three segments which make it up. The operation code is then transferred to the two-digit operation register where it is decoded to set up the circuits to perform the proper operation. The data address is transferred to the address register, and the circuits are set up to transfer information from that drum address to the distributor or from the distributor to that drum address the next time it comes under the reading heads. After this transfer between the drum and the distributor is completed, the instruction address is transferred into the address register, and the circuitry is set up to transfer the next instruction into the program register when it is available.

To complete our discussion of Figure 6–9, it should be noticed that the distributor, the upper accumulator, and the lower accumulator are addressable—that is to say that their contents can be obtained by using 8001, 8002, or 8003 as the data address or instruction address of an instruction. There are also the storage-entry switches (address 8000) on the control console of the 650 into which a ten-digit number with its sign can be manually set. As can be seen from Figure 6–9, this number can be entered into the distributor or into the program register when the address 8000 is used. It should also be noted that information can be transferred from the distributor, upper accumulator, and lower accumulator directly to the program register without first returning the information to the drum.

Programming

To understand what an electronic computer can do, what it cannot do, and what is involved in preparing a problem for machine solution, we will need to study machine programming. Roughly speaking, programming refers to the process of breaking the problem down into a sequence of steps which the machine can follow and then expressing these steps in terms of the specific instructions which the machine can perform. To understand what is involved in programming, it is necessary first to understand the basic operations that the machine can perform. This provides the raw materials with which we must work. However, the task of assembling these elementary operations together in the proper sequence to most efficiently accomplish the desired result involves an extremely complex synthesizing process. In the following pages, we will discuss many of the operations of the 650, and attempt to provide some ideas and techniques that will be useful in this creative synthesizing process.[6]

As we prepare a program, we will write it on a planning chart (see Figure 6–11) which includes space for the location of the instruction, the operation code, the data address, and the instruction address. In addition, the planning chart provides an area for the accumulator and distributor which may be filled in to follow through an example and to show the exact numbers that will be present in these registers after each instruction has been executed. There is also space for remarks which describe what each small group of instructions is designed to accomplish. These remarks are most helpful when reading a program after it has been set aside for a few hours.

---

[6] Additional information concerning the IBM 650 may be obtained from the sources cited in the supplemental readings at the end of this chapter.

Input-Output

Bl.	No.	Loc.	Op.	D.	I.	U.A.	L.A.	Dist.	Remarks

FIG. 6–11.

In order to program the machine, it is not sufficient to have a hazy idea what the instructions accomplish. The machine will do exactly what it is told, and you must know exactly what it does or the program may not accomplish what you intended. Thus, you must *clearly understand* what each operation code accomplishes. However, it is not necessary to memorize the operation code numbers, for you may use the operation abbreviations when first writing the program and fill in the operation codes later.

It should be noted that the 650 computes with signed numbers— it handles these positive and negative numbers automatically according to the proper rules of arithmetic.[7] Therefore, it behooves us

[7] For those whose arithmetic is a bit rusty, four rules may be used to add and subtract signed numbers. (1) The sum of two positive numbers is a positive number. (2) The sum of two negative numbers is a negative number. (3) The sum of a positive and a negative number is obtained as follows: (a) Ignore the signs of the two numbers; (b) subtract the smaller of the two numbers from the larger of the two numbers; (c) give this result the sign of the larger of the two numbers. (4) In order to subtract one number from another, change the sign of the number to be subtracted and add the resulting two numbers.

In the following illustrations, the signs inside of the parentheses denote the algebraic signs of the numbers, while the plus and minus signs between the parentheses denote the operations of addition or subtraction.

$$(+5) + (+7) = +12 \quad \text{(Rule 1)}$$
$$(-7) + (-5) = -12 \quad \text{(Rule 2)}$$
$$(+7) + (-5) = +2 \quad \text{(Rule 3)} \quad (Cont.)$$

to know these rules of arithmetic so that we will know what to expect from the machine.

Add, Subtract, and Store Operations

There are a separate set of add, subtract, and store operations for the upper accumulator and another set of operations for the lower accumulator. Let us first consider the lower accumulator.

The illustrations in this section will be presented in a form similar to the planning chart, with a line to indicate the contents of the upper and lower accumulators and the distributor before the instruction is executed, and a second line giving the instruction and the results obtained from that instruction. An additional column will be used to indicate the contents of the location given by the data address of the instruction, and the location of the instruction and the instruction address columns are eliminated in these illustrations.

65 RAL (Reset and Add to Lower). This operation code resets the entire 20-position accumulator to zero and then adds the contents of the data-address location into the low-order ten positions of the accumulator. Notice in Examples 6–1 and 6–2 that the number obtained from the drum with its sign not only appears in the lower accumulator, but it also appears in the distributor after this operation is completed.

15 ALO (Add to Lower). This operation code causes the contents of the data-address location to be added to the contents of the low-order ten positions of the 20-digit number in the accumulator. Note in Examples 6–3, 6–4, and 6–5 that the number added from the drum appears in the distributor at the completion of the operation, and that the machine follows the rules of signs. Example 6–6 illustrates that operations in the lower accumulator may cause a one to overflow into the upper accumulator. Examples 6–7 and 6–8 bring out the fact that the entire 20 positions of the accumulator must be considered when the signs of the numbers are different.

20 STL (Store Lower Accumulator). This operation code causes the contents of the lower half of the accumulator with the accumulator sign to be stored in the location specified by the data address of

$(-7) + (+5) = -2$	(Rule 3)
$(+7) - (-5) = (+7) + (+5) = +12$	(Rules 4 and 1)
$(-7) - (+5) = (-7) + (-5) = -12$	(Rules 4 and 2)
$(+7) - (+5) = (+7) + (-5) = +2$	(Rules 4 and 3)
$(-7) - (-5) = (-7) + (+5) = -2$	(Rules 4 and 3)

the instruction. The contents of the lower half of the accumulator remain undisturbed. The data address for all store instructions must be between 0000 and 1999. Notice in Example 6–9 that at the completion of this operation the contents of the data-address location, the lower accumulator, and the distributor are the same.

Example Number	Operation	Contents of Data-Address Location	Upper Accumulator	Lower Accumulator	Distributor
6–1	RAL	0000012345 + 0000012345 +	5555555555 0000000000	4444444444 + 0000012345 +	2233445566 − 0000012345 +
6–2	RAL	0000012345 − 0000012345 −	5555555555 0000000000	4444444444 + 0000012345 −	2233445566 − 0000012345 −
6–3	ALO	0000022222 + 0000022222 +	0000000000 0000000000	0000033333 + 0000055555 +	1234567890 + 0000022222 +
6–4	ALO	0000022222 − 0000022222 −	0000000000 0000000000	0000033333 + 0000011111 +	1234567890 + 0000022222 −
6–5	ALO	0000044444 − 0000044444 −	0000000000 0000000000	0000033333 + 0000011111 −	1234567890 + 0000044444 −
6–6	ALO	5555555555 + 5555555555 +	0123456789 0123456790	8888888888 + 4444444443 +	1234567890 − 5555555555 +
6–7	ALO	0000066666 − 0000066666 −	0123456789 0123456788	0000033333 + 9999966667 +	1234567890 + 0000066666 −
6–8	ALO	8888888888 + 8888888888 +	0123456789 0123456788	3333333333 − 4444444445 −	1234567890 + 8888888888 +
6–9	STL	0123456789 + 0000055555 −	2222222222 2222222222	0000055555 − 0000055555 −	0000000006 + 0000055555 −

As our first illustration of how these instructions may be combined to accomplish useful results, suppose that we wish to add two numbers that are in memory and to store the result in memory. To be specific, suppose that the two numbers to be added are stored in drum locations 0100 and 0101, and we wish to place their sum in drum location 0102. Notice at this point that, in general, we are not concerned with two specific numbers—whatever the contents of these two drum locations may be, we wish to find their sum and place it in location 0102. In the usual situation, these numbers will change with each transaction that is processed. Therefore, the program can process the various transactions one after another. In other words, the program of a machine corresponds to an algebraic formula, and the various values of the different symbols of this formula are inserted for each transaction.

However, in order to visualize what is going on within the machine, let us suppose that the contents of 0100 are 0000001111+, and the contents of 0101 are 0000002222+. The following program will produce the desired result:

Loc.	Op.	D.	I.	U.A.	L.A.	Dist.
1005	RAL	0100	1006	0000000000	0000001111+	0000001111+
1006	ALO	0101	1007	0000000000	0000003333+	0000002222+
1007	STL	0102	1008	0000000000	0000003333+	0000003333+

Notice in the above illustration that we have arbitrarily decided to allocate memory locations 1005, 1006, and 1007 to this portion of the program itself. Any of the 2,000 drum locations that are not used for some other purpose might have been used to store these instructions.

Observe that each storage location is cleared only when new information is entered—the same information may be read out of storage over and over without being affected, but the previous information is lost when a new number is entered (or stored) in the location.

66 RSL (Reset and Subtract from Lower). This operation code resets the entire accumulator to plus zero and subtracts the contents of the data-address location from the lower half of the accumulator. Notice in Examples 6–10 and 6–11 that this results in entering the number from the drum into the lower accumulator with its sign changed. However, upon completing the operation, the distributor has the same sign as the number on the drum—the sign is not changed until we reach the accumulator.

16 SLO (Subtract from Lower). This operation code causes the contents of the data-address location to be subtracted from the low-order 10 position of the 20-position accumulator. Examples 6–12 and 6–13 illustrate how the operation can affect the contents of the upper accumulator as well as the contents of the lower accumulator. Example 6–14 is an illustration of the fact that subtracting a negative number from a negative number can produce a positive result.

Corresponding to each of the instructions involving the lower accumulator is a similar instruction which involves the upper half of the accumulator. More complete discussions of these five operation codes can be found in the *650 Data Processing System Bulletins*.[8]

---

[8] Cited in the supplemental readings at the end of the chapter.

Example Number	Operation	Contents of Data-Address Location	Upper Accumulator	Lower Accumulator	Distributor
6–10	RSL	0123456789+ 0123456789+	9876543210 0000000000	0005678999− 0123456789−	2431507673− 0123456789+
6–11	RSL	0123456789− 0123456789−	9876543210 0000000000	0005678999− 0123456789+	2431507673− 0123456789−
6–12	SLO	0000044444+ 0000044444+	0000055555 0000055556	9999998765− 0000043209−	0000000333+ 0000044444+
6–13	SLO	0000044444+ 0000044444+	0000055555 0000055554	0000033333+ 9999988889+	0000004321− 0000044444+
6–14	SLO	0000044444− 0000044444−	0000000000 0000000000	0000033333− 0000011111+	0000000007+ 0000044444−

The operation code, operation abbreviation, and name of each of these instructions are included in the following list:

    60 RAU (*Reset and Add to Upper*)
    10 AUP (*Add to Upper*)
    21 STU (*Store Upper Accumulator*)
    61 RSU (*Reset and Subtract from Upper*)
    11 SUP (*Subtract from Upper*)

In Example 6–15, an overflow occurs out of the upper end of the accumulator. The 650 has a console switch whose setting determines the effect of such an occurrence. If this overflow switch is set to "stop," the machine will stop when an overflow occurs. If this switch is set to "sense," an overflow sets the overflow circuit, which affects the operation of the *Branch on Overflow* instruction, which will be discussed under branching in Chapter 7.

Because the accumulator is treated as a single 20-digit number, whenever an operation in the upper accumulator causes the accumulator to change sign, the lower accumulator will be complemented, and the units position of the upper accumulator will be reduced by one.[9] Example 6–16 illustrates the results of such an occurrence.

Example Number	Operation	Contents of Data-Address Location	Upper Accumulator	Lower Accumulator	Distributor
6–15	AUP	5555555555− 5555555555−	7666543052 3222098607	0123456789− 0123456789−	0000000009+ 5555555555−
6–16	SUP	6666666666+ 6666666666+	5555555555 1111111110	0123456789+ 9876543211−	2000000000+ 6666666666+

[9] The complement of a positive ten-digit number is obtained by subtracting it from 10000000000. More specifically, this is the tens' complement. The nines' complement of this number would be obtained by subtracting it from 9999999999.

In most cases, the part of the accumulator that is not being used is cleared, so these abnormal conditions do not arise. However, it is sometimes extremely convenient to be able to utilize the upper and lower portions of the accumulator for different purposes simultaneously, but it is then necessary to make sure that the numbers in the upper and lower accumulators *always* have the same sign so that erroneous results will not be obtained.

The fact that the upper accumulator, lower accumulator, and distributor are all addressable may be used to perform some interesting operations. It should be pointed out that whenever an addition or subtraction is performed, the first thing done by the machine is to place the contents of the location given by the data address into the distributor. Therefore, in Example 6–17, when we reset-add the upper to itself, the contents of the upper are placed in the distributor before the accumulator is cleared, and then the distributor is added to the upper accumulator, producing the result of clearing the lower accumulator. In Example 6–18, the accumulator is effectively shifted 10 positions to the left by reset adding from the lower into the upper accumulator, and in Example 6–19, the contents of the lower accumulator are doubled by adding the lower accumulator to itself. Since the registers involved have instantaneous access, the operations involving the 8000 addresses are executed quite rapidly, and are preferred for this reason to operations that would produce the same results by referring to the drum memory or by shifting.

Example Number	Operation	Data Address	Upper Accumulator	Lower Accumulator	Distributor
6–17			0000000077	0000012345 −	3300000000 +
	RAU	8003	0000000077	0000000000 −	0000000077 −
6–18			7777777777	0000012345 −	9900000077 +
	RAU	8002	0000012345	0000000000 −	0000012345 −
6–19			0000000000	0000022222 +	0000000001 +
	ALO	8002	0000000000	0000044444 +	0000022222 +

Two instructions do not involve arithmetic but are frequently used together for transferring information from one part of memory to another.

69 LDD (*Load Distributor*). This operation code causes the contents of the data-address location of the instruction to be placed in the distributor.

24 STD (*Store Distributor*). This operation code causes the contents of the distributor with the distributor sign to be stored in the location specified by the data address of the instruction. The contents of the distributor remain undisturbed. The data address for *all* store instructions must be between 0000 and 1999.

Input and Output Instructions

Since the reading and punching of cards is a mechanical process, it is relatively slow as compared with the electronic processes involved in computing. Thus, it is highly desirable that these mechanical processes be handled in a way that will allow computation to proceed with a minimum of delay. Devices called *buffers* are used to overlap the card reading, calculation, and punching. A buffer is a memory device that receives information at the speed at which cards are read and assembles it so that it may be transferred into main memory at the speed at which information can be recorded in memory. In the 650, separate ten-word input and output buffers are provided by a "blind" band on the drum—a band that is not addressable by the program.[10] As can be seen in Figure 6–12, these buffer areas physi-

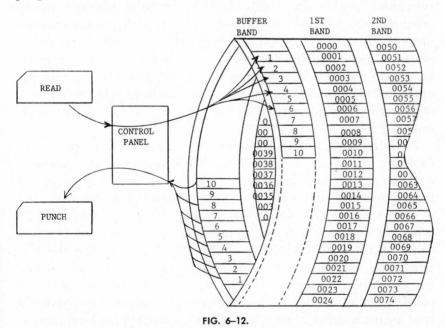

FIG. 6–12.

---

[10] In the basic 650, which has only one read-punch unit, only one input and one output buffer are provided. If an additional input-output unit is attached to the machine, two additional buffers are located between these on the same band. If a third input-output unit is attached, it is necessary to add a second buffer band.

cally correspond to words whose addresses end in 01 through 10 (or 51 through 60) for the read buffer and addresses ending in 27 through 36 (or 77 through 86) for the punch buffer.

As a card is read, the wiring of the control panel determines which field of the card is entered into which of the ten available buffer words, and as a card is punched, the wiring of the control panel determines in which field each of the ten output words is punched. Thus, the control panel allows information to be rearranged or eliminated as cards are read or punched. Since we are primarily interested in the characteristics of the stored program, the details of control-panel wiring will not be discussed. Likewise, the button-pushing details of operating the machine will not be covered, except that Appendix A presents detailed instructions for those who wish to use a 650 to run the problems at the end of the chapter. The IBM manuals cited in the supplemental readings may be consulted for more information on the control panel and operation of the console.

After the card has physically passed the reading brushes and its information has been assembled in the read buffer, the contents of the buffer may quickly be transferred into main memory by simply connecting the read heads of the buffer band (through amplifying circuits, of course) to the writing heads of the proper band in memory. Thus, while a digit is being read in the buffer, it is simultaneously being written in memory; consequently, it can *only* be written in the areas of the drum which correspond to the position of the buffer. Similarly, information can *only* be punched from areas of the drum that correspond to the physical position of the punch buffer.

70 RD1 (Read). This operation code causes the machine to read cards by a two-step process. First, the contents of the ten-word read buffer are transferred into the corresponding ten words of the band designated by the data address of the instruction. Secondly, the next card is fed under the reading brushes, and the information read is entered into buffer storage for the next read instruction. The execution of the machine instructions is only delayed during the first portion of this process, and computing may take place during all or part of the time during which the second step of the process is taking place. Thus, of the 300 milliseconds that are required to physically read a card, around 240 milliseconds are available for computation without slowing the card-feeding speed below 200 cards per minute. Of course, if another read instruction is encountered before the completion of the second step of this process, an interlock delays the execution of the second read instruction until the card has been read and the buffer completely filled, so the programming cannot get ahead of the card reading and thereby miss part of a card.

The address of the first word of the input area into which the contents of the buffer are to be transferred is usually given as the data address of the read instruction. For example, to enter the contents of the input buffer into words 1951 through 1960, the data address of the read instruction would ordinarily be 1951. However, since the only place in a band into which the contents of the buffer may be entered is determined by the way the machine is constructed, the machine only interprets enough of the data address to determine which band is involved. Thus, a read instruction with a data address of 1972, 1999, 1950, or any other address within this band would also result in the information being entered into words 1951 through 1960.

Of all the instructions in the basic 650, the read instruction is unique in that it alone may alter more than one word of memory. Even if only one or two words are actually read from a card, the entire ten-word block of input storage will be replaced by the contents of the read buffer, which will contain one or two words of data, and the remaining words will be zeros or blanks, depending upon control-panel wiring.[11] Thus, unused words in the input block into which a card is read can seldom be used for any other purpose, for they are erased each time a card is read. On the other hand, the ten potential input words of bands that are not used for input may be treated just like the rest of drum memory.

In order to enter the program into the memory of the machine, certain cards may be designated as *load* cards by means of a twelve (or Y) punch in a specified column. When a load card is read, the control-panel wiring is ignored so that the card is read column by column into the first eight words of the buffer, and the 650 takes its next instruction from the location given by the data address. This condition will be more fully discussed in subsequent sections on branching and on loading the program.

71 WR1 (Write). This operation code causes a card to be punched by a two-step process. First, the machine transfers a ten-word block of output storage from the band designated by the data address of the instruction to the output buffer. Secondly, the card is punched with information in the buffer storage. Of the 600 milli-

---

[11] Here the word *blank* indicates that there are no bits present in the biquinary representation, so this represents an invalid code to the machine.

seconds required to punch a card, only about 60 milliseconds are necessary to perform the first part of this operation. During the second part of the operation, about 540 milliseconds are available, during which other instructions may be executed.

As in the read instruction, the data address of a write instruction only selects the band from which the information will be punched—the physical location of the output buffer requires that the information be punched from a block of words whose addresses end in 27 through 36 or 77 through 86. Thus, the 71 instruction with a data address of 1201, 1215, 1227, 1228, or 1243 will cause the information in the ten-word block from 1227 to 1236 to be punched into the card. Unlike the operation of the read instruction, punching from a block of output storage does not alter the contents of that block.

As was mentioned in connection with the read instruction, although buffers allow overlapping of reading, computing, and punching, they do not physically speed up the punching of cards beyond the rate of 100 cards per minute. Thus, for example, if the computing time required between two separate write instructions is less than 540 milliseconds, the programming will be delayed until the completion of punching of the current card before transferring the information for the following card into the punch buffer.

As an example of an extremely simple but nevertheless complete 650 program, let us consider a situation where we have a deck of punched cards, each of which contains two numbers (designated A and B). From each of these cards, we would like to produce a card in which A, B, and their sum, C, are punched.

In this problem, we need to read a card, compute the sum of A and B, store A, B, and C for punching, and finally punch the output card. Whenever we begin to plan a program, the first thing is to decide what steps must be accomplished and in what sequence they must be done to provide the desired results. This planning is best done by means of a *block diagram*. Although in the simple problems which we will use for exercises it may appear that a block diagram is superfluous, in any practical program, requiring hundreds of separate instructions, the situation is almost impossibly confusing unless a block diagram is actually written before programming is started. As a matter of fact, in a complicated situation, the development of a satisfactory block diagram may be more difficult and time consuming than the subsequent writing of the program itself. Furthermore, it is usually necessary to explain a program to others (or for them to be able to read what you have done), and a block diagram is the best means of transmitting the basic logic of the approach that has been taken. A block diagram for this illustration might appear as in Figure 6–13.

Notice that there is an arrow leading from block 4 to block 1 which indicates that after the first card is punched we read the second card, and after it is completed we read the third, and so forth. Thus, no

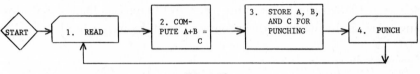

FIG. 6–13.

matter how many cards we have to compute, the machine will continue to feed them and process them until the machine either runs out of cards or the operator pushes the stop button.

As in all programs, in Example 6–20 we must allocate the memory to various functions that it must serve. We must decide what area to use for input storage, what area to use for output storage, and where to locate the instructions themselves. In the program which follows, we have arbitrarily decided to read the card into the block 1951 to 1960, to punch from the block 1977 to 1986, and to locate the instructions starting in location 0100. We will assume that by control-panel wiring, factor A is entered into word 1951, and factor B is entered into word 1952. Likewise, we will punch A from 1977, B from 1978, and their sum C from 1979. For illustrative purposes, we will let A = 0000000005+ and B = 0000000007+.

Example 6–20

Loc.	Op.	D.	I.	U.A.	L.A.	Dist.	Remarks
0100	RD1	1951	0101				
0101	RAL	1951	0102	0000000000	0000000005+	0000000005+	Read
0102	ALO	1952	0103	0000000000	0000000012+	0000000007+	Compute
0103	STL	1979	0104	0000000000	0000000012+	0000000012+	A+B=C
0104	LDD	1951	0105	0000000000	0000000012+	0000000005+	Store A for
0105	STD	1977	0106	0000000000	0000000012+	0000000005+	punching
0106	LDD	1952	0107	0000000000	0000000012+	0000000007+	Store B for
0107	STD	1978	0108	0000000000	0000000012+	0000000007+	punching
0108	WR1	1977	0100				Punch

It is obvious that several arbitrary decisions were made when the above program was written. For example, the upper accumulator could have been used rather than the lower, B could have been added before A, A and B could have been transferred to output storage by using reset add and store accumulator instructions, and these transfers to output storage could have been accomplished prior to the addition (which would involve a modification of the block diagram). Moreover, in the above program factor A is available in the distributor after the step located in 0101 and could be stored in 1977 with a single instruction at this point. Likewise, factor B is available after the step located in 0102 and could be stored in location 1978 at this point. Thus, we would save two load-distributor instructions by writing the program as in Example 6–21.

Example 6–21

Loc.	Op.	D.	I.	U.A.	L.A.	Dist.	Remarks
0100	RD1	1951	0101				Read
0101	RAL	1951	0102	0000000000	0000000005+	0000000005+	Add and
0102	STD	1977	0103	0000000000	0000000005+	0000000005+	Store A
0103	ALO	1952	0104	0000000000	0000000012+	0000000007+	Add and
0104	STD	1978	0105	0000000000	0000000012+	0000000007+	Store B
0105	STL	1979	0106	0000000000	0000000012+	0000000012+	Store C
0106	WR1	1977	0100				Punch

Thus, we see that there are many possible programs to accomplish a given result, some of which are more efficient than others. A really creative programmer will succeed in producing an efficient program, not one which merely works. The improvement illustrated above also requires a change in the block diagram itself. Frequently, improvements in a program will require changes in the block diagram or even in the over-all procedure, which may involve several machine runs and the design of the input and output formats.

Multiplication and Shifting

One of the reasons that the accumulator in the 650 includes 20 positions becomes apparent when we consider the multiply instruction, for the product of two 10-digit numbers can be a 20-digit number.

19 MPY (Multiply). This operation causes the multiplier (which must be in the upper accumulator) to be multiplied by the multiplicand (obtained from the data-address location) to form a 20-digit product which appears with the proper sign in the entire accumulator.[12] At the completion of this operation, the multiplicand appears in the distributor, and the multiplier is no longer available, for it has been replaced in the upper accumulator by the upper 10 positions of the product.

---

[12] The sign rule in multiplication is simple. The product of two numbers with the same sign is positive, while the product of two numbers with unlike signs is negative.

It should be noted that it usually requires two program steps to accomplish a multiplication—one to place the multiplier in the upper accumulator and the second to perform the multiplication. If we wish to multiply A (located in 0100) by B (located in 0101) and store the result, C, in 0102, the program in Example 6–22 would be satisfactory (supposing that 0000000027+ is in 0100 and that 0000000062+ is in 0101).

Example 6–22

Loc.	Op.	D.	I.	U.A.	L.A	Dist.
0976	RAU	0100	0977	0000000027	0000000000+	0000000027+
0977	MPY	0101	0978	0000000000	0000001674+	0000000062+
0978	STL	0102	0979	0000000000	0000001674+	0000001674+

If the numbers in Example 6–22 had been 2700000000+ and 6200000000+, the resulting number in the accumulator would have been 1674000000 0000000000+, and if the numbers had been 0012345678− and 0094271365+, the result in the accumulator would have been 0000116384 3916910470−. In this latter case, it would have required both a store-upper and a store-lower instruction to save the entire result, and the contents of the upper accumulator (with the minus sign) might have been stored in 0102, while the contents of the lower accumulator (with the minus sign) might have been stored in 0103.

The 650 multiplies by repeated addition, one multiplier digit at a time, starting with the high-order position of the upper accumulator. First, the multiplicand is placed in the distributor. Then the entire accumulator is shifted left one position, thus shifting the high-order digit out of the accumulator into a special storage position where it is analyzed, and the multiplicand is added from the distributor into the lower accumulator the number of times indicated by the digit being analyzed. Then the entire accumulator is shifted one more place to the left, the next digit is analyzed, and the multiplicand is added into the lower accumulator the proper number of times. After ten such shifts, all ten digits of the multiplier have been analyzed, and the partial product obtained from the high-order digit has been shifted nine places into the upper accumulator. We are ordinarily taught to multiply from right to left rather than from left to right, but the two procedures are equivalent.

If the lower accumulator is not cleared to zeros before the multiply instruction is given, the contents of the lower accumulator (without sign) will be added to the portion of the product developed in the upper half of the accumulator, and any resulting carry-over into the twenty-first digit of the result will affect the low-order positions of the product by effectively increasing the low-order digit of the multiplier by one before multiplication is started, as illustrated in Example 6–23. In this illustration, 8000000000+ times 9000000000+ is 7200000000 0000000000+. Adding 6666666666+ to the upper accumulator gives 13866666666 0000000000+, but the 1 is an overflow into the lowest multiplier position (since it actually occurs when accumulating the first partial product in the lower accumulator), making the multiplier 9000000001+. Multiplying 8000000000+ by 9000000001+ gives 7200000000 8000000000+, and adding the string of sixes to the upper accumulator gives the result shown in the example. Obviously, unless there are extenuating circumstances, we always reset add the multiplier into the upper accumulator to avoid these difficulties.

Example 6–23

Operation	Contents of Data-Address Location	Upper Accumulator	Lower Accumulator	Distributor
MPY	8000000000+ 8000000000+	9000000000 3866666666	6666666666+ 8000000000+	1357900000+ 8000000000+

The time required to multiply depends upon the number of additions, which is determined by the sum of the digits in the upper accumulator. For example, a multiplier of 195 would require 15 additions, while a multiplier of 1020000000 would require only three additions. Therefore, to achieve maximum speed, the factor whose digits will average to the smallest sum should be used in the upper accumulator as the multiplier.

Although we have so far ignored its influence, in the arithmetic operations, the location of the decimal point is extremely important. In order to properly align the decimal point and to drop or round unnecessary figures after multiplication, several instructions are available which shift the entire contents of the accumulator to the left or to the right. Notice that in each of these instructions, the data address no longer refers to a location on the drum (since no drum location is involved), but in these instructions, the data address indicates the number of positions to be shifted.

30 SRT (Shift Right). This operation code causes the contents of the entire accumulator to be shifted to the right the number of places specified by the units digit of the data address of the instruction. All numbers shifted off of the right end of the accumulator are lost, and zeros are inserted at the left of the accumulator to replace the digits that have been shifted away. A maximum shift of nine positions is possible with a single shift-right instruction, and a data address with a units digit of zero will result in no shift. As can be seen in Example 6–24, the sign of the accumulator is not affected by the shift-right instruction.

35 SLT (Shift Left). This operation code causes the contents of the entire accumulator to be shifted to the left the number of places specified by the units digit of the data address of the instruction. All numbers shifted off the left end of the accumulator are lost (without setting the overflow circuit), and zeros are inserted at the right end of the accumulator to replace numbers that are shifted to the left. Again, a maximum shift of nine positions is possible, and a data address with the units digit of zero will result in no shift. Example 6–25 illustrates that the shift-left instruction only examines the units position of the data address to determine how many positions to shift the accumulator.

31 SRD (Shift Right and Round). This operation code causes the contents of the entire accumulator to be shifted right the number of places specified by the units digit of the data address of the instruction. To compensate for the digits thus dropped, a five is added (with a plus sign if the accumulator is positive or a minus sign if the accumulator is negative) to the number in the last position that was dropped because of the shift. Thus, if the highest-order digit dropped is a five or greater, an overflow increases the resulting units digit by one, while if the highest-order digit lost is four or less, no overflow will occur and the units position of the result will not be affected. Notice that in this instruction, a data address with a units digit of zero will result in a right shift of ten positions with rounding. Examples 6–26 and 6–27 illustrate the shift and round instruction.

Example Number	Operation	Data Address	Upper Accumulator	Lower Accumulator	Distributor
6–24			0000012345	0345436724 −	0000044444 +
	SRT	0003	0000000012	3450345436 −	0000044444 +
6–25			6789012345	9876543211 +	9700000000 −
	SLT	0417	3459876543	2110000000 +	9700000000 −
6–26			0057233119	0023447632 −	9700000000 −
	SRD	0005	0000000572	3311900234 −	9700000000 −
6–27			0000000000	0052961234 +	0000000888 +
	SRD	0005	0000000000	0000000530 +	0000000888 +

The 650 computes as though the decimal point in the numbers were at the extreme right. In other words, it handles numbers as though they were integers, and we must make allowance in our program for the proper placing of the decimal point. Notice in the following discussion that the decimal point never explicitly appears in the memory of the machine, but we must know where the decimal should appear in each number, and we must program the machine so that the results will appear in the desired form.

Let us consider an example of multiplication with decimals. Suppose that we have a number of cards in which are punched the numbers A and B. A has the form xxx.xx, and B has the form x.xxx. We would like to find their product, C, and punch it into a card, saving only two decimal places. In this discussion, the number of x's involved denotes the maximum size that the numbers can assume. For example, xxx.xx represents any number between 000.00 and 999.99. The placement of a decimal point in multiplication is quite simple— the maximum possible number of figures in a result is the sum of the maximum number of figures that can be in each of the factors, and the decimal point is placed by counting the total number of digits to the right of the decimal point in the two factors and by placing the decimal point the resulting number of places from the right end of the answer. Thus, A × B would have the form xxxx.xxxxx. Again, this symbolism only indicates that the resulting number will be between 0000.00000 and 9999.99999. Thus, we see that this result must be rounded by dropping three positions.

If we desire to punch A, B, and C into the output card, the block diagram in Figure 6–14 would be satisfactory. Assume that we wire

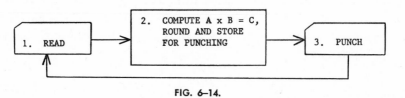

FIG. 6–14.

the control panel so that A enters the first word of the buffer and B enters the second word of the buffer, and that we wire the output part of the control panel so that A is punched from the first word, B is punched from a second word, and C is punched from a third word. One satisfactory program for this problem is shown in Example 6–28. For purposes of illustration let A equal 23.46 and B equal 1.225.

Example 6–28

Loc.	Op.	D.	I.	U.A.	L.A.	Dist.
0001	RD1	1951	0002			
0002	RAU	1952	0003	0000001.225	0000000000+	0000001.225+
0003	STD	1978	0004	0000001.225	0000000000+	0000001.225+
0004	MPY	1951	0005	0000000000	00028.73850+	00000023.46+
0005	STD	1977	0006	0000000000	00028.73850+	00000023.46+
0006	SRD	0003	0007	0000000000	00000028.74+	00000023.46+
0007	STL	1979	0008	0000000000	00000028.74+	00000028.74+
0008	WR1	1977	0001			

It should be noted that in Example 6–28 the instructions in location 0003 and 0005 are used to store B and A for punching. Also, the steps located in 0005 and 0006 could have been interchanged without any effect on the operation of the resulting program. Furthermore, although we include the decimal points on our program form for our own convenience, they do not appear in the memory or registers of the machine.

Division

Among the arithmetic operations, division is by far the most troublesome to both the mathematician and the computer programmer. The mathematician must always guard against the possibility of dividing by zero.[13] The machine programmer must likewise guard against this possibility, but he must also be certain that the size of the result of a division does not exceed the limits specified by the design of the machine. In other words, to the 650, any quotient that has more than ten digits is essentially equivalent to infinity.

14 DIV (Divide). This operation code causes a 20-digit dividend located in the accumulator to be divided by a 10-digit divisor whose location is given by the data address of the instruction. The resulting quotient appears in the lower accumulator (with its proper sign), and the remainder appears in the upper accumulator

---

[13] As an example of the difficulties that may arise, there is a well-known "proof" that two equals one.

(1) Let $\qquad a = b$

(2) $\qquad a^2 = ab \qquad$ (multiplying both sides by a)

(3) $\qquad a^2 - b^2 = ab - b^2 \qquad$ (subtracting b^2 from both sides)

(4) $(a - b)(a + b) = b(a - b) \qquad$ (factoring both sides)

(5) $\qquad a + b = b \qquad$ (cancelling the factor $a - b$)

(6) $\qquad b + b = b \qquad$ (substituting b for a)

(7) $\qquad 2b = b$

(8) $\qquad 2 = 1 \qquad$ (dividing both sides by b)

Of course, in step 5 when we canceled the factor $(a - b)$, we were actually dividing by $(a - b)$, and since $a = b$ we were dividing by zero.

(with its proper sign) . At the completion of the divide operation, the divisor is located in the distributor. In order to prevent the development of a quotient of more than ten positions, *the portion of the dividend that is located in the upper accumulator must be smaller than the divisor* in absolute value. If this rule is violated or if division by zero is attempted, a quotient overflow will occur, and the machine will stop.

It should be noted that if the sign of the remainder and the sign of the quotient are different, the upper and lower accumulators will have different signs.[14] This is *the only case* in which the accumulator can have two different signs. If it is desired to preserve the sign of the remainder, the upper accumulator should be stored immediately after the divide operation. Then the accumulator should be reset with a reset-add or reset-subtract operation to return to the normal situation in which the accumulator has but one sign, for very odd results can be obtained when manipulating numbers in the accumulator when the signs of the upper and lower accumulators are different.

64 DVR (Divide and Reset Upper) . This operation code causes the machine to divide as explained under operation code 14; but, at the completion of the operation, it resets the upper accumulator (containing the remainder and its sign) to zero. If the remainder is not to be used in subsequent processing, this code should be used in preference to the code 14.

Notice in Example 6–29 that the 650 does not automatically add zeros to obtain more decimal places in the quotient—it merely leaves the remainder in the upper accumulator so that it can be used. Example 6–30 illustrates that the sign of the upper and lower accumulators can be different, while Example 6–31 is an illustration of how a full 20-digit number can be divided by a 10-digit number to produce a 10-digit quotient. Example 6–32 shows how a violation of the rule that the divisor must exceed the portion of the dividend in the upper accumulator leads to a quotient overflow stop; while Example 6–33 illustrates the results of the divide and reset upper instruction.

---

[14] The rule for determining signs in division is as follows: (1) The quotient is positive if the divisor and the dividend have the same sign; the quotient is negative if the divisor and the dividend have different signs. (2) The remainder always has the sign of the dividend. For example, −21 divided by −5 gives a quotient of +4 with a remainder of −1. This may be checked by verifying that −5 times +4 plus −1 equals to −21, since A divided by B equals C with a remainder of R, if and only if A is equal to B times C plus R. Likewise, +21 divided by −5 equals −4 with a remainder of +1.

Example Number	Operation	Contents of Data-Address Location	Upper Accumulator	Lower Accumulator	Distributor
6–29	DIV	0000000050+ 0000000050+	0000000000 0000000027	0000000627+ 0000000012+	0000000887− 0000000050+
6–30	DIV	0000000050− 0000000050−	0000000000 0000000030+	0000062730+ 0000001254−	0000000023+ 0000000050−
6–31	DIV	9000000000+ 9000000000+	4570000000 7000000000	0000000000+ 5077777777+	0000000003+ 9000000000+
6–32	DIV	0000000002+ 0000000002+	0000000004 Quotient overflow stop.	4000000000+	0000000777− 0000000002+
6–33	DVR	0000000050− 0000000050−	0000000000 0000000000	0000062730+ 0000001254−	0000000023+ 0000000050−

One of the interesting aspects of division is that it is easy to determine the number of *decimal places* that will be found in the quotient, but it is difficult to determine the exact number of *figures* in the quotient. The number of decimals in the quotient may be found by subtracting the number of decimal places in the divisor from the number of decimal places in the dividend. This is equivalent to the rule for marking off the decimal place in the process of long division. However, we must remember that the 650 does not automatically add zeros at the right of the dividend, and if we wish more quotient decimal places than this rule produces, it is necessary to insert zeros at the right by shifting the accumulator to the left before division.

For example, if we wish to divide A of the form xxxxxx.xx by B of the form xxxx.xx and produce a quotient, C, which is rounded to three decimal places, it will be necessary to add zeros to the dividend before dividing. In order to determine how many zeros to add, it is convenient to set up the problem just as you would set it up to divide out by hand:

$$\begin{array}{r} \text{xxx.xxxx} \\ \text{xxxx.xx} \overline{)\text{xxxxxx.xx}_\wedge\text{0000}} \end{array}$$

In order to round to three positions, we must produce four, so the above illustration shows that we will have to add four zeros to the dividend before dividing. If A is located in 0100, B is located in 0101, and we wish to store C in 0102, the program shown in Example 6–34 will suffice. In this example, we let A = 140.00 and B = 65.24.

Example 6-34

Loc.	Op.	D.	I.	U. A.	L. A.	Dist.
0001	RAL	0100	0002	0000000000	00000140.00+	00000140.00+
0002	SLT	0004	0003	0000000000	0140.000000+	00000140.00+
0003	DVR	0101	0004	0000000000	000002.1459+	00000065.24+
0004	SRD	0001	0005	0000000000	0000002.146+	00000065.24+
0005	STL	0102		0000000000	0000002.146+	0000002.146+

Perhaps the basic difficulty with the division process is illustrated by the fact that without additional information we do not know that the result, C, will have only the six figures indicated in the above analysis—the program in Example 6-34 could actually cause a divide overflow stop. We must remember that the notation xxxx.xx merely indicates a number between 0000.00 and 9,999.99. If the number B were 0000.02 and the number A were 400,000.00, after shifting A left four positions, the upper accumulator would exceed the divisor, and the machine would stop.

In other words, to determine the maximum size of a quotient, it is not sufficient to simultaneously consider the maximum divisor and the maximum dividend. Basically, it is necessary to consider the maximum dividend with the minimum divisor to get an upper limit on the size of the quotient. However, this approach may also be misleading, for the maximum dividend may never occur with the minimum divisor.

This problem is akin to the problem which we faced in the design of cards, when we had to decide how many digits to include in a given field. Sometimes we have additional information concerning the size of the numbers with which we are working that enables us to determine that the numbers obtained will never be large enough to overflow the accumulator (or a certain field size). If we have no such additional information, it is necessary to be extremely careful when programming the machine. Occasionally, it is necessary to do a division in two steps (utilizing the remainder) to handle cases where a quotient of more than 10 digits might conceivably arise.

In data-processing work, we are extremely fortunate because we usually do have a considerable amount of additional information concerning size of the numbers that can arise. However, in scientific or engineering calculations, which often involve tens of thousands of steps, the scientist frequently has a pretty good idea concerning the size of the numbers he is putting into the calculations and the size of the numbers which he will receive as answers, but he often has meager knowledge of the size of the intermediate results which may be obtained in the process of these thousands of computations. In order to handle such situations conveniently, the machines designed as scientific computers quite frequently utilize special circuitry or automatic programming techniques that enable them to operate with so-called "floating decimal" numbers.[15]

EXERCISES

In the following group of exercises, fill in the contents of the data-address location, the accumulator, and the distributor after the specified instruction has been executed. These exercises are independent in that there is no carry-over from one exercise to the next, but some are designed to illustrate the differences between similar situations.

Exercise Number	Operation	Contents of Data-Address Location	Upper Accumulator	Lower Accumulator	Distributor
6.1	66–RSL	0000000044 −	0000000009	0000066666 +	0000000088 +
6.2	61–RSU	0000000044 +	0000000009	0000066666 +	0000000088 +
6.3	15–ALO	0000000066 −	0000000099	0000000077 +	0000000033 −
6.4	16–SLO	0000000066 +	0000000099	0000000077 +	0000000012 +
6.5	16–SLO	0000000066 −	0000000099	0000000077 +	0000000012 +
6.6	16–SLO	0000000066 +	0000000099	0000000055 +	0000000012 +
6.7	16–SLO	0000000066 +	0000000000	0000000055 +	0000000012 +
6.8	15–ALO	0000000066 +	0000000000	0000000055 −	0000000012 +
6.9	15–ALO	0006666666 +	0000000123	9997777777 +	0000000012 +
6.10	10–AUP	0000000066 +	0000000055	0000000022 −	0000000012 +
6.11	10–AUP	0000000066 +	0000000055	0000000000 −	0000000012 +

---

[15] Floating decimal notation is discussed in Appendix D.

Exercise Number	Operation	Contents of Data-Address Location	Upper Accumulator	Lower Accumulator	Distributor
6.12	11–SUP	0000000066 +	0000000055	0000000022 +	0000000012 +
6.13	11–SUP	9800000000 +	2300000000	0000000022 −	0000000012 +
6.14	21–STU	0000000066 +	0000000012	0000000066 −	0000000012 +
6.15	21–STU	0000000066 +	0000000000	0000000066 −	0000000012 +
6.16	19–MPY	0000000008 +	0000000006	0000000000 −	0000000012 +
6.17	19–MPY	0000008000 −	0000060000	0000000000 −	0000000012 +
6.18	19–MPY	8000000000 −	6000000000	0000000000 +	0000000012 +
6.19	19–MPY	8000000000 +	6000000000	0000022222 +	0000000012 +
6.20	19–MPY	8000000000 +	6000000000	7770000000 +	0000000012 +
6.21	14–DIV	0000000003 +	0000000000	0000000007 +	0000000012 +
6.22	14–DIV	0000000003 −	0000000000	0000000007 +	0000000012 +
6.23	14–DIV	0000000003 −	0000000000	7000000000 +	0000000012 +
6.24	14–DIV	3000000000 +	0700000000	0000000002 +	0000000012 +
6.25	64–DVR	0000000003 −	0000000000	7000000000 +	0000000012 +
6.26	64–DVR	3000000000 −	7000000000	0000000000 +	0000000012 +

Exercise Number	Operation	Data-Address	Upper Accumulation	Lower Accumulation	Distributor
6.27	35–SLT	0015	2222222222	3333333333+	0000000012+
6.28	30–SRT	0003	2222222222	3333333333−	0000000012+
6.29	31–SRD	0007	0000012345	6789012345−	0000000012+
6.30	31–SRD	0007	0000012345	4321012345+	0000000012+
6.31	65–RAL	8002	0000055555	0000000066−	0000000012+
6.32	65–RAL	8003	0000055555	0000000066−	0000000012+
6.33	10–AUP	8003	0000055555	0000000066−	0000000012+
6.34	11–SUP	8003	0000055555	0000000066−	0000000012+
6.35	19–MPY	8003	0000060000	0000000000−	0000000012+

6.36 Considering an instruction represented in biquinary form, precisely which bits of the data address must be interpreted by the machine when a *Read* instruction is executed to determine the band into which the contents of the buffer are to be transferred?

In the following exercises, prepare a block diagram and write a program to accomplish the desired results. You may use operation abbreviations rather than the numeric operation codes when writing these programs.

6.37 We have a group of time cards in which are punched man number, regular hours, overtime hours. The control panel is wired so that these are entered into the buffer in the following form:

Man Number	00000xxxxx	Word 1.
Regular Hours	0000000xx.x	Word 2.
Overtime Hours	00000000x.x	Word 3.

For each such card, we wish to punch a card containing man number and total hours. The control panel is wired so that we must punch the information from the buffer in the following form:

Word 1.	00000xxxxx	Man Number.
Word 2.	0000000xx.x	Total Hours.

At what speed would this program cause the 650 to read cards?

6.38   Suppose that the input cards in Exercise 6.37 also contain the regular hourly rate, and the control panel is wired so as to place it in the fourth word of the input buffer in the form x.xx. For each such card, we wish to punch a card containing man number, regular hours, and regular pay (regular hours times regular hourly rate rounded to the nearest cent). The control panel is wired so that we must punch the information from the buffer in the following form.

Word 1.	00000xxxxx	Man Number.
Word 2.	0000000xx.x	Regular Hours.
Word 3.	00000xxx.xx	Regular Pay.

6.39   Given the input cards in Exercise 6.38 and assuming that we pay time and a half for overtime, we wish to punch a card for each man containing man number, regular hours, overtime hours, and total gross pay. The control panel is wired so that we must punch the information from the buffer in the following form:

Word 1.	00000xxxxx	Man Number.
Word 2.	0000000xx.x	Regular Hours.
Word 3.	00000000x.x	Overtime Hours.
Word 4.	00000xxx.xx	Gross Pay.

Hint: It will help to store in memory as a part of the program itself the constant 1.5. Then gross pay is regular rate times (regular hours plus 1.5 times overtime hours).

6.40   Modify the program in Exercise 6.39 so as to also accumulate total gross pay for all the cards so that it will be available in some memory location at the conclusion of the machine run. It will be desirable to make sure that this location is cleared to zero before the first card is read.

6.41   We have a group of cards in which are punched item number, total dollar sales of the item during the first month, total dollar sales of the item during the second month, and total dollar sales of the item during the third month. The control panel is wired so as to enter this information into the input buffer in the following form:

Item Number	0000xxxxxx	Word 1.
Sales 1st Month	000xx,xxx.xx	Word 2.
Sales 2d Month	000xx,xxx.xx	Word 3.
Sales 3d Month	000xx,xxx.xx	Word 4.

For each item, we wish to punch a card containing item number, average dollar sales for the three months, and per cent of the total three-month sales that was sold in each of the three months. You may assume that some of each item was sold. Round these per cent calculations to the nearest tenth of a per cent. The control panel is wired so that we must punch the information from the buffer in the following form:

Word 1.	0000xxxxxx	Item Number.
Word 2.	000xx,xxx.xx	Average Sales.
Word 3.	000000xxx.x	% First Month.

Word 4.   000000xxx.x   % Second Month.
Word 5.   000000xxx.x   % Third Month.

SUPPLEMENTAL READINGS

ANDREE, RICHARD V. *Programming the IBM 650 Magnetic Drum Computer and Data-Processing Machine*. New York: Henry Holt & Co., Inc., 1958.

This book provides an introduction to programming of the 650. Although it is designed for students with an interest in computation rather than data processing, it should be helpful to one who wishes to understand 650 programming.

IBM 650 Data-Processing System Bulletins. New York: International Business Machines Corp., 590 Madison Ave., 1958.

General Information, Console Operation, Special Devices (Form G24–5000)

533 Card Read Punch, 537 Card Read Punch, 407 Accounting Machine (Form G24–5001)

Basic Operation Codes, Program Optimizing, Program Loading (Form G24–5002)

These booklets are designed to present the characteristics of the IBM 650. Although they are not easy reading for the beginner, whenever questions of fact arise concerning the characteristics of the machine, reference to these booklets can usually provide an answer.

CHAPTER 7 · An Intermediate Computer—Part II

IN THE previous chapter, the basic arithmetic instructions of the 650 were discussed. Frankly, were the computers merely able to perform arithmetic rapidly, they would be of quite limited usefulness to the scientist and engineer and of practically no interest to those interested in business data processing. In this chapter, the logical and decision-making capabilities which make these machines such powerful tools for calculation and data processing will be considered.

Branching

Among the most important characteristics of the electronic computer is its ability to follow simple "yes-or-no" decisions. This capability is obtained through the use of branching instructions. Each of these instructions asks a question which can be answered either yes or no. If the answer is no, the normal sequence of instructions is followed by the machine. However, if the answer to this question is yes, then the machine executes an alternate sequence of instructions. Thus, it is possible to follow different procedures depending upon the answer to this question.

All of the 650 branching instructions operate in essentially the same way. If the answer to the yes-or-no question is no, the next instruction is taken from the location specified by the instruction address, while if the answer is yes, the location of the next instruction is given by the data address. Thus, the data address in a branching instruction is an *alternate* instruction address.

46 BMI (Branch on Minus Accumulator). This instruction causes the 650 to examine the sign of the accumulator. If the sign of the accumulator is minus, the next instruction is taken from the location given by the data address. If the sign of the accumulator is

136

plus, the next instruction is taken from the location given by the instruction address. The contents of the accumulator are ignored.

It should be noted that in the case of a division, when the sign of the upper accumulator may be different from that of the lower, this instruction considers only the sign of the lower accumulator. Also, it is possible for the accumulator sign to be negative while its contents are zero.

As an illustration of the use of branching instructions, suppose we are using the 650 to maintain finished-goods inventory records, and for a given item number, we have within memory the previous on-hand balance and the number shipped. We wish to determine the current on-hand balance by subtracting shipments from the old balance. Although it appears impossible to ship more of an item than you have, occasionally records will be in error; for this reason, it is desirable to make sure that our data-processing system does not produce nonsensical negative inventories. At any rate, we wish to detect and investigate such situations if they arise, so we might consider the partial block diagram shown in Figure 7–1. Notice in Figure

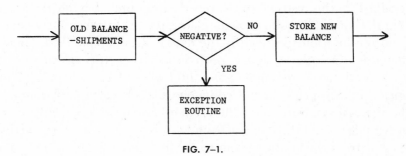

FIG. 7–1.

7–1 that decision points are indicated by the use of diamond-shaped symbols in the block diagram.

Let us assume that the old balance (98, for example) is in location 1200, the amount of the shipment (35, for example) is in location 1201, and we wish to store the new balance (if not negative) in 1202. Also assume that we have decided to place the first word of the exception routine in location 0200. Then we might write the program shown in Example 7–1. Notice that the data address of the *Branch Minus* instruction is circled. This indicates to someone reading the program that the next instruction to be executed may not be the next instruction written on the programming form. If the program is lengthy, it is helpful to indicate (as shown) where the instruction referred to by this address may be found.

Example 7–1

Location	Operation	Data Address	Instruction Address	Upper Accumulator	Lower Accumulator	Distributor
0100	RAL	1200	0101	0000000000	0000000098+	0000000098+
0101	SLO	1201	0102	0000000000	0000000063+	0000000035+
0102	BMI	⟨0200*⟩	0103	0000000000	0000000063+	0000000035+
0103	STL	1202	XXXX	0000000000	0000000063+	0000000063+

*See page 4 of program.

It should be observed in Example 7–1 that if the old balance were 20 and the shipments were 35, then the instruction in location 0103 would not be executed, but the machine would go to location 0200 for its next instruction.

Two 650-branching instructions are concerned with the possibility of zero or nonzero in the accumulator. In most machines, these instructions would branch on zero, but in the 650 they are designed to branch on nonzero.

45 NZE (Branch on Nonzero Accumulator). This operation code causes the machine to examine the entire accumulator. If the entire accumulator is zero, the next instruction is taken from the location specified by the instruction address. If any number other than zero is in the entire 20-position accumulator, the next instruction is taken from the location specified by the data address. It should be noted that the accumulator sign is not considered in this instruction.

44 NZU (Branch on Nonzero in Upper Accumulator). This operation is just like the preceding one, except that it only examines the upper ten positions of the accumulator to determine whether or not it is zero. If the upper accumulator is zero, the next instruction is taken from the location given by the instruction address, but if the upper accumulator is not zero, the next instruction is taken from the location given by the data address.

Programming Group Control

A frequent problem in data processing is that of determining whether the card just read pertains to the same man, account number, or item number as the previous card. This situation (which is handled so simply and neatly by group control on the punched card accounting machine) must be handled by programming in an electronic computer.

For example, suppose we wish to use the 650 to summarize a deck of transaction cards instead of summary punching with the accounting machine. We have a set of punched card labor tickets containing man number, job number, and hours which we wish to summarize by job number. As we will see later, it is possible to take other approaches to this problem, but when using the 650 in the same way that we use the accounting machine, our first step would be to sort these cards into account-number sequence, thus grouping together all the transactions pertaining to each account. Then we would like to process these cards through the 650 and punch a card for each account containing account number and total hours.

Here, for the first time, we are faced with a problem for which the block diagram is not immediately obvious, although the basic approach is relatively straightforward. For each card that is read, we must ask the question "Is this card for the same job?" If the answer is yes, then we should add these hours to the total. If the answer is no, then we should punch a total card for the job that was just processed. This partial block diagram is shown in Figure 7–2.

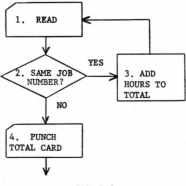

FIG. 7–2.

In this situation, it is apparent that we can program the question "Is this the same job number?" by subtracting the job number of the card just read from the previous job number and using the *Branch on Nonzero* instruction. Although, in this case, it might be possible to use the upper accumulator for the branching and the lower accumulator to accumulate the total hours, it is not desirable to maintain a total in the accumulator from card to card. Thus, we will use a memory location (say 1978) as an accumulator by reset adding the contents of 1978 into the lower accumulator, adding hours from the current card and storing the result back in 1978, where it will be available for punching into the summary card when we desire.

The major question left, then, is "What do we do after we punch the total card?" Our first temptation is to take an arrow back to block 1, but upon analysis we find that this would cause the first card of each group to be ignored. We wish to process this card, but we do not wish to do it by going to block 3, since this would add the hours from the first card of the new group to the total hours for the previous group. Thus, we are led to merely store the job number (in 1977) for punching and the hours from the card (in 1978) to start the new group. Incidentally, storing the new job number gives us something to compare with when we read the next card.

One question still remains: "How do we get started?" If we start with block number 1, on the first card there is no previous job number to compare with, so we would progress along the "no branch and punch an extra total card. A more desirable solution would be to start as shown in the diagram of Figure 7–3. A possible

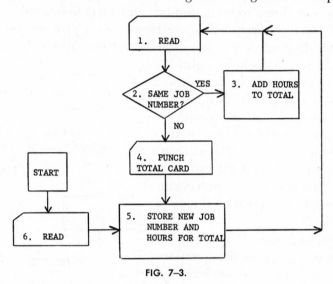

FIG. 7–3.

program for this problem is given in Example 7–2. For illustrative purposes, we assume two input cards. The first card has job number 123 (wired into word one) and 32.4 hours (in word 2), and the sec-

Example 7–2

Block No.	Inst. No.	Loc.	Op.	Data Addr.	Inst. Addr.	Upper Accumulator	Lower Accumulator	Distributor
6	1	0001	RD1	1951	0002			
5	1	0002	LDD	1951	0003			0000000123+
5	2	0003	STD	1977	0004			0000000123+
5	3	0004	LDD	1952	0005			000000032.4+
5	4	0005	STD	1978	0006			000000032.4+
1	1	0006	RD1	1951	0007			000000032.4+
2	1	0007	RAL	1951	0008	0000000000	0000000123+	0000000123+
2	2	0008	SLO	1977	0009	0000000000	0000000000+	0000000123+
2	3	0009	NZE	⓪013	0010	0000000000	0000000000+	0000000123+
3	1	0010	RAL	1978	0011	0000000000	000000032.4+	000000032.4+
3	2	0011	ALO	1952	0012	0000000000	000000048.7+	000000016.3+
3	3	0012	STL	1978	⓪006	0000000000	000000048.7+	000000048.7+
4	1	0013	WR1	1977	⓪002			

ond also has job number 123 with 16.3 hours. We start our program with block 6.

Incidentally, in writing the program in Example 7–2, the data address of the instruction in location 0009 was not inserted until after the next-to-the-last instruction had been written. Again, the circled addresses indicate possible deviations in the sequence of execution of the instructions as compared with the sequence in which they are written on the programming sheet.

Overflow Detection

As we mentioned in our discussion of the instructions pertaining to the upper accumulator, the result of an overflow out of the upper accumulator depends upon the setting of the overflow switch on the 650 console. If this switch is set to *stop*, an overflow causes the machine to stop. If this switch is set to *sense*, an overflow out of the upper accumulator *sets the overflow circuit*. This essentially means that when an overflow occurs a circuit is set just as a person would turn on a light switch. Subsequent overflows after the circuit is set do not affect the circuit (unless in the meantime it has been reset).

47 BOV (Branch on Overflow). This operation code causes the machine to examine the overflow circuit. If the overflow circuit is set to the *on* position, the *Branch on Overflow* instruction causes the next instruction to be taken from the location given by the data address, and it also resets the overflow circuit. If the overflow circuit is not set, this instruction causes the next instruction to be taken from the location given by the instruction address.

An overflow may occur inadvertently because of errors in the program logic or input data, or it may be a normally expected event used by the programmer in the logical design of his program. If it is desired to be aware of each overflow that occurs, it is obvious that a *Branch on Overflow* instruction should be given after each addition that could cause an overflow. Otherwise, more than one overflow might occur between branching instructions.

70 RD1 (Read). As was discussed in Chapter 6, in addition to performing the function of reading a card, the read instruction is actually a branch instruction. If the card contains a punch designating it as a "load card," the read instruction causes the next instruction to be taken from the location designated by the data address, rather than from the location given by the instruction address. Thus, we see a possible motivation for using some address other than the first word of the read-in block as the data address of a read instruction. The use of this instruction as a branch instruction will be discussed in a subsequent section on "Loading the Program."

Control Words

Since the basic numeric 650 cannot store anything but numeric information, the X punches used to distinguish one type of card from another cannot be entered into the 650 memory in their usual form. By the use of control-panel selectors (as shown in Figure 7–4), the presence of an X in a certain column is translated into an 8 in a specific position of an input word, and the absence of an X in this column is translated into a 9 in that position.[1] When several different types of cards are being used in a given procedure, each of the various X's are wired to translate into a digit of a single input word (usually the tenth) called the control word. Likewise, through control-panel wiring, 8's in certain positions of output word ten may be used to punch X punches in the output cards.

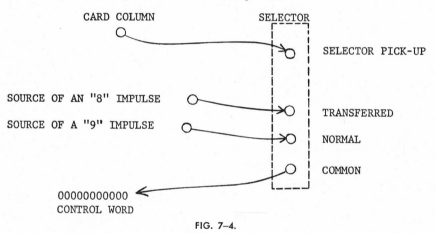

FIG. 7–4.

In order to determine the type of card that has been read and branch to the proper part of the program to handle this type of card, the control word is loaded into the distributor, and a special set of branching instructions is used to test this control word. Since these instructions (*Branch on Digit Eight in a Distributor Position*— operation codes 90–99) are not typical of stored program machines, they will not be discussed in detail here.

It should be remarked that the X's in the card are also used to control selectors which vary the control-panel wiring upon entry so that the information on each card form is entered into the most convenient positions of the input storage words. Likewise, the 8's in word ten of output storage (which can be translated into X's in the

---

[1] See the discussion on selectors in Chapter 3.

card) can also be used to vary the format of the output. Thus, in effect, a separate control panel is available for each type of input and output card. This ability to vary the format on input and output reduces the amount of rearrangement of information that must be programmed.

At this point, we have completed our detailed study of the operation codes available in the 650. Because they are not typical of computers in general, discussion of a number of interesting and useful operation codes of the basic 650 have been omitted. These include all of the *absolute value* operations, stop, store data address and store instruction address, and shift and count. The *Table Look-up* instruction will be mentioned later in the section on table look-up. For similar reasons, the features of the control panel and its wiring have not been discussed. The operation of the machine and the use of the console are discussed in Appendix A.

The major motivation for our discussion of the 650 instructions and their use has been to obtain an understanding of the stored program, its capabilities and limitations, and the considerations involved in programming. The remainder of this chapter will be devoted to some interesting ways in which these instructions may be used.

Instruction Modification

One of the most powerful characteristics of the stored program electronic data-processing machine is its ability to compute with its own instructions, and thus modify or synthesize instructions that it will execute later on in the program. Although this capability seems at first glance to be so complex that it would be almost unusable, it is actually used quite routinely in almost every program of any complexity.

Looping

One of the more common techniques involving instruction modification is called *looping,* where a set of instructions are executed, then modified slightly, then executed again, then modified, then executed, and so on.

As an example of a program involving looping, suppose we have accumulated upon the drum a set of labor cost balances for 500 job numbers. These balances are located so that the cost for job number 1 is accumulated in storage location 0001, the cost for job number 2 is in storage location 0002, and so on. In other words, for any job number between 1 and 500, the drum location corresponding to the job number has been used to accumulate total cost. Our problem is to get this information off the drum into cards, each card containing the balance for a single job.

Our first approach might be to write a program of the following type: load distributor from 0001, store distributor in 1977, punch from 1977, load distributor from 0002, store distributor in 1977, punch from 1977, load distributor from 0003, store distributor in 1977, punch from 1977, and so on. However, this approach would require 1,500 locations for the program itself, which together with punch-out locations and the 500 balances would exceed the capacity of the drum.

Although unsuccessful, this attempt gives us an indication of what may be done. If we examine this program in groups of three instructions, we notice that only the first instruction of each group has changed, namely the load distributor instruction. And we notice that the data address of this instruction has merely been increased by one in each group. Thus, we might consider the block diagram shown in Figure 7–5. Notice that portions of the block diagram associated with instruction modification are indicated through the use of a hexagonal box.

The block diagram of Figure 7–5 would accomplish our purpose of punching out the 500 balances, but, unfortunately, it would not stop with that. It would continue to punch out the entire drum, and stop only when the data address of the load distributor instruction reached 2,000, which is an invalid address. Thus, we are forced to modify our diagram to obtain Figure 7–6.

In order to write any computer program, it is apparent that it is necessary to understand what the program is to accomplish. Thus, when writing the portion of a program that accomplishes instruction modification, we must first understand the portion of the program that is being modified. Therefore, we will start by writing the instructions associated with blocks 1 and 2 of Figure 7–6 for the first job. Notice that we enclose in parentheses addresses that are to be modified.

Example 7–3

Block No.	Inst. No.	Loc.	Op.	Data Addr.	Inst. Addr.	Upper Accumulator	Lower Accumulator	Distributor
1	1	1000	LDD	(0001)	1001			Hours
1	2	1001	STD	1977	1002			Hours
2	1	1002	WR1	1977	1003			Hours

How can we answer the question posed in block 3 of Figure 7–6? We will have punched the last balance when the instruction in 1000 becomes LDD 0500 1001. Thus, we need to store the constant

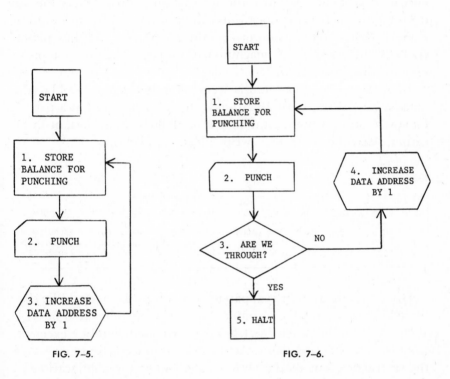

FIG. 7–5.   FIG. 7–6.

6905001001+ in memory (say in 1050) as part of our program so that we may subtract it from the *Load Distributor* instruction and *Branch on Nonzero*.

Example 7–4

Block No.	Inst. No.	Loc.	Op.	Data Addr.	Inst. Addr.	Upper Accumulator	Lower Accumulator	Distributor
3	1	1003	RAL	1000	1004	0000000000	6900011001+	6900011001+
3	2	1004	SLO	1050	1005	0000000000	0004990000−	6905001001+
3	3	1005	NZE	(1007)	1006	0000000000	0004990000−	6905001001+
5	1	1006	NOP	0000	9999			

The instruction in 1006 is used to stop the machine at the conclusion of the program. The *No-operation* instruction (NOP-00) tells the machine to look for its next instruction in location 9999. Since there is no location 9999, the machine stops when 9999 enters the address register. Actually, we could have made the instruction in 1005 NZE 1007 9999, and the machine would stop when the difference is zero. However, since the instruction address enters the address register before the operation code is interpreted, we could not stop the machine on a nonzero condition by using the instruction NZU 9999 1006, since the machine will stop each time it attempts to execute this instruction.

In order to write block 4, it is necessary to have a one to add to the data address of the *Load Distributor* instruction. Thus, as a part of our program we store the number 0000010000+ as a constant in location 1051. Then we may write block 4 as follows:

Example 7–5

Block No.	Inst. No.	Loc.	Op.	Data Addr.	Inst. Addr.	Upper Accumulator	Lower Accumulator	Distributor
4	1	1007	RAL	1000	1008	0000000000	6900011001+	6900011001+
4	2	1008	ALO	1051	1009	0000000000	6900021001+	0000010000+
4	3	1009	STL	1000	1000	0000000000	6900021001+	6900021001+

Upon examination, it is apparent that this program could be simplified in many ways. For example, the last instruction could be STL 1000 8002, and the *Load Distributor* instruction would be executed from the lower accumulator. Actually, it is unnecessary to ever take the instruction out of the accumulator either for modification or execution. Furthermore, if we let N be the data address of the instruction in 1000, at the end of block 3 we have in the accumulator N-500. If we add 501 to this, we get N + 1 in a single step. Thus, if we store in 1051 the number 6905011001+, we can replace the instructions in locations 1007 and 1008 by the instruction ALO 1051 1009.

To make the above problem realistic, it would be necessary to punch the department number along with the balance for that department. The only necessary modification to the block diagram would be in block 4, which would be modified to read: Increase the data address and the department number by one. This, however, would give us the option of doing our comparison against either the instruction being modified or the department number itself. This program will be left as an exercise for the reader.

It should be apparent that any time spent executing instructions that modify other instructions is essentially nonproductive. If a program can be written which accomplishes the desired result and does not involve instruction modification, it will usually operate faster than a similar program involving instruction modification. On the other hand, memory space is often conserved by using the technique of instruction modification. When there is a choice, the technique used should be determined by the over-all balance among operating speed, programming effort, and available memory.

Instruction Synthesis

When utilizing computers, it is frequently necessary to refer to information stored in memory under circumstances in which it is impossible for the programmer (at the time the program is written) to know where the information is stored, for this depends upon the transaction itself.

For example, let us consider the following situation: Suppose we have 50,000 cards in random sequence, each containing a job number and a number of hours worked on that job. Just as in the example in the section on "Programming Group Control," we would like to obtain from these cards a total of the hours worked on each of the 500 jobs, except that we would prefer not to sort the cards. Assuming that the job numbers range from 001 to 500, we could assign the 650 memory in the following way: Use storage location 0001 to accumulate the hours for job number 001, use storage location 0002 to accumulate the hours for job number 002, and use storage location 0500 to accumulate the hours for job number 500. Assuming that these 500 drum locations contain zeros at the beginning, our first approximation of a block diagram might appear as in Figure 7–7.

However, we would soon discover that it is not quite this simple, because we have difficulty obtaining the proper previous total from among the 500 possible totals stored on the drum, and we have the same difficulty when returning the new total to storage. Thus, we are led to reason that we need an instruction whose data address is the same as the job number to obtain the previous total, and another similar instruction to return the new total to storage. Since we cannot write these instructions, perhaps we can design a program to write them for each card read, and we prepare the block diagram shown in Figure 7–8.

Let us assume that the department number (represented by

xxx) is read into the low-order positions of buffer word 1, and that hours are read into buffer word 2. In order to synthesize an instruction, it is necessary to know what we are attempting to construct, so we first write the part of the program that does the work, namely block 4. In the following program, we are assuming that the

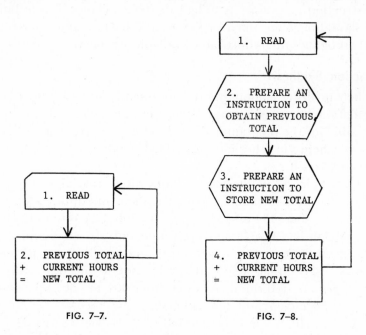

FIG. 7–7.   FIG. 7–8.

read instruction in block 1 is located in 1000 and reads the cards into the input area starting in 1951.

Example 7–6

Block No.	Inst. No.	Loc.	Op.	Data Addr.	Inst. Addr.	Upper Accumulator	Lower Accumulator	Distributor
4	1	1020	RAL	(0XXX)	1021	0000000000	Prev. Total	Prev. Total
4	2	1021	ALO	1952	1022	0000000000	New Total	Current Hrs.
4	3	1022	STL	(0XXX)	1000	0000000000	New Total	New Total

In constructing the instruction in location 1020, we must combine the operation code 65 and the instruction address 1021 with the job number as the data address. Thus, if we shift the job number left four positions and add it to the constant 6500001021+, we will obtain the desired result. Therefore, we will store the instructional constant 6500001021+ in location 1050 as a part of our program and write block 2 as follows:

Example 7-7

Block No.	Inst. No.	Loc.	Op.	Data Addr.	Inst. Addr.	Upper Accumulator	Lower Accumulator	Distributor
2	1	1001	RAL	1951	1002	0000000000	0000000XXX+	0000000XXX+
2	2	1002	SLT	0004	1003	0000000000	000XXX0000+	0000000XXX+
2	3	1003	ALO	1050	1004	0000000000	650XXX1021+	6500001021+
2	4	1004	STL	1020	1005	0000000000	650XXX1021+	650XXX1021+

By a similar reasoning process, we decide to store the instructional constant 2000001000+ in location 1051 and write the following program for block 3:

Example 7-8

Block No.	Inst. No.	Loc.	Op.	Data Addr.	Inst. Addr.	Upper Accumulator	Lower Accumulator	Distributor
3	1	1005	RAL	1951	1006	0000000000	0000000XXX+	0000000XXX+
3	2	1006	SLT	0004	1007	0000000000	000XXX0000+	0000000XXX+
3	3	1007	ALO	1051	1008	0000000000	200XXX1000+	2000001000+
3	4	1008	STL	1022	1020	0000000000	200XXX1000+	200XXX1000+

In order to better understand how this program would operate, let us go through it with a specific example. Suppose the card read contains 47.3 hours for job number 327, and at the time it is read, the previous total hours for job number 327 are 467.9.

Example 7-9

Block No.	Inst. No.	Loc.	Op.	Data Addr.	Inst. Addr.	Upper Accumulator	Lower Accumulator	Distributor
1	1	1000	RD1	1951	1001			
2	1	1001	RAL	1951	1002	0000000000	0000000327+	0000000327+
2	2	1002	SLT	0004	1003	0000000000	0003270000+	0000000327+
2	3	1003	ALO	1050	1004	0000000000	6503271021+	6500001021+
2	4	1004	STL	1020	1005	0000000000	6503271021+	6503271021+
3	1	1005	RAL	1951	1006	0000000000	0000000327+	0000000327+
3	2	1006	SLT	0004	1007	0000000000	0003270000+	0000000327+
3	3	1007	ALO	1051	1008	0000000000	2003271000+	2000001000+
3	4	1008	STL	1022	1020	0000000000	2003271000+	2003271000+
4	1	1020	65	(0327)	1021	0000000000	000000467.9+	000000467.9+
4	2	1021	ALO	1952	1022	0000000000	000000515.2+	000000047.3+
4	3	1022	20	(0327)	(1000)	0000000000	000000515.2+	000000515.2+

Upon reflection, it is apparent that several steps in the above program are unnecessary. For example, if we were to modify the block diagram to construct the first instruction of block 4 last, then we could execute it from the accumulator without storing it on the drum. Also, blocks 2 and 3 include much needless duplication. We may note that (2000001000+) plus (4500000021) equals

6500001021+; so by using the constant 4500000021+ in 1050 rather than 6500001021+ we may immediately construct the first instruction of block 4 after we have created the last instruction.

Example 7–10

Block No.	Inst. No.	Loc.	Op.	Data Addr.	Inst. Addr.	Upper Accumulator	Lower Accumulator	Distributor
1	1	1000	RD1	1951	1001			
3	1	1001	RAL	1951	1002	0000000000	0000000327+	0000000327+
3	2	1002	SLT	0004	1003	0000000000	0003270000+	0000000327+
3	3	1003	ALO	1051	1004	0000000000	2003271000+	2000001000+
3	4	1004	STL	1022	1005	0000000000	2003271000+	2003271000+
2	1	1005	ALO	1050	8002	0000000000	6503271021+	4500000021+
4	1	8002	RAL	(0327)	1021	0000000000	000000467.9+	000000467.9+
4	2	1021	ALO	1952	1022	0000000000	000000515.2+	000000047.3+
4	3	1022	STL	(0327)	(1000)	0000000000	000000515.2+	000000515.2+

The use of the 650 *Store Data Address* instruction would have saved the locations occupied by the two instructional constants in the above program, but it would have been necessary to execute one more instruction and utilize one other storage location if the instruction had been used. Since this instruction is not typical of most machines, it will be omitted from this discussion.

Table Look-up

Because of the way identifying codes are assigned, it is frequently inconvenient or impossible to assign the memory location to be the same as the code, as was done in the previous example. Most identifying codes contain more digits than the memory address allows, and codes usually are rather sparsely distributed over their range of values. For example, the item numbers identifying the parts in a production control system might contain seven digits, which allows for 9,999,999 different parts. However, there may be only 15,000 parts in the system, in which case only 15,000 of these part numbers would be used. Likewise, there may be a five-digit job number and only 400 active jobs. How can we handle such situations?

In the first place, we might attempt to devise a formula to compute a drum location from the identifying number. For example, if the 400 job numbers ranged from 45027 to 45426, we could subtract 45027 from each to obtain drum locations ranging from 0000 to 0399. Unfortunately, because the identifying numbers are widely scattered, it is usually impractical to attempt to find a usable formula.

In such cases, we must store a table in memory, including both the identifying number (called the *argument*) and the information desired (called the *function*). The telephone book is an example of such a table, where the name is the argument and the telephone number is the function. A table may have more than one function for the same argument. For example, in the telephone book both address and telephone number are associated with name.

The telephone book illustrates another important characteristic of usable tables. The usefulness of the telephone book depends upon the fact that the names are in alphabetical order. Otherwise, we would not be able to easily find any name. For example, if you know a telephone number, can you easily find the person's name? Not from the telephone book, but if you had a book in telephone number order, you could easily refer to it to find in whose name a phone is listed, and where it is located.

Thus, for ease of reference, tables are arranged in the computer memory in sequence according to the argument. Usually, the arguments are stored in one block of memory and the functions in a separate block of memory a specified number of locations away. For example, if job numbers are stored in locations 0001 to 0400, the corresponding hourly totals might be stored in locations 0401 to 0800. To locate the total for a given job number (called the *search argument*), we first find the location of the job number in the table and then add 400 to this location to obtain the location of its balance.

How, then, can we write a program that can be used to find the argument that is stored in memory? One approach would be to start at the beginning of the table and examine each argument in sequence until an argument greater than or equal to the search argument is found. This might be accomplished through the use of the block diagram shown in Figure 7–9. Here the notation arg (i) means the table argument stored in memory location i.

In the 650, the program for the above block diagram would require about three drum revolutions for each time around the loop until the argument is found. If the table contained 400 entries, this would mean an average of $200 (3) (4.8) = 2,880$ milliseconds, or 2.88 seconds, which is rather slow. However, the 650 has a special instruction (84 TLU *Table Look-up*) that searches through the arguments in a table at a rate of 48 arguments per drum revolution. Before the TLU operation is begun, the search argument must be placed in the distributor. The location of the first table argument greater than or equal to the search argument is inserted into the positions of the lower accumulator corresponding to the data-address positions of an instruction. Since the *Table Look-up* instruction is found in few machines other than the 650, it will not be discussed in detail here, but it is worth remarking that this instruction makes it possible to search a 400-entry table in an average of about 20 milliseconds.[2]

It should be emphasized that the block diagram in Figure 7–9 presents a very inefficient approach to programming a table look-up. In machines that do not have an automatic *Table Look-up* in-

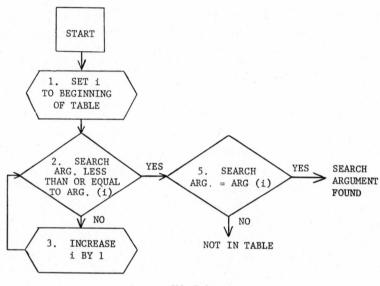

FIG. 7–9.

struction, a so-called *binary search* is frequently programmed. The basic idea of the binary search is to look first at the middle of the table and decide which way to go from there. Then look halfway to the end in the proper direction and decide which way to go, and continue this process, cutting the length of the step in half each time. In Figure 7–10, let N be the number of entries in the table and K be the location of the first table entry. The notation arg (i) means the table argument stored in memory location i.

The program for Figure 7–10 would execute about 14 instructions for every time around the loop, but for a 400-entry table we would only have to go around the loop a maximum of nine times. For machines that can execute instructions almost as rapidly as the automatic table look-up can scan memory, the binary search is at least as efficient for large tables as an automatic *Table Look-up* instruction.

---

[2] The IBM 7070 has a similar instruction.

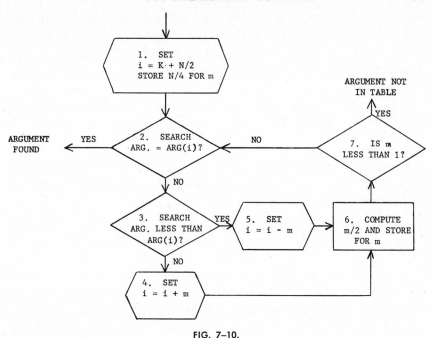

FIG. 7–10.

Index Registers

One or more index registers are available as standard or optional equipment on several electronic computers. The same size as the address register, index registers are used in modifying addresses of instructions and in looping. These registers may be added into, subtracted from, and branched on, much the same as an accumulator. In addition, for any "tagged" instructions, the contents of the index register are added to (or subtracted from) the data address of the instruction before that instruction is executed and without changing the instruction as it is stored in memory. One way to "tag" an instruction is by making its sign negative.

Designating the index register by capital B (RAB stands for *Reset Add to Index Register*), let us consider how it could be used in the illustration concerned with accumulating total hours for each of 500 jobs. The block diagram associated with this illustration is shown in Figure 7–8 (see p. 148). By entering the department number into the index register, we would

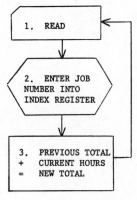

FIG. 7–11.

automatically insert the proper data address into the instruction which obtains the old balance and the instruction which stores the new balance (both of which would be tagged with a minus sign). Thus, our block diagram could be simplified to that shown in Figure 7–11.

The program associated with this block diagram would be as shown in Example 7–11.

Example 7–11

Block No.	Loc.	Op.	Data Addr.	Inst. Addr.	Index Reg.	Upper Accumulator	Lower Accumulator	Distributor
1	1000	RD1	1951	1001				
2	1001	RAB	1951	1002	0327			
3	1002	RAL	0000	1003–	0327	0000000000	000000467.9+	000000467.9+
3	1003	ALO	1952	1004	0327	0000000000	000000515.2+	000000047.3+
3	1004	STL	0000	⟨1000⟩	0327	0000000000	000000515.2+	000000515.2+

Notice in the above program that the instructions located in 1002 and 1004 are tagged with a minus sign, so the instructions actually executed by the machine (in the above example) would be RAL 0327 1003 and STL 0327 1000.

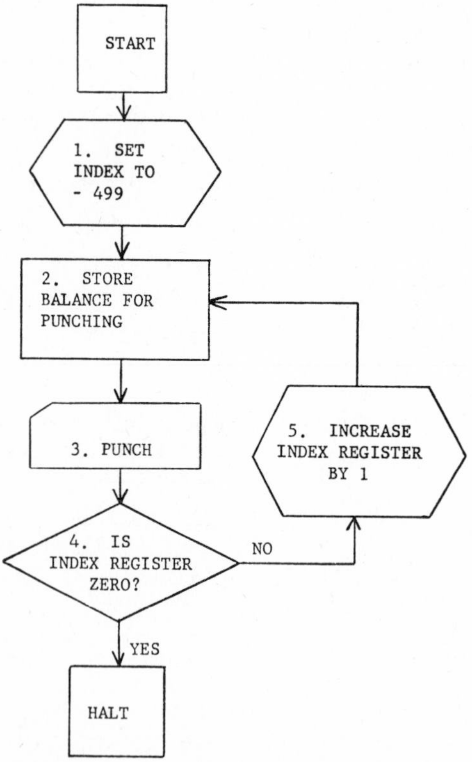

Index registers can also be used to simplify the programming involved in looping, for they can both modify the addresses and serve as the criteria for determining when to come out of the loop. For example, consider the problem of punching into cards the totals that were accumulated on the drum. Figure 7–6 (see p. 145) provides a block diagram for writing this program without the use of an index register. With an index register available, we might use the block diagram shown in Figure 7–12.

Assuming that we have instructions AXB (*Add to Index Register*) and NZB

FIG. 7–12.

(*Branch on Nonzero in Index Register*) that operate like similar instructions for the accumulator, and that the constant 0000000499— is stored in location 1050 and 0000000001+ is stored in location 1051, we might write the program as seen in Example 7–12.

Example 7–12

Block No.	Loc.	Op.	Data Addr.	Inst. Addr.	Index Reg.	Upper Accumulator	Lower Accumulator	Distributor
1	1000	RAB	1050	1001	0499–			0000000499–
2	1001	LDD	0500	1002–	0499–			Total Hrs. +
2	1002	STD	1977	1003	0499–			Total Hrs. +
3	1003	WR1	1977	1004	0499–			Total Hrs. +
4	1004	NZB	1005	9999	0499–			Total Hrs. +
5	1005	AXB	1051	(1001)	0498–			0000000001+

When the index register reaches zero, the instruction in location 1004 will stop the machine, since it will not branch, and the invalid address 9999 will enter the address register.

As can be seen by comparing Example 7–12 with Examples 7–3 and 7–4 (see p. 144–5), the use of an index register to modify a single instruction does not spectacularly increase efficiency. However, when several instructions are to be modified in the same manner, frequently they can all be changed by a single operation on the index register.

Although 3 index registers are available as optional equipment on the IBM 650, the above description differs in several details from the operation of those registers, particularly with respect to the method of tagging instructions. The Datatron 205, Datatron 220, IBM 704, and IBM 709 all include from 1 to 3 index registers as standard equipment, while the Minneapolis-Honeywell 800 has 64 index registers, and the IBM 7070 includes 99 index registers.

Switches

Frequently a condition detected at one place in a program requires that modification be made at one or more other places in the program that may be executed later. The "remembering" of these conditions is accomplished by the use of *switches* which are quite analogous to the switches which control traffic on a railroad.

As a simple illustration, suppose that we have, in man-number sequence, a file of cards which contains a variable number of cards for each man number. For some of the man numbers in the file, the group of cards will contain one or more X-79 cards, placed at random in the group. We would like to process the file under the following conditions: For each man-number group, process all of the cards up to and including an X-79 card (if one is present), and ignore all of the cards after the X-79 card has been reached.

A switch is denoted by the following symbol in the block diagram:

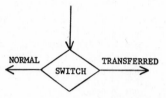

It should be noted that of the two or more possible paths away from the symbol, one and only one can be active at any given time. This is controlled elsewhere in the program by setting the switch to the desired position, as illustrated in the block diagram in Figure 7–13.[3]

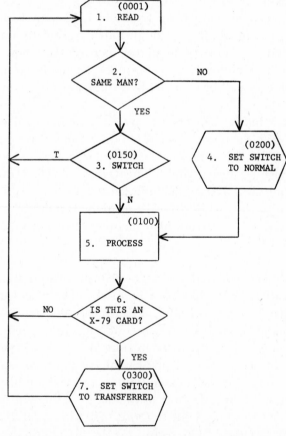

FIG. 7–13.

---

[3] Other block diagrams could handle this problem, some of which do not involve the use of switches.

In this figure, cards for a given man number are read and processed until an X-79 card is detected. At this time, the switch is set to the transferred position so that subsequent cards are simply checked to see if the man number has changed, and, if not, they are ignored. When the man number does change, the switch is reset to the normal position, and the first card and all following cards are processed until again an X-79 card is detected.

There are many ways that this switching function can be accomplished. Perhaps the most straightforward of these ways is through the use of an unconditional transfer instruction, which in the 650 is represented by the *No Operation* instruction (NOP, code 00) which merely directs the machine to the location specified by the instruction address to obtain the next instruction.

Assuming that the read instruction of block 1 is located in 0001 and that the first instruction of block 5 is located in 0100, we could store the constant 0000000100+ in location 0500 and the constant 0000000001+ in location 0501 and write programs for blocks 4 and 7 as shown in Example 7–13. Note that the *No Operation* instruction in location 0150 is the switch.

Example 7–13

Block No.	Inst. No.	Loc.	Op.	Data Addr.	Inst. Addr.	Upper Accumulator	Lower Accumulator	Distributor
4	1	0200	LDD	0500	0201			0000000100+
4	2	0201	STD	0150	(0100)			0000000100+
7	1	0300	LDD	0501	0301			0000000001+
7	2	0301	STD	0150	(0001)			0000000001+

It should be observed that the switch must be set to the normal position at the start of the program, so that the first card will be processed properly. This can be accomplished through the use of an *initialization* routine that will be executed but once at the start of the program. This initialization routine may also be used to set certain storage locations to their proper value (frequently zero) and to set instructions that may be modified to their starting condition. Although all of these things may be accomplished as the program itself is loaded, it is frequently convenient to do them in an initialization routine because then the program can be restarted (without reloading the instructions) by merely starting the machine at the beginning of the initialization routine.

Loading the Program

As we consider the use of a computer in which the instructions to be executed are stored in the memory of the machine, the question naturally arises as to how these instructions are entered into the memory. The process of entering the program into the memory of a machine is called *loading* the machine. The simplest method of loading the 650 involves the use of *single-word load cards* illustrated in Figure 7–14 (ignore columns 41 through 80).

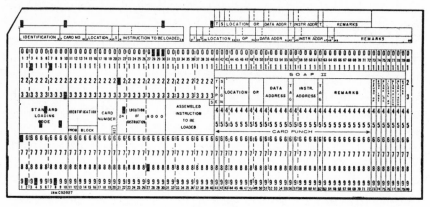

FIG. 7–14.

When the program written on the planning chart is presented to the key punch operator, she inserts single-word load cards into the key punch. These cards are prepunched as follows: Columns 1 through 10 are punched with 6919541953; columns 21 and 22 are punched 24; and columns 27 through 30 are punched 8000. For each line on the coding sheet, the key punch operator produces a load card which contains, in addition to the identifying information and the operation abbreviation as shown in Figure 7–14, the memory location of the instruction to be entered (which she punches into columns 23 through 26) and the instruction to be loaded (which is punched into columns 31 through 40). All of these cards are identified as load cards by a 12 punch in a specified column (for example, column 1).

As previously discussed, when the 650 reads a load card several abnormal functions take place. In the first place, all control-panel wiring is ignored; the 80 columns of the card are transferred directly into the first 80 positions (the first 8 words) of the read-in area of the specified drum band. Secondly, the read instruction is actually a *Branch on Load Card* instruction, so when a load card is read, the next instruction is taken from the location given by the data address of the read instruction, rather than the location given by the instruction address. Therefore, in this illustration the next instruction would be taken from the first word of the card.

Now let's see how all of this works. To load the program, the program cards are inserted into the read hopper, and the number 701951xxxx (where the xxxx may represent an invalid address or the location of the first instruction of the program itself) is manually set into the storage entry switches, which have the address 8000. When the computer reset button is pressed, the number 8000 is automatically inserted into the address register, so that when the start button is pressed, the machine takes its first instruction from the storage entry switches. This instruction 701951xxxx says "read into the 10-word area starting with location 1951, and as the card is a load card (which branches), the next instruction is taken from location 1951." This instruction is 69 1954 1953, which tells the machine to load the distributor with the instruction that was punched into this card (and which was read into location 1954). The next instruction is taken from location 1953, which contains the instruction 24 yyyy 8000, where yyyy indicates the location at which the instruction is to be stored. This tells the machine to store the distributor (which contains the instruction to be loaded) at the proper location and go to address 8000 (which is the storage entry switches) for the next instruction. Thus, the next card is read, and the same process is followed with it, except that the instruction and the location at which it is to be stored are different.

Thus, the single-word loading routine would appear on the planning chart as shown in Example 7–14, assuming the instruction to be loaded from the card is 65 0743 0452, and it is to be located in 0451.

Example 7–14

Loc.	Op.	Data Addr.	Inst. Addr.	Upper Accumulator	Lower Accumulator	Distributor
8000	RD1	1951	XXXX			
1951	LDD	1954	1953			6507430452+
1953	STD	(0451)	(8000)			6507430452+

Although the single-word loading routine is simple and convenient for checking out programs, when file storage space and machine loading time become important, it is desirable to have routines which load several instructions from each card. The card form for a routine that will load four words from each card is illustrated in Figure 7–15.

In addition to the instructions punched into the loading cards

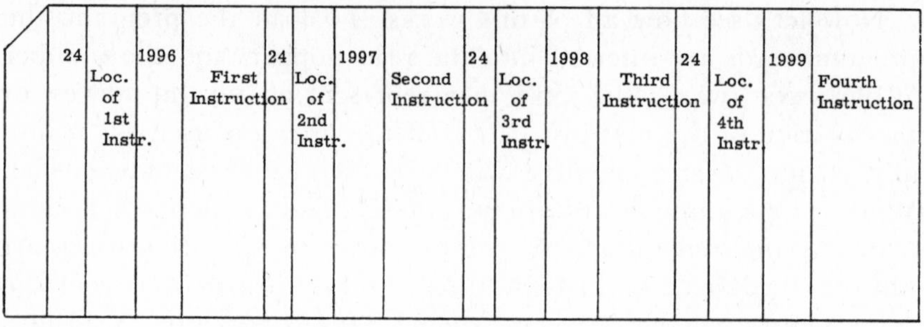

24		1996		24		1997		24		1998		24		1999	
	Loc. of 1st Instr.		First Instruction		Loc. of 2nd Instr.		Second Instruction		Loc. of 3rd Instr		Third Instruction		Loc. of 4th Instr		Fourth Instruction

FIG. 7–15.

themselves, the instructions in Example 7–15 are loaded onto the drum by means of single-word loaders.

Example 7–15

Location	Op.	Data Addr.	Inst. Addr.
1999	RD1	1995	9999
1995	LDD	1952	1951
1996	LDD	1954	1953
1997	LDD	1956	1955
1998	LDD	1958	1957

The first instruction to be executed is the *Read* instruction (RD1 1995 9999) which reads the first card into the 1950 band (locations 1951 through 1958).[4] Combining the instructions above with those that have just been read in from the card, we obtain the program shown in Example 7–16.

Example 7–16

Location	Op.	Data Addr.	Inst. Addr.
1999	RD1	1995	9999
1995	LDD	1952	1951
1951	STD	wwww	1996*
1996	LDD	1954	1953
1953	STD	xxxx	1997*
1997	LDD	1956	1955
1955	STD	yyyy	1998*
1998	LDD	1958	1957
1957	STD	zzzz	1999*

---

[4] As was discussed in Chapter 6, the data address of a *Read* instruction merely selects the band, and the information from the card is placed in the read-in area of that band. This is an example of a case where we do not wish to use the first word of the read-in area (1951) as the data address.

In this example, the (*) indicates that the instruction comes from the loading card, while wwww, xxxx, yyyy, and zzzz represent the respective memory locations at which the four instructions are to be stored.

Since these are load cards, the *Read* instruction branches and the next instruction is taken from 1995. This instruction loads the distributor with the contents of the 1952, which is the first instruction to be entered from the load card. Then the machine goes to location 1951 for the next instruction, which says to store the distributor (containing the instruction to be loaded) in the proper location. This process is then repeated for the second, third, and fourth instructions to be loaded from this card, and the machine goes to location 1999 for the instruction to read the next card.

It is interesting to note that no more than five instructions can be loaded into random locations from a single card, because there are not enough card columns to load six instructions and six four-digit addresses (a total of 84 columns). However, if it is desired to load into sequential locations, a routine has been developed to use the card form shown in Figure 7–16 to load as many as seven instructions from a single card. In the first word of the card in Fig. 7–16,

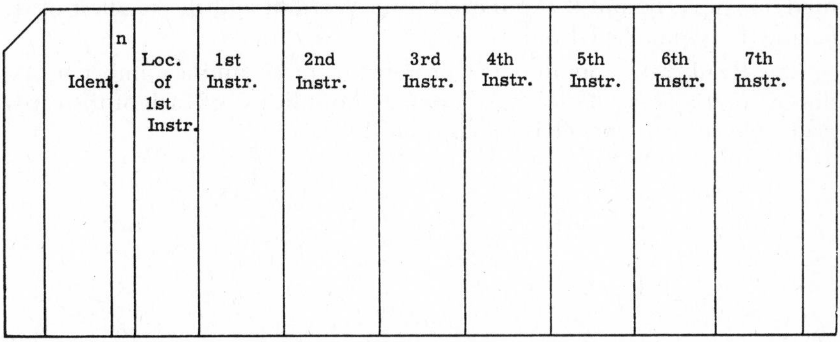

Ident.	n	Loc. of 1st Instr.	1st Instr.	2nd Instr.	3rd Instr.	4th Instr.	5th Instr.	6th Instr.	7th Instr.

FIG. 7–16.

n is the number of words to be loaded from the card (n may range from one to seven).

As was mentioned previously, programs are originally punched into the single-card loaders, and the program is debugged in this form. After the program is in a form that can be used in a routine fashion, it can be condensed into four instructions per card or seven instructions per card by means of automatic conversion routines, which read the single-card loaders into the 650 and punch out loading cards in one of the condensed forms.

EXERCISES

Prepare a block diagram and a program for each of the following exercises.

7.1 Read cards containing an identification number and two quantities, A and B. The control panel is wired so that this information enters the buffer in the following way:

Identification	xxxxxx	Word 1.
Quantity A	xxx.xx	Word 2.
Quantity B	xxx.xx	Word 3.

If $A = B$, ignore the card. Otherwise, punch an output card in which the identification is punched from Word 1 of the buffer, and the larger of A and B is punched from Word 2 of the buffer.

7.2 Read cards containing an identification number and three quantities, $A, B,$ and C. The control panel is wired so that the information enters the buffer in the following way:

Identification	xxxxxx	Word 1.
Quantity A	xxx.xx	Word 2.
Quantity B	xxx.xx	Word 3.
Quantity C	xxx.xx	Word 4.

Punch a card in which the identification is punched from Word 1 of the buffer; the largest of $A, B,$ and C is punched from Word 2; the middle-sized one of $A, B,$ and C is punched from Word 3; and the smallest of $A, B,$ and C is punched from Word 4.

7.3 Read cards containing item number, price, and a number n. Assuming that n is greater than zero, punch n duplicates of each of the cards read. The control panel is wired as follows:

		Input	Output
Item Number	xxxxxx	Word 1.	Word 1.
Price	xxx.xx	Word 2.	Word 2.
n	xx	Word 3.	

7.4 Three different types of cards are involved in a 650 procedure: balance cards (X–75), sales cards (X–43), and returns cards (X–50). Prepare a *partial* block diagram that will read a card and direct the program to the balance card routine if the card is a balance card, to the sales card routine if the card is a sales card, and to the returns card routine if the card is a returns card. In this diagram, you may use general questions such as "Is this an X–75 card?" Do not write the program, but answer the following questions:

a) What would happen if a card without any X punch in it came along?

b) What would happen if a card came along that had an X in 75 and an X in 50?

c) In what sequence should the questions be asked? Why?

d) Modify the block diagram to assure that the machine would stop for all possible mistakes such as those in (*a*) and (*b*).

7.5 There are 600 numbers of the form xxxxxx.xx stored on the 650 drum in locations 1000 to 1599. Prepare a block diagram and program that will add these numbers and punch a card with their sum.

7.6 Prepare a block diagram and program that will set drum locations 0100 through 1999 to zero.

7.7 There are 300 job numbers stored on the 650 drum in locations 1001 to 1300. Associated with each job number is a total of hours worked on that job, and these totals are stored on the drum in locations 1501 to 1800. If the job number is stored in location *n*, then the total for that job is stored in location $n + 500$. Prepare a block diagram and write a program to punch a card for each job containing job number and total hours. The control panel is wired so that job number should be punched from Word 1 of the output buffer and total hours should be punched from Word 2 of the output buffer.

7.8 Consider a generalization of Exercise 7.7 in which there are *n* job numbers starting in location *k*. If the job number is in location *i*, then the total for that job is stored in location $i + m$. Assuming that *k* is greater than 99, and that *n* and *m* are not large enough to make the table exceed the size of memory, prepare a block diagram and write a program that will read a card containing *n*, *k*, and *m* and punch a card for each of the *n* jobs containing job number and total hours. Assume that the control panel is wired so that *n* is read into Word 1, *k* into Word 2, and *m* into Word 3, and that the output is wired as in Exercise 7.7.

In the following four exercises, assume that a job rate table for job numbers 1 through 500 is stored on the drum so that the rate (of form x.xx) for job number *i* is stored in drum location *i*. Prepare a block diagram and program for Exercises 7.9, 7.10, 7.11, and 7.12.

7.9 We wish to read cards containing man number, job number, and hours, and for each such card, punch a card containing man number, job number, hours, and pay (job rate times hours). The form of the numbers and the control-panel wiring are described below.

		Input	Output
Man Number	xxxxxx	Word 1.	Word 1.
Job Number	xxx	Word 2.	Word 2.
Hours	xx.x	Word 3.	Word 3.
Pay	xxx.xx		Word 4.

7.10   We wish to read cards containing man number, job number, hours, and guaranteed rate, and for each such card, punch a card containing man number, job number, hours, and pay. In this case, pay is computed as hours times the larger of job rate and guaranteed rate. The control panel is wired the same as in Exercise 7.9, except that guaranteed rate (x.xx) is wired into Word 4 on input.

7.11   Assume that there are several cards for each man number in Exercise 7.10, and that they are sorted into man-number sequence. We wish to produce a single card for each man containing man number, total hours, and total pay. Pay is computed as in Exercise 7.10, and the control panel is wired as shown below.

		Input	Output
Man Number	xxxxxx	Word 1.	Word 1.
Job Number	xxx	Word 2.	
Hours	xx.x	Word 3.	
Guaranteed Rate	x.xx	Word 4.	
Total Hours	xx.x		Word 2.
Total Pay	xxx.xx		Word 3.

7.12   With the input and output cards and the computation the same as in Exercise 7.11, we wish to accumulate total job cost for each job number by using the locations 0501 to 1000 for this purpose. Thus, the total dollars for job number i would be accumulated in location $i + 500$. Assume that locations 0501 to 1000 have been cleared to zero prior to the start of this program.

7.13   Given an input card containing loan number, loan amount, yearly interest rate, and payment amount, we wish to prepare a schedule of the monthly payments on this loan by punching an output card for each such payment containing payment number, payment amount, remaining balance of loan after the payment, the amount of the payment applied to principal, the amount of the payment applied to interest, and the loan number.

The interest for a payment is computed on the basis of the remaining balance, and this is subtracted from the payment amount to obtain the amount of the payment applied to reduction of the principal. However, on the last payment, the standard payment amount may be too much to make the loan come out even, so this payment should be adjusted to exactly repay the loan. At the conclusion of one loan, read the next card and repeat the process for the next loan.

The form of the numbers and the wiring of the control panel are described below.

		Input	Output
Loan Number	xxxx	Word 1.	Word 6.
Loan Amount	xx,xxx.xx	Word 2.	
Yearly Per Cent Interest	xx.xx	Word 3.	
Payment Amount	x,xxx.xx	Word 4.	Word 2.
Payment Number	xxxx		Word 1.
Remaining Balance	xx,xxx.xx		Word 3.
Amount to Principal	x,xxx.xx		Word 4.
Amount to Interest	x,xxx.xx		Word 5.

SUPPLEMENTAL READINGS

Same as Chapter VI.

CHAPTER 8 · Development of a Computer Processing System

IN THE previous discussion, we have concentrated our attention upon the stored program and how it may be used to control the electronic data-processing machine. It is necessary to understand the stored-program concept to comprehend the capabilities and the limitations of electronic data-processing machines. Moreover, a knowledge of the stored program also enables us to comprehend why electronic computers are so dependent upon people. But there is much more to the use of computers than programming, and we are now in a position to consider the entire process involved in converting a data-processing area from manual or punched card methods to electronic data processing.

Although the machine program, in a sense, represents the culmination of the over-all process, writing the machine instructions is only one of several steps, and it usually requires only around 20 to 30 per cent of the total time involved. It should be emphasized that the entire process must be properly carried out or the proposed electronic data-processing application will not be successful. Like the weakest link in a chain, each step is potentially of great importance, for failure of any of these steps can lead to an unsatisfactory result.

Defining the Problem

The first step in this process is that of defining the data-processing problem itself. It is necessary to determine what information is required from the system in the form of reports; what is required from this portion of the system to integrate it into the over-all data-processing system; where the input information arises; what exceptions can arise and under what circumstances; how many transactions and exceptions of each type are involved; how each transaction and exception should be handled; what files are involved and what information is involved in them; whether results are required on schedule or on demand; and so forth ad infinitum. Even if we are merely converting an area as is, the answers to these questions may be far from obvious, for a data-processing system is so complex that it usually must be defined by observing it in operation to determine what is being done. Only in the most extraordinary circumstances is it possible to find some individual in the organization who can define in sufficient detail an existing data-processing area.

Furthermore, when converting an area to electronic data processing, it is not uncommon to attempt to improve the results obtained from the system. Often, this improvement is one of the major motivations for the use of a computer, so the problem of defining the data-processing area frequently becomes entwined with the fundamental question: What information should be processed and what results should be obtained? Thus, defining the data-processing area may not only involve finding out what is being done at the present, but it may also include answering the difficult question: What should be done? This subject will be discussed in greater detail in Chapter 14, Systems Analysis and Design.

It is obvious then that the data-processing area must be properly defined; that it may be a time-consuming process; and that it is of crucial importance. It is not so obvious, but it is equally true, that the question "What results should we produce?" cannot be adequately answered without first answering the question "What results *can* we produce, and what are the *costs* involved?" In other words, the desirability of data-processing results depends heavily upon the cost of obtaining them. This is a complex situation in which we should attempt to minimize the total of two costs: (1) the cost of data processing; and (2) the cost of poor decisions caused by inadequate data processing.

Thus, to determine the most desirable end products, we must move into the succeeding steps of the process, for costs cannot be reliably estimated until some further steps have been undertaken.

Devise Procedure

The second step in the process is that of devising a procedure for converting the input information into the results that are required. A procedure usually is expressed in the form of a flow chart showing where the information enters the system, any manual steps that are involved, the files that are maintained, the various machine runs required, and the output reports that are produced. A procedure is similar to a block diagram for a program, except that each block represents an entire machine program, and the procedure integrates these programs together with auxiliary machine processing and manual data-processing steps to produce the required results. It may be somewhat surprising to discover that, despite the speed of the computer and the power of the stored program, it is usually necessary to break a data-processing problem down into several machine runs. Not only does the size of the machine memory restrict the size of the program that can be accommodated, but also the fact that files may be maintained in different sequences, and that a variety of different outputs are required may combine to make it necessary to split the processing into a number of different machine runs.

In order to illustrate the over-all process involved in converting to electronic data processing, let us consider a rather simple hypothetical example. Since it would be almost impossible to present an undefined problem on paper without defining it, we will assume that the area is already well defined.

Let us consider a payroll similar to the one illustrating the use of punched card equipment in Chapter 4, except that rather than having a single rate, each man will be paid the larger of his guaranteed rate and the rate for the job on which he worked (as in Exercises 7–10 through 7–12 at the end of Chapter 7).

It may be possible to use different procedures to accomplish the results required from a payroll data-processing system. For example, the punched card procedure described in Chapter 4 could be utilized with a computer taking the place of the punched card calculator. However, this would hardly be desirable, for it would involve substituting a machine costing $4,000 per month for one costing $600 per month without substantially decreasing the processing time involved. Thus, we should consider other alternatives.

In the procedure presented in Figure 8–1, the time cards are prepunched with identifying information, and regular and overtime hours are mark-sensed. The time cards arrive in the data-processing center batched by department, and after they are sorted on man number, they may be matched with the year-to-date cards for that department so that the current hours may be mark-sense punched into the year-to-date cards.

The job cards are prepunched with job information and department number; man number, regular hours, and overtime hours are mark-sensed. They also arrive in the data-processing center batched by department, but they require no sorting since the procedure is designed to accept them in random sequence. The format of the in-

PAYROLL PROCEDURE

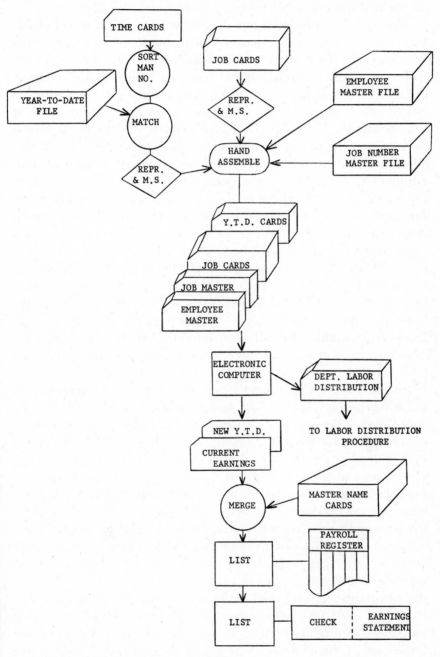

FIG. 8–1.

put and output records, which should be considered at this stage, is shown in Figure 8–2.

The payroll is processed one department at a time, utilizing several different sets of cards that may be manually removed from files and placed by hand in the proper sequence to enter the computer.

The procedure illustrated in Figure 8–1 utilizes the memory capability of the computer to eliminate the sorting steps that are required in the punched card procedure, while, at the same time, it consolidates the labor distribution procedure with the main payroll calculation. The payroll is processed one department at a time, with all of the job cards from that department entering the procedure in random sequence. The basic approach is to establish a table within the memory of the machine with space for the information concerning each man, so that total hours and total pay for each man can be accumulated as the job cards are processed. When all of the job cards for a given department have been processed, the gross pay for each man will have been accumulated in the memory table, and the information is available for the calculation of net earnings. Likewise, by maintaining a table in memory containing an entry for each active job within the department, it is possible to simultaneously accumulate job costs so that when all of the job cards have been processed the labor distribution totals of job cost by department can be punched from memory.

In processing a department's payroll, the employee master cards are fed into the machine first, so that the employee table may be established. Then the job master cards are fed into the machine to establish the job-cost table. As each job card is read into the machine, the employee record is found within the table, and the job and guaranteed rates are compared so that the larger of these may be applied to this job. Hours are accumulated to balance against attendance time, and the product of hours times rate is added to the record for the man and to the record for the proper job. After all of the job cards have been processed for the department, the year-to-date cards are then read. As each year-to-date card is read, the completed record for that man may be found in memory so that the gross-to-net payroll calculation may be made, and the total hours worked, according to the job cards, may be compared with the attendance hours which have been reproduced into the year-to-date cards. If attendance hours and job hours do not balance, an indication may be punched into the new year-to-date card and current earnings card so that the reason for the out-of-balance condition may be determined before the checks are printed for that particular man.

PAYROLL CARD FORMS

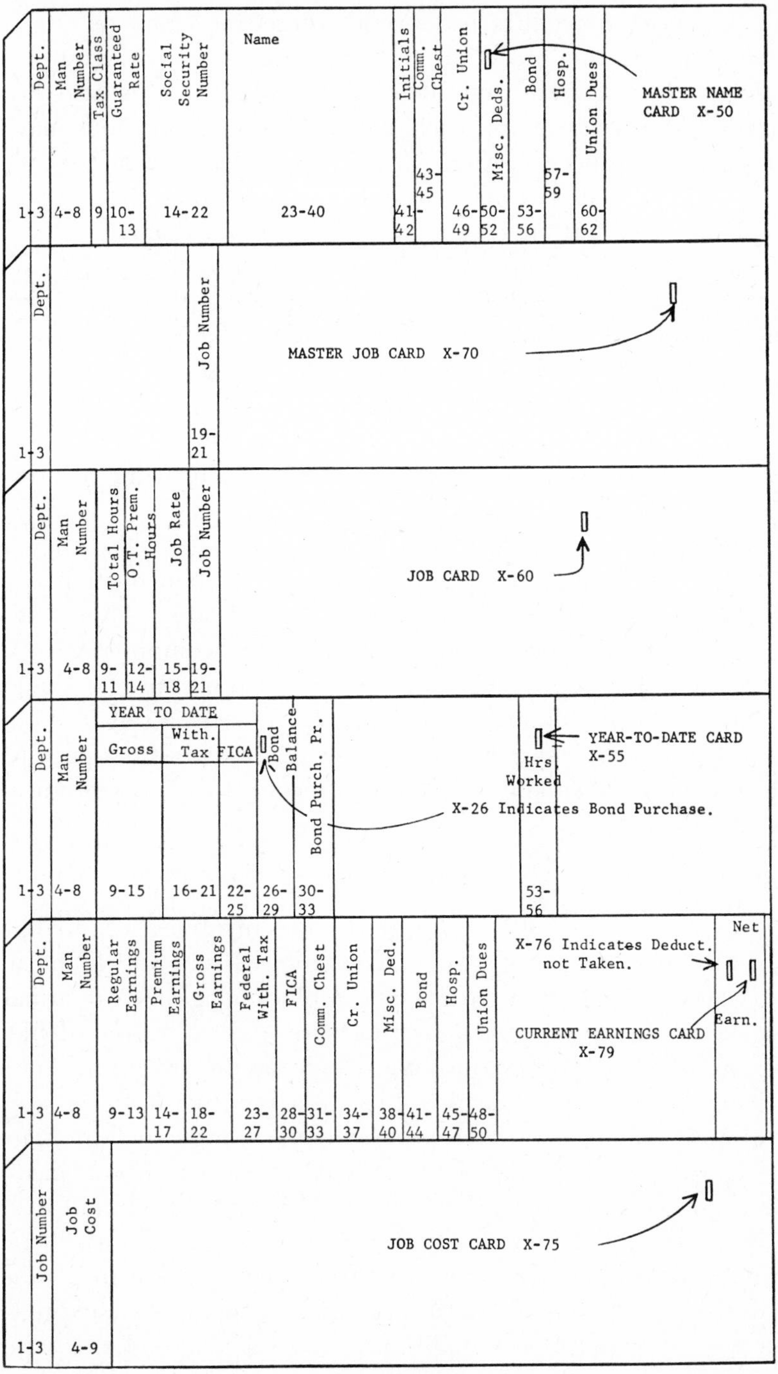

MASTER NAME CARD X-50

Dept. | Man Number | Tax Class | Guaranteed Rate | Social Security Number | Name | Initials | Comm. Chest | Cr. Union | Misc. Deds. | Bond | Hosp. | Union Dues

1-3 | 4-8 | 9 | 10-13 | 14-22 | 23-40 | 41-42 | 43-45 | 46-49 | 50-52 | 53-56 | 57-59 | 60-62

MASTER JOB CARD X-70

Dept. | Job Number

1-3 | 19-21

JOB CARD X-60

Dept. | Man Number | Total Hours | O.T. Prem. Hours | Job Rate | Job Number

1-3 | 4-8 | 9-11 | 12-14 | 15-18 | 19-21

YEAR-TO-DATE CARD X-55

X-26 Indicates Bond Purchase.

		YEAR TO DATE					Hrs Worked
Dept.	Man Number	Gross	With. Tax	FICA	Bond Balance	Bond Purch. Pr.	
1-3	4-8	9-15	16-21	22-25	26-29	30-33	53-56

CURRENT EARNINGS CARD X-79

X-76 Indicates Deduct. not Taken.

Net Earn.

Dept. | Man Number | Regular Earnings | Premium Earnings | Gross Earnings | Federal With. Tax | FICA | Comm. Chest | Cr. Union | Misc. Ded. | Bond | Hosp. | Union Dues

1-3 | 4-8 | 9-13 | 14-17 | 18-22 | 23-27 | 28-30 | 31-33 | 34-37 | 38-40 | 41-44 | 45-47 | 48-50

JOB COST CARD X-75

Job Number | Job Cost

1-3 | 4-9

FIG. 8-2.

Although it is by no means the conventional way to process a payroll, the above procedure has several interesting characteristics. In the first place, the procedure is simple and straightforward, involving very few steps and little card handling. It is also faster than the punched card approach, especially since operations may be overlapped by processing the checks for each department as soon as the cards for that department have been completed by the computer. The labor distribution is also available without delay.

The major point, however, is that there are usually many possible procedures, which may differ from one another rather radically. As another example, we might combine some of the ideas involved in the above procedure with portions of the punched card procedure so that the main payroll processing would follow the punched card procedure, but the departmental labor-cost distribution would be accumulated as a by-product of this processing by utilizing a job-cost table within memory.

Not only are there many possible procedures, but also they are likely to differ widely in efficiency, depending upon the job to be done and the capabilities of the equipment available. Thus, one of the major problems involved in utilizing the computer for data processing is that of devising the most efficient procedure for the job, utilizing the available machine. If a good procedure can be found, the mechanization may prove to be quite effective, but if a poor procedure is used, it is likely that the application will be economically unsound.

Block Diagrams

For each machine run in any procedure involving a stored-program machine, diagrams must be constructed from which the machine program can be written. These block diagrams are usually constructed in several stages, starting with a general over-all block diagram which expresses the major logic of the program. An interesting illustration of a general block diagram that has been going the rounds among computer programmers is presented in Figure 8–3. An over-all block diagram for the computer run in our payroll illustration is presented in Figure 8–4. Although the amount of detail which should be included in this type of block diagram will vary from one individual to another and from one situation to another, the over-all block diagram should be simple enough to be expressed on a piece of paper of reasonable size, and yet it should adequately exhibit the relationships between the various types of input and out-

HOW TO GET TO WORK IN THE MORNING

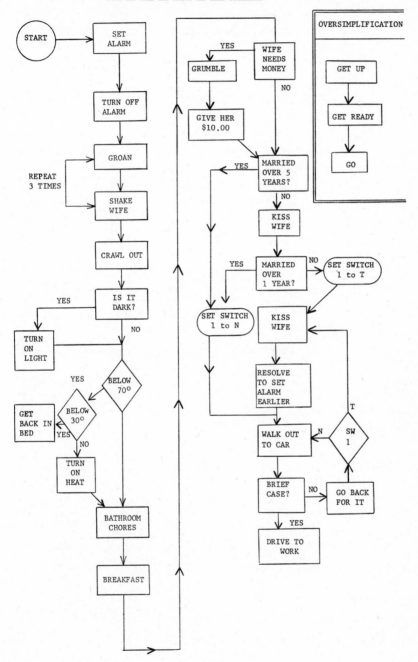

FIG. 8–3.

OVER-ALL BLOCK DIAGRAM (PAYROLL)

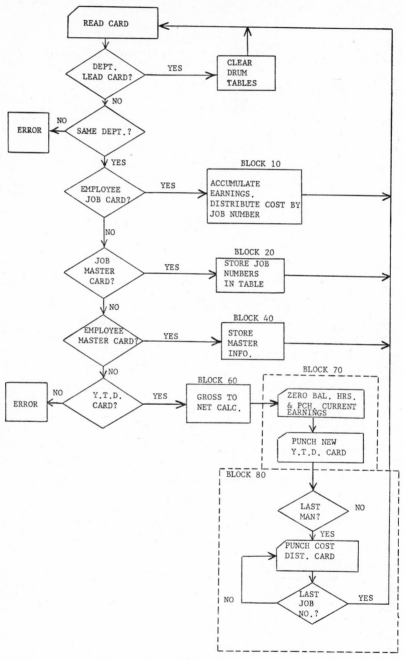

FIG. 8–4.

put and the general processing steps involved in the machine run. Not only is the over-all block diagram valuable in communicating to others the general ideas involved in the machine run, but it also forces the person who constructs it to rigorously formalize the basic logic of the program before becoming involved in the myriads of details which may conceal important logical errors.

Since a block in the over-all block diagram may represent several hundred machine instructions, a further breakdown and a more detailed block diagram may be prepared for each of these blocks. In this illustration, we have used multiples of ten to identify these blocks in the over-all block diagram so that in the next breakdown we may use the units digit to identify the individual blocks. A more detailed breakdown of block 60 of the over-all block diagram is shown in Figure 8–5 in which the blocks are identified by the numbers 61, 62, 63, and so forth.

The resulting diagram may include sufficient detail to enable a program to be written. On the other hand, further breakdowns may be desirable for certain of the blocks in the semidetailed block diagram, as illustrated in Figure 8–5 for block 62. The notational system may be expanded by inserting an additional digit beyond the decimal point, and this may be further extended if additional detail is necessary. Thus, the blocks in Figure 8–6 are numbered 62.1, 62.2, 62.3, and so on.

It should be obvious that the process of *construction* of block diagrams and the *presentation* of the final results in block diagram form are two separate and distinct entities. The process that one goes through to arrive at a completed block diagram is a complex trial and error procedure that is extremely difficult to formalize. Some individuals prefer to follow a logical step-by-step process involving several progressive stages, each in more detail than the previous one. On the other hand, others prefer to go directly from the over-all block diagram to a quite detailed result. However, no matter which approach is attempted there are likely to be many revisions before a completed product is achieved, for even after the diagram is logically complete there remains the problem of revising the geometrical presentation so that the eye can easily follow the flow.

Coding

The over-all process of preparing a machine program is called *programming*. This includes the preparation of the block diagrams

SEMIDETAIL BLOCK DIAGRAM (BLOCK 60)

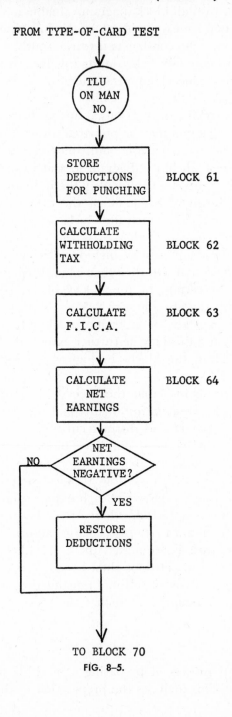

FROM TYPE-OF-CARD TEST

TLU
ON MAN
NO.

STORE
DEDUCTIONS   BLOCK 61
FOR PUNCHING

CALCULATE
WITHHOLDING   BLOCK 62
TAX

CALCULATE   BLOCK 63
F.I.C.A.

CALCULATE   BLOCK 64
NET
EARNINGS

NET
NO ── EARNINGS
NEGATIVE?

YES

RESTORE
DEDUCTIONS

TO BLOCK 70

FIG. 8–5.

DETAIL BLOCK DIAGRAM (BLOCK 62)

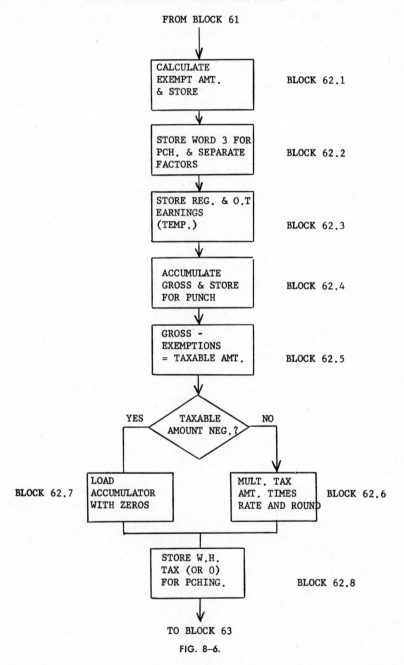

FROM BLOCK 61

CALCULATE EXEMPT AMT. & STORE — BLOCK 62.1

STORE WORD 3 FOR PCH. & SEPARATE FACTORS — BLOCK 62.2

STORE REG. & O.T EARNINGS (TEMP.) — BLOCK 62.3

ACCUMULATE GROSS & STORE FOR PUNCH — BLOCK 62.4

GROSS - EXEMPTIONS = TAXABLE AMT. — BLOCK 62.5

TAXABLE AMOUNT NEG.? YES / NO

BLOCK 62.7 — LOAD ACCUMULATOR WITH ZEROS

MULT. TAX AMT. TIMES RATE AND ROUND — BLOCK 62.6

STORE W.H. TAX (OR 0) FOR PCHING. — BLOCK 62.8

TO BLOCK 63

FIG. 8-6.

to write the program. The process of converting a detailed block diagram into the machine instructions which are stored in memory is called *coding*. To perform this function, it is necessary to specify the precise locations and form in which the input information and the output results will appear in memory, for the memory locations for the various fields of information must be known in order to address them when they are required in the program (see Figure 8–7).

INPUT-OUTPUT STORAGE LAYOUT

Input or Output Storage Word No.	Master Name Card	Job Number Card	Job Card	Old Year-to-Date Card	Current Earnings Card	New Year-to-Date Card	Job Cost Card
1	Dept. Number 0000000XXX	Dept. Number 0000000XXX	Dept. Number 0000000XXX	Dept. Number 0000000XXX	Man No. | Dept. No. XXXXX00XXX	Man No. | Dept. No. XXXXX00XXX	Job No. | Job Cost XXX0XXXXXX
2	Man Number 00000XXXXX		Man Number 00000XXXXX	Man Number 00000XXXXX	Com. Cr. Misc. / Ch. Union XXXXXXXXXX		
3	Guar. Rate 000000XXXX		Regular Hours 0000000XXX	Y.T.D. F.I.C.A. 000000XXXX	Reg. Earn. | Prem. Earn. XXXXX0XXXX	Bond Price 000000XXXX	
4		Job Number XXX0000000	Prem. Hours 0000000XXX	Y.T.D. Gross 000XXXXXXX	Bond Hosp. Union / Ded. | Dues XXXXXXXXXX	Bond Bal. 000000XXXX	
5			Job Rate 000000XXXX	Y.T.D. W.H. Tax 0000XXXXXX	Gross 00000XXXXX	New Y.T.D. Gross 000XXXXXXX	
6	Tax Class 000000000X		Job Number XXX0000000	Bond Bal. 000000XXXX	With. Tax 00000XXXXX	New Y.T.D. W.H. Tax 0000XXXXXX	
7	Com. Cr. Misc. / Ch. Union XXX XXX XXX			Bond Price 000000XXXX	F.I.C.A. 0000000XXX	New Y.T.D. F.I.C.A. 000000XXXX	
8	Bond Hosp. Union XXXX XXX XXX			Hours Worked 0000000XX.X	Net Pay 00000XXXXX		
9							
10	Control Word 0000090998	Control Word 0000080999	Control Word 0000090899	Control Word 0000090989	Control Word X0800X0000	Control Word 00000X0X08	Control Word 0000080000

"8" if Deductions not taken

"8" if Bond to be purchased

"8" if hours do not balance

FIG. 8–7.

Likewise, the memory of the machine must be allocated among the various functions which it must perform, including input and output areas, reference tables, working storage, and the program itself. For our payroll illustration, the memory allocation is shown in Figure 8–8.

Once the detailed block diagram has been written, the input and output format specified, and the memory allocated, it should be a relatively straightforward process to prepare a program for the machine. This is not intended to imply that the coding process requires no creativity or that its proper completion is a trivial matter, but, if the preceding steps have been properly completed, the coding process should require a relatively small percentage of the total time involved. Moreover, the processes of coding and block diagram-

MEMORY ALLOCATION

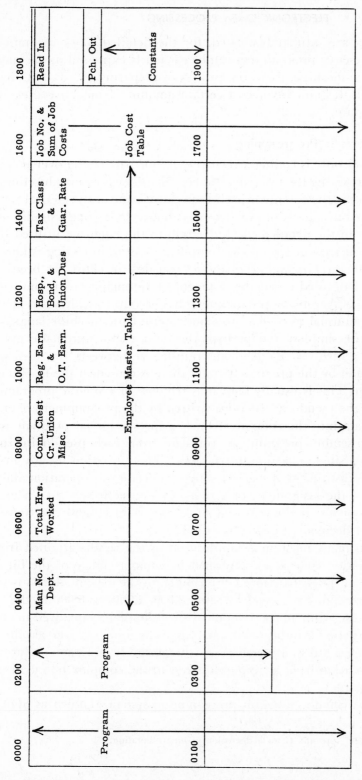

FIG. 8-8.

ming are intimately related, for the detailed block diagram must represent a program that can be efficiently expressed in the language of the machine. Thus the process of preparing an efficient, detailed block diagram involves a certain amount of mental coding of the program.

Automatic Programming

Not only is coding a relatively minor part of the over-all process of preparing the program, but considerable effort may be eliminated by using the computer itself to perform some of the clerical work involved in coding, or even to translate from a language similar to that used in the detailed block diagram to the language utilized by the machine itself. Use of the computer to assist in coding is known as *automatic programming,* and a great deal of effort has been and is being devoted to the development of automatic programming techniques. Automatic programming has become so widely accepted that it is unusual to code a problem in pure basic machine language.

The simplest and perhaps the most useful automatic programming involves a one-to-one translation between the instructions written by the programmer and those executed in the machine program. This is usually known as *regional* or *symbolic* programming, and the pseudo instructions written by the programmer are entered as data into the computer which utilizes a special program (called an assembly program) to translate from each pseudo instruction into a single machine instruction. This translation usually involves the substitution of machine operation codes for operation abbreviations, the assignment of actual machine addresses for "names" of data or instructions, as well as (in binary machines) the translation from decimal to binary notation.[1]

In many machines, modification of the results attained from an operation code is accomplished by complex usage of the bit structure of the instruction. For example, in the 650 an address is tagged for an index register by adding 2,000, 4,000, or 6,000 to the actual address; while in the 705 one of 16 accumulators involved in an *Add* instruction is indicated by analysis of the zone bits over certain digits of the address. In such cases, the assembly program performs the translation from a simple notation to the complex one used in the machine.

A symbolic assembly-programming system (known as SOAP) is

---

[1] See Appendix C for a discussion of binary notation.

widely used for programming the IBM 650. SOAP allows the use of operation symbols (such as RAL for the operation *Reset Add to Lower*) and also permits the use of alphabetic symbols to represent addresses for both data and instructions. Also, addresses which refer to the location of the next instruction in the program may simply be left blank, so that most of the instruction addresses need not be written on the programming form. Not only does the SOAP program substitute actual machine addresses for the symbolic addresses written by the programmer, but the first time the symbol appears in the program, the most optimum address available is substituted. Thus, the machine program written by the use of SOAP is semi-optimized so that the program will operate at a relatively high speed.

However, a SOAP program is not as efficient as could be produced directly by a good programmer, for the assembly program simply considers the first use of a symbol when deciding where on the drum to assign it, while that symbol may be subsequently utilized many times within the program. Furthermore, the sequence in which instructions should be written for execution may depend upon optimization considerations, and the SOAP program does not alter the sequence in which instructions are executed. Thus, SOAP is most useful in situations in which the amount of machine running time does not justify the effort involved in hand optimization or in which the SOAP program will allow the machine to operate at maximum card input and output speeds. But hand optimization should still be used whenever a program is to deal with a sufficiently high volume of work in which the SOAP version would result in less than maximum card reading and punching speeds. Figure 8–9 shows a portion of a program written in SOAP language side by side with the machine language program produced by SOAP.

Aside from the optimization (which is peculiar to the IBM 650 and certain other drum machines), symbolic programming allows the programmer to allocate memory after the program has been written rather than before. This is important, for the programmer can only estimate the amount of memory that will be required for the program itself before it is written, while after the symbolic program has been written he can count the number of steps so he knows precisely how many memory locations are required. Corrections can easily be inserted in a symbolic program. It also allows several different programmers to work simultaneously on different parts of the same program, for they need only use the same symbols for data that

	SOAP				MACHINE LANGUAGE		
Loc. of Instr.	Op. Code	Data Addr.	Inst. Addr.	Loc. of Instr.	Op. Code	Data Addr.	Inst. Addr.
	RAU	1652		0518	60	1652	0408
	SUP	1662		0408	11	1662	1117
	STU	DIFF		1117	21	0472	0525
	BMI	OK	OVERC	0525	46	1230	1330
OVERC	MPY	WORK		1330	19	0025	0346
	SLT	0009		0346	35	0009	1167
	MPY	1903		1167	19	1903	0873
	SRD	0006		0873	31	0006	1139
	ALO	WORK5		1139	15	1215	0569
	STL	WORK5	OK	0569	20	1215	1230
OK	LDD	WORK5		1230	69	1215	0568
	STD	E0047		0568	24	1432	0488
	RAU	E0247		0488	60	1632	0538
	MPY	1652		0538	19	1652	1023
	SRD	0003		1023	31	0003	0533
	STL	E0055		0533	20	1440	0544
	RAL	BASE8		0544	65	1017	0522
	ALO	1964		0522	15	1964	0619

FIG. 8–9.

are utilized in two or more portions of the program, and the assembly program will integrate the individual pieces into an over-all program when it assigns actual machine locations.

Library Subroutines

The early users of computers quickly noticed that certain sequences of program steps recurred so often that it appeared wasteful to write them over and over again. Thus, one of the early automatic programming techniques involves writing portions of programs that occur repeatedly in a form in which they may be incorporated into any program in which that sequence of steps may be required. These "building blocks," known as subroutines, have been of great value in the area of scientific computing, for the same mathematical operations frequently reappear within the same program or in different programs. For example, subroutines for computing the square root of a number, the logarithm of a number, the sine of an angle, the cosine of an angle, or for floating decimal point operations have found widespread use in computing installations.[2]

Some interesting considerations are involved in linking these pieces of programs into a specific program, for it may be inconvenient to place a subroutine in the same memory locations in each

---

[2] Floating decimal notation is explained in Appendix D.

program in which it may be used. This problem is usually handled by writing subroutines in symbolic form so that they may be integrated into the program when it is assembled.

Subroutines which are used over and over within the same program are usually stored in memory but once and utilized repeatedly by the master program. To use a subroutine several times within a program and return to the proper place in the master program each time, it is necessary to provide the subroutine with the location to which the machine should go for the next instruction after the subroutine has been executed. Instruction modification is then used within the subroutine to insure that upon its completion the proper step of the master program will be executed. Also, subroutines usually operate upon data from the memory of the machine, so the subroutine must be provided with the memory locations in which these data are stored. The location to which the program control should be returned upon completion of the subroutine, along with the location of any data that are to be manipulated by the subroutine, is usually provided through a standardized *calling sequence* which specifies how the programmer enters the routine.

Interpretive Routines

The next major step in automatic programming involved writing of pseudo instructions that could be analyzed by a supervisory program to call in the proper subroutine and provide it with the required information. Thus, since a single pseudo instruction written by the programmer results in the execution of many machine instructions, programming effort is considerably reduced. In an interpretive system, the pseudo instructions are analyzed each time they are executed, the proper subroutine is executed, then the next pseudo instruction is analyzed, and the process is repeated. Thus, not only must the subroutines be in memory at all times, but also the program that performs the analysis must be located in the memory of the machine, and the steps necessary to analyze the pseudo code must be performed each time the program is executed. The Bell Laboratories System for the IBM 650 is an example of an interpretive program in which the pseudo instructions cause the 650 to simulate a three-address machine with automatic floating decimal point operations and with operations that take square roots, evaluate trigonometric and logarithmic functions, and provide a form of index registers. Such interpretive systems have been widely used in engineering computing because people with little experience in programming computers can easily be taught to program their own problems. The major drawback of these systems is the inefficient utilization of machine time which results from the time lost in interpretation each time a pseudo instruction is executed.

Compilers

A compiler is similar to an interpretive system in that it produces many machine instructions from a single pseudo instruction. However, in a compiler, the translation from the pseudo language to the machine instructions is performed in a special machine run before the actual use of the program is attempted. Thus, the compilation of a program of this type is similar to the assembly of a symbolic program, and, in fact, the two are frequently combined into programming systems that involve both assembly and compiling. The output of this machine run is, then, a machine language program which may be utilized just as any other machine language program.

Compilers have many advantages over interpretive systems. In the first place, the compiler itself does not have to be in the machine memory while the program is being executed, so the program being run can utilize the entire machine memory. Furthermore, the instructions are only translated once in a compiling system as opposed to being translated each time they are executed in an interpretive system.

However, the most important advantage of compilers as opposed to interpreters is that, since the entire capability of the machine can be concentrated upon the process of translation from the pseudo code to the machine language, and since this translation is done but once, the pseudo code in which the programmer writes need not be as closely tied to the structure of the machine as is necessary in the interpretive systems. In other words, the translation process can be much more complex, so that the language utilized by the programmer can be a closer approximation of the language in which he normally expresses himself. For example, the IBM FORTRAN system for the 704 and 709 allows the program to be written in the form of mathematical equations which are translated by the compiler into a machine program which performs the operations indicated by the equations. Likewise, data-processing compilers such as the Remington Rand Flo-matic system and the IBM Commercial Translator allow data-processing programs to be written in a language that is similar to that used in a detailed block diagram involving English words and flow-charting symbols.

Thus, it is claimed that the programmer need know nothing about the actual machine language itself, for the coding step as a manual operation is entirely eliminated when the sophisticated compiling systems are utilized. As a matter of fact, one of the major advantages of these systems may be that they are relatively independent of the particular machine that is to be used to run the program. There are several examples of such compiler languages for which translators exist that will produce machine language programs for several different machines. For example, Fortran statements can be translated into programs for the 704, 709, 7090, 7070, and even (with some minor modifications) for the 650. And COBOL (COmmon Business Oriented Language) has been designed with the objective of translating from this language into programs for many different computers manufactured by different companies. Thus, it is possible that the use of this technique can overcome the tremendous reprogramming costs associated with replacing an obsolete machine with a new one, for the compiler language programs could merely be recompiled into a program for the new machine.

Efficiency of Automatic Programming

Although these compiling systems are of great value when properly used, at their best, they can only eliminate the coding process, which involves but a relatively modest percentage of the over-all time and cost of preparing a program. Moreover, certain questions arise concerning the efficiency of the machine program produced by a compiler. Is the resulting program as efficient in terms of machine running time as a program coded by the average human programmer? The answer to this question has not yet been completely determined, but it appears reasonable that compiled programs may be as efficient as those produced by the average programmer, although it is doubtful that they will ever achieve the efficiency of outstanding programmers.

The previous paragraph is only concerned with the translation from the detailed block diagram to the machine program. The really important question is: Will the over-all process of preparing the program utilizing a compiler produce as efficient a program as would be produced by the over-all process utilizing manual coding? As we have seen, the machine program and the detailed block diagram are intimately related, and a good detailed block diagram cannot be produced without taking into consideration the complexities of the coding involved. Thus, when compilers eliminate the necessity for considering machine coding, they are likely also to eliminate the consideration of the machine language program itself when the detailed block diagram is prepared. Likewise, since the compiler allocates memory, there is less necessity for the programmer to consider the machine characteristics when designing the over-all procedure, which may also result in substantially less efficient machine programs. When changing from one machine to another, major procedural changes frequently are required to take full advantage of the characteristics of the new machine.

Since the use of compilers could result in less efficient programs, it may be necessary to balance the cost savings obtained by eliminating the manual-coding step against the losses resulting from more machine running time required because of less efficient programs. In view of the above, it does not appear likely at present that sophisticated compilers will completely eliminate coding of high-volume data-processing applications in symbolic systems based upon machine language. However, these sophisticated systems will be extensively used, for they provide a welcome reduction in the time and effort necessary to get work running on computers, and they are extremely convenient when modifying a program or converting to a new machine.

Incidentally, research into the construction of sophisticated compiling systems has focused attention upon the language problems involved in expressing data-processing procedures. Unfortunately, it seems that we have no better language than English in which to express these problems and, as compared with the language of mathematics for expressing scientific problems, ordinary English is quite unsatisfactory. Although English is supposedly an easy language for the programmer to learn, it suffers from a lack of precision and from the fact that the same thing may be said in so many different ways. Perhaps a more symbolic language, peculiarly adapted to expressing data-processing procedures, will result from the research being conducted in this area.

Debugging

After the program has been written, errors must be eliminated before the machine procedure can be used on a routine basis. Checking out, or "debugging," is the process of ascertaining that the program accomplishes the results for which it was intended. It is important to realize that the process of debugging must begin when the program is originally planned and must be continued as the program is written, for a program that is well planned and carefully written will contain few errors of commission or omission as compared with one that is poorly planned and sloppily written.

Two major types of errors cause difficulty in a program. The first type is the "logical" error, where the original planning of the program does not adequately represent the data-processing situation involved. A simple example of this type of error occurs in planning a payroll application, when the planner may ignore the fact that the total of a man's deductions and taxes may well exceed his gross pay in certain circumstances, thus producing a negative net pay amount. The second type of error is the clerical error, such as the assignment of two different instructions or pieces of data to the same memory location, the use of a wrong operation code by mistake, or the omission of one or more instructions. While the detection and elimination of clerical errors is by no means a trivial problem, techniques have been developed that enable us to cope fairly well with this type of error. However, the logical errors present an entirely different problem, for they usually represent a fundamental lack of understanding of the data-processing situation, and they are usually detected only after a more comprehensive understanding of the situation itself has been attained. Thus, the debugging process may occasionally turn out to be a continuous affair, with no absolute certainty that it has ever been completed.

As the size and complexity of the program increases, the problem of debugging increases geometrically; it may be very simple to check out a program involving only 30 instructions (quite possibly no mistakes and, consequently, no debugging may be involved), while a program involving several thousand instructions may require several days or even weeks of work. Thus, it becomes apparent that the cost of debugging becomes more important as we go to larger and larger equipment, for we are likely to be attempting larger and more complicated programs, while at the same time the hourly cost of the equipment is higher. Where a machine costs several hundred dollars an hour, it is obviously important that the process of debugging be approached efficiently so that a maximum amount of it can be done in a given amount of machine time. Thus, it is important that efficient techniques for debugging be developed and that these techniques be used. The following discussion outlines some of the techniques that have been developed for debugging.

In the first place, the program should be well documented, and the block diagram should be complete and legible. The program must be legible, and it should be keyed into the block diagram so that the program steps can be associated with the block to which they contribute. Also, the program should be accompanied by brief remarks explaining what the instructions are intended to accomplish.

After the program has been key-punched into cards, verified, and listed on the accounting machine, the cards should be sorted by instruction location, operation code, and data address, and lists of the program should be made in each of these orders. These lists are useful in eliminating clerical errors before they ever reach the machine. For example, the list in instruction location sequence can be scanned easily to pick out any errors in which two instructions have been inadvertently assigned to the same location. If the operation abbreviation has been punched into the card, the list in operation code sequence will highlight any instructions which have been designated by an incorrect operation code. Furthermore, these lists are practically indispensable for reference purposes when errors are detected during the check-out procedure itself. For example, if it is ascertained that an instruction is being incorrectly modified, the list in data-address sequence can be used to quickly ascertain all instructions that refer to the instruction being modified.

To know whether or not the program is producing the results desired, it is necessary to test it with input data. Usually these input data are of a hypothetical nature, designed to test the various branches of the program with as little machine time as possible. The correct answers for these input data must also be available at the time of testing. In addition, it is quite helpful if at least one case can be carried completely through on the programming chart itself, showing the intermediate results in the machine registers. Not only must suitable input data and precalculated results be available, but the input data must be in the input form so that they can actually be read into the machine and processed by the program.

Although most machines are designed so that a person can sit at the console and examine any registers within the machine and execute a test program one step at a time, this is an extremely slow process and should be avoided. Therefore, many techniques have been developed to use the machine itself as an aid in diagnosing programming errors. One of the most valuable of such techniques is called a *tracing routine*. This takes over control of the machine, and as each instruction of the program being debugged is executed, the instruction and the contents of the various registers, after the instruction is executed, are punched or printed from the machine.

Thus, a list may be produced which shows the instructions executed and the status of the machine at the completion of each of these instructions.[3] This list may then be compared with the program listing itself (which represents what the programmer expected), and errors may be isolated and analyzed away from the machine. Even tracing, however, can be abused because of time considerations. For example, the 650 executes around 200 to 500 instructions per minute. Thus, to trace even one second of machine running time requires from two to five minutes. To trace a program that would require five minutes to run would involve between 10 and 25 machine-hours, in addition to a minimum of 60,000 cards.

The process of checking out a long and complicated program usually involves several brief periods of testing on the machine itself, interspersed with long periods of thought (away from the machine) during which the mistakes are diagnosed by a logical process similar to that employed to discover the murderer in an old-fashioned detective story. Most well-run installations have rules and procedures governing the debugging process which are designed to discourage programmers from sitting at the console and tying up the expensive computer while searching for errors.

Not only is debugging a complex and expensive task, but it is practically impossible to prove with certainty that a complex data-processing program is free from error. In the first place, debugging procedures are relatively ineffective in eliminating logical errors, for it is not likely that synthetic test data, devised to determine whether the program operates as the programmer thinks it should, will include situations adequate to bring to light the subtle misunderstandings that are embodied in logical errors. For example, it is not likely that the programmer will include in the test data an exception, the existence of which he is unaware.

Indeed, a complex program has so many branches that it is almost impossible to design test data that will insure that each instruction in the program will be executed in the process of debugging to detect clerical errors. Even when adequate test data have actually been used, it would require substantial additional effort to actually *prove* that such is the case. Thus, we may conclude that debugging should eliminate most of the errors in a program and reduce the likelihood that there are others, but it does not entirely eliminate the possibility that errors will exist in a program.

---

[3] A trace routine for the 650 is described in Appendix B.

It should be noted that the use of automatic programming techniques both increases and decreases the problems of debugging. In one sense, debugging is more difficult, for the machine language program is almost meaningless to the programmer. On the other hand, fewer clerical errors are involved, since the machine is performing most of the clerical tasks. Special provisions are frequently provided within the automatic programming system itself to aid in the debugging process.

Conversion

After the program is thought to be free of error, the final step in the process is that of converting the application to the use of the electronic computer. This process is far from trivial, for it frequently involves significant changes in the way information (both input and output) is handled by people outside the data-processing portion of the organization. The mechanized system must always be integrated into an organization composed of people, and not only is it difficult to foresee all of the consequences involved in the changes that are necessary, but it is also imperative that we understand that the success of the use of the computer may depend upon the human factors outside of the mechanized procedures.

To gain confidence in the machine program and procedures involved, as well as to allow the people of the organization to gradually adjust to the changes, it is customary to convert an application to computer processing before abandoning the previous processing method. Thus, there is a period of *parallel operation* during which "bugs" in the mechanized procedures and difficulties of adapting people to the new procedures can be eliminated. Parallel operation usually requires a minimum of two or three processing cycles, and in situations in which major difficulties arise the period of parallel operation may extend over a period of several weeks or months.

As an illustration of the problems that can arise in parallel operation and debugging, consider the following selections abstracted from a diary prepared by Fred Gruenberger of the General Electric Company at Hanford, Washington.[4] The application involved was a file maintenance problem in which a magnetic tape file of some 11,000 300-character master records was updated daily by some 2,000 to 4,000 transactions. This application was converted from a manual

---

[4] Reproduced by permission from *Computing News*, Vol. 5, No. 8, April 5, 1957.

processing system and went into parallel operation on December 10, 1956.

The conversion job shown here was fairly clean and straight-forward. The problem was well-defined, and the customers were co-operative and able to learn rapidly. Even so it took six weeks of daily processing to uncover all the troubles and subtle bugs (assuming they are all out now).

Near the end of December, a log book was begun which recorded events of each day's run. The following are excerpts from this log. Man-number 88888 is a fictitious one included for debugging purposes.

December 29: . . . An overflow condition stopped the machine on man-number 88888. . . . Corrected at console by subtracting a large amount from bucket in question and noting action. Two output tapes disappeared without being printed.

January 6: Job went on at 3:00 A.M. and promptly collapsed. Main parameter card had invalid identification. Error discovered when F. wandered in at 1:00 P.M.

Rerun started at 8:00 P.M. Collapsed again due to some data cards with batch numbers not represented in batch parameter cards. The chief customer was notified and started for his office to get missing data.

Rerun again at 11:00 P.M. with complete data. New trouble: 83 tape read errors. Here F. pulled a boner. Changed typewriter address to address of an on-line printer without noting transfer-back address . . .

January 7: On machine at 9:00 P.M. All went well till the first of five input cards with an invalid month code. . . . F. batched a console patching. Reloaded and restarted. 20 minutes shot. . . . One report out of balance today.

It seems last three correction cards for 88888 were not processed. No non-metaphysical explanation leaps to mind.

January 9: On at 8:30 P.M. for a special pass—edit the master tape. Pass collapsed immediately due to our cleverness in writing instructions at same place in memory as the tape input area. Correction made and pass proceeded. However, for some 12,000 master records it produced about 20,000 error messages. This program was debugged?

January 17: . . . Regular daily business was processed today by operators, with no intervention on the part of the analysts.

January 21: Utter chaos today. January 21 report shows figures which are impossible. Something is seriously wrong in the master records.

January 22: Glorious recovery. GG found two errors in the program transferring payroll information to our tape. . . . The organization code was at the far end of the master record, not where it belonged. This accounts for a great deal of the trouble of recent dates.

January 28: Another demonstration given today: Smooth as silk. The regular daily run was moved up 2:00 P.M. for this purpose. Fifth consecutive daily processing handled by operators only. We are tempted to conclude that the job is now successful.

The duplication of activities involved in parallel processing may cause serious personnel difficulties, for someone must process the information in the old way, someone must process it in the new way, and it is frequently necessary for others to assume the task of reconciling the differences found in the results. Thus, when the total work force is about to be reduced because of the mechanization, it must be increased during the conversion process. This duplication of effort may occur outside of the data-processing organization, for those associated with preparing the input information may be forced to follow two different procedures, one of which is new and the other of which is soon to be discarded. These problems will be discussed further in Chapter 15.

Relationships between the Steps

As has been described above, the over-all process of converting a data-processing area from a previous method to the use of an electronic computer involves the following steps: defining the problem, devising the procedure, preparing over-all and detailed block diagrams, coding, debugging, and finally converting. Unfortunately, however, the process is far from straightforward, for the steps cannot be performed independently of one another. For example, to devise an adequate procedure, it is necessary to determine how much work can be accomplished on a given machine run. This involves a rough block diagram of the run and perhaps estimates of the amount of memory required for the tables, program steps, and input and output storage.

Frequently, it is necessary to return from a step near the end of the process to an early step and redo previous work. For example, when preparing a detailed block diagram it may become obvious that the program would operate more efficiently if the over-all block diagram were modified. At the coding stage, we may find that the procedure which breaks the processing down into machine runs is not adequate, for the program may require more memory capacity than the machine has available, making it necessary to return to the problem of devising an adequate procedure. Logical errors, discovered during the debugging or conversion process, can force a return clear back to the problem definition step, and consequent reworking of all intervening steps in the process.

It may be observed that the objective of this whole process is to attain an adequate understanding of the data-processing problem and to express this understanding in the form of workable procedures and machine programs. Since the problems of data processing are quite complex, it is not likely that a complete understanding of the data-processing problem will be obtained at the first attempt. It is usually necessary to begin with a less than adequate understanding, and to improve upon this knowledge as we continue through the process, making corrections and repeating steps whenever necessary.

Organization and Personnel

The close interrelationships between the steps in the process of placing an application on the computer has implications as to how the over-all process should be carried out. For example, it has been suggested that the problem definition and procedures preparation should be performed by one group of people, the over-all and detailed block diagramming by another group, and the coding by a third group. However, in view of the interrelationships between these steps, someone should be assigned responsibility for the entire process, so a team approach is usually taken in which procedures analysts, programmers, and coders work together on a given application from the beginning to the end of the process. Thus, at each step in the process the viewpoints of the procedures analyst, the programmer, and the coder can be taken into consideration.

It is also apparent that in a complex process such as this, in which each step is dependent upon the previous step, a thorough and painstaking job must be done from start to finish. There is no place for sloppy work or inattention to detail. The persons who are involved must be thorough, painstaking, and well organized, and some speed may be sacrificed in the interest of accuracy and precision. A rather broad background is required of the person who aspires to work as a procedures analyst, for he must thoroughly understand the possibilities of the machine so that he can devise procedures for which efficient programs can be prepared.

The organization and staffing of a data-processing center are discussed in more detail in Chapter 16.

The entire process must be well documented, for data processing is a dynamic activity, and even the best of systems will eventually be modified. Human memory has a low reliability, and, even if it were accurate, those involved in the original development may no longer be available. Also, it is an extremely complex task to modify a well-documented machine program, and it is almost impossible to modify a poorly documented program. In fact, in this situation it may be easier to go back and redo the entire job rather than attempt to utilize that which has already been done. Not only does the process of detailed documentation provide reference material for future use, but it also forces those preparing the system to perform their task with thoroughness and precision.

Cost Estimation

Furthermore, an understanding of the interrelationships between these steps provides an explanation for the difficulties that have been encountered in estimating the savings or costs associated with acquiring a computer or placing an application on a machine that is already available. Machine running-time estimates must be made on the basis of original definitions of the problem area, and the first approximation to a procedure, block diagram, and machine program. Frequently, these estimates are excellent, but it is not uncommon for them to be quite misleading, for as a more adequate understanding of the problem area is developed, the machine time involved may expand by several hundred per cent. This is not to imply that accurate estimates can never be made, or that it is undesirable to attempt to make estimates. It is simply a recognition that at an early stage in the process it is possible for estimates of machine time to be significantly in error, usually on the low side.

The cost of the systems analysis and programming itself is also extremely important and difficult to estimate. Several man-years of work may be involved, and it is difficult to control these costs because exerting pressure to assure that the individual steps are completed expeditiously may only postpone the recognition and correction of basic difficulties until the latter stages of the process, at which time more work must be repeated. Such work is difficult to administer, for it is not easy to determine how much time pressure should be exerted or even to estimate the amount of time and effort that should be required to complete the over-all process.

Control of Accuracy

A major problem in the design of mechanized data-processing systems is that of control of accuracy. As compared with humans, machines are exceptionally accurate. However, this does not imply that machine errors do not occur, for errors are made by the best machines. Moreover, any errors that exist in the input information will cause erroneous results.

People appear to have a built-in armor of skepticism with which they view the results of manual processing, so manual data processing is repeatedly scrutinized at each step in the process, and the results are accepted with caution. On the other hand, the results produced by a machine tend to be accepted with blind faith, and since the intermediate results are not subject to careful scrutiny by humans, special care must be given to the design of procedures by which errors may be detected and corrected.

Three aspects of control of accuracy must be considered in the design of procedures. In the first place, checks must be included which reduce the probability of an undetected error producing erroneous results. Second, once an error has been detected, the cost of its correction is influenced by the design of the system. The previous two points are concerned with accidental errors. There is also the possibility of purposeful errors introduced to perpetrate fraud, so the system should be designed so as to discourage fraud by increasing the probability that it will be detected.

The objective in control of accuracy is not necessarily to eliminate all errors. Rather, we should attempt to minimize the total costs associated with the detection and correction of errors plus the costs caused by the uncorrected errors that are produced.

Considerations associated with the control of accuracy are involved in each step of the over-all process of converting to mechanized data processing. At the problem definition stage, for example, the accuracy required of the system must be determined. Procedures must include provision for insuring the accuracy of input information and for the establishment of controls by means of which the accuracy of processing can be checked. Block diagrams and programs must not only produce the desired results but must also include provisions for the detection of errors. The design of procedures and programs may also be influenced by the desirability of developing restart procedures by means of which correct processing can be resumed after errors are detected. Debugging is an important consideration in the control of accuracy, for the objective of debugging is to eliminate errors in the program itself, and erroneous programs produce inaccurate results.

Auditors are also concerned with determining the accuracy of data-processing results. It is important that the procedures be designed so as to include provisions for an adequate audit trail. Furthermore, the auditor has a viewpoint and training that makes him valuable in establishing accuracy controls and in designing adequate test data for use in debugging.

The auditors should take an active part in the over-all process of design and installation of a mechanized data-processing system. If efficient procedures are to be developed, the auditor must understand the capabilities and limitations of computers so that he can adapt his requirements to the new equipment without undue injury to the efficiency of the system.

Summary

To convert an area from manual processing to electronic data processing, it is necessary to obtain an understanding of the data-processing problem and to express this understanding in the form of procedures and machine programs. There are several steps involved in this process, including defining the problem, devising procedures and block diagrams, writing and debugging the programs, and finally parallel operation and conversion. Each of these steps presents its own peculiar problems, but the major difficulty is associated with the fact that the over-all process is not straightforward, but loops back upon itself as misunderstandings come to light.

In the first step of this process, problem definition, it is necessary to decide upon the results to be obtained. But it is illogical to specify the results to be produced by a data-processing system without regard to the cost of obtaining them, and costs are related to the procedures used, the equipment available, the form in which the results are presented, and the type and amount of information obtained. Thus, it is important that management, who in the final analysis must specify the results required, be aware of the necessity for adapting results to the requirements of technology and co-operate with and encourage efforts to design effective systems, taking into account both the cost and the value of information. It is equally important that management realistically plan for the time and costs involved in the preparation necessary to produce programs and convert to electronic data processing.

EXERCISES

8.1 a) Describe each of the steps involved in converting a data-processing area from manual processing to electronic data processing.
  b) How are these steps interrelated?

c) Why is it important that this process and the interrelationships between the steps be understood?

8.2 *a*) What is automatic programming?

b) Describe the various types of automatic programming systems and distinguish between them.

c) What are the advantages of automatic programming?

d) What are the limitations of automatic programming?

8.3 *a*) What is a trace routine?

b) Define and distinguish between logical and clerical errors that may exist in a program.

c) Why is it difficult to devise test data adequate to debug a program?

d) How can you prove that a complex program is free of errors?

8.4 Why does the most efficient procedure for a particular application depend upon the characteristics of the machine to be used? What influence does this have on the possibility of using a compiler language to make it easy to change from one machine to another?

SUPPLEMENTAL READINGS

The Auditor Encounters Electronic Data Processing. Prepared by Price Waterhouse & Co., and published as Form Number 32–7489 by International Business Machines Corp., New York.

An excellent presentation of the effect of the use of electronic data-processing equipment upon the auditor and of techniques that can be used in the control of accuracy.

CHAPIN, NED. *An Introduction to Automatic Computers.* Princeton, N.J.: D. Van Nostrand Co., Inc., 1957.

Pages 106 to 128 discuss approaches to the process of defining the data-processing problem.

FACT—A New Business Language. Wellesley Hill 81, Massachusetts: Minneapolis-Honeywell, Datamatic Division, 1960.

A manual describing a data processing compiler language.

HOPPER, GRACE M. "Automatic Programming for Business Applications," *Computers and Automation,* Vol. 7, No. 2 (February, 1958), pp. 14–16.

A discussion of automatic programming for data-processing applications.

McCRACKEN, D. D.; WEISS, H., and LEE, T. *Programming Business Computers.* New York: John Wiley & Sons, Inc., 1959.

Chapter 3 discusses flow charting and various types of block diagrams and their use.

SHONTING, D. M., and STONE, L. D. "Audit Techniques for Electronic Systems," *Journal of Accountancy,* Vol. 106 (October, 1958), pp. 54–61.

This article discusses the problems of control of accuracy from the viewpoint of the auditor, and presents some of the techniques that the auditor can use with computer systems.

WRUBEL, M. H. *A Primer of Programming for Digital Computers,* New York: McGraw-Hill Book Co., Inc., 1959.

Discusses several automatic programming techniques commonly used with the 650 for scientific and engineering calculation, including subroutines, SOAP, the Bell Laboratories Interpretive System, and the Fortransit compiler. It also discusses debugging.

CHAPTER 9 · Applications of Magnetic Drum Machines

INTERMEDIATE electronic data-processing machines, such as the basic 650, may be integrated into a punched card data-processing system, providing it with the capabilities of the stored program and the processing advantages of a memory of several thousand digits. Such machines have achieved a remarkable popularity—it is estimated that in 1960 more than 1,500 of them were in use in the United States.

As one would expect, a general-purpose computer is usually used in many different data-processing procedures. Because almost every organization has a payroll, this is probably the most frequent application area for intermediate computers. Payroll is certainly not the most important application for most such machines, but when a computer is obtained for several uses, payroll is likely to be included among them.

Other areas in which intermediate computers are frequently used include inventory accounting, cost accounting, sales analysis, material control, and engineering calculations. In reference to the latter, it is not uncommon for firms that obtain a computer primarily for data processing to allocate a portion of its time to the engineering department, and this frequently results in a significant improvement in the effectiveness of the engineering effort.

The above discussion has been concerned with the use of intermediate computers in general manufacturing organizations. However, a surprising percentage of the intermediate computers have been used in special industries, such as fire and casualty insurance, public utilities, wholesale, life insurance, federal and state governments, railroads, and petroleum. For example, of the first 400 IBM 650 computers ordered, about 60 per cent were in special industries. In such industries, the use of an intermediate computer may be justified on the basis of one or two special jobs that have suf-

199

ficient volume or importance to support the cost of the computer. It should be emphasized that a tremendous amount of ingenuity goes into most data-processing applications. Frequently, applications that are called by the same name are completely dissimilar when examined closely. Each use of a data-processing machine must be expressly tailored to the situation in which the machine is being used—so far, it has not been found possible to merely transplant applications from one industry to another (or even from one company to another within the same industry) without extensive revision.

Therefore, the illustrations included in this chapter have not been chosen primarily to illustrate how an electronic computer should be used in typical situations. The primary purpose of each of these illustrations is to present interesting ways in which the capabilities of the computer can be applied to data processing. In particular, several of these examples provide illustrations of how an ingenious use of memory can simplify data-processing procedures.

Parts Requirement Planning

Manufacturing organizations frequently produce a variety of end products. However, although the same factory may be producing hundreds of different items, for purposes of efficiency, it is common for these items to be constructed from a relatively small number of standard parts or components. For example, in the automotive and home appliance industries, it is customary to produce a basic stripped model, a standard model, and a de luxe model of each product that are identical in 90 per cent of their parts. And even in industries that produce to customers' specifications, most products are primarily composed of standard assemblies and parts.

The above discussion is not intended to prove that a small number of parts is involved in production of our modern complex mechanisms, but it does indicate that the number of parts involved is much less than if each end item were entirely different from every other end item. This interchangeability of parts which allows production efficiencies also provides some difficulty in planning for production. To break a production schedule down into the quantities of the individual parts that are required, it is necessary to consider (for each individual part) all of the end items in which it appears, and add together these separate requirements to obtain a total requirement for the part.

This process of "exploding" the production schedule to the individual parts involved is necessary to procure those parts that are purchased and to plan production for those parts that are produced within the organization. Unfortunately, however, a production schedule is usually dynamic rather than static—it is subject to frequent changes as the result of variations in the demands of the market, labor conditions, raw material prices, inventory policies, and moods of management.

When a schedule changes, it is necessary to reflect the effect of the changes upon the required parts, and if several thousand parts and several hundred items are involved, it is apparent that large amounts of data processing are also involved. Furthermore, *time* is an extremely important consideration, for the ability to meet the new schedule depends upon acquiring the required parts in the proper amounts at the right time. Any delay in exploding the schedule to parts is too much to suit those who are charged with the responsibility for obtaining, canceling, or scheduling the parts involved and for controlling the inventories of these parts.

Parts requirement explosion has therefore been one of the popular applications of standard punch card equipment, and the following approach has frequently been used. Two basic types of information are necessary to explode a schedule to basic parts: the schedule itself and a bill of materials for each end item.

For planning purposes, most schedules involve several periods of time (days, weeks, or months). In this case, the first period is a firm schedule, the next period is less definite, and succeeding periods are usually forecasts for planning purposes only. Such a schedule is presented in Figure 9–1.

| Model | Periods | | | | | |
Number	1	2	3	4	5	6
12A	50	50	75	70	60	40
12B	25	30	30	30	30	35
127C	0	0	20	30	40	50
203X	100	100	100	100	100	100
204	30	20	10	0	0	0
607	0	0	25	0	0	25

FIG. 9–1.

The schedule is punched into cards, with one card for each line on the schedule, as shown in Figure 9–2.

For each end item, hereafter referred to as a model, a bill of materials is required. A bill of materials is a list of the parts and materials required to build the model, along with the required quantity of each part or material (see Figure 9–3).

Model Number	1	2	3	4	5	6	
0012B	00025	00030	00030	00030	00030	00035	

FIG. 9–2.

A card is also required for each line on each bill of materials. In fact, the bill of materials is frequently maintained in punched card form and printed (when required) by means of a punched card ac-

BILL OF MATERIALS	
	Model 12B
Part #	Usage Quantity
123	4
2322	1
2323	1
4460	5
4723	1
4725	8

FIG. 9–3.

counting machine. Thus, we have a permanent file of cards, such as the one shown in Figure 9–4.

Model Number	Part Number	Usage	
0012B	00123	004	

FIG. 9–4.

The usual punched card procedure (see Figure 9–5) involves key-punching the schedule cards, sorting them to model-number sequence, and hand-pulling or selecting by use of a collator the bill of materials decks for each of the models appearing in the schedule. These bill of materials decks are reproduced to obtain working decks, and the proper schedule card is filed ahead of each active bill of materials deck. A punched card calculator can then be used to pick up the scheduled quantities for each period for a given model, multiply these quantities by the usage of each part, and punch in the part card itself the resulting requirement of that part for each period of the schedule.

Then the resulting cards may be sorted to part-number sequence

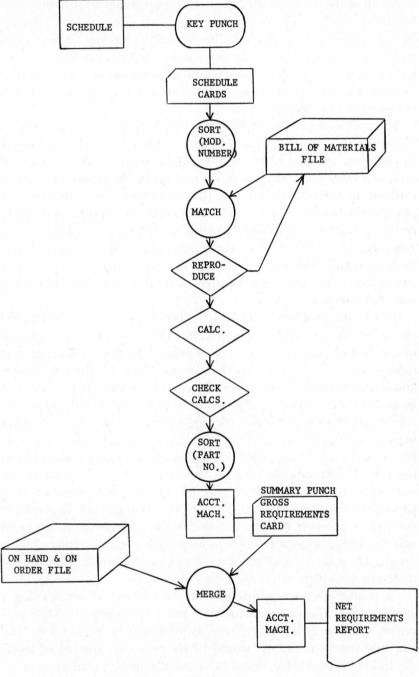

FIG. 9–5.

to get all of the cards for each part number together so that they may be summarized on the accounting machine, where a total requirements card for each part may be summary-punched. These cards may then be merged with a file of inventory balance cards to produce a net requirements report showing the on-hand balance, the on-order balance, the requirements for each of the coming periods, and the net shortage or overage resulting.

The above procedure is relatively simple in principle and suffers from only two major defects. The first of these is the time necessary to complete the procedure. For example, if there were a total of around 15,000 active parts and 500 end items, there may be 180,000 cards in the bill of materials file, 100,000 of which may be active for any given schedule. Even with considerable overlapping and duplication of machines, it would still require about a week of processing (on a two-shift basis) before the requirements reports would begin to be printed. Although a week is not particularly long for this amount of work, any time required to do this processing is usually just that much too much.

The second problem is one which cannot be disposed of easily, and one which we may tend to overlook. It is the problem of maintenance of the bill of materials file—the continual process of adding new models and keeping up with the changes made by the production and engineering departments on the current models. If this file is to be useful for forecasting purposes, it must accurately reflect the current shop practice, and it is surprising to discover how many changes must be made each week to keep this file current. Usually, a second file (called a *where-used* file) is maintained to make it easier to keep the bill of materials file current. A where-used file has exactly the same cards in it as the bill of materials file, but it is maintained in part-number sequence. Thus, when the engineering department substitutes one part for another, the cards which are to be replaced may be found together in the where-used file and replaced as a group. These cards can then be used to locate the individual bills of materials in which cards must be changed.

Of course, several approaches may be considered when using a computer for the determination of parts requirements. One procedure that has been widely used is presented in Figure 9–6. The schedule for all models is stored in the memory. Instead of using the bill of materials file (as in the normal punched card approach), the where-used file is used. It is passed through the computer (in part-number sequence) and, as each card for a given part number is read, the forecast for the model number involved is found in memory, and the contribution of that model to the requirements for the part is computed. Thus, after all of the cards for a given part number have been read, the total requirement for that part is avail-

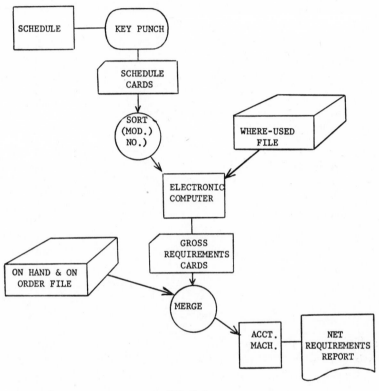

FIG. 9–6.

able for punching into an output card. A general block diagram for this computer run is shown in Figure 9–7.

For the volumes discussed above, the computer procedure would require only about three days' work on a two-shift basis, which is an important time improvement. However, this time is misleading, for it refers to the total time to complete the entire job. But, in this procedure, the first results would become available after only a few hours' time, and the planners could begin to work with them almost immediately. As a matter of fact, it is likely that the high-value or long-lead-time parts would be put through the computer first, and the critical items would be handled almost immediately, while the nuts and bolts could be processed later.

It should be noted that there are several serious limitations to this approach, which must be considered in light of the individual circumstances. The first of these is the size of the memory. If the schedule involves a large number of models or extends over a considerable number of periods, the memory of the computer may not

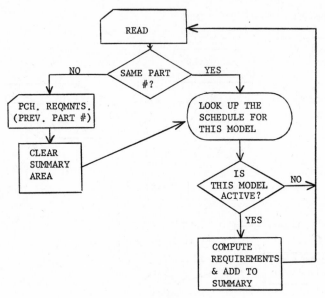

FIG. 9–7.

be sufficient to store the entire schedule. Furthermore, it is frequently desirable (in order to reduce the size of the bill of materials file) to first break the model schedule down into requirements in terms of subassemblies, and then repeat the process to find the individual parts requirements. This is known as a two-stage explosion. Frequently, the situation will call for a multistage explosion. Where the explosion involves more than one stage, the output of the first stage becomes the schedule for the second, and the memory requirements for succeeding stages may get quite large. In these cases, however, it may be possible in individual situations to divide the end items into small groups (which have little or no interchangeability of parts between them) for processing separately, thus reducing the over-all problem to several smaller problems that can be handled individually.

It is also readily apparent that the above computer procedure is rather inefficient when only a small percentage of the models are active in a given production schedule, for in this case, only a relatively small proportion of the cards read by the computer would actually be involved in the requirements calculation. In such situations, it may be possible to separate the models into active and inactive categories. Then the active models may be processed by using the above approach, while the bills of materials for any models from the inactive file that are included in the current schedule may be hand-pulled and processed using the regular punched card approach.

Automobile Insurance Rate Checking and Coding

When an automobile insurance policy is sold, a copy of the completed application is usually forwarded to the home office of the insurance company. Here it is checked for accuracy of the premiums, and statistical and management codes, required by the various rating organizations, are assigned. These codes enable the rating organizations to make studies of insurance in force and losses in various categories with which they are concerned. Until recently, it was impossible to mechanize the functions of rate checking and coding— they were performed by clerks who referred to rating books and coding tables to assign the proper codes and rates to the individual coverages afforded by the policy.

With the advent of the memory capacity of the intermediate electronic computer, it became possible to mechanize this process and to perform both of these operations at the same time. Seven types of coverages (bodily injury and property damage, medical, collision, comprehensive, wind, combined additional, and towing and labor) may be involved in any automobile insurance policy, and the premium for each of these depends upon from one to six different factors (such as state, private passenger classification, age of driver, type of car, and medical limits desired) . In addition, at least ten different codes must be assigned to each policy to facilitate later statistical analysis.

To enable its salesmen to determine the premium on a given policy, most companies publish a rating manual containing as many as 100 pages of instructions and tables. For a computer to be able to check the rating, it would appear that the entire book would have to be stored in the computer's memory. This seems impossible, for if we calculate the amount of memory required to store all of the tables in the book, it will usually add up to many times the memory available. Herein lies the interest in this application, for by examining the tables involved, and combining the knowledge of how the tables were originally arrived at with the computing capabilities of the machine, it is possible to reduce the memory requirements to the amount available in most intermediate computers.

The rating manuals were prepared with the capabilities and limitations of people as the primary consideration. Thus, whenever possible tables were substituted for computations. Of course, the numbers in these tables did not occur by happenstance—they are based upon underlying relationships that enabled the table to be constructed in the first place. Furthermore, the rating manuals use many techniques to minimize the possibility of human errors and confusion, such as printing the same table in several places when it is to be used under a number of different circumstances.

Thus, there are a number of ways in which the memory required can be reduced. In the first place, consideration can be restricted to the tables involved in rating policies for one state at a time, for the policies for one state can be easily processed as a group before proceeding to the next state. In addition, an examination of the tables which apply to a given state reveals that a tremendous amount of duplication is involved among them. For example, there may be 35 territories within a state, with a large table for each of these territories, but actually only five *different* tables in this group.

As an illustration of how calculation may be substituted for memory, consider the determination of the premium for bodily injury or property damage. To find the premium for bodily injury coverage, a table in the rating manual is used which provides the premium for limits 5/10 (meaning $5,000 per person and $10,000 per accident) on the basis of a territorial schedule and the private passenger class, as shown in Figure 9–8. If the limits are other than 5/10, we must also refer to the table in Figure 9–9 to find the premium. Thus, to find the premium for bodily injury for class 1B in territory 7 with

Type and Class	Terr. 5		Terr. 6		Terr. 7		Terr. 8	
	B.I.	P.D.	B.I.	P.D.	B.I.	P.D.	B.I.	P.D.
Private Pass.								
Class 1A	$19	$19	$25	$19	$18	$14	$14	$17
Class 1B	21	20	29	22	21	17	16	20
Class 1C	27	27	35	26	26	20	20.	24
Class 2A	35	35	45	34	33	26	25	31
Class 2B	40	40	51	39	38	30	29	35
Class 2C	48	48	62	47	45	36	35	42
Class 3	32	32	41	31	30	24	23	28

FIG. 9–8.

| | | | | | MASTER INCREASED LIMITS | | | | | |
| | | | | | (Even Dollar Rates) | | | | | |

Rate	10/20	15/30	20/40	25/25	25/50	50/50	50/100	100/100	100/300	200/200	250/250
$10	$12.00	$12.80	$13.30	$13.00	$13.60	$13.90	$14.50	$14.70	$15.40	$15.50	$15.80
11	13.20	14.08	14.63	14.30	14.96	15.29	15.95	16.17	16.94	17.05	17.38
12	14.40	15.36	15.96	15.60	16.32	16.68	17.40	17.64	18.48	18.60	18.96
13	15.60	16.64	17.29	16.90	17.68	18.07	18.85	19.11	20.02	20.15	20.54
14	16.80	17.92	18.62	18.20	19.04	19.46	20.30	20.58	21.56	21.70	22.12
15	18.00	19.20	19.95	19.50	20.40	20.85	21.75	22.05	23.10	23.25	23.70
16	19.20	20.48	21.28	20.80	21.76	22.24	23.20	23.52	24.64	24.80	25.28
17	20.40	21.76	22.61	22.10	23.12	23.63	24.65	24.99	26.18	26.35	26.86
18	21.60	23.04	23.94	23.40	24.48	25.02	26.10	26.46	27.72	27.90	28.44
19	22.80	24.32	25.27	23.70	25.84	26.41	27.55	27.93	29.26	29.45	30.02
20	24.00	25.60	26.60	26.00	27.20	27.80	29.00	29.40	30.80	31.00	31.60
21	25.20	26.88	27.93	27.30	28.56	29.19	30.45	30.87	32.34	32.55	33.18
22	26.40	28.16	29.26	28.60	29.92	30.58	31.90	32.34	33.88	34.10	34.76
23	27.60	29.44	30.59	29.90	31.28	31.97	33.35	33.81	35.42	35.65	36.34
24	28.80	30.72	31.92	31.20	32.64	33.36	34.80	35.28	36.96	37.20	37.92

FIG. 9–9.

limits of 15/30, we would find $21.00, and under 15/30 in Figure 9–9 we would find the premium of $26.88. With a computer, we can replace the table in Figure 9–9 by simply noting that there are certain percentage relationships between the 5/10 rate and all of the other rates, as shown below:

10/20	120%	50/100	145%
15/30	128	100/100	147
20/40	133	100/300	154
25/25	130	200/200	155
25/50	136	250/250	158
50/50	139		

Thus, in the illustration with territory 7, class 1B, and increased limits of 15/30, we would find the basic rate of $21.00 and multiply it by 128 per cent to obtain a premium of $26.88.

For collision insurance, the table in the rating manual is quite complex, with the premium being determined by territory, symbol (for type and model of automobile), deductible amount, class, and age group, as shown in Figure 9–10. For example, to find the $150 deductible collision premium in territory 4 for a car corresponding to symbol C, class 1, and driver age group 3, we would find $10 corresponding to the circled identifications in Figure 9–10. However, it is only necessary to store the premiums for two deductible amounts ($50 and $100), since all of the others may be expressed in terms of these. For example, the $150 deductible premium is 80 per cent of the $100 deductible premium, while the $75 deductible premium is the average of the $50 premium and the $100 premium.

Likewise, the premiums for the various age groups may be expressed as a percentage of the premium for age group 1, and the class premium may be expressed as a percentage of class 3. Thus Figure 9–10 can be reduced to the small table in Figure 9–11 with a certain amount of computation. Note that the table in Figure 9–11 (for 17 different symbols) involves only 17 words of storage, if the information is tightly packed.

For the example circled in Figure 9–10, looking up the $100 deductible and symbol C in Figure 9–11 we find $18.00. To convert to $150 deductible, we multiply by .8, getting $14.40, and to convert to age group 3, we multiply this by .9, obtaining $12.96. The amount for class 1 is 80 per cent of this, so, rounding to the nearest dollar, we obtain the $10.00 premium found in Figure 9–10. By use of such

PRIVATE PASSENGER AUTOMOBILE SECTION Territory 4													
$50 Ded. (72) Class			$100 Ded. (74) Class			($150 Ded.) (75) Class			$250 Ded. (76) Class			Age	Symbols
1	2	3	1	2	3	①	2	3	1	2	3	Groups	
$22	$31	$27	$10	$14	$12	$ 8	$12	$10	$ 6	$ 8	$ 7	1	
21	29	26	10	13	11	8	11	10	6	8	7	2	A
20	28	24	9	13	11	7	11	9	5	7	6	3	
19	26	23	9	12	10	7	10	9	5	7	6	4	
26	37	32	12	17	15	10	14	12	7	10	9	1	
25	35	30	11	16	14	10	13	11	7	10	9	2	B
23	33	29	11	15	14	9	13	11	6	9	8	3	
22	31	27	10	14	13	9	12	10	6	9	8	4	
30	43	37	14	21	18	11	16	14	9	13	11	1	
29	41	35	13	20	17	10	15	13	9	12	10	2	ⓒ
27	39	33	13	19	16	⑩	14	13	8	12	10	③	
26	37	31	12	18	15	9	14	12	8	11	9	4	
34	49	43	16	23	20	13	18	16	10	14	12	1	
32	47	41	15	22	19	12	17	15	10	13	11	2	D
31	44	39	14	21	18	12	16	14	9	13	11	3	
29	42	37	14	20	17	11	15	14	9	12	10	4	

FIG. 9–10.

techniques, it is possible to store all of the information necessary to check the rates for and assign codes to policies written in a typical state in less than 1,000 words of memory. It should be mentioned that mathematicians frequently store tables in condensed form to save memory. When necessary, they use high-order interpolation techniques to reconstruct the detailed results.

In this application, input to the computer would be a card (punched from the policy application) containing the pertinent information concerning the type of automobile, age of the driver, location, types of coverage, the premium assigned, etc. The output would be a statistics card which could be used for statistical analysis, and where the agent made a mistake in assigning the premium the machine would punch out a corrected rating card.

One of the casualty insurance companies that uses an electronic computer for this application operates on a decentralized basis, with about ten regional offices which handle the billing for the policies. At these regional offices, the cards are punched from the policies and sent by a transceiver to the home office where they are checked and coded by the computer. For renewal policies, billing cards are sent to the regional of-

Territory 4		
$50 Ded.	($100 Ded)	Symbol
$27	$12	A
32	15	B
37	(18)	(C)
43	20	D
47	23	E

FIG. 9–11.

fices to write bills in advance of renewal. Their volume of around 5,000 policies per day is handled in about $2\frac{1}{2}$ hours computer time, which replaces about 20 clerks under the previous manual procedure. The computer is available for the rest of the working day for such applications as payroll, life insurance calculations, and statistical applications.

Public Utility Billing

The calculation of gas, water, and electric bills for public utilities has been a popular punched card application. Basically, it is quite simple—given a card in which the current meter reading and previous readings are punched, it is only necessary to apply a rather simple rate and calculate the amount of the bill. If it were actually this simple, there would be no need for a computer in this application. The need for an electronic computer is apparent only after an investigation of the by-products required and the great variety of exceptions which can occur.

The exceptions involved include checking "reasonableness" of the consumption in order to detect meter reading errors, estimating consumption for meters that were not read, prorating bills that are for less than the normal billing period, and handling the various types of meters that may be used in a single city.

In the computer approach to utility billing, all of the exceptional situations can be handled in a single run; in the standard punch card approach, each situation requires a special procedure (or manual handling or review). Furthermore, in the computer procedure no sorting is involved—the meter cards are processed in the same sequence in which they are read and need never be removed from this sequence.

When the card is read into the machine, the previous reading is subtracted from the present reading to determine the consumption. Reading dates are subtracted to determine whether the account to be billed is for a full month or a prorated period, and the accounts are processed accordingly.

The computed consumption is compared with previous months, and an audit is performed to determine the accuracy of the reading. If this month's use compares reasonably with the preceding month's, the normal calculation routine is followed. However, if the use is high or low a *subroutine* is followed, and the account is given further programmed scrutiny to check for the "obvious" meter errors, which can be corrected by suitable programming. If the type of error cannot be determined, the bill may be calculated as is and an indication punched in the card so that the card may be selected for clerical review or discussion with the customer.

In cases of missed readings, an estimated consumption is calculated by utilizing an average of the previous months' usage. Factors such as season can be taken into account, duplicating the process an estimating clerk would follow. Where the preceding month was also estimated, the computer can find the last actual meter reading, and from it recalculate successive preceding usages to project an estimated current reading and consumption. Usually, company policy limits the number of times that a bill can be estimated without actually reading the meter, and the computer can check to see whether the preceding month's estimation was the last one allowed. If this is the case, it can prepare a special card to indicate that the meter must be read.

In a given city, there may be several rate structures, depending upon the type of customer and the type of service he receives. Each of these different rate structures is divided into several *consumption steps,* and a different rate is charged for consumption within each step (the rate usually decreases as the consumption increases). For example, in a typical rate structure there may be a flat charge of $1.00 for the first 15 kilowatt hours (K.W.H.) or less, the next 35 K.W.H. cost $.05 apiece, the next 50 K.W.H. cost $.04 apiece, the next 100 K.W.H. cost $.03 apiece, and everything over 200 K.W.H. costs $.02 per K.W.H.

This rate structure may be expressed in the computer by means of the table shown in Figure 9–12. In this table, the correction factor for each rate step is obtained by substracting from the total bill at the maximum consumption of the previous step the product of the rate under consideration times the same consumption. The $1.00 correction factor in the illustration is a flat charge. To obtain the second correction factor, we subtract from the $1.00 the product 15 times $.05 (or $.75), to obtain the $.25 correction factor. The total bill for 50 K.W.H. would be 50 times $.05 plus $.25, or $2.75. Subtracting 50 times $.04 (or $2.00) from $2.75, we obtain the third correction factor of $.75, and so forth. Then to compute the bill for 250 K.W.H. we would multiply 250 times $.02 and add the correction factor of $3.75 to obtain $8.75, which agrees with the long calculation based upon the original statement of the rate structure.

Step (K.W.H.)	Multiplier	Correction Factor
15	.00	1.00
50	.05	.25
100	.04	.75
200	.03	1.75
9999	.02	3.75

FIG. 9–12.

The rate structure is stored in the computer memory drum, with each step requiring one location. Thus, if a company has 30 rates, each of which has five steps, only 150 storage locations are required. The computer calculates the bill by locating the appropriate rate and step by means of table look-up, multiplying the consumption by the rate, and adding the correction factor to the product. Prorated bills are computed by projecting the consumption to a one month base, performing the bill calculation at that base, and adjusting the calculated amount by the prorate percentage previously figured. The ability to store all of the applicable rates together within the machine ensures that bills for all of the various types of customers can be calculated without any prior review or sorting operation.

Among the most interesting aspects of this application are the by-products which are desired. The rate departments of many companies find it necessary to have complete statistics on the number and size of bills rendered customers for each of the company's rates. For example, for each rate, they may wish to construct a graph for which the horizontal axis represents the number of kilowatt hours for each bill, and the vertical axis tabulates the number of bills at each consumption (as illustrated in Figure 9–13).

We would prefer to accumulate all of these statistics in summary form in memory (as a by-product of computing the bills), but since there may be 30 rates and up to 99,999 consumption steps in each rate, it is easy to see that it is not possible to store these summarized statistics for the entire rate structure. However, an analysis shows that most customers are billed on relatively few rates, and that the great majority of customers' consumption falls within definite

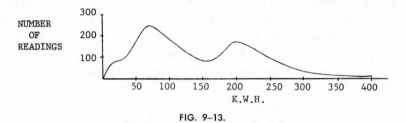

FIG. 9–13.

limits. If storage is reserved for the most frequently occurring rates and bill sizes, over 90 per cent of all bill statistics can be stored, with the remaining 10 per cent punched into detail bill frequency cards during the bill calculation. These detail cards, together with summary frequency cards punched from the drum, represent a complete summarization of all bill statistics.

Frequently, a summarization by dollar amounts of the bills within each rate structure is desired. As in the above case, the summaries may be developed during the bill calculation by accumulating totals for the most frequently occurring classifications in memory and punching special cards for classifications which occur infrequently. Also a total of customers, meters, consumption, and gross and net billing amounts is accumulated during bill calculation and is punched in a control card when the last account of each control unit is completed. This card is later used for automatic control of the accounts receivable cycle balancing operation.

The above discussion is a greatly simplified description of the program involved in public utility bill calculation. It may be deduced, therefore, that the computer program itself is quite complex. The ability of the stored program machine to handle all of these complexities in a single run makes it possible to replace an extremely cumbersome combination of punched card and manual procedures with a relatively straightforward and highly automated process.

Overhead Cost Distribution

The distribution of costs between the various operating and service departments in a business can be a complex problem, for the total costs for any one department are not known until the costs from other departments are distributed to it, while the total costs of the other departments may also be dependent upon the total cost of the first department. Although many approximate solutions to this problem have been developed, it can be solved with mathematical precision through the solution of a set of simultaneous linear equations. Since the advent of the electronic computer, it is not only practical to use this mathematical solution, but it is actually much less expensive to get a mathematical solution than it would be to obtain an approximate solution manually.

The technique used is an iterative procedure in which approximate solutions are improved by repeated calculation until the desired accuracy is reached. To illustrate the method itself, we will consider a case in which only four departments are involved (denoted by A, B, C, and D). The first column of the table in Figure 9–14 indicates that 15 per cent of the total costs of department A are

Dept. to \ Dept. from	A	B	C	D	Direct Costs
A	--	10%	15%	15%	$ 8,000
B	15%	--	20	10	7,000
C	--	10	--	30	9,000
D	15	15	10	--	12,000
TOTAL	30%	35%	45%	55%	$36,000

FIG. 9–14.

charged to department B, and 15 per cent of the total expense of department A is charged to department D. The initial direct costs (totaling $36,000) are given by the last column. Our objective is to redistribute this $36,000 total, taking into account the transfers indicated in the body of the table.

In order to calculate the total cost associated with each department, the information in Figure 9.14 may be expressed in equation form as follows:

$$(1) \quad A_T = .10B_T + .15C_T + .15D_T + 8,000$$
$$(2) \quad B_T = .15A_T + .20C_T + .10D_T + 7,000$$
$$(3) \quad C_T = .10B_T + .30D_T + 9,000$$
$$(4) \quad D_T = .15A_T + .15B_T + .10C_T + 12,000$$

Using the initial direct costs for each department as our first approximation for the total costs for the departments $(A_T = 8,000, B_T = 7,000, C_T = 9,000, D_T = 12,000)$, and substituting these values into the right-hand side of equation 1 we obtain a better approximation for A_T:

$$A_T = .10 (7,000) + .15 (9,000) + .15 (12,000) + 8,000$$
$$= 700 + 1,350 + 1,800 + 8,000$$
$$= 11,850$$

Then, using this new value for A_T, along with the old estimates for B_T, C_T, and D_T, and by substituting in equation 2 we obtain:

$$B_T = .15 (11,850) + .20 (9,000) + .10 (12,000) + 7,000$$
$$= 11,777.50$$

Likewise, using $A_T = 11,850$, $B_T = 11,777.50$, $C_T = 9,000$, and $D_T = 12,000$, and substituting in equation 3 we obtain:

$$C_T = .10 (11,777.50) + .30 (12,000) + 9,000$$
$$= 13,777.75$$

Now, using $A_T = 11,850$, $B_T = 11,777.50$, $C_T = 13,777.50$, and substituting in equation 4 we find:

$$D_T = .15 (11,850) + .15 (11,777.50) + .10 (13,777.75)$$
$$= 16,921.91$$

This completes the first iteration. For the second iteration, we repeat the above process, always substituting the latest available approximation for A_T, B_T, C_T, and D_T:

$$A_T = .10 (11,777.50) + .15 (13,777.75) + .15 (16,921.91) + 8,000$$
$$= 13,782.70$$
$$B_T = .15 (13,782.70) + .20 (13,777.75) + .10 (16,921.91 + 7,000$$
$$= 13,515.15$$
$$C_T = .10 (13,515.15) + 30 (16,921.91) + 9,000$$
$$= 15,428.09$$
$$D_T = .15 (13,782.70) + .15 (13,515.15) + .10 (15,428.09) + 12,000$$
$$= 17,637.49$$

The results of succeeding iterations are summarized in Figure 9–15. In this table, we may observe the process of convergence toward the correct solution. Notice that the improvement in accuracy of the totals between iterations 6 and 7 is less than $4.00, while the last two iterations agree to the nearest dollar for each department. Although even better accuracy could be obtained by a few more iterations, in view of the usual inaccuracies in the assignment of the original percentages, this accuracy is probably ample. To determine a formal stopping point, we may compare the total of all of the departments (last line in the table in Figure 9–15) for a given iteration with the same total for the previous iteration and agree to terminate the procedure when this difference is less than a specified amount (in this case $1.00).

Having obtained the total cost, it is easy to use the column totals

Iteration Dept.	3	4	5	6	7	8
A_T	$14,311.35	$14,411.56	$14,446.78	$14,453.65	$14,455.07	$14,455.37
B_T	13,996.07	14,071.30	14,101.81	14,106.80	14,108.01	14,108.26
C_T	15,642.77	15,750.19	15,764.42	15,768.30	15,769.07	15,769.24
D_T	17,810.21	17,847.45	17,858.73	17,860.90	17,861.37	17,861.47
Total	$61,760.40	$62,080.50	$62,171.74	$62,189.65	$62,193.52	$62,194.34

FIG. 9–15.

of the table in Figure 9–14 to determine the percentage of the total costs remaining, and calculate the net costs for each department as below:

$$A_N = A_T - .30A_T = .7A_T = \$10,118.76$$
$$B_N = B_T - .35B_T = .65B_T = 9,170.37$$
$$C_N = C_T - .45C_T = .55C_T = 8,673.08$$
$$D_N = D_T - .55D_T = .45D_T = 8,037.66$$
$$\text{Total} = \overline{\$35,999.87}$$

Since the total direct charges were $36,000, this procedure produced excellent accuracy in the above illustration. It should be noted that this method may not converge for all sets of simultaneous linear equations, but it is satisfactory for the equations arising in overhead cost allocation.

It is not difficult to program the above procedure for a computer. This has been done for a firm which has 90 departments with around 625 interdepartmental transfers. In this case, the percentages involved in the equations to be solved were stored in memory in the following form:

Per Cent	Dept. to	Dept. from
xx.xx	xxo	oxx

These percentages are stored in sequential locations, with a zero word between equations. Words 0000 through 0090 may be used to record the approximate solutions as they are developed. Assuming that the percentages are stored properly on the drum, and that the direct cost for the departments are stored (in location 0000 through 0090) as the first approximation, the block diagram in Figure 9–16

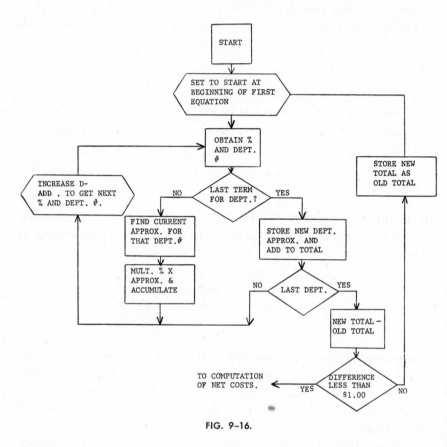

FIG. 9–16.

may be used to calculate the total costs for each of the 90 departments.

The entire program for reading all the information into the memory of the computer, computing the total costs for each of the departments, computing the net costs for each department, and punching the results into cards requires less than 300 program steps. Adding 100 locations for accumulating the department totals and 100 locations for the initial direct costs, 1,300 locations remain for departmental distribution percentages.

For the problem in the firm just cited, the solution, using a 650, requires about ten iterations at 40 seconds per iteration. The total problem, including loading the program, loading the percentages and initial direct costs, and punching the results, requires less than 15 minutes. This replaces around 300 hours of desk calculator labor required for an approximate solution.

Summary

Each of the above illustrations provides an example of the ingenuity required in the design of computer applications. In the material-requirement explosion, an entirely different file sequence was necessary to take advantage of the capabilities of the computer. In the automobile insurance rating and coding procedure, it was necessary to analyze how extensive tables, developed for use by the insurance salesman, had been constructed so that they could be condensed to fit into the computer's memory. In this illustration, the proper entry in the full table is recomputed each time it is needed. A similar approach is often taken to the determination of the surrender value of life insurance policies.

The public utility billing illustration shows how the branching capability of the electronic computer makes it possible to handle numerous and rather complicated exceptions in a computer program. It also demonstrates how memory may be effectively conserved when accumulating summary information by only allocating memory to the high-volume categories, while handling the low-volume categories in another way.

The use of mathematical techniques in an accounting problem is shown in the overhead cost allocation example. When a computer is available, powerful mathematical techniques may become practical—the use of mathematics may not only simplify the data-processing problem, but also provide a better solution.

EXERCISES

9.1 Describe the difference between a bill of materials file and a where-used file. Outline a data-processing procedure to determine parts requirements using each of these files.

9.2 If carried to its logical conclusion, what should be the outputs from a material control system? Does the procedure discussed in this chapter provide these outputs? What is needed before such outputs could be produced?

9.3 Describe some techniques for conserving memory when storing tables. Why don't we use these techniques when the tables are to be used by people?

9.4   Suppose we have utility bills representing consumptions ranging from 1 to 10,000 K.W.H. If we wish to tally the number of bills of each size between 40 and 140 K.W.H., how could we exclude the other bills? (Answer with a block diagram.)

9.5   *a)*   What is an iterative procedure?

b)   What is meant by convergence of an iterative procedure?

c)   What is a set of simultaneous linear equations?

d)   Are there other ways to solve simultaneous linear equations? How?

e)   How can overhead cost allocation be expressed in terms of simultaneous linear equations?

SUPPLEMENTAL READINGS

Application Development 19—Type 650 for Public Utility Customer Accounting.   Form Number 32–6153. New York: International Business Machines Corp., 590 Madison Avenue.

A description of the use of a 650 computer for utility billing as discussed in this chapter.

Application Report 75—Overhead Cost Allocation.   Form Number 32–9360. New York: International Business Machines Corp., 590 Madison Avenue.

This presents the example of overhead cost allocation included in this chapter and briefly discusses the solution of the equations using punched card calculators.

JEWETT, GRANDJEAN G.   "Distribution of Overhead with Electronic Calculators," *The Journal of Accountancy* (June, 1954), pp. 698–701.

Discusses distribution of overhead and the use of electronic computers to solve the resulting equations.

Type 650 for Fire and Casualty Insurance Applications.   Form Number 32–6160. New York: International Business Machines Corp., 590 Madison Avenue.

Presents a discussion of rate checking and coding of automobile insurance policies using the 650.

CHAPTER 10 · Large Electronic Data-Processing Machines

IN CHAPTERS 6 and 7, the IBM 650 was discussed to illustrate the major concepts associated with the stored program and its use. From the general description of the electronic computer in Chapter 5, it is apparent that the basic 650 has rather limited input and output, and that it includes no facilities for storage of file information. It was noted in passing, however, that it is possible to expand the basic 650 to include additional input-output and file storage units.

To provide a broader background of machine characteristics, large-scale electronic data-processing machines will be discussed instead of an expanded 650. However, this discussion will be based upon the understanding of the stored program, obtained through our study of the 650, discussing only those characteristics which differ from those with which we are familiar.

The large electronic-data processing machines are distinguished by their speed, by the fact that the primary method of input and output is magnetic tape, and by their cost. The typical large computer installation usually consists of several other machines in addition to the main frame of the computer. However, rather than being supported primarily by auxiliary punched card equipment, the large-scale electronic data-processing machine may have its own complement of auxiliary equipment, based upon magnetic tape as a processing medium.

A typical large-scale installation might consist of: (1) the basic computer and memory; (2) ten magnetic tape units; (3) a punched card–to–magnetic tape converter; (4) a magnetic tape–operated high-speed printer; (5) a magnetic tape–to–punched card converter. This installation of machines might rent for a total of $30,-000 per month on a single-shift basis, or sell for around $1,500,000.

221

Alpha-Numeric

In contrast to the 650, the typical large-scale computer is able to represent both numeric and alphabetic characters directly in memory. A popular character coding system utilizes seven bits for each character, four of which correspond to the numeric punches in a punched card, two of which correspond to the zone punches, and one of which is used for checking accuracy.[1] As can be seen in Figure 10–1, the four numeric bits have values corresponding to 1, 2, 4,

```
            0123456789 ABCDEFGHIJKLMNOPQRSTUVWXYZ  &.¤-$*/,%#@

Check   {C   XX X  XX   XX X  XX    X XX  X X XX   X   X X X   XX
         B              XXXXXXXXXXXXXXXXXXX            XXXXXX
Zone    {A              XXXXXXXXX          XXXXXXXX XXX    XXX
         8   X      XX         XX        XX        XX  XX XX XXXX
Numeric {4       XXXX      XXXX      XXXX      XXXX     X  X X X
         2   X XX  XX    XX XX    XX  XX  XX  XX      X  X  X X
         1   X X X X X X X X X X XX X X X X X X X X   X   X XX X
```

FIG. 10–1.

and 8, so that any number from zero to 9 can be represented by a combination of bits in this code, while the two zone bits together give four combinations corresponding to no-zone, Y-zone, X-zone, and O-zone. The check bit is present in those characters where it is required to make the total number of bits even.

To process files of alphabetic information, it is necessary to be able to compare two alpha-numeric fields to determine which is the lower. Since normal arithmetic operations cannot be performed with alphabetic characters to subtract one field from another, it is necessary to have instructions which directly compare one field with another and determine which field should come first in dictionary sequence. In some cases it is desirable to compare fields containing a mixture of numbers, alphabetic characters, and special symbols. Thus, for any machine the designer must specify the sequence under which comparison instructions are to operate.[2] One possible such sequence is that which is normally produced by the punched card sorter, which places blanks first, then the special characters, then the alphabet, and then the numbers zero through 9. Specifically, this sequence of characters is as follows:

---

[1] Used in the IBM 705 and the IBM 7080.

[2] This is called the sorting sequence, sometimes the collation sequence, of the machine.

Blank & ☒ - $ * / , % # @   A through Z   0 through 9

In order to program a comparison, several instructions might be provided.

CMP (Compare). This instruction compares the contents of some register (such as the accumulator) with the contents of the memory location specified by the data address. This comparison begins with the high-order position of the word and proceeds toward the right, as we would do in an ordinary dictionary. Associated with this instruction are two indicators similar to the overflow indicator. If the accumulator is higher than the specified memory word, the *high* indicator is set. If the accumulator is equal to the specified memory location, the *equal* indicator is set. If the accumulator is lower than the specified memory word, no indicator is set. These indicators remain set until the next *Compare* instruction is executed.

BRH (Branch on High). This instruction interrogates the *high* indicator. If this indicator is on, the program branches; if this indicator is off, the normal sequence of instructions is executed.

BRE (Branch on Equal). This instruction interrogates the *equal* indicator. If this indicator is on, the program branches; if the indicator is off, the normal sequence of instructions is executed.

Various Representations of Information

As we have seen, information is recorded in the memory of machines as various combinations of "bits" of information. These codes must be used because computers are constructed of binary elements —elements that have exactly two states, such as *off* and *on*.[3] Each such element can represent a "bit" of information.

The 650 uses the biquinary code which utilizes combinations of seven bits to record the digits zero through 9, while the code mentioned above uses seven bits to represent the numbers, alphabet, and special characters. It was also mentioned in Chapter 6 that a two-out-of-five bit code is used on the 650 drum.

This raises the following question: How many bits are required to represent the numbers zero through 9 or the alphabetic characters? Since each character represented must have a distinct combination, this latter question reduces to the question: How many different combinations can be constructed out of a single bit, or two bits, or three bits, or four bits, etc?

---

[3] This is similar to, but not identical with, the concept of binary numbers which is discussed in Appendix C.

To discuss this question, let us represent the *on* condition of an element by a 1 and the *off* condition by a zero. Then a single bit gives two combinations, zero and 1. Two bits give four combinations: 00, 01, 10, 11. If we add a third bit, then there are eight possible combinations, since each of the above can be combined with both a 1 and a zero to obtain the following combinations:

$$
\begin{array}{ccc}
001 & & 000 \\
011 & \text{and} & 010 \\
101 & & 100 \\
111 & & 110
\end{array}
$$

Thus, each time we add a bit, we double the number of combinations, thus N bits give 2^N combinations.

Since $2^3 = 8$ and there are 10 digits, three bits are not enough to represent the numeric digits. However, $2^4 = 16$, so four bits are more than enough to represent the 10 digits. Perhaps the most common numeric representation is the binary-coded-decimal representation which uses four bits with values corresponding to 1, 2, 4, and 8 to represent zero through 9. Thus, in this code, the digits are represented as shown in Figure 10–2.

A slight variation of the binary-coded-decimal notation is to represent zero as 1 0 1 0 (which would correspond to ten) so that the combination 0000 is not used. The Burroughs Datatron 205, the Burroughs Datatron 220, and the IBM 604 use the binary-coded-decimal representation. It should be observed that this representation has little self-checking capability, for the dropping of a bit always results in another "valid" number, and the addition of a bit may result in a "valid" number.

An important variation of binary coded decimal is the *excess-three* binary-coded-decimal notation, in which three is added to the digit before it is expressed in binary-coded-decimal form (see Figure 10–3). The excess-three notation has a valuable property for subtraction, since the nines' complement of any digit may be obtained by substituting zeros for ones and ones for zeros in the bit representation.

The two-out-of-five representation used on the 650 drum is also shown in Figure 10–3. This representation has self-checking properties, since the dropping of a bit or the adding of a bit results in an invalid representation.

If we wish to represent both the numeric digits and the alphabet, we have 36 different characters. Since $2^5 = 32$, five bits are too few, so six bits are required. Since $2^6 = 64$, with a six-bit code we have combinations available to handle any reasonable number of special characters in addition to the alphabet and numeric digits.

The most popular alpha-numeric codes are based on the logic of

	8	4	2	1
Zero	0	0	0	0
One	0	0	0	1
Two	0	0	1	0
Three	0	0	1	1
Four	0	1	0	0
Five	0	1	0	1
Six	0	1	1	0
Seven	0	1	1	1
Eight	1	0	0	0
Nine	1	0	0	1

FIG. 10–2.

	Excess Three				Two-Out-of-Five				
	8	4	2	1	0	1	2	3	6
Zero	0	0	1	1	0	1	1	0	0
One	0	1	0	0	1	1	0	0	0
Two	0	1	0	1	1	0	1	0	0
Three	0	1	1	0	1	0	0	1	0
Four	0	1	1	1	0	1	0	1	0
Five	1	0	0	0	0	0	1	1	0
Six	1	0	0	1	1	0	0	0	1
Seven	1	0	1	0	0	1	0	0	1
Eight	1	0	1	1	0	0	1	0	1
Nine	1	1	0	0	0	0	0	1	1

FIG. 10–3.

the punched card code, using four bits (binary-coded-decimal or excess-three representation) to represent the numeric punch and the other two bits (four combinations) to represent the no-zone, 12-zone, 11-zone, and zero-zone possibilities.

Since errors are not detected by these codes, a seventh bit position is frequently added to the code to make it self-checking. This bit, called a *redundancy* or *parity* bit, is added so as to make the total number of one bits in each valid character even (or in some machines odd), so that if a single bit is added or dropped an invalid character results. An example of this type of code has been shown in Figure 10–1.

When representing pure numeric information, the number of bits required is minimized when the numbers are converted to the pure binary system discussed in Appendix C. However, numbers cannot be translated digit by digit into this notation, so a considerable amount of computation is required to make the conversion. Thus, most computers designed for data processing use one of the notations discussed above. However, several machines are designed to operate on numbers in either pure binary or binary-coded-decimal form, depending upon which is the most convenient. In these machines, binary representation is used to store instructions, and it can be used for data in suitable circumstances.

Magnetic Core Memory

Rather than performing from 200 to 500 operations per second as does the 650, the large-scale electronic data-processing machines operate at from 5,000 to 200,000 operations per second. Since each operation usually involves two accesses to memory, it is obvious that such speeds can only be attained if the memory operates hundreds of times as fast as the 650 magnetic drum memory.

The tremendous speed of the large-scale electronic data-processing machines is attained through the use of a memory which has an access time of only a few microseconds.[4] Although various devices (mercury delay lines and cathode-ray tubes) have been used for these memories, the standard fast-access memory is constructed of magnetic cores. A magnetic core is a doughnut-shaped ring, less than one tenth of an inch in outside diameter, made of a magnetizable ceramic material. These small beads, each of which can remember one "bit" of information, are strung on lattices of wire as illustrated in Figure 10–4.

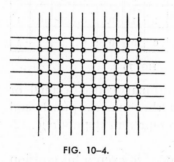

FIG. 10–4.

As was mentioned in the discussion of magnetic drum read-write heads in Chapter 6, when a current is sent through a wire wrapped around a piece of iron, the iron is magnetized, and the direction of the magnetization depends upon the direction of the current through the wire. The read-write head is made of an alloy for which the magnetization disappears when the current is removed, but there are other alloys for which the magnetization remains present after the current is removed (until it is changed by sending current through the wire again).

Magnetic cores are made of materials in which the magnetization remains after the current is removed. Also, the core is wrapped around the wire. The magnetic core has the property that if a pulse

---

[4] A microsecond is one millionth of a second. Thus, a millisecond is one thousand microseconds, and a second is one million microseconds. Since light (and electricity) travels at 186,000 miles per second, light travels about .186 miles (or about 982 feet) in one microsecond.

of electricity is sent through the wire in one direction, the core will remain magnetized in a clockwise direction, while if the current in the wire is reversed, the core will remain in a counterclockwise state. As shown in Figure 10–5, these two states can be used to remember one "bit" of information.

The magnetic cores have one additional property that enables the machine to conveniently select the particular core in which to record

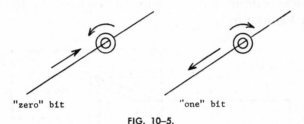

"zero" bit   "one" bit

FIG. 10–5.

a bit of information. If the core is magnetized in one direction, it takes a suitably strong current to cause it to "flip" to the opposite state. If the current required to flip a core is denoted by I, then a current of $\frac{1}{2}$I will not affect the cores. Thus, we are able to record a bit of information where we desire by selecting one horizontal wire and one vertical wire and sending a current of magnitude $\frac{1}{2}$I through each of these wires. As shown in Figure 10–6, only the core at the intersection of these two wires will have a current sufficient to flip the core, so a bit will be recorded in this core and nowhere else.

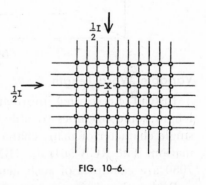

FIG. 10–6.

To read information from a magnetic core memory, another wire is threaded through all of the cores in a plane.[5] When a core flips, a current is generated in this wire. Thus, to read out a core, current is sent through the proper pair of wires to record a zero. If the core flips, a pulse is available on the read-out wire, indicating that a "1" was present in the core. If it does not flip, no pulse is available on the read-out wire, and a "0" was present. This process always sets the core to the zero state, destroying the information stored, so the information that was read out must

---

[5] Actually, in order to make it possible to more easily select an entire word from memory, a fourth wire (called an *inhibit wire*) is also threaded through all the cores in a plane. Thus, each core has four wires passing through it.

be immediately rewritten so that it will be available for later reference.

The magnetic core memory consists of several planes, each of which contains a single bit of each word of memory. For example, if the character code requires six bits and the word size is ten digits plus sign, 62 planes of 4,000 cores each would provide 4,000 words of memory. A word would be read or written in this memory by selecting corresponding pairs of wires in each of the 62 planes, as shown in Figure 10–7.

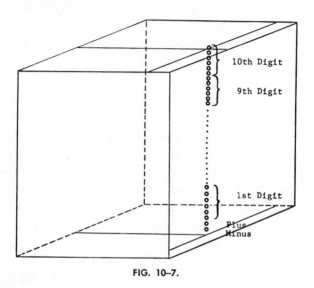

FIG. 10–7.

Variable Word Length

Instead of recording information in memory in words of a specific length, some machines are able to handle each field (whether it be a single character or many characters) as an individual unit of information. The RCA 501, the IBM 1401, the IBM 705, and the IBM 7080 are examples of such machines.

Rather than being composed of words of a fixed length, the memory of such machines is organized so that each character has its own address. A field is addressed by its units position in memory, so the left limit of the field must be designated by a special character, a special bit position in the character code, or by sensing the sign over the units position of the next field to the left.

Assuming that we denote the upper limit of a field by a special bit position, the memory would be organized into groups of seven planes, and each character would be represented by a combination of six bits and a field definition bit. Suppose that Mr. T. C. Mits, man-number 12345, with an hourly rate of $2.50, worked for 40 regular hours and 8.3 overtime hours. If we denote the field definition bit by a circumflex ($\wedge$) over the character, the record for Mr. Mits might appear as in Figure 10–8. Thus, to obtain his man num-

| | | | | $\wedge$ | | $+$ $\wedge$ | $+$ $\wedge$ | | $+$ $\wedge$ | | $+$ |
| M I T S | | T C | 1 2 3 | 4 | 5 | 2 5 | 0 0 | 8 | 3 | 4 0 | 0 |

20 21 22 23 24 25 26 27 28 29 30 31 32 33 34 35 36 37 38 39 40 41 42 43 44 45 46

FIG. 10–8.

ber, we would address 00034; to obtain his regular hours worked, we would address 00043; and to obtain his overtime hours, we would address 00040.

Notice that the allocation of memory in such a machine is quite similar to the allocation of columns in a punched card—the maximum number of positions that a field can require must be allotted to that field (as shown in the field for overtime hours). Since we must locate the fields by means of the address of the units position, the number of characters devoted to each field must remain fixed so that these addresses will be the same from record to record.

Machines in which memory is organized as described above are said to have *variable field* (or *word*) *length*. However, the length of a particular field is not really variable; it must be fixed, just as the size of a field on punched cards must be fixed.[6] But the ability to allocate the required number of positions (and only the required number of positions) of memory (or of magnetic tape) to each field allows us to make the maximum use of the memory available. On the other hand, an additional digit is required in the data address on a machine in which each memory position is addressable. Also, since characters must be obtained from memory one at a time, such machines inherently operate in a serial fashion—they operate on one character at a time, so that the time to perform an operation is proportional to the size of the field.

Order Structure

Since magnetic core memory is truly random—it requires exactly the same amount of time to refer to any word—little is gained from

---

[6] Some machines have true variable field length, for they need not record high-order zeros in a field. This is advantageous for magnetic tape, where the time to read the tape depends upon the number of characters recorded.

having an instruction address portion of the instruction (as in the 650). Therefore, many large machines are *single-address* machines. They have an operation code and a data address, but no instruction address. The next instruction is taken from the next memory location except when a branch instruction is executed.

With but an operation code and a data address, only six digits are required for an instruction. In a variable-field-length machine, this presents no problem; but in a machine with ten-digit words, four digits positions are wasted for each instruction stored in a word. Thus, some single-address machines have a word length of 12 digits, so that two instructions may be placed in each word. Other machines use the extra positions to denote the index register whose contents are to be added to the address, or to obtain the advantages of variable field length in a fixed-word-length machine. In the latter case, any portion of a word (containing several fields) may be operated upon by an instruction, with two digits being used to denote the limits within the word of the field. For example, if memory-location 1642 contains man number and rate as shown below, the instruction RAL XX *04* 1642 will Reset Add man number (positions zero through 4) into the accumulator without affecting the rest of the

Man Number		Rate
1 2 3 4 5	0 0	2.5 0

word. Thus, information may be packed and unpacked without shifting in the accumulator.

In some machines, an instruction is composed of an operation code and two data addresses. Such *two-address* instructions allow the machine, for example, to multiply two numbers together without first placing one in a register, since one address can give the location of the first factor and the other address can give the location of the second factor. Likewise, it is possible to transfer a word from one part of memory to another with a single instruction, and to have a three-way branch in which the machine branches to one location if the accumulator is minus, to another location if the accumulator is zero, and goes to the next location if the accumulator is positive and nonzero.

There are also *three-address* machines, in which an instruction has an operation code and three data addresses, A, B, and C.

Op.	A	B	C
XX	XXXX	XXXX	XXXX

Such a machine requires no accumulator, for A denotes the location of one factor, B denotes the location of the other factor, and C denotes the location at which the result of the operation is to be stored. It should be observed that the word size may be large here unless the memory is small or alphabetic addressing is used so that each address can be expressed with three characters.

Also variable-field-length machines are in existence for which the instructions have a variable number of addresses (ranging from zero to three), depending upon the operation code. For example, the stop code requires no data address, an instruction to add field A to field B and store the result in location B requires two addresses, and so forth. Thus, each instruction uses a minimum of memory space.

Magnetic Tapes

It is apparent that the speeds of computation discussed above would be useless for data-processing purposes if we were not able to move information into and out of the machines at a correspondingly high speed. Thus, the use of magnetic tape as the primary method of input and output is one of the most important characteristics of the large-scale computers.

Magnetic tapes provide a concise, accurate, speedy, and relatively inexpensive method of recording information in a form in which it can be processed by machine. In addition to their use for input and output, magnetic tapes are also used for storage of file information. The magnetic tape used for electronic data processing is similar to the plastic material used for ordinary tape recorders, except that it is usually wider, and it must be manufactured to more rigid quality specifications. Although some machines have used tape up to 3 inches wide, most magnetic tapes are between ½ and 1 inch wide, and a single reel will contain from 1,500 to 3,000 feet of tape.

Information is read from and recorded on magnetic tapes by read-write heads similar to those used with magnetic drums. Although information can be organized for recording on tape in many ways, one of the most popular methods is to record parallel by bit and serial by character. Thus, for the seven-bit character code shown in Figure 10–1, seven read-write heads would be used, and each would record a single bit of the character code in a separate *channel* (or track) on the tape.

A magnetic tape unit is constructed so that a reel may be easily mounted for processing and removed after processing is completed.

The tape unit is designed to transport the tape over the read-write heads between two reels. To make it possible to start the tape in a few milliseconds, the movement of the tape itself is isolated from the motion of the reels by providing some slack tape between the tape reels and the mechanism which pulls the tape over the read-write heads (as shown in Figure 10–9).

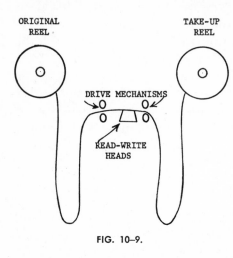

Depending upon the machine, information may be recorded on tape at a density between 100 and 600 bits per inch per channel, and the tape may move at from 50 to about 150 inches per second. Thus, information may be transferred from magnetic tape into memory at a speed between 5,000 and about 90,000 characters per second on tape units that are serial by character, and even faster on tapes which employ more channels in parallel.

FIG. 10–9.

On an ordinary tape recorder, sound is recorded continuously from one end of the tape to the other, and the tape is in continuous motion. In contrast to this, information on the computer tape is recorded in blocks, with a gap between each block so that the tape can come to a stop and start again between blocks as shown in Figure 10–10. The time required to start the tape and get it up to speed for reading each record has an important influence upon the effective speed of reading or writing the tape. For the various machines, this start time ranges between about 3 and 40 milliseconds.

Thus, magnetic tapes are similar to punched cards in the sense that a single *Read* instruction reads an entire block of information into memory, and a single *Write* instruction writes an entire block from memory. In most machines, a tape block has no address while on tape, but each *Read* instruction enters the next block into a specified group of words in the memory of the machine. However, on magnetic tapes, the blocks are usually considerably larger than 80 characters. Also, magnetic tape may be reused, since, when new information is written, the old is erased.

On some machines, a tape block is of fixed length, while on others, the length of a block may be determined by the programmer. Be-

BEFORE REALING BLOCK N.

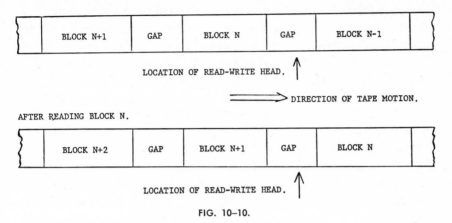

LOCATION OF READ-WRITE HEAD.

⟹ DIRECTION OF TAPE MOTION.

AFTER READING BLOCK N.

LOCATION OF READ-WRITE HEAD.

FIG. 10–10.

cause of the necessity for starting the tape for each block and the amount of tape wasted in interrecord gaps, it is desirable to have long blocks. On the other hand, the memory space required for input and output areas increases as the blocks get longer, so the available memory limits the length of the block that can be used.

However, the length of the record being processed need not coincide with the length of the tape block. In the usual case, several records are grouped together to form a tape block as shown in Figure 10–11. Thus, the difference between the fixed-block-length and the

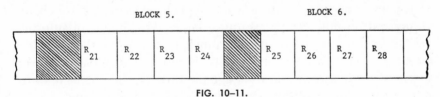

FIG. 10–11.

variable-block-length machines is not as important as it might appear. However, in a fixed-block-length machine, it is necessary to waste some of the room in a block whenever the length of the record does not divide the length of the block. For example, if the block length is 60 words, and a record requires 8 words, only 7 records can go in a block, and 4 words will be wasted.

Magnetic Tape Instructions

Several interesting programming considerations are involved in the use of magnetic tapes for input and output. The machine must be informed which of the possible tape units to read from or to write on. Some method must be devised for determining when the end of a reel of tape has been reached, and provision must be made for rewinding tapes so that they can be removed from the machine. There is the possibility of backspacing to reread a record, so it may be possible to correct certain tape errors through programming instead of merely stopping the machine. Also, it is possible to read a tape backwards as well as forwards on some machines, which is advantageous in certain circumstances.

Since many tape units are attached to a large-scale machine, either separate *Read* and *Write* instructions must be associated with each tape unit, or some other method must be devised for indicating the particular unit to be operated. In addition, the machine must be told where in memory to place the information or where to read it from. Thus, if a two-address machine is used, the first address can designate the number of the tape unit involved, and the second address can give the memory location of the first word of the record. In a single-address machine, the data address of a *Select* instruction may be used to designate the tape unit which is to be activated by the next tape instruction. Thus, to read a block from tape unit 1 into a memory block starting in location 1000, it is necessary to give a pair of instructions: SEL 0001 and RD1 1000.

In using the basic 650, the process of transferring information from the read-in areas to the punch-out area is a cumbersome and time-consuming process. In a magnetic tape machine, in which the input and output records are quite large, the amount of information that must be transferred is much greater, and therefore the problem is more acute. Fortunately, the use of magnetic core memory makes it relatively easy to design circuitry that allows us to move a large amount of information with very few instructions.

For example, in a three-address machine we might have a *Move* instruction in which the first address would give the memory location of the first word of the block to be moved, the second address would give the memory location at which we wish to place the first word of the block, and the third address would indicate the number of words to be moved. Thus, the instruction MVE 0120 1900 0050 would move the 50 words in location 0120 through 0169, into locations 1900 through 1949.

End-of-File Procedures

One of the considerations involved in the use of magnetic tape is that of rewinding the tape when its end has been reached. Unfortunately, this problem cannot be satisfactorily solved by simply allowing the tape to run completely out as we might with a motion picture projector. A method must be devised for detecting the end of the tape and rewinding it through machine programming. This is further complicated by the necessity to detect and correct (when possible) tape reading and writing errors.

Actually, the meaning of *end of file* depends upon whether the tape is being written on or read from. If we are writing on a tape, it is necessary to detect the physical end of the tape so that we do not attempt to write beyond the end. On the other hand, when reading the tape, we wish to know when we have read all of the information that was written on the tape, even if the physical end of the tape has not been reached.

Both of these end-of-file conditions may be handled by a *Branch on End-of-File* (BEF) instruction, which interrogates the end-of-file indicator, and branches if it is on. When writing on tape, the end-of-file indicator is turned on by a signal from the tape unit when the end of the tape is reached. When reading from tape, the end-of-file indicator is turned on when a special end-of-file character is encountered on the tape. Thus, a *Write End-of-File* (WEF) instruction is given after writing on a tape has been concluded. So, when the end of the tape is detected when writing, it is necessary to *Write End-of-File* so that this condition can be detected when the tape is read.

Error Detection

Because the magnetic tape units are mechanical devices which must operate within very stringent tolerances, they are usually the least reliable component of an electronic data-processing system. When information is recorded at a density of several hundred bits per inch on a flexible tape, even a small particle of dust can interfere with the reading or writing of the information. This is not to imply that magnetic tape units do not perform satisfactorily, but it does indicate that built-in checks should be incorporated in their design whenever possible, and that they must be properly maintained and carefully used.

Therefore, in most machines, information is recorded on magnetic tape in some self-checking code, with the most prevalent technique being the use of a redundancy bit as illustrated in Figure 10–1 (p. 222) , in which each valid character is composed of an even number of "one" bits. Thus, when the tape is read, the machine counts the number of bits in each character, and, if this is odd, an error is

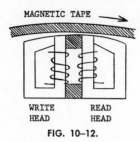

MAGNETIC TAPE

WRITE HEAD   READ HEAD

FIG. 10–12.

indicated by setting an error indicator which may be interrogated by a *Branch on Error* (BER) instruction. In some machines, an additional bit of information is recorded for each channel at the end of a block to make the number of bits in each channel of the block even, thus providing both a vertical and horizontal redundancy check.[7]

Unfortunately, however, when a writing error occurs, it is not detected until the tape is read. Thus, it may be several hours (or even weeks) after processing has been completed before it is discovered

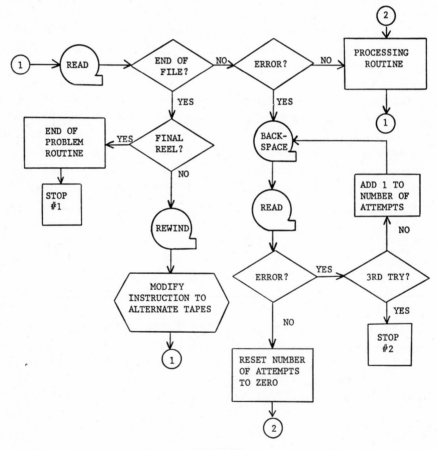

FIG. 10–13.

---

[7] By recording check characters at the end of the blocks for each channel, in addition to the vertical redundancy bits, it is possible to automatically reconstruct the correct information in most error situations.

that the results are unreadable. To detect such errors immediately after they occur, some machines utilize "dual-gap" read-write heads. As shown in Figure 10–12, each character is read and checked for validity a few milliseconds after it is written, so that writing errors are detected at a time when corrective action can most conveniently be taken.

When a single file requires several reels of tape, it is usually desirable to use two tape units for input and two for output for the file. By alternating between two tape units, when a reel is completed, it can be rewound and replaced by a new reel while the machine is processing the reel on the other tape unit, thus overlapping several minutes of tape-handling time for each reel involved. This tape unit switching is accomplished by instruction modification.

A typical end-of-file routine for an input tape is illustrated in the block diagram in Figure 10–13. When a read error occurs, three attempts are made to read the record correctly before stopping the machine. Input tape units are alternated by the end-of-file procedure. Similar routines are required for each of the *Read* or *Write* instructions in the program.

Tape Handling and Control

As was mentioned previously, the high density of recording and rapid motion of the tapes combine to make magnetic tapes the least reliable components of the computer. The performance of tape units does not depend entirely upon the equipment itself, but tape reliability may be significantly influenced by how the tapes are handled and stored by the machine operators. For optimum performance, magnetic tape should be handled very carefully to protect it from damage and from dirt when it is being stored and when the reels are being mounted on the tape units.

Particles of dust on the surface of the tape can cause reading or writing errors by increasing the distance between the tape and the read-write heads. Dropping or squeezing a reel of tape can crimp or nick the edges of the tape and thus affect the alignment of the channels with respect to the read-write heads. Extreme care must be taken when mounting, transporting, and storing magnetic tape reels to assure that the tapes acquire an absolute minimum of dust and wear. This involves intensive training and constant supervision of personnel, spotless housekeeping, and humidity and dust control in the machine room and tape storage areas.

Furthermore, a human cannot read the information on a piece of magnetic tape—a machine must be used to read it. Thus, to the machine operators, one reel of tape looks very much like any other reel, and a typical installation may have several thousand reels of tape involved in its various processing runs. It is, therefore, necessary to establish identification procedures that can insure that the proper tape reels are being used at the correct time. This problem is complicated by the fact that magnetic tape may be used over and over and over, so that a reel of tape that cannot be used today (because the information recorded upon it is still needed) may become available for use next week. If the wrong reel of tape is placed on the machine for input, the processing will be in error. This situation is usually easily detected and corrected. However, if the wrong reel of tape is mounted on the machine for output, the information on that reel is destroyed when the new information is written. For this reason, many tape units are constructed so that a special plastic *file protect ring* must be affixed to a tape reel before the tape unit can record on the tape.

A visible label must be placed on each tape as it is written, showing the job on which the tape is used, the tape unit on which it must be mounted, the date when it was written, the date after which it may be re-used for other purposes, and so forth. Most well-run installations employ a tape librarian, whose full-time job it is to maintain control over the magnetic tapes and see that the proper reels are used at all times.

In addition to the written labels for human use, it is usually desirable to write a magnetic label on each tape so that the machine program can check to see that the proper tapes are mounted on the correct tape unit. This is accomplished by using the first record that is written on the tape as an identification record, containing such information as the tape serial number; the date when the tape was placed in service; the number of times the tape has been passed through the machine; the date on which the present information was written; the date when it may be used for other purposes; and program identification information such as the run number, tape unit address, and reel number.

Instructions can then be incorporated in the starting routines and the end-of-file procedures which will check to see that all of the input tapes are properly mounted and that the output tapes may safely be written upon, as well as placing a current label on the output tapes. These tape labels may also be used for gathering usage statistics which can be analyzed to determine when the tapes are worn to the point where they should be retired from service.

Needless to say, these extra routines complicate the programming and (more importantly) require a considerable amount of memory. In this connection, it should be noted that an extra tape unit may be used to store parts of the program that are executed infrequently. For example, we may store the end-of-file and error-correction routines on such a tape unit and read these routines into the main memory of the machine only when they are needed. If several such routines are written on one reel of tape, bringing the proper one into the memory may involve searching through several records on the tape to find the desired routine. This searching process may seriously delay the programming, so this technique is most useful for storing portions of the program (such as those discussed above) which are seldom used.

Overlapping Operations

One of the most important questions that can be asked when evaluating machines is: How much overlapping can be done? To illustrate the importance of this question, suppose we are concerned with an application involving two input files (A and B) and two output files (C and D). Thus, each processing cycle involves the following steps: *Read* Tape A, *Read* Tape B, process, *Write* Tape C, and *Write* Tape D.

In a machine in which the tapes are unbuffered, only one of these functions can be performed at a time, as shown in Figure 10–14 (in which time is represented by the horizontal axis).

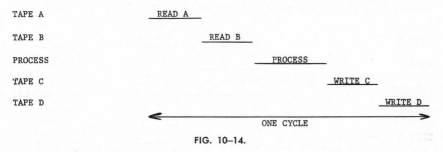

FIG. 10–14.

Machines exist in which it is possible to read and write on tape simultaneously, but not to compute at the same time. In Figure 10–15, let A_N denote the Nth block on Tape A, A_{N+1} denote the $(N + 1)^{st}$ block on Tape A, and similarly for tapes B, C, and D.

Here a complete cycle requires only the time to *Read* A, *Read* B, and process, since *Writing* Tapes C and D is overlapped.

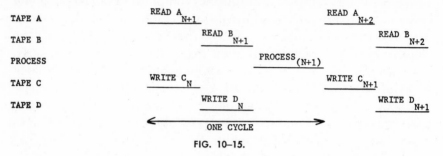

FIG. 10–15.

If our machine had one input and one output buffer, like the 650 has for reading and punching cards, a complete cycle would only require the time to *Read* A and *Read* B (as shown in Figure 10–16).

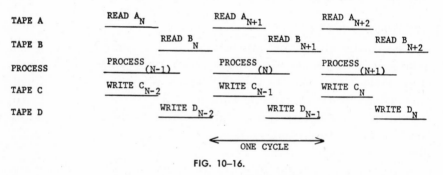

FIG. 10–16.

With *two* input and *two* output buffers available, a complete cycle would only require the time to process, since all reading and writing would be overlapped as shown in Figure 10–17.

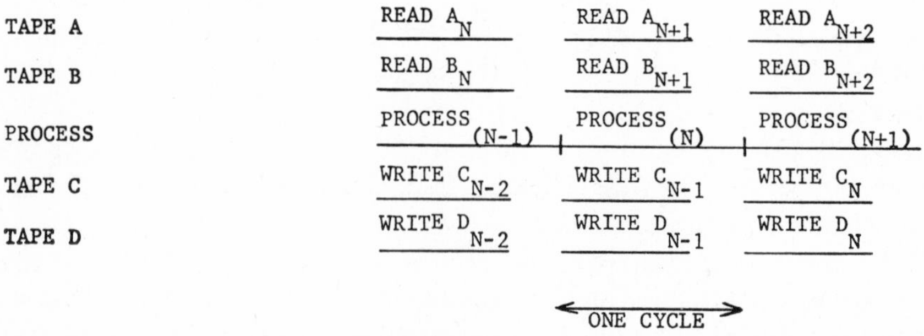

TAPE A   READ A$_N$ READ A$_{N+1}$ READ A$_{N+2}$

TAPE B   READ B$_N$ READ B$_{N+1}$ READ B$_{N+2}$

PROCESS   PROCESS$_{(N-1)}$ PROCESS$_{(N)}$ PROCESS$_{(N+1)}$

TAPE C   WRITE C$_{N-2}$ WRITE C$_{N-1}$ WRITE C$_N$

TAPE D   WRITE D$_{N-2}$ WRITE D$_{N-1}$ WRITE D$_N$

ONE CYCLE

FIG. 10–17.

There are two basic approaches used to buffer magnetic tape input and output. The first approach used was to provide a buffer that holds a complete tape block (see Figure 10–18). This type of buffer operates like the input and output buffers on the 650. A *Tape Read* instruction, for example, operates in two steps: (1) Transfer the contents of the buffer into memory; (2) start the designated tape unit to read a record that will refill the buffer.

The newer method of buffering uses the memory of the machine itself to assemble the record being read, with two single-word buffers and a special address register being used to co-ordinate the tape units with the memory. In this system, the tape is connected to the single-word buffer A. When this buffer is full, it transfers its contents to buffer B so that buffer A can be refilled from the tape. Then the machine processing is interrupted for one memory cycle while the contents of buffer B are stored in the location given by the special address register, one is added to the contents of the register, and the machine continues processing while the next word is read from tape. (See Figure 10–19.)

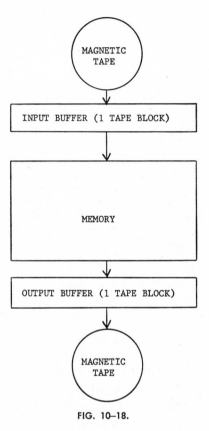

FIG. 10–18.

If the tape reads at 60,000 characters per second, it requires 167 microseconds to read a ten-digit word. For a machine in which a memory cycle requires 6 microseconds, less than 4 per cent of the time necessary to read the tape is devoted to transfers between buffer B and the memory, so the remaining 96 per cent of the time may be devoted to internal processing. Actually, programming is interrupted for the same amount of time under either method, but this interruption occurs at one time in the first method rather than being scattered out as in the second.

On a buffered machine, it is usually necessary to provide two input areas for each file to utilize the buffers effectively. For example, when the second method of buffering is used, alternate input areas must be provided for a single file so that the information in one area can be

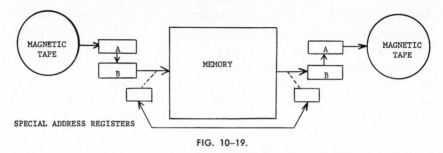

FIG. 10–19.

processed while the other area is being filled from tape. Thus, if there are several files and the tape blocks are large, a considerable amount of memory must be devoted to input and output areas.

Other Input-Output Equipment

Fast mechanical input-output devices have been developed for use with the large-scale computers. For example, punched card readers are available that will read at speeds up to around 600 cards per minute, and punched paper tape can be read photoelectrically at about 1,800 characters per second. Output speeds are somewhat slower, with card punching at 250 cards per minute and paper tape punching at about 300 characters per second.

The most spectacular devices associated with computers are the high-speed mechanical line printers that can print at from 600 to 1,500 lines per minute. Several photographic and xerographic techniques are also used for page-at-a-time printing.

One type of high-speed printing mechanism consists of a group of rapidly rotating print wheels, each of which has on its circumference each of the alphabetic, numeric, and special characters. These print wheels are rigidly joined together to form a cylinder that revolves rapidly on its axis. The paper is fed between this cylinder and a set of hammers, with one hammer for each printing position on a line (and thus for each print wheel). To print a line, each hammer is electronically fired when the desired character on the print wheel is in position to print.

Another method of high-speed line printing utilizes a 5 by 7-inch matrix of wires to form each character (see Figure 10–20). In a wire printer, the proper combination of wires to form the desired character is pushed forward before the head is forced against the ribbon.[8] In this method of printing, carbon copies are frequently more read-

---

[8] Incidentally, the IBM printing key punch uses this method to print along the top of the card as it punches.

able than is the original, for the dots tend to blend together better on the carbons.

FIG. 10–20.

On-Line and Off-Line Operation

In several computers, some or all of the above input-output devices can be attached directly to the computer (with or without buffers, depending upon the machine). When they are operating under direct control of the computer, they are said to be *on-line*.

Since magnetic tapes are considerably faster than these devices, it is frequently desirable to utilize magnetic tape for all (or most) input and output. In this case, it is possible to use a card reader, a magnetic tape unit, and a control unit to form a card-to-tape converter, so that information that has been punched into cards can be converted to magnetic tape in an *off-line* operation without involving the computer itself. Likewise, it is possible to use magnetic tape-to-card equipment and magnetic tape-operated printers for off-line conversion of magnetic tape to other forms of output.

It is possible to prepare magnetic tapes for some machines directly through use of an electric typewriter that also records on magnetic tape. Because of problems involved in detecting and correcting errors, this method has not become popular, and most transaction information is key-punched into cards, verified, and then converted to magnetic tape through use of off-line card-to-tape converters.

Summary

Two major characteristics distinguish the large electronic data-processing machines from computers similar to the basic 650: (1) the use of high-speed magnetic core memory; and (2) the use of magnetic tape for file memory and as the major input and output medium.

Magnetic core memory provides random access in a few microseconds, thus making possible processing speeds of tens of thousands of operations per second (or more). Since it is not possible to arrange instructions in memory to provide faster operation, instructions are stored sequentially in magnetic core memory, so no instruction address is provided in the instruction format. However, some of these machines use two or three data addresses in their instruction formats.

Information is recorded on magnetic tape in blocks, each of which is read or written by a single instruction, as are the cards in the 650. However, magnetic tape input and output is much faster than other methods. Magnetic tapes may also be read backwards, backspaced, and rewound, and several tape units are usually connected to the same machine. It is advantageous for tapes to be buffered so that reading, writing, and processing can take place simultaneously.

Input from punched cards and output through cards and line printers may be accomplished directly on some machines. However, because of the high speed of magnetic tape and the resulting savings in main frame time, card-to-tape, tape-to-card, and tape-printer auxiliary equipment are frequently utilized with large-scale electronic data-processing machines.

EXERCISES

10.1 If the two-out-of-five code is used, how many magnetic cores would be required in the memory of a machine that contains 5,000 ten-digit words (with the sign represented by an additional digit)?

10.2 How many bits would be required in a code to represent the digits zero through nine, 10 special characters, and both the upper and lower case alphabet?

10.3 Using but three positions, design an addressing system for a 3,000-word memory. Hint: Let the high-order digit of the address be both alphabetic and numeric.

10.4 In a three-address machine we have an instruction that adds one number to another and stores the result.

    a) How many single-address instructions would be required to obtain the result of this instruction?

    b) If we wish to obtain and store the sum of 10 numbers, how many three-address instructions would be required?

    c) If we wish to obtain and store the sum of 10 numbers, how many single-address instructions would be required?

10.5 Suppose we have a machine in which information is recorded on magnetic tape at a density of 500 characters per inch, with a $\frac{1}{2}$-inch gap between blocks. The tape moves at 100 inches per second, so information is transferred at a rate of 50,000 characters per second. Five milliseconds are required to start the tape between blocks. We have 30,000 records of 120 characters to record on such tape.

    a) If these records were recorded in 120-character blocks, how many feet of tape would be required, and how much time would be required to read the tape?

b) If these records are recorded in 2,400-character blocks, how many feet of tape would be required, and how much time would be required to read the tape?

10.6 At 1,000 lines per minute, how long would it take to print 30,000 lines on an on-line printer? How much main frame time could be saved by writing this information on magnetic tape (as in part (*a*) of Problem 10.5) and using an off-line printer?

10.7 Some machines have a *Branch on Signal* instruction that branches when either an end-of-file condition or an error condition arises. How would such an instruction affect the block diagram in Figure 10–13? In what sense is this advantageous?

10.8 Since magnetic tape can be read so fast, is buffering of tapes as important as was buffering the cards on the 650? Why?

SUPPLEMENTAL READINGS

An Introduction to Coding the Burroughs 220. Bulletin 5019. Pasadena, Calif.: Burroughs Corp., 1958.

An introduction to computer coding based upon the Burroughs 220.

Honeywell 800 Transistorized Data Processing System—Preliminary Programming Manual. Newton Highlands 61, Mass.: Minneapolis-Honeywell Regulator Co., Datamatic Division: 1959.

A brief description of the major features of the Honeywell 800. Includes a discussion of the binary number system.

IBM 705 Data Processing System—Reference Manual. Form Number A22–6506. New York: International Business Machines Corp., 590 Madison Ave., 1959.

This manual presents the characteristics of several versions of the 705, assuming that the reader is acquainted with electronic data-processing machines.

IBM 7070 Data Processing System—General Information Manual. Form Number D24–7004. New York: International Business Machines Corp., 590 Madison Ave., 1959.

A brief presentation of the characteristics of the IBM 7070 system, with emphasis on the features that are peculiar to this machine.

RCA 501 Electronic Data Processing System—Programmers' Reference Manual. Form Number P501–2. Camden, N.J.: Radio Corp. of America, Electronic Data Processing Division, 1958.

A description of the RCA 501, with major emphasis on the description of its instructions, including timing.

CHAPTER 11 · Processing Magnetic Tape Files

SOME OF the characteristics of large-scale electronic data-processing machines were presented in Chapter 10. However, no attempt was made to directly relate these character- istics to their use in data processing, so this chapter will be devoted to how the large-scale machines, and especially magnetic tapes, are used in data processing.

Magnetic tapes are used for input of transactions, output of re- sults, and for maintaining file information. Since on most ma- chines the tape records are not addressable, a record must be read into the machine memory before it can be identified. To obtain a single record from a magnetic tape file, it is usually necessary to start at the beginning of the tape and examine each record until the ma- chine reaches the record for which it is searching. The above ap- proach is not efficient, for on the average it would be necessary to examine half of the file to obtain an item from the file. Although magnetic tapes operate rapidly, it still takes several minutes to read a reel of tape, and to spend a minute (or even a few million micro- seconds) for each file reference is too time consuming.

Therefore, magnetic tape files are utilized in a way that is quite similar to the use of the punched card collator, as described in Chapter 3. The master file is maintained in sequence upon tape, and it corresponds to the file in the primary feed of the collator. The transaction tape, sorted into the same sequence as the file, corresponds to the cards in the secondary feed of the collator. Thus, the active items from the file may be selected by using the branching ability of the computer to program the functions of the collator. Moreover, through the use of the computers, the active items can be processed and returned to the file concurrently with this process of collation. Thus, instead of merely selecting active items for further processing in other machines (as does the collator), the computer with mag-

246

netic tapes combines the processing function with that of file reference and updating.

Thus, to use magnetic tape files efficiently, the same approach that is basic to the use of punched card equipment is adopted. It is necessary to collect a batch of transactions, sort them into the same sequence as the master file, and proceed through the master file in sequence to process the entire batch. Since magnetic tapes are processed in a sequential manner, they may be called *sequential access* files, as opposed to the *direct access* files in which it is feasible to go directly to any item and process it individually. Direct access files will be discussed in Chapter 12.

For technical reasons, in most machines it is impossible to read a record from a magnetic tape, alter it, and write it back on the magnetic tape to replace the old record.[1] Even if it were possible to perform this operation, it might not be desirable because the original file information is destroyed in this process, so it is difficult to go back and reconstruct a correct record when the machine malfunctions or errors are made.

When the transactions affect the contents of the file, the master file is usually read and rewritten on a new tape, with those records that must be altered being changed and the inactive records merely rewritten without change. Then the updated master file is used as input during the next processing cycle. This basic approach is illustrated in Figure 11–1.

It should be noted that the approach of rewriting the entire file

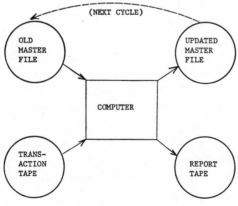

FIG. 11–1.

---

[1] On some machines, notably the Burroughs Datatron 220, it is possible to perform this type of operation.

each time it is processed makes accuracy of tape writing an important consideration, for there is the possibility of creating errors in records that are not even processed. Also, if the machine is buffered, or if it can read and write tapes simultaneously, it takes no extra time to rewrite the file. But if the machine cannot overlap operations, the approach of rewriting the entire file may be so uneconomical that more complex techniques must be devised for efficient processing with unbuffered machines.

Sorting Magnetic Tape

As has been discussed previously, magnetic tape machines usually process transactions against a file that is in sequence, and the transactions must be placed in that same sequence to process efficiently. Thus, it is necessary to be able to sort information on magnetic tapes. However, a magnetic tape is a continuous ribbon, so the individual records cannot be physically shuffled as can punched cards. Fortunately, it is possible to use the computer itself to rearrange the information on magnetic tapes and thereby accomplish the same result obtained with a punched card sorter.

The most common method of sorting magnetic tapes involves a process of merging together the small sequences on the original tape to form longer sequences, repeating the merging process with these sequences to form longer sequences, and so on, until a single sequence is built up. At least four tape units are used for this process—a minimum of two for input and two for output.

To illustrate the process, suppose we have a magnetic tape containing records identified by the three-digit numbers shown in Figure 11–2. It should be emphasized that we are concerned not only with these numbers, but also with the records which they identify. We wish to sort the records so that they are in sequence according to these identifying numbers (as the sorting key).

In Figure 11–2, it is readily apparent that the first four numbers are already in sequence, that the next five form a sequence, that the next three form a sequence, and that the last three form a sequence. The end of a sequence is indicated by a step-down condition—a number followed by a smaller one.

021
142
343
565
007
380
786
960
965
253
275
613
849
376
477
814

FIG. 11–2. To merge these sequences together to form longer sequences, we first separate this original tape into two tapes, so that they can be merged. If we place the original tape on unit A, on the

first pass we will produce Tapes C and D, as shown in Figure 11–3. In this procedure, we write records on Tape C until the end of the first sequence is reached, then we write on Tape D until the end of the next sequence, then on C till the end of the next sequence, then

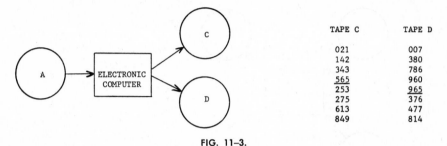

TAPE C	TAPE D
021	007
142	380
343	786
565	960
253	965
275	376
613	477
849	814

FIG. 11–3.

on D till the end of the next sequence, and so on, switching output tapes at the end of each sequence.

At the conclusion of this pass, we may remove the input tape from Tape Unit A and replace it with another reel of tape, thus preserving the information in its original sequence. The next pass requires a fourth tape unit, and Tapes C and D become the input, and A and B are the output, as shown in Figure 11–4. As we merge Tapes C and D together, we write on Tape A until the end of the first output sequence, then we write the next sequences on B, then switch back to A, and so on.

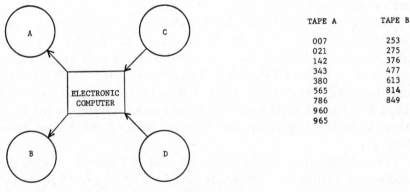

TAPE A	TAPE B
007	253
021	275
142	376
343	477
380	613
565	814
786	849
960	
965	

FIG. 11–4.

On the next pass, Tape Units A and B become the input and C and D the output. However, as shown in Figure 11–5, only one sequence is produced, so we never switch to Tape D, and the sorting process is completed.

The foregoing process is accomplished by a series of comparisons between the record just read from the first input tape, the record read from the second input tape, and the last record which has been written. Records are thus written in ascending sequence on one out-

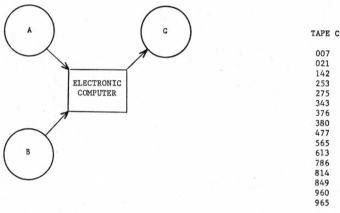

	TAPE C
	007
	021
	142
	253
	275
	343
	376
	380
	477
	565
	613
	786
	814
	849
	960
	965

FIG. 11–5.

put tape until both input records are smaller than the last record that was written, when a new sequence is started on the other output tape. The block diagram in Figure 11–6 illustrates the basic logic of a single sorting pass. In this diagram, A represents the sorting key of the last record read from Tape A, B represents the sorting key of the last record read from Tape B, and L represents the key of the last output record.[2]

Although it only applies directly to passes in which there are two input tapes, with a small change in interpretation, the block diagram of Figure 11–6 will also serve for the first pass. If we substitute the words "read from Tape A into Input Area A" for "read Tape A," and the words "read from Tape A into Input Area B" for "read Tape B," then A represents the identification of the record from Area A, and B represents the identification of the record from Area B.

Let us follow through the block diagram of Figure 11–6 with the example of Figure 11–2 to obtain the result of Figure 11–3. At the start, we read 021 into Area A and 142 into Area B. The number 021 is less than 142, so we ask if 021 is greater than the last record written. Since we have written no previous records, the answer is yes, so we go to ③ and write 021 on Tape C, read 343 into Area A,

---

[2] The notation "$A \geq B$?" is read: Is A greater than or equal to B?

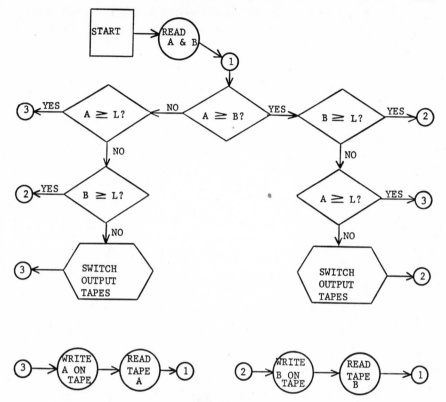

FIG. 11–6.

and go to ①. Now 343 is greater than 142, so we ask if 142 is greater than the last record written. Since 142 is greater than 021, we go to ② and write 142 on Tape C, read 565 into Area B, and go to ①. At this point $A = 343$, $B = 565$, and $L = 142$. Thus, $A \geqq B$? is answered no, but 343 is greater than 142, so we write 343 on Tape C and read 007 into Area A. Now $A = 007$, $B = 565$, and $L = 343$, so again we take the left path on the block diagram. But A is not greater than L, so we ask if B is greater than L. The answer is yes, so we go to ② and write 565 on Tape C, read 380 into Area B, and return to ①.

At this stage $A = 007$, $B = 380$, and $L = 565$. Thus, A is not greater than B, A is not greater than L, and B is not greater than L, so we switch from Tape C to Tape D and go to ③. Thus, we write 007 on Tape D, read 786 into Area A and return to ①. This may be continued with the remainder of the input records.

By a similar process, it is easy to verify that the block diagram of Figure 11–6 produces the result shown in Figure 11–4 from those shown in Figure 11–3, assuming that we always call the input Tapes A and B and the output Tapes C and D. Likewise, we can verify that the results of Figure 11–5 are produced from the results of Figure 11–4.

In the above procedure, the total number of sequences on the output tapes is cut in half on each pass after the first. Working backwards from the last pass (which has but one sequence), we see in Figure 11–7 that the preceding pass had two sequences, the one be-

	Number of Sequences	N = Number of Passes to Complete the Sort	2^N
At the end of the last pass	1		
At the beginning of the last pass	2	1	2
At the beginning of the next-to-last pass	4	2	4
At the beginning of the 3rd-from-last pass	8	3	8
At the beginning of the 4th-from-last pass	16	4	16
At the beginning of the 5th-from-last pass	32	5	32
At the beginning of the 6th-from-last pass	64	6	64

FIG. 11–7.

fore that had four sequences, the one before that had eight sequences, the one before that had sixteen sequences, and so forth. Thus, at the start of a process requiring N passes (after the first), there were a maximum of 2^N sequences.[3]

If we know the number of sequences on the two tapes at the end of the first pass (denoted by K), then we can determine the number of additional passes (denoted by N) that will be required to complete the sort by choosing N as the smallest whole number that will satisfy the relationship $2^N \geqq K$.[4]

For example, if there are 1,500 sequences after the first pass, 11 more passes will be required, because $2^{11} = 2,048$ (which is greater than 1,500), while $2^{10} = 1,024$ (which is less than 1,500). The diffi-

---

[3] 2^N is read "2 to the Nth power," and means the product of N twos. Thus, $2^1 = 2$, $2^2 = 4$, $2^3 = 8$, $2^4 = 16$, and so on.

[4] As will be seen in Exercise 11.1 at the end of this chapter, in addition to splitting the original tape into two, the first pass may reduce the total number of sequences on the tapes. Thus, K may not be the number of sequences on the original tape.

culty involved in this process of estimating the number of passes required to sort a tape is that we usually do not know the number of sequences on a tape at the start—we only know the number of records. Thus, we are forced to estimate the number of sequences, using whatever information we have. It is helpful to know that if the file is already in order, there is but one sequence, while if the file is originally in reverse sequence, it is easily verified that the first pass produces sequences of length two.

Actually, however, the accuracy of the estimate of the number of sequences is usually not as crucial as one might suppose. For example, in the foregoing illustration any estimate between 1,025 and 2,048 would still indicate 11 passes after the first. Furthermore, the machine will take the necessary number of passes—our estimates are only attempts to predict the number of passes required, and do not influence the operation of the machine.

This process is called a two-tape merge. It is possible to use three input tapes and three output tapes and obtain a three-way merge, and corresponding higher-order merges may be devised. If we let T represent the number of input tapes used, the corresponding formula obtained is:

$$T^N \geqq K.$$

A Hypothetical Machine

To discuss the time required for sorting and the costs of this process, some of the characteristics of the particular machine under consideration must be specified. Rather than an actual machine, a hypothetical machine that includes characteristics typical of many available large-scale machines will be considered as an example.

It will be assumed that this machine has 4,000 10-character alphanumeric words in its magnetic core memory. It will execute an average of 10,000 single-address instructions per second. It will include 10 magnetic tape units that record at a density of 500 characters per inch and read at 50,000 characters per second with a start-stop time of 5 milliseconds (one-half inch gap) and variable block length. The machine includes one set of input-output buffers that move information into and out of the machine one word at a time. The magnetic tape units can read and write in the forward direction only, and it requires one minute to rewind a tape. Also a card reader is attached to the main frame that reads a maximum of 400 cards per minute.

In addition, the installation includes a card-to-tape converter that converts cards to tape at 400 cards per minute, producing grouped records with 100 characters per record and 10 records per tape block. The tape printer prints 600 120-character lines per minute from tape blocks 1,200 characters long, each containing ten lines. The tape-to-card converter produces 200 cards per minute from tape blocks 1,000 characters long with 10 cards per block.

On a one-shift basis, the main frame, 10 tape units, and the card reader rent for a total of $21,500 per month. The card-to-tape converter rents for $3,000, the tape printer rents for $3,500, and the tape-to-card converter rents for $2,000. Thus, the total installation rents for $30,000 per month on a single-shift basis. Assuming that an extra shift rental is 50 per cent of the single-shift rate, on a two-shift basis, the above equipment would rent for $45,000 per month.

Assuming two-shift utilization, we may compute an hourly rate for each of the above machines. There are about 176 hours per month in a single shift. Thus, the hourly cost of the main frame and associated equipment is $32,250 divided by 352, which equals about $92 per hour, assuming 100 per cent utilization. Because of downtime, machine errors, operator errors, etc., we can only expect about 80 per cent utilization, so $115 per hour is a reasonable estimate of the minimum machine cost. Likewise, we may estimate the cost of the card-to-tape converter to be $16 per hour, the tape printer to be $18 per hour, and the tape-to-card converter to be about $17 per hour. None of these costs include operators or overhead.

Costs and Time for Sorting

To estimate the total time for a given sort, we need to know both the number of passes required and the amount of time for each pass. For the low-order merges, we can assume that the processing time is overlapped by the tape time (for reasonable record sizes) so that the total time per pass is determined by the number of blocks in the file.

Suppose we have 10,000 80-character records to be sorted, and that they are recorded on tape with 40 records per tape block. Thus, we have 250 tape blocks of 3,200 characters per block. Since the tape reads at 50,000 characters per second, each block requires 64 milliseconds to read plus 5 milliseconds to start, for a total of 69 milliseconds per block. Thus, the time for a pass would be .069 times 250, which equals $17\frac{1}{4}$ seconds. Rewind time will be the same as the write time until we reach one minute, but since we are writing on two tapes, only 9 seconds is required for each, and all rewinding can be done at the same time. Thus, the total time for a pass is approximately 26 seconds (except for the last pass, where a full $17\frac{1}{4}$ seconds of rewind must be allowed).

If we assume that we have 3,000 sequences at the end of the first pass, then 12 additional passes will be required, since:

$$2^{12} = 4,096 > 3,000 > 2^{11} = 2,048$$

Therefore, 13 passes are required, for a total of 346 seconds (including 8 extra seconds of rewind time on the last pass). About 2 minutes will be required to mount and dismount the tapes, so the sort will require about $7\frac{3}{4}$ minutes.

If the tapes could be read backwards, as they can on several machines, the total time per pass can be reduced to $17\frac{1}{4}$ seconds by merging backwards and thus eliminating rewind time (except on the last pass). Thus, the total time would be reduced to about 6 minutes.

It should be noted that the two-way merge is probably the least efficient method of sorting on magnetic tape. For example, a three-way merge would reduce the number of passes after the first to eight, since:

$$3^8 = 6,561 > 3,000 > 3^7 = 2,187$$

Taking into account the resulting slight reduction in tape rewind time, and assuming that we cannot read backwards, with a three-way merge the sorting time would be reduced to about $5\frac{2}{3}$ minutes.

Incidentally, in the three-way merge each input tape would require two input areas, and two output areas would be needed also, for a total of eight areas of 320 words each. Thus, 2,560 words of memory would be used for input-output areas. This illustrates the pressure that is placed upon memory space by input-output areas, and suggests one reason why large memories are desirable on large-scale computers.

Another approach that may reduce sorting time is that of sorting several records into sequence in the memory of the machine during the first pass. Thus, we might internally sort each tape block into sequence, so that at the end of the first pass we would have only 250 sequences. In this case, six passes after the first would then be required, since:

$$3^6 = 729 > 250 > 3^5 = 243$$

The internal sort of the block of 40 records could be programmed as a two-way merge, using memory areas instead of tapes.

It would probably take at least 150 milliseconds for each block, so the first pass would require about 37.5 seconds plus rewind time. Therefore, the total time required would be about $5\frac{1}{4}$ minutes, which is not a startling improvement over the plain three-way merge. However, on machines in which the tapes are slower relative to the internal programming, and on applications where the records are of larger size, an internal sort on the first pass produces a significant improvement.[5]

It should be noted that we assumed that setup would require two minutes, or 38 per cent of the total time involved in this sort. Thus, the best way to increase efficiency would be to reduce this setup time. By providing extra tape units and utilizing automatic executive routines to load and start a new program (using other tape units) immediately when the old one is completed, it is possible to use the machine almost continuously while the reels are being mounted and removed. Many efficiently run data-processing organizations utilize such techniques to improve efficiency.

At $115 per hour, the main frame of our hypothetical machine costs about $2 per minute, without overhead or operators. Thus, the sort just discussed, which requires a minimum of a little more than 5 minutes, would cost about $10.

If this same file were represented by 10,000 cards, and we were sorting on a 6-digit numeric key, 6 passes would be required. Using a 1,000-card-per-minute sorter, and assuming an operating efficiency of 60 per cent, it would require 60,000 card passes, or about 100 minutes to sort the file. However, the punched card sorter rents for less than $1.00 per hour, and an operator can be obtained for about $2.25 per hour, so the total cost of sorting the punched card file would be about $5.40.

Since the time for comparisons is small compared to the tape time, the time required for sorting magnetic tapes is essentially independent of the length of the sorting key. But the time necessary to sort punched cards depends upon the number of card passes required, which depends upon the number of columns involved in the sorting key, and whether they are alphabetic or numeric. If our sorting key were 11 digits or 6 alphabetic characters, the costs of tape sorting

---

[5] It should be obvious at this point that there are many variations in method that may be used to sort magnetic tapes. Likewise, there are a number of techniques for internal sorting. The best method for any given situation will depend upon the characteristics of both the equipment and of the file that is to be sorted.

and card sorting would be about the same, and tape sorting would be less expensive than card sorting for larger fields.

However, it should be emphasized that the total cost of all the applications must be considered—not just the costs of sorting—when comparing the economics of a punched card system with those of a magnetic tape electronic data-processing system. Furthermore, when desirable, it is frequently possible to sort transaction cards on a punched card sorter before converting the resulting sorted file to magnetic tape for processing through the computer. It should also be noted that it is frequently possible to utilize the memory of the computer to eliminate or reduce the necessity for sorting, and thus reduce the cost and complexity of the procedures involved.

It has been repeatedly pointed out by data-processing experts that a special-purpose machine (requiring only limited capabilities as compared with a computer) could be designed to take over the tape sorting burden from the expensive computer main frame, as well as to perform the functions of extraction from a file and merging. The sort-collate device for the Remington Rand File Computer and the IBM 1401 tape system both show promise for off-line tape sorting. However, these machines are restricted to a low-order merge with small records; thus, they cannot employ the powerful techniques that can be used with the large computers, so they show no spectacular economic advantage. Also, as will be discussed later,[6] some machines are able to perform such functions as sorting simultaneously with other work, and the sorting only delays the other work by the amount of internal processing time involved in the sort. Since internal processing time may be substantially less than the tape time involved, the cost of the sorting is reduced.

Generalized Sort Routines

Almost every magnetic tape to be sorted requires a slightly different program. This is caused by differences in the record size, the number of records per block, and in the location of the sorting key (or keys) within the record. However, it is not usually necessary to write a new sorting program for each different tape that is to be sorted—a "generalized sort routine" may be devised (and is usually available from the machine manufacturer or from another machine user) which utilizes a particular sorting technique and is capable of modi-

---

[6] See the section in this chapter on multiprogramming.

fying itself to fit various formats of files. The record size, the number of records per block, and the location within each record of the sorting key (or keys), may be entered into the machine by means of a punched card or the first record on the tape. The first phase of the generalized sort program then utilizes this information to modify the sorting routine itself to produce (for example) a three-way merge which will apply to the particular tape under consideration. This process requires but a few seconds to be completed, and then the machine proceeds to use the modified program to sort the file.

Inventory Control, Accounts Receivable, and Billing Application

To illustrate how a tape data-processing machine may be used, let us consider a hypothetical illustration combining into one procedure elements of invoicing, billing, accounts receivable, and inventory control. Let us assume that we carry about 50,000 different items in inventory, that we receive an average of 2,000 orders each day with an average of 6 items on each order, that there is an average of 2,000 receipts and adjustments per day, and that these 14,000 line items each day involve a considerable amount of duplication—there is an average of only 8,000 different items active each day.

As each order arrives, we would like to check it against the inventory record to see whether or not we can ship the items requested, and, if not, backorder them for later shipment. Then we write a priced and extended invoice which shows warehouse location so that the stock can be conveniently pulled from a copy of the invoice. Before writing the invoice, however, we update the accounts receivable record and check to see that the customer's credit limitations have not been exceeded. Periodically, the accounts receivable file can be analyzed for collection follow-up.

Although the processing described above requires a considerable amount of record keeping and clerical effort, the area of inventory control provides the major motivation for the use of an electronic computer in this situation. By maintaining accurate and adequate usage information, along with on-hand and on-order balances, it is possible to reflect the effect of each transaction upon the inventory status and to signal immediately when it is desirable to procure, expedite, or dispose of surplus. Furthermore, when some action should be taken, adequate information concerning the status of the item, the various vendors, and the probable usage can be automatically provided to the person in charge of controlling the inventory for that particular item. This allows the people involved to concentrate on the problems associated with managing the inventory rather than spending their time looking up records and checking balances to determine which items need their attention. By reducing outages and preventing the accumulation of excessive quantities of obsolete items, this "management by exception" technique should provide significant increases in the return on the money invested in inventory.

It should be apparent, however, that the effectiveness of inventory control will depend upon the decision rules that are devised for setting reorder levels, expedite levels, and for deciding when to dispose of surplus. If we do not know enough about our inventory problems to devise effective rules, we cannot expect the computer to do a satisfactory job of inventory control, for the computer is utterly dependent upon the rules that we devise and the program that we write. At least one organization that tried this approach has found to their dismay that they did not know enough about their inventory control problems to make it successful.

Procedure

As the customer orders are received, a card (containing the customer number, item number, and quantity ordered) is punched for each item on each order. These cards are combined with similar cards for those items that are received into the warehouse and for those items that are being ordered from the vendors. The resulting 14,000 cards are sorted into item-number sequence and converted to magnetic tape for processing against the master inventory file (which is also in item-number sequence) in Run No. 1, as shown in Figure 11–8.

The master inventory file contains such information as item number, description, unit price, unit cost, total orders and backorders for each of the past six months, on-hand balance, on-order balance, backorder balance, reorder level, expedite level, disposal level, warehouse locations, a maximum of three vendors, an indication of the person in charge of inventory control for this item, and codes indicating the inventory control rules to be applied to this item. We will assume that each master inventory record requires 30 words, and that these are grouped six records to each tape block.

As discussed previously, this machine cannot selectively alter records within a tape file, so it is necessary to read and rewrite the entire master inventory file to change the 8,000 active records among the total of 50,000 inventory records in the file. Since the machine

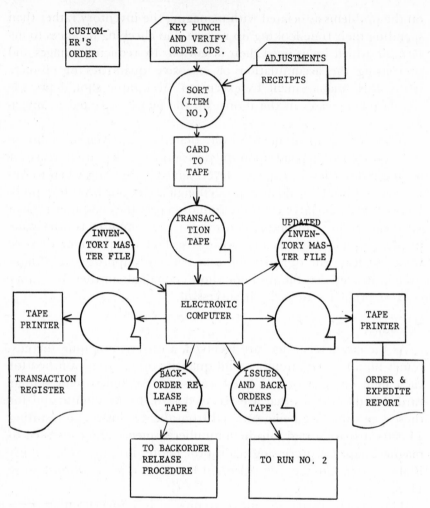

FIG. 11–8.

can read and write at the same time, no additional time is required, and an important safeguard against machine malfunctioning is obtained because the input information is not destroyed. If the output is found to be in error (or unreadable), it can be reconstructed by reprocessing the old input tape.

To have something to refer to when questions arise, and to provide an audit trail, a transaction register is produced that lists each inventory activity, showing the item number, type of transaction, old balance, transaction amount, and resulting new balance, as well as the date of the last transaction, so that the activities on an item may be traced by hand if there is any question concerning that item.

Each active item is examined to determine whether it should be reordered, expedited, or disposed of. For each condition that requires any of these actions, a report is prepared that contains most of the information in a master inventory record, so that the proper person has the information necessary to take the indicated action.

The receipt of some items may allow backorders to be released, and a tape indicating the items and quantities involved is provided to go into a backorder release procedure.

The issues and backorders tape is actually an invoice tape—it contains (for each item that has been ordered) all of the information necessary to write a line on the proper invoice. However, this tape is in item-number sequence, so that the items for a given invoice are scattered more or less at random on this tape. This tape then becomes the input to Run No. 2, which sorts it to customer-number sequence so that the body information may be combined with heading information to write an invoice.

In Run No. 3, this tape is combined with a customer master tape, maintained in customer-number sequence, which contains name and address, standard shipping instructions, and accounts receivable information. The output from Run No. 3, shown in Figure 11–9, includes a tape from which invoices may be printed, an updated customer master tape, a transaction register tape, and an exception tape, which notes such situations as missing customer records or the exceeding of allowable credit.

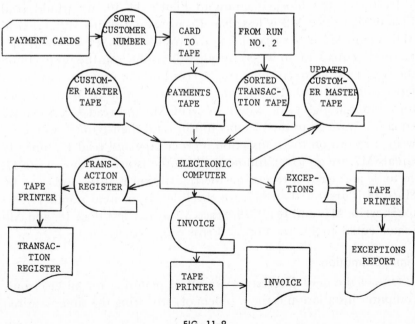

FIG. 11–9.

Let us consider Run No. 1 in greater detail. The general block diagram shown in Figure 11–10 represents an acceptable over-all logic for this run, assuming that we understand that the symbols referring to tape reading really mean "read another block if we have exhausted all of the records from the previous block." If the block is not exhausted, a read-tape symbol simply means to process the next record of the tape block. The write-tape blocks should be similarly interpreted. In Figure 11–10, the symbol T represents the item number of the record being processed from the transaction tape, and the symbol M represents the item number of the record being processed from the inventory master tape.

The block diagram of Figure 11–10 should be tested through the use of simple synthetic data to demonstrate that each logical possibility is handled properly. Consider the following sequence of transactions and master inventory records (I represents an issue transaction, R represents a receipts transaction, and M represents a master inventory record) :

Transaction	Master
I5	M2
R7	M4
I7	M5
I8	M7
	M9
	M11

Following the block diagram in Figure 11–10, we would read I5 and M2. Since M2 is less than I5, we would write M2 and read M4. Again, M4 is less than I5, so we would write M4 and read M5. Here M5 equals I5, so we go through the issues routine, write I5 on the issue tape, go to ③ and write a record on the transaction register tape. Then we read R7, and since R7 is not equal to M5, we check for reorder and go to ①, where we write M5 and read M7. Since R7 equals M7, we go to the receipts routine and thence to ③, where we write a record on the transaction register tape and read I7. Since I7 equals M7, we go to ②, follow through the issues routine, write I7, go to ③ and write a record on the transaction register and read I8. Since I8 is greater than M7, we check levels on item number 7, go to ①, write M7, and read M9. Since M9 is not less than I8, and M9 is not equal to I8, we stop at Error Stop No. 1.

Time Estimation

One of the most interesting aspects of planning for an electronic computer installation is the problem of estimating the time required

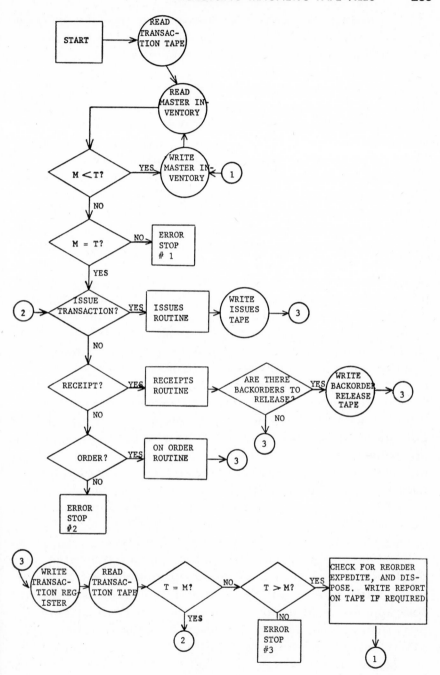

FIG. 11–10.

for each processing run. This is an extremely important problem when deciding whether or not to install such a machine, or when deciding whether or not to place a given application on the electronic computer.

Historically speaking, there are numerous instances when the time estimates upon which the decision to procure a machine was based turned out to be low by a factor of several hundred per cent. Perhaps the classic example of this difficulty occurred at one of the pioneer installations of a large-scale computer, where it was originally estimated that the payroll for 12,000 employees could be processed in 2 hours per week. As the problem was originally programmed, it would have required around 20 hours per week to process this payroll. After three years of reprogramming, it was possible to reduce the processing time to approximately 8 hours per week for some 7,000 employees.

It is not an easy job to take a *completed* program (of some complexity) and estimate the amount of time that will be required to process a given volume of transactions. However, this is not the primary source of our difficulty. The difficulty arises because we usually know so little about the problem at the time that we require the estimates. We must estimate on the basis of a hypothetical procedure involving a certain number of machine runs. Usually, we ignore at first a large number of seemingly trivial exceptions that can occur, and when we get to the point of programming we may find that the program actually requires several times as many steps as we had originally estimated.[7] The point is that accurate time estimates require a thorough understanding of the problems involved, combined with excellent estimates of the amount of memory that will be required for the various usages and the number of program steps that will be involved.

Even after the program has been written, it is not a trivial job to estimate the amount of time that will be required. To illustrate some of the difficulties involved, let us attempt to estimate the time required for Run No. 1 of the previous illustration, assuming that our basic approach is satisfactory and that we know the number of program steps in each block of the block diagram of Figure 11–10.

First, let us consider the tape time involved. The master file consists of 50,000 30-word records, grouped 6 records per tape block.

---

[7] See Chapter 8 for a further discussion of this problem.

Thus, we have 8,334 blocks of 180 words each in our inventory master tape. Each tape block requires 3.6 inches plus a ½-inch gap, for a total of 4.1 inches per block. Thus, we require about 2,847 feet of tape, or a little more than one full reel. At 50,000 characters per second, each block will require 36 milliseconds to read, and adding 5 milliseconds start time, we obtain a total of 41 milliseconds per block. Thus, our inventory master file will require about 342 seconds to read and rewrite.

After conversion to tape, the 14,000 cards produce 1,400 tape blocks of 1,000 characters each, and we will assume that the issues and backorders tape is of a similar form, but contains only 1,200 blocks. The transaction register tape will be composed of 1,400 blocks of 1,200 characters each, and its writing can be overlapped with the reading of the transaction tape. Thus, we require 30 seconds to write the issues and backorders tape and 41 seconds to write the transaction register tape. The amount of time for the backorder release tape and the order and expedite report tape is quite difficult to estimate, for we do not know how many backorders will occur a day, or how many order and expedite reports will be written per day, for they depend upon the effectiveness of our inventory control methods. If we estimate 1,000 four-line order and expedite reports per day, and 500 backorders to release per day, then about 13 seconds will suffice for these tape outputs. Total tape time will therefore be estimated as $342 + 30 + 41 + 13 = 426$ seconds, excluding rewind time.

Referring to Figure 11–10, let us assume that the issues routine averages 300 executed instructions, the receipts routine averages 200 executed instructions, the on-order routine averages 100 executed instructions, and the checking for reorder level block averages 275 executed instructions. Also assume that each master record requires 20 instructions to move it into the processing area and to determine whether or not it is active. Thus, a tape block that has a single issue activity requires $6 \times 20 + 300 + 275 = 695$ executed instructions, which require 69.5 milliseconds (at 10,000 operations per second). Of the 41 milliseconds required to read a block, about 38 will be available for computations, leaving 31.5 milliseconds of additional computation time required. It is easy to verify that two issues activities on a single record in a tape block would require about $6(20) + 2(300) + 275 = 995$ instructions, or 99.5 milliseconds. Thus, 61.5 milliseconds of additional computation would be required. On the other hand, if two different records were active in the same tape block, then about $6(20) + 2(300) + 2(275) = 1,270$ instructions would be executed, and 89 milliseconds of computation would not be overlapped.

From the foregoing discussion it is obvious that we must face questions such as: How many tape blocks will have one issues activity? How many tape blocks will have one receipt activity? How many tape blocks will have two different items active? How many tape blocks will have three different items active? There are many more such questions, none of which we can easily answer, even to give an average figure.

We can easily get an upper limit on the total time by assuming that our 14,000 activities on 8,000 items occur in 1,334 blocks (the minimum number possible), thus providing a minimum of .038 $\times$ (1,334) = 50.7 seconds of overlapped computing time. Assuming that there are 1,000 receipts and 1,000 orders, the total number of executed instructions would be about $(1,334)(120) + 8,000$ $(275) + 12,000(300) + 1,000(100) + 1,000(200) = 6,260,080$, requiring 626 seconds. Neglecting overlapping from other tapes, our unoverlapped computing time would be about 575 seconds.

On the other hand, if we assume a maximum of overlapping (only one activity per tape block), we would have .038 (8,000) = 304 seconds of overlapped computing time, but the first term in the expression for the total number of instructions executed would be (8,000) 120, adding 80 seconds to the total, leaving 402 seconds. Assuming 250 seconds of overlapping, we would have 456 seconds extra computing time, 426 seconds of tape time, 60 seconds rewind time, 120 seconds setup time, or a total of 1,062 seconds (17.7 minutes) for Run No. 1.

The above is obviously not intended to provide an accurate estimate of the time required for Run No. 1. It may not even provide an understandable illustration of how such estimates can be obtained. But it should provide an illustration of the difficulties involved in obtaining such time estimates.

Electronic Data Processing in Life Insurance Companies

A life insurance company does not produce a product in the ordinary sense of the word—the main "production" in the life insurance "factory" (home office) is paper work. Thousands of clerks may be employed in the process of maintaining the necessary information and records associated with the hundreds of thousands (or even millions) of life insurance policies in force with the company.

Acutely aware that their major home office costs are associated with paper work, the life insurance companies were among the first nongovernmental organizations to investigate the use of electronic data-processing equipment. Metropolitan, Prudential, John Hancock, Pacific Mutual, and Franklin Life Insurance companies all installed large-scale electronic data-processing systems before 1957.

Most of the processing involved in home office operations is concerned with the maintenance and processing of files of information concerning the various aspects of the individual policies. Before the introduction of the computer, it was necessary to maintain between 10 and 20 separate files of policy information for punched card and manual processing.[8] Punched card files might include the name and address file, the billing file, the policy loan file, the dividend file, the valuation file, and the commission file. Manually processed files might include the application file, the alphabetic index file, the policy register file, the premium history file, the dividend file, and the loan history file.

Under the multiple file system, information concerning any given policy was spread out in many files. This multiplicity of files was necessary because of the limited size of the punched card, and because of the physical difficulties associated with reference by large numbers of people to a single file. For the information to be conveniently available to the people using it, a separate file was provided for each different use to which the information was to be put. The existence of these many files containing overlapping information required a considerable amount of duplication of effort, and led to confusion when it was necessary to make changes or to answer inquiries concerning a given policy. Perhaps the major objective in using electronic data-processing equipment is that of consolidating these files for processing and reference purposes.

The ability of the computer to handle long and complex programs involving large numbers of decisions, combined with the large record length available on magnetic tape, makes it possible to consolidate these many files into one master file containing information such as: policy number, amount of insurance, date of issue, age at issue, premium anniversary date, dividend option, rating, basic dividend rate, gross premium, net single premium, name of insured, address of insured, loan principal, loan interest, rate of loan interest, com-

---

[8] Much of the information contained herein concerning insurance files was obtained from notes on a talk given by R. M. Roehm at Endicott, New York, on July 15, 1955, on the subject "Application of the Type 650 with Tapes to Ordinary Life Insurance."

mission, commission-split per cent and agent number for two or more agents, office, and so forth. The length of this record ranges from around 240 to 500 characters, depending upon the company involved.

From the machine standpoint, three basically different types of operations are involved. The first of these is file maintenance—the process of keeping the master record up to date with respect to changes that can occur affecting the policy (such as changes in name or address of the insured, changes in the method of premium payment, instituting a loan on the policy, cancellation of the policy, changing a beneficiary, or starting a new policy). Almost all magnetic tape data processing involves a surprisingly large amount of file maintenance—this is the hidden, nonproductive aspect of data processing which may turn out to be more time consuming than the productive processing.

The second type of processing arises primarily as a function of time or of payment associated with the policy. Bills must be sent, commissions and dividends must be calculated, payments must be accounted for, loan payments must be billed and accounted for, and accounting and statistical information must be gathered.

The third basic type of operation is the process of answering inquiries concerning the status of the various policies. Although the volume of inquiries is not significant as compared with the other two types of operations, the basic procedural approach is usually determined by the company policy with respect to handling inquiries. Most of the file maintenance and processing operations could be accomplished on the basis of a monthly cycle. When it is realized that hundreds of thousands or even millions of records may be involved in the master file, it can be seen that it is desirable to pass this file through the machine as seldom as possible. However, inquiries concerning status must be handled with reasonable promptness. Several basic approaches have been taken which represent compromises between the problem of file reference and the economics of processing.[9] A few of these are outlined below:

1. Back up the magnetic tape file with visible records in the home office which may be used for answering inquiries. In this case, the processing cycle can be weekly or monthly.
2. Decentralize the handling of inquiries to the field (usually district

---

[9] See *Electronic Data Processing System—Ordinary Life Insurance* (Form Number 32-6804) (New York: the International Business Machines Corporation, 590 Madison Ave.).

office). In this situation, the home office furnishes machine-prepared status records to the field for visual reference when answering inquiries. This decentralization usually provides excellent service to the policyholder.

3. Process the master file daily for 24-hour service on inquiries.
4. Process the file and handle references on a weekly basis.
5. Process on a daily basis an abbreviated premium status tape containing the information needed to answer the usual questions along with the date of the last transaction (so that other questions can be answered by reference to the transaction register). The complete master file can be processed on a weekly or monthly cycle basis.

Ideally, it would be highly desirable to process all of the different types of transactions and file references against the master file in one machine run, as shown in Figure 11–11.[10]

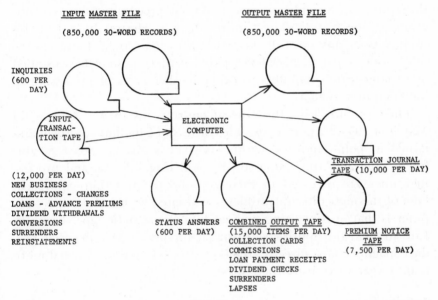

INPUT MASTER FILE

(850,000 30-WORD RECORDS)

OUTPUT MASTER FILE

(850,000 30-WORD RECORDS)

INQUIRIES
(600 PER
DAY)

INPUT TRANSAC-TION TAPE

ELECTRONIC COMPUTER

(12,000 PER DAY)
NEW BUSINESS
COLLECTIONS - CHANGES
LOANS - ADVANCE PREMIUMS
DIVIDEND WITHDRAWALS
CONVERSIONS
SURRENDERS
REINSTATEMENTS

STATUS ANSWERS
(600 PER DAY)

COMBINED OUTPUT TAPE
(15,000 ITEMS PER DAY)
COLLECTION CARDS
COMMISSIONS
LOAN PAYMENT RECEIPTS
DIVIDEND CHECKS
SURRENDERS
LAPSES

TRANSACTION JOURNAL
TAPE (10,000 PER DAY)

PREMIUM NOTICE
TAPE
(7,500 PER DAY)

FIG. 11–11.

However, because of the large variety of transactions, the amount of processing to be accomplished, and the many different types of insurance that are in force in a given company, an extremely large and complex program would be required. Because of the size of the program and the many input-output areas involved in the approach illustrated in Figure 11–11, it is unlikely that the 4,000 words of memory of our hypothetical machine would be enough, so we

---

[10] Figures 11–11 and 11–12 are adapted from similar illustrations in *IBM 705–III Consolidated Functions—Ordinary Life Insurance* (Form No. 32–7924) (New York: International Business Machines Corporation, 590 Madison Ave.).

would probably be forced to split this into two or more machine runs (as illustrated in Figure 11–12).

The first run (and the *only* run involving the entire master file) is used to select from the master file those records that are actually active for processing on one or more subsequent runs. As can be seen from the diagram, the output of these subsequent runs is merged back into the file the next time the master file is processed.

The approach described above is known as the *consolidated functions* approach, in which all of the processing associated with the insurance policy is accomplished through the use of the machine. For a small- or medium-sized company, such an approach is necessary to justify the cost of a machine. However, some of the largest insurance companies have been able to economically justify the use of the equipment for only one or two of these processing functions. For example, the first Univac acquired by the Metropolitan Life Insurance Company was fully occupied with the actuarial and reserve calculations on their 37,000,000 policies. Metropolitan has installed more large-scale computers to convert other areas of processing to the computer systems.

The Franklin Life Insurance Company installed a Univac in March of 1955.[11] Their master file consists of 240-digit records maintained in policy number within due-date sequence. Some 80 different programs (including sorting, collating, editing, and processing runs) are involved in their consolidated functions approach. One of the most difficult problems associated with installing a computer is that of converting manual files to magnetic tape. Franklin Life adopted the approach of using Unitypers (machines that produce magnetic tape directly from key strokes), and it required more than a year to convert their files.

Activity Ratio

The previous illustration brings up the important question: Can we afford to read 850,000 30-word records to process 10,000 records? The ratio of the number of active file records to the total number of file records, called the *activity ratio*, is approximately 1 to 85 in this example. Thus, on 84 out of 85 records, the machine is essentially idle.

[11] The information in this paragraph was obtained from A. C. Vanselow, "Franklin Life Installs a Computer," *Pioneering in Electronic Data Processing* (Proceedings of the Second Annual American Management Association Electronics Conference, Feb. 27–29, 1956).

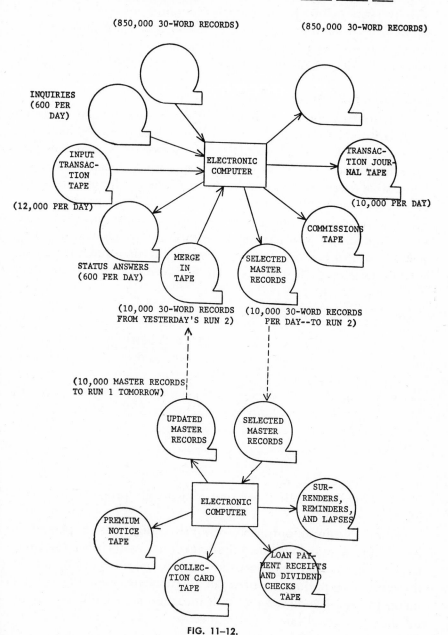

INPUT MASTER FILE

(850,000 30-WORD RECORDS)

OUTPUT MASTER FILE

(850,000 30-WORD RECORDS)

INQUIRIES
(600 PER
DAY)

INPUT
TRANSAC-
TION
TAPE

(12,000 PER DAY)

ELECTRONIC
COMPUTER

TRANSAC-
TION JOUR-
NAL TAPE

(10,000 PER DAY)

COMMISSIONS
TAPE

STATUS ANSWERS
(600 PER DAY)

MERGE
IN
TAPE

SELECTED
MASTER
RECORDS

(10,000 30-WORD RECORDS
FROM YESTERDAY'S RUN 2)

(10,000 30-WORD RECORDS
PER DAY--TO RUN 2)

(10,000 MASTER RECORDS
TO RUN 1 TOMORROW)

UPDATED
MASTER
RECORDS

SELECTED
MASTER
RECORDS

ELECTRONIC
COMPUTER

SUR-
RENDERS,
REMINDERS,
AND LAPSES

PREMIUM
NOTICE
TAPE

COLLEC-
TION CARD
TAPE

LOAN PAY-
MENT RECEIPTS
AND DIVIDEND
CHECKS
TAPE

FIG. 11-12.

There are many other instances of file processing in which the activity ratio is low. In such cases, economic pressure to build up larger batches before processing is considerable, and much of the pressure for development of faster magnetic tape units has come from the desire to economically process such files.

Multiprogramming

The fact that the processing ability of the machines is not effectively utilized in some file processing has led to the development of machines in which it is possible to run two or more programs on a time-shared basis. Thus, in the life insurance application, it might be possible to use the computing ability of the machine for actuarial calculations about 90 per cent of the time, while processing the low activity file at maximum speed. This may be accomplished by providing the ability to interrupt the computing program whenever a new file record has been read so that an alternate program can be used for processing the file, as shown in Figure 11–13. It is also neces-

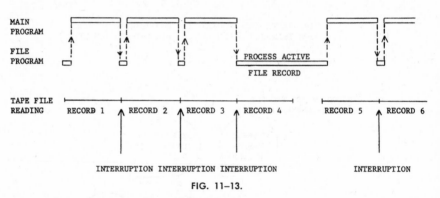

FIG. 11–13.

sary to provide a method for returning to the proper place in the interrupted program.

If multiple input-output buffers are available, it is possible to process two low-activity files simultaneously, or to perform card-to-tape or tape printer operations as a by-product of other processing, therefore eliminating the need for this expensive auxiliary equipment. It should be noted that multiprogramming requires that two (or more) programs be stored in memory at once, so its effective use depends upon having a large capacity memory. It should also be emphasized that, as far as processing is concerned, only one program is operating at a time—only the input-output functions are being overlapped. But this approach does allow the most expensive and powerful component of the machine—the processing unit—to be in continuous use.

Some Characteristics of Batch Processing

The processing of sequential access files, such as magnetic tapes and punched card files, involves the accumulation of a suitable batch of transactions to be processed as a group. This is necessary for efficient operation, because the transactions must be sorted into the same sequence as the file (or files), and the entire file passed through the equipment to process the transactions. The cost involved in processing an individual transaction is roughly proportional to the quotient obtained by dividing the time necessary to pass the files through the machine by the number of transactions. Thus, the more transactions that can be accumulated into each batch, the more efficient the processing will be from the standpoint of costs.

To obtain a batch of transactions, it may be necessary to accumulate transactions for several days, so the average delay time (the average total time between the time when the transaction arises and the time when the results are available) may be on the order of 24 to 36 hours. Thus, tape processing may involve a compromise between the average processing time and the average delay time. When the average processing time is the controlling factor, the batch-processing technique may be quite satisfactory, but when a low delay time is of paramount importance, batch processing may be entirely unsatisfactory.

Summary

The processing of magnetic tape files is generally similar to the basic approach used in punched card processing. Batches of transactions are accumulated, sorted into the same sequence as the file, and processed as a group while reading (and usually updating) the entire file.

Thus, it is necessary to be able to sort records on magnetic tape. Although a number of techniques may be used, the basic method of tape sorting involves the merging together of sequences to obtain longer sequences until a single sequence is finally produced. Unlike the punched card operation, the amount of time required is essentially independent of the number of characters in the sorting key.

The activity ratio of a file-processing run is the number of active file records divided by the total number of records in the file. If the activity ratio is low, the central processor is idle much of the time.

Thus, there is motivation to increase the activity ratio by increasing the size of the batch, thereby increasing the average delay involved in the processing. Faster magnetic tape units and the ability to multi-program are machine developments that make low-activity file processing more efficient.

EXERCISES

11.1 Consider the sequence of records identified by the numbers 25, 03, 17, 80, 46, 15, 77, 17, 03, 01, 25, 98, 62, 02, 33, 17.

   a) How many sequences are represented in the above list?
   b) Follow through the block diagram in Figure 11–6 with the above list. How many sequences are on the output tapes?
   c) How many passes, after the first, will be required to sort the above list using a two-way merge?

11.2 Consider a file containing 15,000 10-word records grouped into blocks of 200 words. This file is estimated to contain 3,700 sequences. The sorting key is a 20-character alphabetic field.

   a) How many passes (including the first) would be required to sort this tape using a two-way merge?
   b) How many passes including the first would be required to sort this file using a three-way merge?
   c) Using the hypothetical machine described in Chapter 11, how much time would be required to sort this file using a two-way merge?
   d) How much time would be required to sort this file using a three-way merge?
   e) Suppose that on the first pass we internally sort the file into sequences of 40 records. How many more passes would be required to sort this file with a two-way merge?

11.3 a) Upon what file characteristics does the time to sort a magnetic tape file depend?
   b) Upon what file characteristics does the time to sort a punched card file depend?
   c) Upon what machine characteristics does the time to sort a magnetic tape file depend?

11.4 a) What are the advantages of magnetic tape over punched cards as a processing medium?
   b) What are the advantages of punched cards over magnetic tape as a processing medium?

11.5 Describe the general approach taken when processing magnetic tape files.

11.6 Some computers can read a tape record, backspace, and write an updated record back on the same area of the tape. For low-activity file processing, should such a machine be buffered? If 10 per cent of the records are active and backspacing requires the same time as reading a record, how much more tape time would such a machine require to process a file than a buffered machine that reads and rewrites on a separate tape?

11.7 Prepare a semi-detailed block diagram for the Read Master Inventory tape symbol in Figure 11–10 to show how the reading of the master inventory file could be handled with six records in each tape block.

11.8 Distinguish between file maintenance and file processing. How does the problem of answering questions affect the procedures that are used for processing files?

11.9 What is multiprogramming? Why is it of importance?

11.10 What are the characteristics of batch processing? What are its advantages? What are its disadvantages?

SUPPLEMENTAL READINGS

GREGORY, R. H., and VAN HORN, R. L. *Automatic Data-Processing Systems*, San Francisco, Calif.: Wadsworth Publishing Co., Inc., 1960.
Chapter 9 discusses file processing and includes a description of various sorting techniques.

Honeywell 800 Transistorized Data-Processing System—Preliminary Programming Manual. Newton Highlands, Mass.: Minneapolis-Honeywell Regulator Co., Datamatic Division, 1959.
This computer includes convenient provision for multiprogramming.

IBM 7070 Data-Processing System—General Information Manual. Form Number D24–7004. New York: International Business Machines Corp., 590 Madison Ave., 1959.
This computer includes provision for multiprogramming.

McCRACKEN, D. D.; WEISS, H., and LEE, T. *Programming Business Computers.* New York: John Wiley & Sons, Inc., 1959.
Chapter 10 describes input and output devices and the use of buffers. Chapter 15 discusses various methods of sorting, both internally and with magnetic tapes.

SLATER, R. E. "Electronic Data-Processing in an Insurance Company," *Pioneering in Electronic Data-Processing.* Proceedings of the second annual AMA Electronics Conference, February 27–29, 1956. Published as Special Report #9 by the American Management Association, New York.
A discussion of the early use of a Univac at John Hancock Mutual Life Insurance Company.

CHAPTER 12 · Random Access Files

AT THE conclusion of the previous chapter it was observed that both magnetic tape and punched card data processing involve the accumulation of a suitable batch of transactions to be processed as a group. Thus, the delay involved in processing a transaction includes not only the processing time itself, but also the time necessary to accumulate the number of transactions necessary to form a batch. In certain situations, the delays involved in batching cannot be tolerated, or the time required to pass the entire file through the machine to process just a few records is excessive. Hence, magnetic tapes are not always suitable for storing file information.

Fortunately, devices have been developed that provide storage for large files of information in such a manner that a single record can be extracted for processing without scanning the other records in the file. Such devices are called *direct access* or *random access* files. Since the time necessary to locate the next active record in most such files depends upon the position in the file of the previous record processed, such files are not truly random access. In one machine, for example, the time necessary to locate a record may vary from two tenths to eight tenths of a second, depending upon how far it is necessary to go from one record to another. But in these files, it is feasible to go directly from one record to another. Thus, the term *direct* access is probably preferable to *random* access, but the latter term is more commonly used.

In the following pages, several types of random access files and various machines with which they are used will be discussed. On several of these machines, it is possible to combine magnetic tape with the use of random access files to obtain the advantages of both.

Large Magnetic Drums

One method of providing random access files is through the use of large magnetic drums. By slowing down the speed of rotation (and

276

thus increasing the average access time) , it is possible to increase the diameter of a magnetic drum, making it possible to store hundreds of thousands of characters of information on its surface. Magnetic drums revolving as slowly as one revolution per second and providing several million digits of storage have been proposed.

Remington Rand File Computer

Perhaps the first commercially available, general-purpose computer with direct access files was the Remington Rand File Computer. The Model 1 File Computer may include as many as 33 magnetic drums, each of which provides storage for 180,000 characters of information.[1] Rotating at about 1,750 revolutions per minute (which gives an average access time of about 17 milliseconds) , each drum contains 300 tracks grouped for addressing purposes into 3 sections of 100 tracks each. Each track can record 600 alphabetic or numeric characters written (serially by bit and by character, with 7 bits per character) by a single read-write head.

Information on these drums is organized into unit records which may contain any multiple of 12 characters up to a total of 120 characters. Records of different lengths may be stored on the same drum so that different types of files may be processed in the same procedure.

RECORD LENGTH	DRUM SECTION	CHANNEL	STARTING POSITION
X	X X	X X	X X

Each unit record is located by means of a seven-digit address. As shown above, the leftmost digit (1 through 9, and zero corresponding to 10) specifies the length of the record in multiples of 12 characters. The next two digits (00 through 98) denote the drum section on which the record is located. The next two digits (00 through 99) give the channel within the drum section, while the low-order two digits (even numbers from 00 through 98) denote one of the 50 possible characters in a channel in which a record may begin. For example, the address 5 07 52 22 locates a 60-character record in channel 52 of section 7 that begins with the twelfth 12-character word in the

---

[1] Model 1 is the second version of the File Computer. This machine differs substantially from Model 0, which was controlled by a wired plugboard and thus was not a stored-program machine. The discussion which follows is restricted to the Model 1 machine.

band. Since this is drum section 7, and there are 3 sections per drum, this system must include at least three file drums.

Channel Search

Given a drum section and channel, the File Computer can search automatically through all the records in that channel to locate the record with a particular identification in a specific field of the records. A search control location for each channel specifies the channel to be automatically searched next, if the record sought is not found on the original channel. This feature is designed to assist in locating records in the file, and will be further discussed later in this chapter, in the section on the Addressing Problem.

The general configuration of the File Computer is shown in Figure 12–1. A wide variety of input-output units may be attached to this machine, including magnetic tape units, punched card read-punch units, paper tape readers, paper tape punches, line printers, and inquiry typewriters. As many as 10 such input-output units may be used with a single system. The sort-collate device employs four magnetic tape units and can be used independently of the computer to perform such functions as collating two tapes together, selecting items from one tape which match those on another, and sorting a tape by means of a simple two-way merge. This device also may operate independently of the main computer until a record requiring computer processing is located, at which time the sort-collate device interrupts the computer which performs the necessary processing.

The working memory of this machine is provided by means of a magnetic drum upon which information is recorded serially by bit and by digit, with 120 characters per channel (see Figure 12–2). There are 87 channels which may be used for data and instructions, and 20 channels which are used to buffer the input and output devices. This drum rotates at 12,000 rpm, giving an average random access time of 2.5 milliseconds.

The 20 input and output channels are grouped together into 10 pairs, each of which may be associated with an input or an output device. At any given time, only one of each pair of bands is directly addressable by the machine, while the other is connected to the input or output device. The role of these two channels may be switched by programming. This permits overlapping input-output operations with computer operations through a simple buffering system. For example, after a card is read into one channel of the input pair, the

UNIVAC FILE COMPUTER

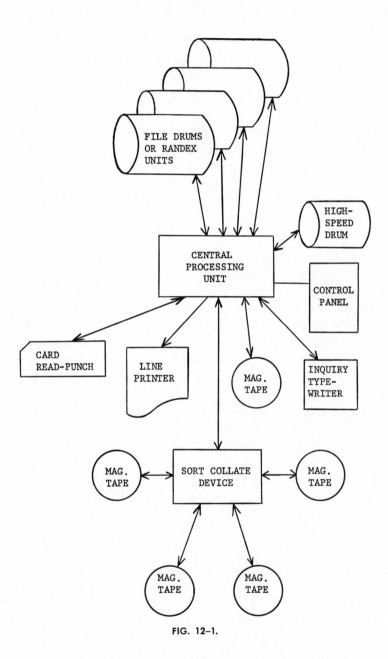

FIG. 12–1.

channels can be switched, allowing the computer to process the information just read from the card while the succeeding card is being recorded on the other channel of the pair.

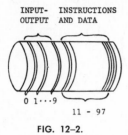

INPUT-OUTPUT / INSTRUCTIONS AND DATA

0 1···9

11 - 97

FIG. 12–2.

The Model 1 File Computer utilizes a combination of the stored program and a wired control panel to provide the advantages of each of these methods of control. A stored instruction consists of 11 digits and the sign position, so that 10 of them can be stored on each channel of the high-speed drum. As can be seen from the instruction format shown below, the File Computer uses the three-address system.

U	V	W	OP	S/C
XXX	XXX	XXX	XX	X

The U address gives the location of one operand (one value involved in the specified operation), the V address gives the location of the other operand, the OP code designates the operation to be performed, and the W address designates the location at which the result is to be stored. The S/C, or special character, defines a secondary operation which extends or modifies the operation specified in the instruction. Operation codes for stored-program instructions lie between 00 and 50, while operation codes 51 through 98 cause the control of the machine to be transferred to the corresponding step on the control panel where a subroutine, consisting of one or more steps, may be executed before control is returned to the stored program. For example, a subroutine to compute square root could be wired in the control panel so that the square root of a number could be computed through the use of the operation code 51.

The monthly rental for a Model 1 File Computer consisting of a 150-card-per-minute read-punch unit, two large file drums, and an inquiry typewriter amounts to approximately $7,750 per month. A File Computer with card input and output, an inquiry typewriter, 10 file drums, a 600-line-per-minute printer, and a sort-collate device with four magnetic tape units would rent for approximately $18,600 per month.

Cost versus Access Speed

One of the major considerations associated with the use of memory files is the cost, usually expressed in terms of cost per digit of information. The second consideration is that of access time. Magnetic drums, such as those used on the File Computer, provide relatively fast access, but the cost per digit of information is relatively high. The cost per digit can be reduced by sacrificing speed of access. Some slower devices with high capacity and lower cost per digit will be discussed.

Movable Read-Write Heads

Since a major cost of magnetic drum memory is associated with the read-write heads, magnetic drums have been constructed utilizing only one read-write head, along with a mechanism which moves it from track to track, as shown in Figure 12–3.

READ-WRITE HEAD

FIG. 12–3.

In the Remington Rand Randex, which provides additional mass storage for the file computer, a movable read-write mechanism is mounted between two large drums. Each drum, 44 inches in length with a 24-inch diameter, rotates at 870 rpm and contains 1,000 tracks, spaced at 25 tracks per inch. Since each track can record 3,000 seven-bit characters, a drum can hold 3,000,000 characters, and the capacity of the pair of drums making up a Randex unit is 6,000,000 characters. As many as 10 such units may be connected to the file computer.

The average time necessary to reposition the read-write mechanism, obtain a 120-character record, and make it available to the computer is approximately 0.4 second, but most of this time can be overlapped with other processing operations.

Magnetic Disk Memory

An extension of the idea of movable read-write heads is used in magnetic disk memory arrays in which the read-write head moves up and down and in and out to locate the proper track.

The IBM magnetic disk memory, called a RAM File, consists of a stack of 50 aluminum disks about 2 feet in diameter rotating on a common vertical shaft at a speed of 1,200 rpm. Information may be recorded on 100 concentric tracks on each face of each disk, giving 10,000 tracks of information (100 disk faces times 100 tracks per face).[2] Information is read from or recorded in these files by means of one or more access arms shaped like tuning forks with two read-

---

[2] RAM storage units are also available with 200 tracks per disk face, thus doubling the storage capacity of the file.

write heads, one on the tip of each prong (see Figure 12–4). By means of a quick-acting servomechanism, this access arm moves from one track of a disk to a position outside the stack, where it then moves up or down to another disk and then in to the desired track of that disk. This total process requires a maximum of eight tenths of a second to go from the innermost track of the top disk to the innermost track of the bottom disk, with an average time of six tenths of a second required to move from one file record to another.

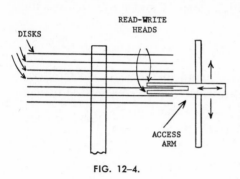

FIG. 12–4.

Two interesting engineering features are incorporated in the access mechanism. The first of these is the use of the Bernoulli principle to position the read-write heads so that they follow slight deviations in the disk to maintain a constant gap between the read-write head and the disk surface. The Bernoulli principle, which states that the pressure of a gas decreases as its velocity increases and explains why airplane wings provide lift, may be illustrated by placing a small sheet of paper firmly against the end of a spool held vertically and trying to blow it off by blowing through the hole, thus causing the paper to stick to the end of the spool. As can be seen from Figure 12–5, compressed air is blown through a "spool" associated with the read-write heads, and the disk takes the place of the piece of paper.

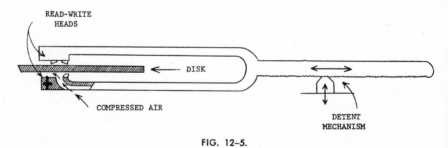

FIG. 12–5.

The second engineering technique of interest, which is also used in the Randex file, is the use of a *detent* mechanism to position the read-write head on the proper track. As can be seen in Figure 12–5, the moving mechanism need only position the read-write head closer to the proper track than to any other, and it is locked into exact position by the meshing of the saw-toothed detent mechanism.

Ramac

Although several IBM computers utilize RAM files, the IBM 305 Ramac was designed specifically for this mechanism. As can be seen in Figure 12–6, the Ramac includes a central processing unit with a

RAMAC   305

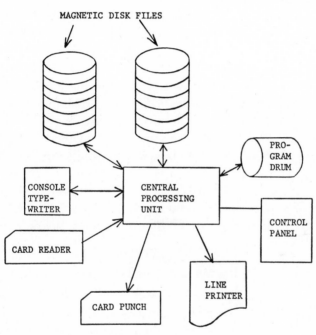

FIG. 12–6.

small drum memory, a card reader, a card punch, a line printer, and one or two magnetic disk files, each of which provides storage for up to 5,000,000 alpha-numeric characters. A console typewriter is also provided which may be used for entry, output, or for interrogating the machine.

Like the File Computer, the Ramac utilizes a combination of stored and wired programming. In the Ramac, however, all branching is done by means of selectors on the control panel. A three-position selector for each of the ten accumulators is set to plus, minus, or zero, according to the contents of the corresponding accumulator.

Another set of selectors is set to equal or unequal, according to the results of program comparisons. At the end of any stored-program step, control may be transferred to the control panel, and the program step to be executed next is determined by wiring through the proper selectors. The three arithmetic operations of addition, subtraction, and multiplication, as well as transfers of information, are performed through the use of stored-program instructions. Division may either be programmed using a subroutine involving addition, subtraction, and branching, or a special device (at additional cost) may be included in the machine to provide a divide operation. In addition to input and output tracks and several processing tracks, the magnetic drum memory provides storage for 200 instructions of ten characters each.

The Ramac magnetic disk file is organized into 100-character records. Since there are two read-write heads on the access arm, a track on each of the upper and lower surfaces of a disk may be read with one position of the access arm. Thus, the addressing system considers ten records as a unit, five on the upper track of the disk and five on the lower track. The record address is a five-digit number. The first two digits give the disk number (ranging from 0 to 49 for the first disk file unit and from 50 to 99 for the second), the next two digits give the track number (from 00 to 99), and the low-order digit (0 through 9) gives the record number, as shown below.

DISK NUMBER	TRACK NUMBER	RECORD NUMBER
X X	X X	X

When the address of a record is placed in the address register, the access arm begins to move toward that record. While the arm is in motion, the machine may continue other processing steps until an instruction is given to read from or write on the disk. If the access arm is properly positioned when a read instruction is given, the record from the disk is transferred onto a track of the drum. However, if the access arm is still in motion when the *Read* instruction is given, the machine interlocks until the arm is properly positioned, and then the record is transferred. When a record is written in the file, it is automatically read back and compared character by character with the information in working memory to insure that correct and readable information is recorded.

The printing is accomplished one character at a time by means of a single octagonal stick which rotates and moves up and down selecting the proper character to be printed in each position and striking the paper from behind with a hammer as the mechanism moves rapidly across the form from left to right (see Figure 12–7). The numbers 0 through 9, the letters of the alphabet, and 11 special characters are arranged on the faces of the stick. A full 80-character line may be printed in 2 seconds, including the time necessary for the printing mechanism to return to the starting position. Thus, the speed of the printer for full lines is 30 lines per minute. However, the speed of printing depends upon the length of the line, and 20-character lines can be printed at 80 lines per minute.

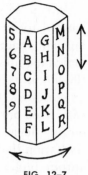

FIG. 12–7.

Compared to a machine like the 650, the Ramac is relatively slow, with each program step requiring a minimum of 30 milliseconds. However, all of the input-output devices are buffered, and the movement of the access arm of the disk file may be overlapped with other processing. Thus, the over-all machine is well balanced so that the overlapping functions may be performed at about the same rate of speed, with a typical transaction requiring about 2 or 3 seconds for processing. While discussing speeds, it is interesting to note that it requires over 8 hours to unload the 50,000 records in a single file into punched cards. With one magnetic disk file, the Ramac rents for $3,200 per month; with two files, it rents for $3,850 per month.

The configuration of the Ramac is relatively flexible. It is possible to obtain an additional access arm for each disk file, so that one arm can be in motion while the other is reading and writing, thus speeding up processing in certain situations. It is also possible to attach two separate Ramac machines to the same disk files, each using its own access arms, so that processing can take place simultaneously on each machine. A punched paper tape reader is available as input, and remotely located typewriter input-output units and a 150-line-per-minute printer may be attached to the machine.

Magnetic Disk Storage for the IBM 650

As many as four magnetic disk storage units may be attached to the IBM 650 system. Although the disk files used with the 650 are almost identical with those used with the Ramac, there are several important differences. In the first place, the 650 is a numeric machine, and the use of a five-bit numeric code rather than a seven-bit code makes it possible to store up to 6,000,000 digits of information in one disk file. Alphabetic information is handled by use of a two-digit code for each alphabetic character, just as it is in the other components of the 650.

Since the 650 calculates at several hundred operations per second, three access arms are provided for each disk unit, all of which can be in motion simultaneously so that by proper programming the processing of one transaction may be overlapped with the location of two others, so as to take advantage of the 650's programming speed.

As can be seen in Figure 12–8, the basic 650 system can be expanded to include several input-output devices and both magnetic tape and magnetic disk files. To incorporate magnetic disk and magnetic tape files, the addition of two units is required, one to control the file units and the other to provide a magnetic core buffer which synchronizes the tapes and disks with the 650 processing unit. A wide variety of punched card, inquiry typewriter, or line printer input-output devices may be attached to a 650 system, restricted by the limitation that only four sets of card, printer, and inquiry input and output buffers are available.

For use with the 650, the RAM magnetic disk file is organized into 10,000 60-word records, one record for each disk track. Of course, one disk record may contain several file records, all of which will be brought into the memory of the 650 simultaneously. Each disk record is addressed through the use of a six-digit number, as shown below.

FILE NUMBER	DISK FACE	TRACK	ACCESS ARM
X	X X	X X	X

The first digit denotes the file unit (from 0 through 3), the next two digits denote the disk face (00 through 99), the next two digits denote the track (00 through 99), and the low-order digit designates the access arm to be used.

To locate a record in the disk file, the address is placed in the distributor, and a *Seek Disk Storage* instruction (operation code 85) is given. Processing may be continued while the access arm is in motion. When it is desired to read (or write) this record, the address is again placed in the distributor and a *Read Disk Storage* (or *Write Disk Storage*) is given (operation codes 86 or 87) which transfers the record from the disk unit to the magnetic core buffer (or from the buffer to the disk unit). Since the magnetic core buffer is directly addressable by the 650 program with zero access time (addresses

9,000 through 9,059), the record may be extracted from the file, processed by the 650 while in the core buffer, and replaced in the file unit.

IBM 650 SYSTEM

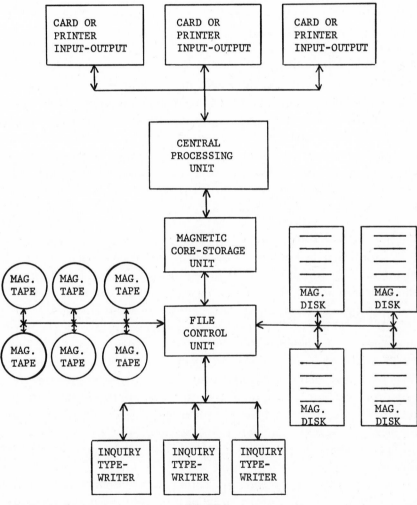

FIG. 12–8.

A basic 650 with a single RAM file and the necessary core storage unit and control unit will rent for around $7,200, with each additional RAM unit renting for $975 per month. A complete 650 Tape-RAM system with all of the auxiliary equipment, including two punched card read-punch units, a line printer, six magnetic tape units, four magnetic disk files, index registers, and automatic floating-decimal arithmetic rents for over $19,000 per month.

RAM files are also available for use with the IBM 7070, IBM 1401, and IBM 1410 data-processing machines. Since the average access time for RAM files is six tenths of a second (600,000 microseconds), it is questionable how widely adaptable the magnetic disk units will be to machines in which processing time is measured in terms of a few microseconds.

Removable Magnetic Disks

Another magnetic disk file unit, manufactured by RCA for use with RCA data-processing systems, resembles the modern juke box. Each unit contains magnetic disks, resembling phonograph records, which may, like magnetic tape reels, be removed from the mechanism and stored when not being processed. With as many as 40 900-character records on each disk, a single unit can contain up to 4,608,000 characters, with an average of $4\frac{1}{4}$ seconds required to read or write a block.

Magnetic Tape Bins

A tape bin is a random access file with larger capacity than the magnetic disk unit and correspondingly slower access. Developed by the Burroughs Corporation for use with their computers, the Datafile tape bin houses 50 separate short lengths of magnetic tape within its cabinet, along with a single read-write mechanism which moves underneath the tapes from one piece of tape to another (see Figure 12–9). Each tape is 250 feet long and contains 2,000 records of 200 characters each, arranged side by side in two lanes of 1,000 records apiece. Thus, each tape bin can store 100,000 200-character records for a total of 20,000,000 digits of information. This unit rents for $825 per month. By increasing the density of recording on the tape, it is possible to store as many as 50,000,000 characters in one file.

To move from one record to another, the mechanism moves the read-write head to the proper piece of tape and then the tape moves at 60 inches per second to the proper record. About one second is required for the read-write head to move from one tape to another. The average time to locate one of the 2,000 blocks on a single tape (assuming that the full 2,000 blocks are used) is 15.3 seconds. Therefore, the average access time to a full Datafile is approximately 16.3

seconds. However, as in the magnetic disk memory, this delay time may be overlapped with other processing. Furthermore, if the data file is not completely filled, the records may be arranged in the file so as to dramatically reduce the average access time. For example, if only 2,000 200-character records are in the file, they may be located

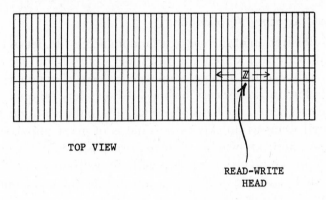

TOP VIEW

READ-WRITE
HEAD

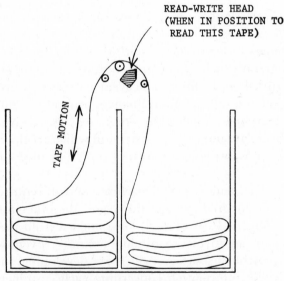

READ-WRITE HEAD
(WHEN IN POSITION TO
READ THIS TAPE)

TAPE MOTION

END VIEW SHOWING ONE OF THE
50 SECTIONS OF THE FILE.

FIG. 12-9.

20 records to a tape lane, and the average random access time is reduced to 1.31 seconds.

To locate a record in the Datafile, a search command is given which designates the lane number (00 to 99), the Datafile unit number (0 through 9), and the number of the tape block (000 through

999). While the search command is being executed, the computer central unit may continue processing. When the record has been located, a write command or a read command is given to transfer information from the computer to the file or from the file to the computer.

Wholesale Grocery Application

As an illustration of the use of a random access file, let us consider the combination of warehouse inventory control, billing, and accounts receivable for a large wholesale grocery. Since markups are relatively low in the grocery business, wholesalers compete actively with one another on the basis of service. Thus, the ability to provide the desired items as quickly as possible is of great importance. An up-to-the-minute knowledge of inventory position, along with the ability to process an order as a unit without waiting for a batch to be accumulated, provide significant advantages for random access processing.

The wholesaler that we will discuss carries about 3,000 items in stock, which he sells to approximately 300 customers in his area. These customers order from a preprinted order form furnished by the wholesaler, on which they simply indicate the number desired of each item printed on the form. The average order will involve about 300 items, and the total volume involves around 35,000 line-items per day. An average of 300 different items are received into the warehouse each day, and a "slot" system, in which receipts are placed in any slot that is available when they arrive, is used in the warehouse.

Within the file memory of the machine, we will require two types of records—one for items in inventory and the other for customer information. On the basis of cards key-punched from the order, we wish to prepare an invoice, maintain accurate inventory records, notify management of shortages which are developing, maintain accounts receivable information concerning each customer, and provide information concerning the warehouse (slot number) so that the order may be easily assembled for shipment.

The record for each inventory item should contain such information as the item number (which, in this case, can correspond to the file address), description, pack and size, unit price, unit cost, unit weight, class of merchandise, minimum stock balance, total on hand, and three or four combinations of slot number and quantity stored in that location. Thus, the item number must include about 75 to 80 characters.

The customer record should include customer number, both the "sold to" and the "ship to" name and address, the routing, and a history of orders for which payment has not yet been received. Thus, each customer record might involve several hundred characters.

Assuming that a Model 1 Univac File Computer is to be used, two file drums would be adequate for the item information, and a third would be used for the customer information. The item record would be 84 characters, with seven records per drum channel, so around 430 drum channels would be required. The customer record for the 300 customers could be accommodated in the form of one record per channel on a drum, which allows a 600-character record for each customer.

The over-all procedure used is shown in Figure 12–10. Input order cards, punched from the preprinted order form, would include store number and eight items (stock number and quantity) spread across the card to reduce the number of cards involved. Receipts would be entered into the computer from cards in which item number, quantity, and slot number would be recorded.

Output from the machine would include heading cards with "sold to" and "ship to" information, along with line-item cards containing item number, slot number, quantity, description, pack and size, unit price, quantity times price, and quantity times weight. Invoices could be printed from these cards, and then the line-item cards could be interpreted, sorted by slot number, and used in the warehouse as picking tickets.

The machine would be programmed to find the item record and multiply quantity by retail price, cost, and unit weight, adjust the inventory balance, test for reorder point and print a notification on the typewriter if reorder is necessary, accumulate total sales and cost by class for 100 classes, punch slot exhaustion cards whenever a slot becomes empty, and punch the output cards described above.

Since the above program should operate at least 100 cards per minute for output, the total processing time should be a little over 6 hours per day (figuring the 35,000-line item cards plus around 1,800 heading cards). Key punching the input cards would involve around 40 hours per day, so seven key punches and operators would be required. The Model 1 File Computer required for this job would rent for around $8,000, and key punches and printers would run the total machine rental to around $9,000. It is likely that the same job could be accomplished for less money through the use of standard punched card equipment, but the procedure described above would provide important advantages in terms of inventory control informa-

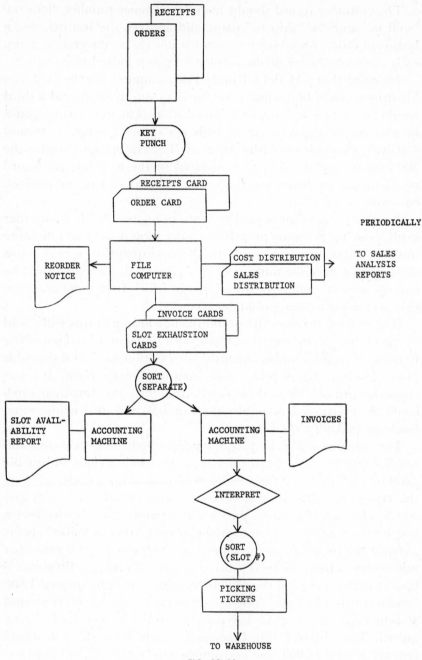

FIG. 12–10.

tion, speed of processing the individual orders, and ability to promptly answer questions concerning the availability of individual items.

Consolidated Manufacturing Control Operations

When utilizing random access files, it may be possible to return to the old manual bookkeeping approach of reflecting the influence of each transaction on various records as the transactions occur, thus keeping all records up to date at all times. In a job-shop situation, the labor ticket prepared for payroll purposes contains information which can also be used to keep track of the progress of each order in the shop and to analyze machine efficiencies.

By maintaining within memory three types of files, it may be possible to use the information on the labor ticket to maintain the employees pay record, to maintain a current status of each job within the shop (including where it stands with respect to the schedule and to standard cost), and to accumulate statistics concerning the performance of each machine in the shop.

Since the record for each active job would include the schedule for that job and standard cost data for each operation, both of which could be compared with actual performance, management could be provided with exception reports highlighting those jobs which are behind schedule or on which excessive costs are occurring. Since the status of each job would be up to date at all times, inquiry stations could be used to interrogate the file whenever desirable to answer questions concerning the status of any order in the shop.

Furthermore, raw material and in-process inventory balances could be maintained, and raw material requirements could be forecast on the basis of the projected production schedules. But the really spectacular potential achievements lie in the relatively unexplored area of shop scheduling. A modest approach to this problem may be taken by working backwards from the due date of the order through each operation to provide a scheduled starting date for each operation that will allow the order to be completed on schedule. Then, given these starting dates for each operation on all orders within the shop, it is possible to prepare a rough forecast of machine load and manpower requirements that may be used to forecast bottlenecks which will arise when attempting to meet the schedule.

A considerable amount of research effort is currently being expended in attempts to devise techniques which can be used to efficiently handle the minute-by-minute decisions concerning which job should be done next when an operation is completed and a machine in the shop becomes available (see Chapter 17). If and when such procedures can be developed, random access files may be used to provide the up-to-date information needed to make these decisions, and thus obtain a substantial increase in operating efficiency.

The Addressing Problem

In the wholesale grocery application described above there was no problem of locating the record for any inventory item because the file location itself was assigned as the item number. This was possible because of the use of preprinted forms for ordering purposes. Frequently it is impossible (or extremely inconvenient) to use the file address itself as an identification number. For example, item numbers are frequently assigned according to coding systems which may be used to classify these items for analysis purposes, or which may be indicative of the particular characteristics of the items themselves. Also, it is seldom convenient to assign item numbers consecutively because new items are always entering the system, while at the same time obsolete items are being removed.

A typical item-numbering system for 10,000 to 15,000 items (which could theoretically be handled through the use of a five-digit code) might involve an item number of eight digits, of which the rightmost two digits might represent a material code, the left-hand two digits might represent an item-use classification, and the remaining four digits might be arbitrarily assigned.

Thus, we are frequently faced with the problem of determining, on the basis of such an identification code (which may include alphabetic characters), a file location at which the corresponding record may be found. At first thought, it appears that this involves converting the identification number into a unique address, one address for each identification number, and only one address for each identification number. However, generally, there is no known method of making such a one-to-one assignment. On the other hand, it is usually possible to devise a method for converting identification codes to file addresses that works well enough for practical use.

In the first place, we may simplify the problem somewhat by dropping the requirement that each identification number must lead to a different file address. This is accomplished by providing "overflow" areas within the file in which records may be located for those items for which duplicate file locations are assigned. The file address of the proper overflow record is then recorded in the original record, so that the location of the duplicate items can be found from the record at the original address. For example, if three item numbers lead to the file address 12345, the first of these items would be located in that record, which would also include the location at which the second item might be found (say 40275), and then that record would include the location at which the third item is stored (say 45337). Thus, it would require three accesses to the file to locate the record for the third item. For obvious reasons this technique is known as the *chaining* method.

The channel search feature on the File Computer is designed to assist in locating records within the file. When the channel in which a record is located is determined, the channel search operation will find the record on that channel with the identification being sought. If there are more different identification codes that produce this channel number than the channel can hold the records for, the search control location contains the number of the overflow channel, and the machine automatically searches until the record is found. On most other machines, this searching and chaining process must be programmed, but it can be accomplished without undue difficulty.

For the chaining method to be effective, it is desirable that there be very few file locations to which large groups of item numbers would be assigned. To insure that the number of duplications is within reasonable bounds, it is frequently desirable to utilize some computing technique which provides random numbers as file addresses. For example, the item identification number may be multiplied by itself, and the middle five digits of the product utilized as the file address. Since the middle five digits are obtained by adding together many digits obtained from individual multiplications, it is likely that they will be relatively random and, thus, suitable for this purpose. Another useful randomization technique is that of dividing the identification number by the number of records to be allocated (increased enough so that the units position becomes a 1, 3, 7, or 9) and taking the remainder from this division as the address of the record.

Suppose, for example, that we consider an application of the 650 with magnetic disk files in which 7,500 records of 200 digits each must be maintained. Since each disk file record contains 600 digits, up to three file records may be contained in the record associated with each disk address. If we assign 3,001 tracks to these records, we would divide the identification by 3,001 and take the remainder as the disk track address. An analysis of the duplications involved in this method of computing addresses for a specific file is presented in the leftmost two columns of the table in Figure 12–11.

Column 3 of Figure 12–11 shows the total number of items for each classification according to column 1. Since there can be as many as three items in an address, only one access per item is required for those addresses in which there are one, two, or three items. However, the fourth item associated with an address will require two accesses, so the total number of accesses for all four items will be five. Likewise, assuming that each overflow item goes into a separate file record, the fifth item will require that the first record be examined, that the record containing the fourth item be examined, and that the fifth item then be located, for a total of three ac-

Items per Address	Number of Addresses	Total Items	Access Needed to Locate All Items Giving Rise to Address	Total Accesses
0	225	0	0	0
1	630	630	1	630
2	782	1564	2	1564
3	644	1932	3	1932
4	400	1600	5	2000
5	200	1000	8	1600
6	80	480	12	960
7	28	196	17	476
8	10	80	23	230
9	2	18	30	60
TOTAL	3001	7500		9452

Reproduced by permission from *IBM Data Processor*, March, 1958.

FIG. 12–11.

cesses. Thus, the total number of accesses required for the five items is eight. This reasoning may be continued to determine the remainder of column four in Figure 12–11. The last column of Figure 12–11 shows the total number of accesses for each classification, and its sum gives the total number of accesses required to refer to the entire file. Thus, the average number of accesses per item is 9,452 divided by 7,500, which gives an average of 1.26 accesses per item.

If some of the items are referred to more frequently than others, the average number of accesses can be effectively reduced by giving the high activity items preference for basic locations, and assigning low activity items to the overflow records. Thus, those items that are referred to most frequently would require but one access, while those that are referred to infrequently would (when necessary) be placed in overflow locations. This can be accomplished by loading the high-activity items into the file first so that low-activity items would be placed in the overflow locations. Incidentally, the file would be loaded by a program that would use the computational technique to compute the location of a record and examine that file location to see if there is room there for that record. If there is no room in the basic location, then the file-loading program follows the chain to the last record and establishes an additional link in which to place the new record.

From the above discussion it is apparent that the addition of new items and the deletion of obsolete items require a rather complex file maintenance program. Also, as the relative frequency of activity of the items change, it may be desirable to reload the file so that items that are currently of high activity may be placed in basic locations.

Control of Accuracy

Several characteristics of random access data processing make control of accuracy more difficult than where batch processing techniques are used. In the first place, transactions may be introduced into the system as they occur, with different types of transactions intermixed and without any reference to the sequence of these transactions. Therefore, it is much more difficult to establish control totals, which are conveniently accummulated in batch processing and which provide much of the basic information for subsequent control of processing accuracy.

Furthermore, when a file record is altered, the original record is destroyed when the updated record is returned to the file. Although current information is always present within the file memory, historical information required to reconstruct the current information is not available within the file. Therefore, if the current record is not readable or if it contains some mistake due to machine malfunctioning or errors in the input information, there may be no convenient way of reconstructing the correct information.

When random access files are utilized, direct manual entry of certain information may be provided through the use of keyboard entry stations. For example, warehouse receipts may be entered into the records by means of a typewriter located in the warehouse. Needless to say, such a method of entering information is likely to introduce errors into the system and is difficult to control, because anyone who has physical access to the remotely located inquiry station can modify the records within the machine. For this reason, it may be desirable to limit, by programming, the use of inquiry stations to the function of extracting information, and to enter all information by means of verified punched cards.

Since the random access processing usually requires no sorting of input information and no intermediate summarizing of the transactions, the usual listings, which are prepared as a by-product of these operations and which serve to provide an audit trail by means of which results may be re-created, are no longer conveniently produced. Thus, it may be necessary to produce a transaction register, with a line for each transaction showing the balances before the transaction, the transaction itself, and the resulting balances, along with a reference to the previous transaction. By means of such information, it is possible to trace back through transactions that have affected a given record by finding the last activity and then referring to the previous one, which refers to the previous one, and so on.[3]

Summary

Files in which it is feasible to obtain records without regard to their sequence make it possible to process transactions in the sequence in which they naturally arise without accumulating batches or sorting. In situations in which intolerable delays are involved in accumulating a suitable batch, random access files present decided advantages. Random access files make it possible to reflect each transaction in all of the files that it affects as the transaction occurs, thus keeping all records on a current basis. Inquiry facilities can be provided that make it possible to extract this current information whenever it is required.

The problem of finding the file record associated with an identification code requires that a suitable addressing technique be developed. The chaining method is used to handle records that give rise to duplicate file locations; and computation of addresses by techniques that produce randomly distributed file locations are frequently utilized to reduce the frequency of long chains.

EXERCISES

12.1 How does the basic approach to processing with random access files differ from the approach used with punched cards or magnetic tape files?

---

[3] This discussion is not intended to indicate that control of accuracy is a major difficulty when utilizing random access equipment, but only to indicate that special attention must be given to the peculiar problems involved. For a more complete discussion of this problem, along with suggested techniques, see *In-Line Electronic Accounting, Internal Control and Audit Trail* by Price Waterhouse & Co., New York, published by IBM as Form No. 32–0753.

12.2 What are the advantages obtained through the use of random access files?

12.3 What are the disadvantages associated with the use of random access files?

12.4 What is the "chaining method," and how is it used in locating records in a file?

12.5 What are the problems involved in devising a suitable address computation technique for a random access file?

12.6 Why do random access files present problems in the area of control of accuracy?

12.7 Suppose we have a random access file in which are stored inventory records indentified by item number. How could we make a list of the items that are out of stock?

12.8 What is involved in inserting a new record in a random access file? In deleting a record? How would these problems be handled in magnetic tape files?

12.9 Suppose we have a random access file in which are stored inventory records identified by item number. We attempt to find a record for an item that is not in the file. What would happen? If we were processing a similar magnetic tape file, what would happen if we attempted to find an item that was not in the file?

SUPPLEMENTAL READINGS

IBM 305 RAMAC—Manual of Operation. Form Number 22–6264–1. New York: International Business Machines Corp., 590 Madison Ave., 1957.

IBM 650 Data-Processing System with 355 Random Access Memory and 838 Inquiry Stations—Manual of Operation. Form Number 22–6270–1. New York: International Business Machines Corp., 590 Madison Ave., 1956.

Model 560 DATAFILE Multiple Bin Tape Unit Handbook—Preliminary Edition. Bulletin 3026. Electrodata Corp., 1956.

RANDEX—General Description. Form U-1722. Remington Rand Univac Division, Sperry Rand Corp., 1959.

The Chaining Method for the 650 RAMAC System. Form No. J28–4002. New York: International Business Machines Corp., 590 Madison Ave., N.Y., 1959.
  Describes various considerations involved in efficient addressing of random access files.

Univac File Computer Model 1—Basic Programming. Form U-1474. Remington Rand Univac Division, Sperry Rand Corp., 1958.

CHAPTER 13 · Classification of Computers

THE STUDY of punched card equipment, magnetic drum computers, large-scale computers, and random access files in the previous chapters has shown that a wide variety of mechanized data-processing equipment exists. The previous presentation has been designed to emphasize the most important characteristics of the equipment and the major ideas involved in its use for data processing.

However, two important categories of equipment have not yet been discussed: scientific computers and special-purpose equipment. Also, a wide variety of computers exists, each with its own unique set of characteristics. To introduce order into this potentially confusing variety, it is desirable to present some characteristics by which electronic computers may be classified. Thus, in this chapter, consideration of electronic data-processing equipment will be completed and the major types of equipment available will be summarized.

Scientific Computers versus Electronic Data-Processing Machines

Historically, one of the first meaningful classifications of computers was in terms of the general broad use for which they were designed. This was originally of great importance because the first machines were designed for scientific calculation, and, although many persons saw the data-processing potential of the computer, these early machines were not suitable for most data-processing purposes. It was several years before computers adequate for data processing were made available.

The most striking contrast between data processing and scientific computation is in the ratio of volume of input and output to the amount of computing involved. In most data-processing problems, tremendous quantities of information are run through the machine, while a good deal of branching and other logical operations are performed but only a relatively modest amount of computation, consisting primarily of addition and subtraction. On the other hand, in a typical mathematical problem, such as the illustration of overhead cost allocation in Chapter 9, relatively small amounts of information are taken in and a fantastic amount of computation is performed in which a much higher proportion of the operations are multiplication and division than in data processing, where these operations are relatively infrequent as compared to addition.

Thus, in the data-processing machine, input and output speed are of primary importance; in the scientific computer, arithmetic speed is paramount. This does not imply that adequate input and output are not important in a scientific computer, or that computation speed is not needed for a data-processing machine. But the most desirable balance between input-output speed and computing speed in the two types of machines is different.

Since the characteristics of electronic data-processing machines have been discussed at length, it may be desirable to consider some of the characteristics of scientific computers.

Binary Notation

To provide as fast an arithmetic unit as possible for a given cost, many scientific computers operate on numbers expressed in binary notation. As explained in Appendix C, zero and one are the only digits used in binary notation, which makes it convenient for machines which are composed of elements that are basically binary or two-state elements. For example, a magnetic core is either magnetized in one direction or the other; an electronic tube is either conducting or not conducting; a condenser is either charged or it is not; a hole appears in a certain position in a card or it does not; and so forth. Furthermore, as discussed in Appendix C, the addition and multiplication tables (which we have to memorize in the primary grades) are quite simple for binary arithmetic. Thus, relatively simple and inexpensive circuits can be used to compute in such a simple system, as compared to those required for numbers expressed in the normal decimal system. Also, it requires fewer bits to represent a number in binary notation than in any coding for the decimal system, so memory elements are more effectively utilized in a binary machine.

Since numbers are not ordinarily expressed in binary notation, the machine must translate (by means of computation) from the decimal system to binary notation whenever information is entered into the machine, and to translate from binary back to decimal on output. The desirability of performing this translation, of course, depends upon the amount of time that it requires relative to the total processing time involved. When there is relatively little input and output, as compared with the amount of computing involved, it may be quite desirable to make this translation because of the additional computing efficiency made possible by the use of binary arithmetic.

Automatic Floating Decimal Point

In long computational problems involving thousands of additions, subtractions, multiplications, and divisions, the intermediate results may be numbers about which we have very little intuitive feeling concerning their size, hence the problem of keeping track of the decimal point when writing the program is quite difficult. So that the machine itself can keep track of the decimal point, many scientific computers include instructions which operate directly upon numbers expressed in floating decimal notation, which is described in Appendix D. Of course, a binary machine uses an automatic floating *binary* point, rather than a floating decimal point.

Index Registers

In large mathematical problems, the repetition necessary to make an electronic computer usable is obtained through the manipulations involved in processing large arrays of numbers rather than by doing the same relatively small problem over and over with different input data. Frequently, simple subroutines are repeated over and over again, each time performing the same computation upon different numbers within the array. This is accomplished by means of instruction modification, with loops frequently occurring within loops. In situations of this type, more time may be required for performing instruction modification than is spent computing. Thus, efficiency in modifying instructions is even more important in a scientific computer than in the data-processing machine, so most scientific computers are equipped with one or more index registers. Index registers and their use were discussed in Chapter 7.

In summary, the typical large-scale scientific computer is likely to be a binary machine with comparatively modest input and output facilities, equipped with a relatively large memory, and including automatic floating decimal point and index registers. With the growing tendency toward the use of quantitative techniques in business and the ever-present possibility of using a computer jointly for data processing and engineering computations, many machines combine the characteristics desirable for data processing and scientific computing. The IBM 709 is basically a 704 (a scientific computer) with improved input-output facilities. On the other hand, the IBM 7070 and the Burroughs Datatron 220 are data-processing machines which include index registers and (at least optionally) automatic floating decimal point instructions.

Special Purpose versus General Purpose

Most of the equipment discussed has been general purpose in the sense that it was not designed specifically to be used for a single application. As was mentioned in Chapter 5, any stored program computer can theoretically be used to solve any problem that can be solved by computation, but this neglects the important practical consideration of memory size, speed, and input and output. Because of the characteristics of certain data-processing areas, it has been necessary to devise special equipment to be able to mechanize data processing. Furthermore, it appears reasonable that added efficiency may sometimes be attained by designing equipment specifically for the particular job, even if general-purpose equipment could be used.

There are two possibilities for special-purpose equipment. One is to design a machine, perhaps not even employing the stored program for control, with only the ability to perform a particular job, eliminating the additional cost of building in general abilities. This approach has disadvantages: (1) If the job changes, the equipment requires modification or becomes useless, and (2) engineering and design costs for such equipment are large, which may make it less expensive to use general-purpose machines whose development costs can be borne by a number of different uses.

The more usual type of special-purpose equipment is composed of a general-purpose central processor with specialized files or input-output equipment that suit it for a particular application.

Airline Reservations

One of the first applications of random access memories occurred in 1952 when American Airlines installed a special-purpose magnetic drum machine, called the Reservisor, to maintain seat availability information for ten days in advance on its flights in and out of New York City. This system has been in successful operation since that time.

A major problem to be solved in such a system is that of input and output, for each ticket agent must have access to the information stored within the machine. This access is provided by means of a small input-output device (about the size of a small adding machine) on the counter beside the agent. To inquire concerning seat availability on a certain flight, the agent selects a metal plate on which the schedule for flights from New York City to the desired destination are printed. When this plate is inserted into a slot in the desk set, notches in the edge of the plate furnish the central machine with the address of the record associated with these flights. By pressing the buttons on the face of the machine, the agent may inquire about a specific flight on a certain date, and lights on the machine will indicate the status of that and other flights to that destination. If one or more seats are to be sold (or canceled), the proper buttons are depressed, and the information is recorded in the memory of the machine, which thus maintains the current status of each flight.

By means of leased telegraph lines and a system of switching devices, more than 100 agent sets can be connected to the main machine. Only one desk set is connected to the machine at a time, but since each set need be connected for only an instant, the delay involved when one desk set must wait for others before being connected is only a second or two.

The Reservisor system has been quite successful, for not only has it released a substantial number of people from the task of manually maintaining a status board, but it has reduced the incidence of errors and speeded up the agent's service to the customer, for he no longer must put up with those embarrassing delays while he (and the customer) wait for someone to answer the telephone. Thus, one agent can handle more and happier customers.

By designing similar switching devices and agent's desk sets, the File Computer has been adapted to the task of maintaining airline seat availability information. Several different airlines are now utilizing these or other such systems for maintaining reservation information.

Processing Checks

Special-purpose equipment has also been designed for use in banks. In terms of total volume, perhaps the largest single data-processing problem consists of the handling of the billions of checks that are processed in the United States each year. From the time that it is issued until it is posted to the proper depositor's account, a check is cleared through an average of 2.3 banks and is sorted and totaled about six times.[1]

Most data processing is concerned with the manipulation of information. However, check processing is more complicated than this, for the check has importance as a document, and the document itself must be processed along with the information.

Since a single check may be processed by many different banks, a common machine-processable language is required to make mechanization practical. The American Bankers Association has established specifications for information content, format, and character design for a magnetic ink recording system that is readable both by people and machines. A sample check, encoded along the bottom with these magnetic ink symbols, is shown in Figure 13–1.

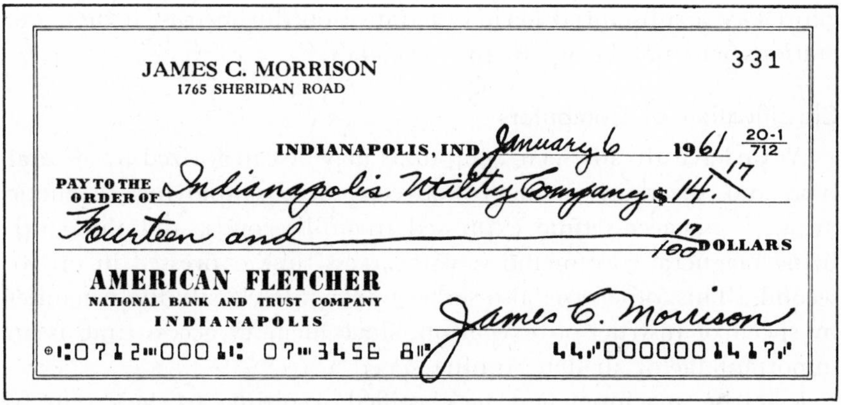
JAMES C. MORRISON
1765 SHERIDAN ROAD
331
INDIANAPOLIS, IND. January 6 1961 20-1/712
PAY TO THE ORDER OF Indianapolis Utility Company $ 14.17
Fourteen and 17/100 DOLLARS
AMERICAN FLETCHER
NATIONAL BANK AND TRUST COMPANY
INDIANAPOLIS
James C. Morrison
0712 0001 07 3456 8 0000001417

FIG. 13–1.

Much of this information, such as the routing symbol, transit number, and account number, may be preprinted on the check before it is issued. Equipment is available from several manufacturers for encoding the variable information, including amount, on the check during the proof operation. Also available is ingenious equipment which can sort checks of intermixed sizes and thickness at high speed, just as punched card equipment sorts cards.

This equipment can also be used to enter the information from the check into computers for posting to accounts maintained on magnetic tape or in random access files. One system of processing equipment, designed to serve the needs of banks with as few as 10,000 accounts, automatically processes files of ledger cards on which in-

[1] See E. L. Van Deusen, "The Coming Victory over Paper," *Fortune,* October, 1955.

formation is printed in the usual way on the front and recorded on magnetic strips on the back. The checks, sorted into account-number sequence, are processed against the ledger cards which are fed through the equipment in the same sequence. The machine selects the ledger cards for active accounts, reads the current status of the account from the magnetic strips, and updates both the front and back of the ledger card.[2]

The development of check-processing equipment has aroused great interest among bankers. But for any bank to take maximum advantage of this equipment, most of the checks it processes must be precoded with magnetic ink characters. This not only requires that competitor banks convert to this system, but it also requires that the people and organizations that issue checks must be motivated to include magnetic ink character recording. Thus, the pioneers in this effort face a substantial period of transition during which their operations will not be up to full efficiency.

Classification of Computers

As we have already seen, computers may be categorized by general type and speed of memory between those employing magnetic drums, with access time expressed in milliseconds, and those utilizing magnetic core memory, with access time expressed in microseconds. This, of course, also serves to roughly classify the machines by speed of instruction execution, since memory access time is an important factor in determining speed.

Likewise, machines may be classified according to their type of input, output, and file storage. There are machines whose input and output are restricted to punched paper tape an an electric typewriter, others with punched card input and output, others which use magnetic tape for input, output, and file storage, and, finally, a group of machines that employ random access files. Of course, these categories occasionally overlap.

One rough classification scheme that is widely accepted is the following:[3]

Large-Scale. The system uses magnetic tapes, and the computer operates at microsecond arithmetic speeds. Price, in general, is in the order of magnitude of one million dollars or more.

---

[2] See "New Breakthrough Scored in Bank Automation Progress," *Burroughs Clearing House,* October, 1959.

[3] Used in the "Computer Census" printed in *Automatic Data Processing Newsletter* (New York: John Diebold and Associates, 40 Wall St.) .

Medium-Scale. The system uses magnetic tapes, and the computer operates at millisecond arithmetic speeds. In general, the price range is from $500,000 to $1,000,000.

Small-Scale. The system does not use magnetic tapes, but the computer is internally programmed.

Miscellaneous Computers. Card calculators and other machines which do not fall into one of the above system classifications.

Although the above classification is useful, it may be desirable to present a slightly more detailed breakdown in terms of the machine characteristics. It should be noted that one machine may appear in several categories, for most machines are obtainable with various configurations of equipment.

Desk-Size Computers

This category of machines is intended primarily to be used as a personal tool by engineers and scientists to solve small- to moderate-sized computational problems. Such machines, selling for between $30,000 and $100,000 or renting for between $1,000 and $3,000 usually require no special installation facilities, and many of them can be plugged into any 110 volt outlet. They usually have relatively slow, punched paper tape input and typewriter output, and many of them are binary magnetic drum machines.

Such machines are frequently operated on an "open shop" basis— that is, the engineers program and run their own problems rather than use an organization of computer specialists for numeric analysis, programming, coding, and running. Examples of machines in this category include the Royal McBee LGP 30, the Bendix G-15, and the IBM 610 and 1620.

Small Data-Processing Machines

These machines are also relatively modest in cost, renting for between $2,000 and $7,000 per month, but they differ from the previous category in that they are usually not binary, and, although they do not process magnetic tape, they have more extensive input-output facilities than the desk computers. This category includes a wide variety of equipment, based upon high-speed paper tape or buffered punched card input and output. The basic 650 is included in this category, as are the Datatron 205, the Remington Rand Univac Solid-State 80 and 90, the Bendix G-15 with card input and output, and the IBM 1401.

Many of these machines are designed to fit into punched card data-processing systems, replacing enough sorters, collators, accounting machines, and calculators to justify their cost. For example, an IBM 1401 can be obtained for less than $3,000 per month that will read 800 cards per minute, punch 250 cards per minute, and print 600 lines per minute. Thus, a 1401 can possibly replace three 407 accounting machines and a 604 calculator at a net reduction in machine rental.

The National Cash Register 390 is an example of a small electronic data processor based upon the concept of a bookkeeping machine. In addition to punched paper tape, punched card, and keyboard input and output, this machine processes visible ledger records upon the back of which information can be magnetically recorded. This provides a novel form of file storage in which the operator manually selects the active records from the file.

Magnetic Tape File Processors

These machines, renting for between $4,000 and $15,000 per month, process magnetic tapes, yet, for some reason, they cannot be classed as large-scale machines. For example, they may use magnetic drum memory, the memory may be too small for complex programs, or the magnetic tapes themselves may be rather slow. Many of these machines are small data-processing machines to which magnetic tapes have been added. Some of them are quite efficient for simple processing of large-volume but low-activity ratio files, some of them may be used as off-line input-output in large-scale computer installations, and some are the equivalent in processing ability of the early large-scale machines.

Examples of equipment in this classification are the Burroughs Datatron 205 with magnetic tapes, the IBM 650 with tapes, the Remington Rand Univac Solid State 80 and 90 with tapes, the Minneapolis-Honeywell 400 system, and the IBM 1401 tape system.

Random Access File Processors

These machines, renting for between $2,000 and $10,000 per month, are designed to process transactions against a random access file. Most of them are rather slow in computing ability and are designed for on-line processing of transactions at speeds of 5 to 20 transactions per minute. Included among the machines in this category are the RCA 301, the IBM Ramac 305, the Remington Rand File Computer, the Burroughs Datatron 205 with Datafiles, the Royal McBee RPC-9000, and the IBM 1401 with RAM files.

Large-Scale Data-Processing Machines

Renting for $15,000 to $50,000 per month, these machines typically process magnetic tapes at speeds between 20,000 and 100,000 characters per second and execute between 5,000 and 30,000 instructions per second. Many of them are building block machines whose input-output facilities, number of buffers, and size of memory may be tailored to fit the needs of each installation. Thus, in certain configurations they may efficiently serve as scientific computers.

Included in this category are the RCA 501, the Minneapolis-Honeywell 800, the Burroughs Datatron 220, the IBM 7070 and 7080, the Bendix G-20, the Remington Rand Univac II, and the General Electric 225.

High-Speed Computers

Renting from around $25,000 per month on up, these machines are usually designed with high computing speed as a primary objective, performing from about 30,000 to around 1,000,000 calculations per second. Many of these machines are also composed of building blocks that may be tailored to the needs of the individual installation, and some of the most powerful include more than one processing unit among the building blocks, so that computing functions may be performed in parallel or several problems may be processed simultaneously.

Just as some configurations of the large data-processing machines may be used effectively as scientific computers, so may these high-speed computers, with fast input-output facilities, be efficient data processors.

Included in this classification are such machines as the Remington Rand Univac Scientific 1103 and 1105, the IBM 709 and 7090, the Control Data 1604, the Philco Transac S-2000, the Remington Rand LARC, and the IBM STRETCH system.

Summary

Many kinds of electronic computers are available, and each has its own advantages and limitations. One of the earliest distinctions was between scientific computers and electronic data processors, but through the use of the building block concept the importance of this classification has been reduced. Another interesting classification contrasts general-purpose and special-purpose machines. Again, the building block concept reduces the distinction, for a special-purpose machine may be composed of a general-purpose computer with specialized input-output or file storage facilities.

Machines may also be classified by size and purpose. Again, because of building block construction, computers with the same name may appear in several categories in their various configurations. Moreover, as technology progresses, the boundaries of the classifications may change or completely new categories may be created. Thus, the lower limit of definition of a high-speed computer rises with each generation of machines.

It should be emphasized that the above classification system is designed primarily to give some orientation to the beginner as he views the profusion of available equipment, not to serve as rules concerning which machines can be used for what purpose or to prohibit a manufacturer from calling his machine anything he sees fit.

EXERCISES

13.1   What are the major differences between scientific computers and electronic data-processing machines?

13.2   In view of your answer to Question 1, how can the same machine be used efficiently for both purposes?

13.3   What is the "building block" concept? Why is this concept of major importance to the producer of computers? Why is it important to the user of computers?

13.4   What is the difference between check processing and most other data processing?

13.5   What problems must be solved in the mechanization of check processing?

13.6   What are the differences between an inventory of airplane seats and inventories of finished goods?

13.7   Prepare a market forecast for computers for the next 10 years. For which types of machines do you forecast the greatest growth?

13.8   Study the computers produced by some computer manufacturer. Does this manufacturer produce machines that compete in each classification discussed in this chapter?

SUPPLEMENTAL READINGS

BELL, W. D. *A Management Guide to Electronic Computers.* New York: McGraw-Hill Book Co., Inc., 1957.

Case History 1 describes the use of a special-purpose machine for inventory control, and Case History 2 describes the use of the Reservisor by American Airlines.

GREGORY, R. H., and VAN HORN, R. L. *Automatic Data-Processing Systems.* San Francisco: Wadsworth Publishing Co., Inc., 1960.

Chapter 7 presents an intensive analysis of characteristics by which computers may be classified, with tables comparing many of the computers available in 1960 according to these characteristics.

IBM 1401 Data Processing System with Tapes and Series 1200 Character Sensing Equipment for Demand Deposit Accounting. Form Number E20–8020. New York: International Business Machines Corp., 1959.

This booklet presents procedures for use of the above equipment for check processing. It includes a description of the combination proof and recording operation, the various card forms, tape records, and machine runs involved, and a block diagram and 1401 program for the posting run.

"NABAC'S Idea Round-Up on Bank Operations," *Burroughs Clearing House* (October, 1959).

This summary of a convention presents various interesting facets of the problems and opportunities involved in automatic check processing.

SELDEN, L. M. "Solving the Input Problem—First Step in MICR," *Burroughs Clearing House* (November, 1959).

Describes Michigan National Bank's approach to the problems of converting to magnetic ink character recording on checks.

CHAPTER 14 · Systems Analysis and Design

MANY OF the previous portions of this book have been concerned with the mechanization of data processing. To explain how computers may be used for this purpose, a substantial portion of the preceding material has been devoted to the characteristics of various types of equipment. However, illustrations of how the equipment is applied to data processing have been included, and the over-all process of converting to an electronic data-processing system has been discussed in Chapter 8. Although a knowledge of this equipment itself is a prerequisite to an understanding of how it may be used, the development of an approach to the use of the equipment is of primary importance. This chapter presents an introduction to a basic approach that may be used, and describes some of the techniques that are useful in the analysis and design of data-processing systems.

As was discussed in Chapter 2, it is important to consider the entire data-processing activity within an organization as an integrated system, the purpose of which is to provide the proper information for adequate management control. Despite the fact that the electronic computer is an extremely powerful data-processing tool, the results obtained from the data-processing system are primarily dependent upon the effectiveness with which the system itself was designed rather than upon the specific equipment employed. Thus, serious consideration must be given to the techniques involved in the analysis and design of data-processing systems.

There are three major steps in the process of designing a data-processing system. First, it is necessary to obtain through systems analysis an understanding of the system as it exists. Then the results that should be obtained from the data-processing system must be specified. Finally, equipment must be specified and procedures devised that efficiently obtain those results. Obviously, these three steps are interrelated both by the techniques used and by their dependence upon each other.

Defining the Present System

The data-processing system of an organization is of almost unimaginable complexity, consisting of information, people, machines, and formal and informal procedures. To specify what such a system should be, it is usually desirable to start by describing the system as it exists, so that the existing system may be used as a point of departure from which a better system may be created. Although it is theoretically possible to specify an abstract system on a theoretical basis alone by simply specifying the results that should be produced from the raw information, with systems of this complexity it is usually impractical to attempt a purely theoretical approach because of the likelihood that important considerations will be omitted. It is difficult enough to comprehend the requirements even after obtaining a representation of the existing system. Furthermore, the cost of the existing system must be determined to provide a basis for comparison of possible improvements.

Thus, the first objective of systems analysis is to obtain an adequate representation or model of the existing data-processing system. It should be noted that any model of a data-processing system (other than the data-processing system itself) is an abstraction of reality, not reality itself. Whatever the form of this abstract representation, it must embody an adequate understanding of the data-processing system that it represents, and it should have enough flexibility so that improvements to the model can be incorporated as an improved system is designed. Thus, two questions arise: (1) What types of models may be used to represent data-processing systems; and (2) how can the construction of such models be approached? In other words, we must be concerned with the "tools" that can be used to represent systems and the techniques by which these tools may be used.

The Total Systems Concept

As an initial approach to studying the data-processing system of an organization, it is possible to view the system as a large "black box" whose contents (whether they be people, transistors, wheels, gears, rocks, electronic computers, or a vacuum) are completely unknown. We might assume that what must go on in this black box is determined by what goes into it and what comes out of it. In a sense, these outputs and inputs define the system. Now, if we were able to peek into this black box, we might find that it is filled with smaller black boxes, whose contents are again unknown, but which are related to one another by flows of information. Again, the operations that must be performed by each of these black boxes is determined by their inputs and outputs. Conceptually, this process of opening black boxes can be continued indefinitely until finally the inputs and outputs of the boxes are related so simply that it is obvious what is going on in each box.

This black box concept provides a basic approach for the analysis of a data-processing system. After specifying the inputs and outputs of the entire system, we may break it down into simpler subsystems which may be related to each other and to the over-all system by the flows of information between them. Each subsystem is defined in terms of its individual inputs and outputs. Then each of these subsystems may be investigated separately in greater detail by subdividing it into smaller subsystems and again expressing the interrelationships between them. This process of subdivision may be continued until the contents of the resulting black boxes are sufficiently simple as to be obvious. This approach is a familiar one, for it has been implied in the previous discussion of procedures flow charts and the various levels of program block diagrams as discussed in Chapter 8.

It should be noted that the above approach starts with the entire data-processing system and breaks it down into simpler and simpler components. Alternatively, another approach might be attempted that would start with the details of the system and combine them to represent the over-all system. Working from the top down is by far the more effective approach, for it provides a framework for organizing the effort in a logical way, and it also produces an integrated representation of the system, for we are always concentrating attention upon the interrelationships between the subsystems rather than viewing them from the inside out and running the risk of ignoring these interrelationships. The above approach is frequently referred to as the *total systems concept*.

To analyze a system, it is necessary to obtain a lot of information about the products of the data-processing system and how they are produced. This information must be gathered and organized to provide a representation of the system. Much of this information must be obtained by following pieces of paper and interviewing those who are involved in the processing. In the following discussion, we will be concerned with some of the tools that are used to organize the information and present it as a comprehensible manner. However, these tools also guide the systems analyst in the process of collecting the information by specifying the information that must be collected and by indicating information gaps that must be filled.

Assuming that the systems analyst is already familiar with the structure of the organization, a logical starting point for his analysis is the collection of samples of the reports, records, and source documents involved in the data-processing system.

A report is the end product of the system used for decision making or planning. For each report it is necessary to prepare a summary description containing information such as the following:

a) The name of the report.
b) How often it is prepared.
c) Who uses it.
d) How it is used.
e) A description of each element of data appearing on the report.
f) An analysis of the control classifications and the sequence of information used in preparing the report.
g) The maximum and average number of lines per page and pages in the report.

The Grid Chart

After the reports produced from the system are collected, a grid chart[1] may be prepared on which these reports are listed horizontally along the top, as shown in Figure 14–1. The source documents, from which comes the information for these reports, are listed vertically along the left side of the grid chart, and an "X" is placed on the chart to indicate relationships between source documents and reports.

When properly prepared, a grid chart of the entire system defines the system as a black box by specifying its inputs and outputs. The preparation of the grid chart provides some organization for the process of collecting source documents and some logical tests of the completeness of the definition of the system, for reports without source documents and source documents that are not used indicate that further investigation is required.

Samples of each of the source documents must be collected, and a

---

[1] This tool was developed by the Army Task Force at Fort Meade, Maryland. It is reported in *An Approach to the Basic Techniques of Systems Analysis* and *The Application Study* (see supplemental readings at the end of this chapter). Much of the discussion is based on these books.

summary description of each source document should be prepared containing:

a) The name of the document.
b) How and where it is prepared.
c) A description of each field of information on the source document, including its name and size.
d) When it is prepared.
e) Average and maximum volumes in terms of lines per form and forms.
f) The reports and records affected by the source document.

FREQUENCY \ OUTPUT	W	D	D	W	M	D	D	W	D	W	M	D
INPUT	REPORT 1	REPORT 2	REPORT 3	REPORT 4	REPORT 5	REPORT 6	REPORT 7	REPORT 8	REPORT 9	REPORT 10	REPORT 11	REPORT 12
FORM A	X			X		X		X				
FORM B		X	X			X	X		X			
FORM C	X			X								
FORM D			X			X		X	X			
FORM E				X	X		X		X			
FORM F		X				X					X	
FORM G	X					X						
FORM H	X								X			
FORM I			X				X	X			X	

GRID CHART

FIG. 14–1.

After the data-processing system has been defined in terms of its inputs and outputs, it should be broken down into smaller black boxes or subsystems. A convenient breakdown is frequently obvious, for subsystems are usually recognized by the organization and are named—the payroll system, inventory control system, purchasing system, and so forth. It should be noted, however, that the relationships between these systems are frequently not recognized, and this is where the system grid chart is valuable, for these relationships are apparent in the grid chart.

The grid chart may be analyzed to discover convenient breakdowns into independent subsystems by taking any report and drawing a vertical line through it. Then a horizontal line is drawn through each source document corresponding to an "X" covered by the vertical line. Then vertical lines are drawn through the reports corresponding to each "X" that has a horizontal line through it, and so forth. If this process terminates before all the reports and source documents are crossed out, those source documents and reports that are covered by lines form an independent subsystem. It can be verified in Figure 14–1 that forms A, C, E, G, H, and reports 1, 4, 5, 7, and 10 form an independent subsystem. Furthermore, those subsystems that are almost independent (connected by only a few x's in the grid chart) can be investigated as a potentially fruitful breakdown of the system.

After the breakdown into subsystems, a separate grid chart can then be prepared for each subsystem to define it in terms of its inputs and outputs. Here, in addition to source documents and reports, it is possible to have two other types of documents involved in the grid chart, namely records (or files) and intermediate documents.

Records are forms or files that are maintained for reference purposes and from which data are extracted for the preparation of reports. For each record a summary should be prepared including the following information:

a) The name of the record.
b) The purpose and use for which it is maintained.
c) A description of each field of information on the record, including its size.
d) The number of records in the file and the turnover of the records (additions and deletions per time period).
e) The sequence of the data and the reason for this sequence.
f) The frequency of maintenance of and reference to the file.

Intermediate documents are products of a data-processing system that are used to facilitate the operation of the system but are not end reports. They usually contain intermediate results in manual or punched card systems and are seldom produced in readable form in electronic data-processing systems. Examples are manual worksheets and most punched cards. A summary should be prepared for each intermediate document similar to those for the source documents and files.

Flow Charting

After the system has been broken down into subsystems of reasonable size and complexity, a flow chart should be prepared for each subsystem showing how the inputs are converted into the outputs. Flow chart symbols for representing mechanized processing steps have been described in Chapter 8. Since most systems include some manual subsystems, or at least manual data-processing operations,

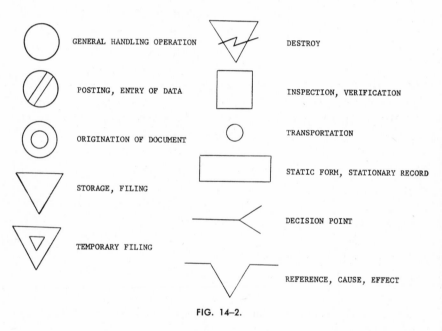

FLOW CHART SYMBOLS

GENERAL HANDLING OPERATION

DESTROY

POSTING, ENTRY OF DATA

INSPECTION, VERIFICATION

ORIGINATION OF DOCUMENT

TRANSPORTATION

STORAGE, FILING

STATIC FORM, STATIONARY RECORD

TEMPORARY FILING

DECISION POINT

REFERENCE, CAUSE, EFFECT

FIG. 14–2.

it is desirable to have flow chart symbols for manual operations. One possible set of such symbols, along with the meaning of each, is presented in Figure 14–2. A hypothetical procedure for processing shop-material orders is illustrated in Figure 14–3. The steps in this procedure are numbered, and a brief description of each step must be included to make the flow chart understandable. These comments are shown below.

1. An original voucher copy and three carbons of the material order is typed by the planning department.
2. The third carbon is held in a suspense file.

3. The voucher copy and two carbons are sent to the material control department.
4. The order is checked for completeness and authenticity.
5. The inventory control record is pulled.
6. The balance is checked against the quantity to be issued.
7. The quantity to be issued is subtracted from the balance, and the new balance is recorded on the inventory control record.
8. The order is stamped "fill" and initialed by the control clerk.
9. The inventory control record is refiled.
10. The second carbon of the material order is filed (authority to delete from inventory control record).
11. The remaining two copies of the order are forwarded to the store-keeper.

SIMPLIFIED FLOW CHART   SHOP MATERIAL ORDER

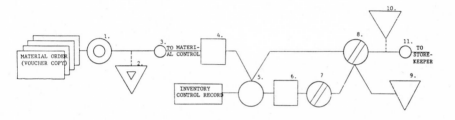

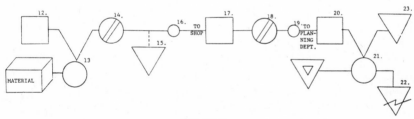

FIG. 14–3.

12. The completeness and authenticity of the order is verified.
13. The material is pulled from stock.
14. The order is stamped "filled" and initialed.
15. The carbon copy is filed (authority to issue material).
16. The original voucher copy of the order is forwarded with the material to the shop department.
17. The quantity received is checked against the order quantity.
18. The voucher copy is signed to provide a receipt.
19. The voucher copy is forwarded to the planning department.
20. The voucher copy is checked to verify that the required actions have been taken and that the necessary signatures are included.
21. The suspense copy is pulled.
22. The suspense copy is destroyed.
23. The voucher copy is filed.

The above illustration represents only a small part of a subsystem. It does not, for example, show how the material orders are created, nor does it show how the inventory control records are analyzed for inventory control purposes.

Also, in the interest of simplicity, the above illustration omits much that is of paramount importance, for it does not include the exceptional occurrences. For example, what is done in the material control department if the stock number on the order is not included in the inventory control records? What action is taken if the inventory control records show that the item requested is out of stock, or that some stock is available, but not enough to completely fill the order? What action does the storekeeper take if the inventory control records show that material is available for issue, but it is not in the storeroom? A knowledge of exceptions such as these, how they can arise, and how each of them is handled is crucial to understanding the system and must eventually be included in the flow chart representation of the system.

Even with the simple subsystem described above, the flow chart becomes quite complicated when sufficient detail is included. Whenever a chart begins to become so complex as to be too large for a reasonably sized piece of paper or too confusing to be comprehensible, it is desirable to break it down into subprocedures of reasonable size. This can be accomplished by restricting the flow chart to a single end product, or to the processing of a specific document, or by producing a separate chart for each organizational activity involved in the processing. In the above illustration, for example, a separate chart could be prepared for the planning department, the material control department, the storekeeper, and the shop. Alternatively, the main flow chart could be used to indicate the detection of the various exceptional conditions, and separate flow charts could be prepared for each exception to indicate how it is handled.

At the completion of the process of systems analysis described above, the existing system is represented by means of:

1. Summary sheets containing pertinent information about the source documents, records, intermediate documents, and reports in the system.
2. A representation of the data-processing system by a grid chart showing its inputs and outputs and the relationships between them.
3. A breakdown of the system into subsystems with a grid chart showing the relationships between the inputs and outputs of each subsystem. There may be several levels of breakdown into subsystems, with a grid chart for each.

4. For each subsystem in the finest breakdown, a flow chart shows how the inputs are converted into the outputs.

It should be noted that the most difficult part of this representation was glossed over in the discussion of the reports, where it was indicated that the use made of each report should be recorded on the report summary. An understanding of the use for which the outputs are prepared is crucial to an understanding of the system, for this end use provides the only justification for the entire processing activity. No matter how much knowledge is obtained of the detailed flows of information within a system, an understanding of the system must include a knowledge of the use made of the output reports. This knowledge is difficult both to obtain and to represent, so the systems analyst should take special care to prepare a complete and accurate description of how each report is used.

Obtaining the Information

The foregoing discussion of techniques which are useful in the representation of data-processing systems and the information which is required indicated that this information must be obtained by interviewing people. One might think that someone, or at most a few individuals, could describe the data-processing system of the organization. One might even expect that in a well-managed company, data-processing procedures would be available in procedures manuals. There are two major reasons why neither of these is likely to be true. In the first place, the data-processing system is not only complex, but it also permeates the entire organization. Secondly, the data-processing system is dynamic, so any representation (whether it be written or mental) rapidly becomes obsolete.

The required information must be obtained from many sources throughout the organization. Any written procedures that are available should be used as a starting point, but they must be thoroughly checked to verify that they are actually being used. Usually, the major source of information is people—clerks who perform routine processing tasks, supervisors who handle exceptions and make judgment decisions where necessary, and the various levels of management that use the results. The only safe way to obtain the required information is through comprehensive interviews with the people involved at all levels, whenever possible checking one person's answers against those of another to eliminate the many misunderstandings that may exist among those associated with the data-processing system.

Even with the whole-hearted co-operation of everyone concerned, the task of describing a complex data-processing system is difficult at best. And without the co-operation of those being interviewed, this task is literally impossible. Thus, a primary prerequisite for success as a systems analyst is the ability to elicit the co-operation of those in the organization who know the details of operation of the present system. The systems analyst who antagonizes everyone with whom he comes in contact is foredoomed to failure.

How can the systems analyst obtain co-operation? This question cannot be answered in a few words, and this book is not intended as a guide to personality development, but a few comments that are pertinent to the specific human relations problems involved in systems analysis may be of value. In the first place, the systems analyst must be careful to go through the recognized organizational channels. The co-operation of the supervisor must be obtained before approaching anyone in a section or justified resentment is likely to result. Courtesy demands that the results of any investigation be reported to the supervisor involved and that gratitude be expressed to him and his subordinates for their co-operation.

The systems analyst should always remember that the mere fact that someone is probing into how people are performing their jobs is likely to make everyone apprehensive and, therefore, somewhat resentful. Also, he is imposing upon the time of everyone with whom he talks, for they are primarily concerned with getting the job done. Even with the most efficient use of time, the interviewing process is quite lengthy and tedious and often involves several interviews with each person. It is important that the systems analyst be well prepared for each interview so that the required information can be obtained as quickly as possible and recorded in an orderly manner. Before each interview, the analyst should carefully study the situation and decide what information he should attempt to obtain. Then he should prepare an outline that can be filled in during the interview to make sure that the desired information is obtained without undue wandering. Of course, excessive efficiency can be most irritating, so the systems analyst must develop a feeling for the attitude of those being interviewed and conduct himself with a suitable mixture of casualness and efficiency.

It is imperative that the systems analyst overcome the temptation to intermix the process of defining the present data-processing system with the process of redesigning and improving the system. Nothing causes resentment faster than for the systems analyst to indicate during an interview that the job is not being done properly. The purpose of the interview is to obtain an understanding of the present data-processing system, and suggestions for improvement not only make it more difficult to obtain information about the system, but also make it harder to implement changes later, for those affected can begin to fight the changes sooner. Also, until a thorough understanding of the entire system is acquired, it is highly desirable that the systems analyst maintain an open mind concerning what the system should be. Since those being interviewed are likely to be quite sensitive to the reaction of the systems analyst, he must be careful not to indicate disapproval by direct comments, questions, facial expression, or tone of voice.

The systems analyst must walk a narrow and difficult line, for without arousing antagonism he must probe deeply into individual conduct and thought processes. Those being interviewed may not understand that a description of the routine part of a job is but the beginning of the task, so they may not comprehend the necessity of isolating and examining each seemingly trivial exception. The systems analyst must continually employ the "honest servingmen" of Kipling:

> I keep six honest servingmen
> (They taught me all I knew) ;
> Their names are What and Why and When
> And How and Where and Who.

But care must be taken to minimize the resentment and antagonism aroused by the use of these servingmen.

Improving the Results of the System

After an understanding and a representation of the existing data-processing system have been obtained, the next step in the process of systems analysis and design is to determine the output results that should be produced by an improved system. Although no simple, direct process can be used to determine the results that should be produced by a data-processing system, it is possible to suggest a helpful general approach to this problem.

In any problem-solving procedure, it is desirable to first specify the objective. As was discussed in Chapter 2, the objective of data processing is to provide a basis for adequate management control of the organization. Thus, the concept of the feedback-control loop (or servomechanism) provides a valuable frame of reference within which to consider the output results which a data-processing system should provide. As shown in Figure 14–4, control depends upon two basic factors: (1) the existence of goals to be obtained; and (2) the flow of information in the control loop. In the control loop, information about the performance of "operations" is collected and organized so that it may be compared with the goals (objectives, expectations, performance criteria) specified. If the goals are being satisfactorily attained, then the control process goes no farther. But, if there are deviations, then it is necessary to decide what to do to produce the desired results, and this decision must be implemented.

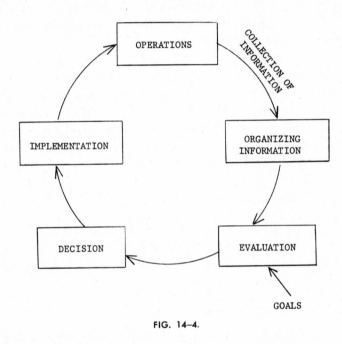

FIG. 14–4.

It may be observed that there is a direct relationship between the form in which the goals specified by management are presented and the results that must be prepared by the data-processing system for comparison with these goals. The goals or plans by which performance is evaluated go a long way toward the determination of the information that must be collected and the processing that must be performed. On the other hand, the information that can be collected and processed provides a constraint upon the criteria which management can use to evaluate performance. Therefore, the systems analyst and the manager must co-operate so that the design of the data-processing system and the establishment of goals (or criteria for evaluation) can be co-ordinated.

It is also desirable that the talents and capabilities of management be used in the control system only where required. Since the screening of results against performance criteria is both a dull and high-volume operation, whenever possible it should be included in the data-processing system so that the system produces results to management only when management's attention is necessary. Thus, the concept of management by exception provides guidance when considering the output that should be produced from the data-processing system.

When the output results that should be produced by the data-processing system are considered, it is desirable to first study this problem in the abstract without consideration of what is being produced by the present system. A completely fresh viewpoint and approach may lead to spectacular improvements in the management control achieved. Of course, any radically new approach must be compared with the representation of the present system to determine whether it can stand the test of realistic complexity.

Although potentially of great value, the abstract approach to such a complex problem may not lead to fruitful results. If this happens, the complexity of the problem can be substantially reduced by referring to the present system and asking how its output results might be modified to achieve improved control. In this situation, the systems analyst, guided by the feedback-control concept, can profitably adopt a "questioning attitude" toward the outputs produced by the present system.

Each output of the system should be skeptically examined to eliminate the unnecessary. A most useful question is: Why is this required? Since most data-processing systems have developed over a period of time without co-ordination and with a minimum of integrated planning, most of them contain a substantial amount of inefficient duplication and produce a variety of anachronistic output reports that are no longer used. Not only should unused reports be ruthlessly eliminated, but even those that are put to some use should be evaluated to determine whether their value justifies their cost.

After each output's use has been determined, it is proper to ask: Is the report adequate for the purpose? Does it contain the required information? Should it be more detailed? Should it be better summarized? Is the information summarized according to the most meaningful classifications? Should additional information be added? Is the user combining it with other reports before he uses it? Is some of the information superfluous? Is the information presented in the most usable form? Is it available at the time that the information is needed for adequate control? Should it be produced upon demand rather than periodically? Thoughtful attention to such questions may result in substantial improvements in the outputs of the system through elimination of reports, combination of reports, further processing of results, and revisions of report content and form.

In the process of determining the output requirements of a data-processing system, it is frequently necessary to ask management, "What information do you need?" Although this question must be asked, the answers do not always provide a solution to the systems problems. The most likely answer is, "Just what I've been getting for the past twenty years, except perhaps a little quicker." On the other hand, a manager may become enthusiastic and ask for information that is impossible or impractical to produce. The latter attitude is not necessarily harmful if the manager is willing to give some serious thought to the problem to arrive at a compromise. However, the systems analyst must be careful not to create the impression that he (or a computer) is a magician who can pull miracles out of a hat at a moment's notice.

Design of an Improved System

After the results that should be produced from the data-processing system have been determined, the problem of how to most effectively produce these results still remains. The data-processing tools must be determined and suitable procedures for their use must be devised. In this book, a number of procedures have been presented for which punched card and electronic data-processing equipment are used. Substantial parts of Chapters 4 and 8 have been devoted to the development of such procedures. At this point, we may ask the question: How do we approach the task of devising data-processing procedures?

When attempting to improve manual procedures,[2] a popular approach is to start with the existing system and attempt to make incremental improvements where they are indicated. Although this approach may lead to an improved manual system, it is definitely to be avoided when designing a mechanized system to replace man-

---

[2] Those who desire more knowledge of techniques that are useful in the improvement of manual systems should refer to a standard book on office systems such as George Terry, *Office Management and Control* (3d ed.; Homewood, Ill.: Richard D. Irwin, Inc., 1958).

ual processing, for the capabilities of machines are radically different from those of humans, and an attempt to pattern the use of machines after manual methods is usually disastrous. Radical restructuring of the system is usually required to produce efficient processing. Thus, the design of a mechanized data-processing system is a creative process, so no "cookbook" procedure can assure success. However, many people have analyzed the process of creative thinking,[3] and the systems analyst may find several approaches that are of value in designing procedures.

The first step in the solution of a problem is to define it so that it can be given concentrated attention. Creative ideas do not occur at random—they are usually the result of hard work and study specifically directed at a well-defined problem. This important step in the design of data-processing systems has been described at length in the preceding portions of this chapter.

Secondly, creativity is based upon knowledge. Thus, the systems analyst should concentrate upon extending his knowledge of data-processing equipment and its use. He must keep up with new developments in a rapidly changing field, and any new machine manual or procedure write-up may contain an idea that will be invaluable sometime in the future. For example, the applications discussed in Chapter 9 include several approaches to the use of memory that may be of great value in entirely different situations. As was emphasized in Chapter 8, it is imperative that the systems designer have a comprehensive knowledge of the equipment for which he is designing procedures, for the efficiency of a procedure often depends upon taking advantage of specific equipment characteristics.

Thirdly, creative systems design depends upon the development of a multitude of alternative approaches to the solution of the problem. In the long run, the systems designer who quits when he discovers a workable solution to the problem at hand is not likely to be successful, for there may be several other radically different approaches, one of which may be definitely superior to all the rest. The designer should let his imagination roam unfettered. He should collect and record all ideas that occur to him without regard to their practicality, consider all existing ideas and knowledge in all possible combinations and relationships, and use each new idea as a steppingstone to another by attempting to combine it with another

---

[3] See references *The Creative Thinking Process* and *How to Solve It* in the supplemental readings.

approach—modifying it, extending it, adapting it, reversing it, and rearranging it. In the design of data-processing systems, as well as in other creative processes, the larger the store of possible alternative solutions that can be created, the more likely is the development of a satisfactory solution.

In the design of mechanized data-processing systems there are several crucial areas upon which the systems designer might profitably concentrate his efforts to develop alternative approaches. The first of these is the area of data recording. As a general rule, the data should be recorded in machine-processable form as near their source as possible. Since recording is a relatively expensive process, the development of the most efficient recording method to suit the situation is of special importance. Another crucial area is that of processing sequence and file organization. Can several files be consolidated so that all required information may be obtained from one reference? Should one file be split in two so that one part can be processed frequently and the other only occasionally? In what possible sequences might this file be maintained? Should this file be processed sequentially or in random order? Such questions as these may lead to the development of a number of alternative basic approaches to the design of procedures to solve a given problem.

As was pointed out in Chapter 8, after a basic procedural approach to the problem has been devised, much effort must still be devoted to block diagramming, writing programs, debugging, and conversion. All of these processes are related to the initial design of the procedure, for problems that arise in these later stages may force major redesign of the procedures.

Relationships between Systems Objectives, Systems Design, and Data-Processing Equipment

In designing a data-processing system, it is necessary to consider the value of the possible alternative variations in output that could be produced from the system. Since management control is the major motivation for producing data-processing outputs, two questions arise in evaluating these outputs: (1) How much does it affect management control? (2) How much is this management control worth? These questions are almost impossible to answer by actual measurement, so management judgment usually must suffice. Assuming that a value can be placed on the various alternative sets of data-processing results, they could then be placed in sequence of increasing value, and their cost could be plotted against their value, as shown in Figure 14–5.

It would be convenient if the relationship between the value of possible alternative outputs from a data-processing system and the cost of producing them were smooth and well-behaved as shown in Figure 14–5. Unfortunately, this relationship is by no means smooth and well-behaved, for seemingly minor changes in the form or con-

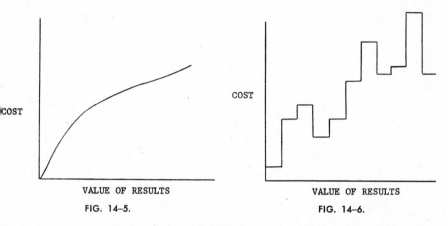

FIG. 14–5.

FIG. 14–6.

tent of data-processing outputs frequently lead to large variations in the cost of producing these results. This is illustrated in Figure 14–6, which shows that it is possible to decrease data-processing costs and at the same time increase the value of the output reports. In this rather chaotic situation, the task of the systems designer is neither to maximize the value of the data-processing results nor to minimize the cost of data processing. The task of the systems designer is to maximize data-processing profit —the difference between the value of the results of data processing and the cost of obtaining these results, which is shown in Figure 14–7.

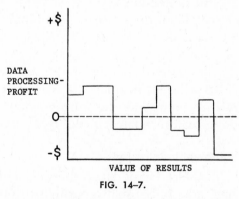

FIG. 14–7.

Because of this complex relationship between cost and value of information, it is not possible to completely separate the task of specifying the results to be obtained through a data-processing system from that of designing the system to obtain the results. That is to say, the results that are most desirable cannot be determined until an attempt has been made to design the system, for the cost of producing these results cannot be reliably estimated until the system has been designed. Therefore, there must be a considerable interplay between the process of systems design and the specification of the results to be obtained from the system. It is imperative that management be adequately educated concerning this interrelationship, and that the systems analyst and the manager who is to use the information produced be able to co-operate in the determination of a set of outputs and a system design that maximizes the difference between cost and value.

The above problem is further complicated by two additional considerations. In the first place, it is the cost of and the value produced by the entire data-processing system that are of concern, not the cost of an individual report in comparison with the value of that specific report. This is merely another way of saying that, for best over-all results, the requirements of the various users of the output information must be interrelated with one another so that an effective over-all system can be designed, and this implies that compromises must be obtained between the conflicting viewpoints of the various managers that may be involved. In the following chapters, we will be concerned with the organizational implications of this necessity of arriving at these compromises in the design and implementation of an effective data-processing system.

Secondly, the costs of a given data-processing procedure are also related to the type of mechanized equipment available, which adds a third dimension to the cost versus value considerations just discussed. Thus, the selection of equipment becomes involved with the analysis and design of data-processing systems. In particular, assuming that the output results to be obtained from a data-processing system are fixed, the data-processing system design that is most efficient will depend upon the type of equipment available. Carrying this reasoning one step further, the output results that should be produced are related to the type of equipment that may be used.

Equipment Selection

The selection of data-processing equipment is a complex and difficult task. It is usually possible to decide on the general type of equipment that can be considered on the basis of a general knowledge of the systems requirements, the volumes of data, and the amount of money available. However, choosing between specific machines and configurations of equipment may be a formidable task. Theoretically, each machine has a data-processing profit graph, similar to Figure 14–7, that should determine the output results and procedures that give a maximum profit for that machine. Then these maximum profits should be compared to decide between machines. Thus, theoretically, it is unfair to set the output requirements and then decide on the best machine with which to produce those outputs.

Actually, it is not unusual for the equipment decision to be made before the systems design is completed. Fortunately, the type of equipment utilized is frequently of secondary importance if a system is designed that is efficient with that particular equipment. Another approach is to specify the output requirements of the system, and then develop an individual system for each alternative machine under consideration. The machine manufacturers can be utilized in this process, for they will usually study a problem, design a system that is efficient for their machine, and present a detailed proposal for evaluation. The evaluation of such proposals is not a simple task, for the analyst must understand the proposal (and the machine) well enough to determine whether the proposed system will actually fulfill the requirements and to evaluate the reliability of the time and cost estimates included. Despite the complexity of evaluation, a variety of proposals is a definite asset, for it usually provides a group of alternative approaches that is valuable when designing the system, no matter which machine is chosen. Furthermore, a knowledge of several different machines and the various approaches to their use is useful to the systems analyst by providing him with an additional stock of ideas which he may use in his creative thinking process.

Summary

Data-processing should be viewed as an integrated system whose basic objective is to provide the necessary information for adequate management control of the organization.

To design a data-processing system, a desirable starting point is an understanding of the present system. Then the outputs required from the system must be determined to contribute to the achievement of the desired management control, the equipment to be used must be chosen, and efficient procedures for the accomplishment of the desired results must be devised.

A variety of tools and techniques may be used in the process of obtaining a representation of the existing data-processing system, including grid charts and various types of flow charts. Most of the required information must be obtained by talking with people who are doing the work or using the results.

It is more difficult to describe the creative process involved in determining the best output information to be produced and in devising efficient procedures for producing these outputs. In creative systems design, it is desirable to concentrate attention upon defining the problem, the development of knowledge relevant to the problem, and the devising of unusual alternative approaches.

The output results desired and the procedures and equipment used are intimately related, since the desirability of a particular set of output results is heavily dependent upon their cost, which is determined by the procedures and equipment employed. Since the basic objective of data processing is to contribute to management control, the systems analyst and the manager must co-operate in the design of a data-processing system that will maximize the data-processing profit, that is, the difference between the value for management control of the information produced and the cost of data processing.

EXERCISES

14.1 What are the most important abilities desirable for success in systems analysis and design work?

14.2 If you were beginning a system study, what types of meaningful intermediate targets might be set when planning the over-all allocation of time and effort on the project?

14.3 What are the most difficult problems involved in obtaining a representation of an existing data-processing system?

14.4 Why and how is management involved in the task of systems analysis and design?

14.5 *a*) It is reasonable to compare two computers feature by feature (that is, amount of memory, arithmetic speed, tape speed and density, word size, instruction format, etc.)? Why?

   b) What information in addition to the above is required to decide upon the type of equipment that should be employed?

14.6 Prepare a flow chart representation of:

   a) The registration- and grade-recording system of your educational institution.
   b) The parking ticket system used by your city.
   c) The chemistry stockroom record-keeping system for your educational institution.

   Can you suggest improvements in these systems?

SUPPLEMENTAL READINGS

An Approach to the Basic Techniques of Systems Analysis. Prepared by the Federal Government Sales Office, Electronic Data Processing Division, Radio Corporation of America, 1725 K Street N.W., Washington 6, D.C.

This is one of the few publications on systems analysis available from equipment manufacturers.

The Application Study. Data Processing Department of the U.S. Army Adjutant General's School, Fort Benjamin Harrison, Indiana.

Although written in military style, this little booklet is the source of several excellent approaches to systems analysis problems. It was developed out of experience of the Army Task Force at Fort George G. Meade, Maryland.

GRAD, BURTON, and CANNING, R. G. "Information Process Analysis," *Journal of Industrial Engineering,* Vol. X, No. 6 (November–December, 1959), pp. 470–76.

This article suggests that, in systems analysis, flows of information should be charted rather than flows of paper. A set of symbols for this purpose is suggested, and simple illustrations are presented. This system appears to give a concise abstract representation of the data-processing system without obscuring this with the details of how it is accomplished.

GREGORY, R. H., and VAN HORN, R. L. *Automatic Data-Processing Systems.* San Francisco: Wadsworth Publishing Co., Inc., 1960.

Chapters 11, 12, 14, and 15 are devoted to the basic principles, techniques, and economics of systems analysis and design. Chapter 10 discusses the cost and value of information.

MEE, JOHN F. "The Creative Thinking Process," *Selected Readings in Management* (ed. Fremont A. Shull, Jr.), pp. 150–55. Homewood, Illinois: Richard D. Irwin, Inc., 1958.

This presents an excellent discussion of the creative thinking process.

OPTNER, STANFORD L. *Systems Analysis for Business Management.* Englewood Cliffs, N.J.: Prentice-Hall, Inc., 1960.

This book is devoted to the principles and techniques of systems analysis and design. In addition to an excellent presentation of the importance of planning and scheduling systems work, it also includes a number of check lists that are useful to the systems analyst. Ten short cases are included at the end of this book.

POLYA, G. *How to Solve It.* Princeton, N.J.: Princeton University Press, 1948.

This interesting little book is concerned with the development of a general approach to the solving of problems. Although written for teachers of mathematics, it is a simple book and is useful for anyone who must solve problems.

CHAPTER 15 · Problems Involved in Introducing a Computer

ALTHOUGH many potential advantages can be gained through the use of electronic data processing, the introduction of an electronic computer into an organization also introduces some important and complex problems. The computer does not automatically solve problems—it is only a tool and someone must devise a way to use it in a particular application. But before we can get around to solving the original problems for which we obtained the computer, it is necessary to face many problems created by the computer itself.

As was discussed in Chapter 2, the data-processing system of an organization is of almost unimaginable complexity. The introduction of a computer usually involves widespread changes in this complex system. Moreover, the data-processing system is inextricably interrelated with the entire organization, so that changes in the data-processing system may have an extreme impact upon the performance of the organization.

Indeed, the potential benefit of the use of the computer may be directly proportional to the disturbance that its introduction creates, for the use of the computer should open new possibilities not attainable with less powerful processing capabilities. Thus a computer that introduces no problems is unlikely to produce significant results.

This chapter discusses some of the most important problems that arise with the introduction of a computer. Our objective here is to present the problems—not to present the solutions. The solutions will be different depending upon the particular circumstances, and, in some cases, there may be no solution. The important thing, however, is that these problems be faced by management before their symptoms become apparent in the form of emergencies.

334

Human Problems

Much of the advantage of mechanization is that it replaces human effort by machines, thus increasing the productivity of the individual worker. One distinction made between the concepts of mechanization and automation is that mechanization replaces muscle power while automation replaces brain power. The electronic computer is *expected* to take over jobs or portions of jobs that were previously performed by human beings. Historically, this process of replacement of man by machines has created widespread sociological and economic problems. The introduction of the first automatic looms in England created vast unemployment; mechanization in the coal mining industry has profoundly affected both the worker and economics of the industry; and mechanization on the American farm is vastly increasing the productivity of the farm worker, but, at the same time, it is destroying the traditional "family" farming operation.

Although they are aware of the many problems associated with automation, most American labor leaders are publicly welcoming the opportunities afforded by automation rather than trying to turn back the clock. For example, when Philip Murray was president of the CIO, he said:

I do not know of a single solitary instance where a great technological gain has taken place in the United States of America that has actually thrown people out of work. I do not know of it, I am not aware of it, because the industrial revolution that has taken place in the United States in the past 25 years has brought into the employment field an additional 20 million people.[1]

And Walter Reuther, in testimony before a congressional subcommittee as president of the CIO, said:

First of all, we fully realize that the potential benefits of automation are great, if properly handled. If only a fraction of what technologists promise for the future is true, within a very few years automation can and should make possible a four-day work-week, longer vacation periods, opportunities for earlier retirement, as well as a vast increase in our material standards of living.

At the same time, automation can bring freedom from the monotonous drudgery of many jobs in which the worker today is no more than a serv-

---

[1] Quoted by Robert C. Tait (Statement before the Subcommittee on Economic Stabilization of the Joint Committee on the Economic Report, 84th Cong.), hearings published under the title "Automation and Technological Change," pp. 204–5.

ant of the machine. It can free workers from routine, repetitious tasks which the new machines can be taught to do, and give to the workers who toil at those tasks the opportunity of developing higher skills.[2]

Despite the attitude expressed in the above quotations, the use of the electronic computer has presented problems to organized labor. Wallace Webber, president of Local 889 of the United Auto Workers, a white-collar local that represents office workers in Chrysler auto plants, has stated:

Three years ago Local 889 had 5,000 members. Now we have 4,000, and the loss mostly is due to the inroads of automation in offices.
. . . In the long run, this (the increasing use of computers) may eliminate half our jobs.[3]

Actually, relatively few office workers are unionized, so the introduction of computers may present organized labor with an important opportunity to organize these workers by exploiting the fear, uncertainity, and changes in status accompanying office automation.

In remarkably few instances has union action affected the use of electronic computers. The major difficulties have arisen when contract seniority provisions have made it difficult to move the most capable people into system analysis and programming work. In one isolated instance, unexpected labor negotiation difficulties appear to have significantly delayed the conversion of some applications to a computer installed by a large railroad.

A study of the effect of the installation of a Univac at a large insurance company was made by the United States Department of Labor.[4] Of the 198 persons formerly required to carry out the function taken over by the computer, only 85 were expected to remain after the computer was completely installed. Table 15–1 shows what happened to the 106 persons who had been displaced at the time of the study.

Of course, the replacement of jobs is only the negative part of the story—new jobs are also created. The Department of Labor study indicated that the insurance company involved required 20 new jobs associated with the actual operation of the computer, as well as 9 new jobs in systems and procedures work. Although the total num-

---

[2] Walter P. Reuther, *ibid.,* p. 101.

[3] "Office Automation Hits UAW," *Business Week,* April 9, 1960, p. 58.

[4] K. G. Van Auken, Jr., "The Introduction of an Electronic Computer in a Large Insurance Company" (Printed as an appendix to the testimony of James P. Mitchell, Secretary of Labor, before the Subcommittee on Economic Stabilization of the 84th Cong. on October 24, 1955). Included in "Automation and Technological Change," pp. 290–300.

TABLE 15–1

Distribution of Releases from Division	Men	Women	Total
Transferred to other jobs within the division..............7		65	72
Transferred to jobs in other divisions.....................2		13	15
Retired...		1	1
Resigned (14 marriages, 2 jobs in another company, 2 moved to other areas).................................		18	18
Total..9		97	106

Source: "Automation and Technological Change" (Hearings before the Subcommittee on Economic Stabilization, 84th Cong.), p. 296.

ber of jobs in the affected section was drastically reduced, the total effect included considerable upgrading—the average salary of the 85 remaining employees was $4,200 per year as opposed to a previous average salary in the section of $3,700 per year. Table 15–2 shows the wage structure of the section before and after the installation of the computer. It is interesting that the major effect of this computer was

TABLE 15–2

Approximate Annual Salary	Number of Employees							
	Originally in Classification Sections		Released or to Be Released for other Assignments		Assigned to the Computer Operations		Expected in New Classification Sections	
	Men	Women	Men	Women	Men	Women	Men	Women
$2,500..........	...	4	...	...	...	...	...	4
2,800..........	...	6	...	1	...	...	...	5
3,000..........	...	35	...	30	...	...	...	5
3,200..........	...	35	...	28	1	1	1	8
3,400..........	...	52	...	34	...	...	...	18
3,600..........	3	...	3	...	1	...	1	...
3,700..........	...	9	...	4	...	...	...	5
4,000..........	...	16	...	9	3	2	3	9
4,300..........	...	8	...	3	1	...	1	5
4,600..........	1	12	1	11	...	1	...	2
5,000..........	...	7	...	3	...	1	...	5
5,400..........	...	1	...	1	...	2	...	2
5,800..........	...	3	...	1	...	1	...	3
6,700..........	...	1	...	1	...	...	...	...
7,200..........	1	...	1	...	2	...	2	...
7,600..........	2	...	1	...	1	...	2	...
8,100..........	...	...	...	...	2	...	2	...
8,500..........	1	...	1	...	...	...	...	...
9,000 and over...	1	...	...	...	1	...	2	...
Total......	9	189	7	126	12	8	14	71

Source: "Automation and Technological Change" (Hearings before the Subcommittee on Economic Stabilization, 84th Cong.), p. 298.

to allow a reduction of 92 women's jobs paying from $250 to $283 per month ($3,000 to $3,400 per year), while the total number of men employed in the section actually increased.

The impact of computers upon clerical workers has been greatest in the large paperwork organizations, such as insurance and certain government agencies, in which very high-volume, specialized operations are involved. For example, in early 1956 the Treasury Department installed an IBM 705 for centralized reconciliation and payment of all U.S. government checks.[5] This single installation reduced the personnel requirements in the sections affected from 755 to 270 and also allowed the Federal Reserve banks to achieve a reduction of an additional 400 employees.

On the other hand, the computers in use in manufacturing organizations for general data-processing work have not achieved such spectacular reductions in clerical forces. They have tended to concentrate on the production of hitherto unavailable information rather than upon replacing clerks.

As was shown in Table 15–2, the other effect of the introduction of computers is the creation of an entirely new class of jobs. This is a significant effect, for in March of 1958 the U.S. government alone had requirements (partially unfilled) for about 4,300 positions created by the computer, and it was estimated that by 1961 the federal government alone would require over 12,000 people to work with computers.[6] In December, 1956, at the dedication of the 100th IBM 700 series computer, IBM vice president L. H. LaMotte said:[7]

> Inside of a decade we expect there will be close to 10,000 stored program computers installed. This means that somewhere around 150,000 to 200,000 people will have to be trained to use the machines. It isn't very often that an entirely new profession of such size is established.

Effect on Individuals

It should be observed that the new jobs that are created frequently require different talents than do the jobs that are eliminated, so entirely different people may be involved. The clerk that is replaced seldom has the ability to become a systems analyst or a programmer, although she may perhaps become a key punch operator.

---

[5] "Use of Electronic Data-Processing Equipment" (Hearing before the Subcommittee on Census and Government Statistics of the Committee on Post Office and Civil Service, House of Representatives, 86th Cong., June 5, 1958), Appendix A.

[6] *Ibid.*, Appendix 6, Exhibit 6, p. 94.

[7] *Computing News,* Vol. 5, No. 94 (February 1, 1957).

Although not too much specific information is available on this subject, it is widely believed that the majority of the workers replaced by the electronic data-processing machine are performing work requiring minimum skills, and consequently drawing minimum pay. These positions are usually filled by young women who plan to work a few years before marriage. Because of the high demand for this type of worker, the rapid turnover involved, and the relative ease with which such workers can be transferred to other unskilled jobs within the company, relatively few difficulties have arisen in this area. The use of an electronic data-processing machine has seldom caused many of these workers to be fired or laid off—the problem is usually solved by slowing down the rate of hiring and replacement, which merely transfers the burden to those just entering the work force. Older workers who have achieved a certain amount of seniority and who are relatively less flexible may cause more serious problems. The skills that they have acquired through years of experience may no longer be required, and these skills may not be transferable to other jobs. The jobs associated primarily with the supervision of clerical people are also eliminated when the computer replaces the clerks, and these supervisors are frequently older workers who have attained their position primarily through seniority.

In addition to the jobs that are eliminated, many other jobs may be substantially changed. Here there are two possibilities: (1) The computer may take over the dull routine part of the job, thus allowing the worker to concentrate his abilities on the creative and challenging aspects; or (2) the computer may take over the interesting parts of the work, leaving only the boring repetitious labor or preparing input information. Undoubtedly, both of these situations arise in practice, so it is impossible to generalize without knowledge of the specific situation.

Morale Problems

Despite everything that can be done to reduce its impact upon the individual, we must face the fact that the introduction of an electronic computer into an organization can and must affect the jobs of some of the workers. And human nature being what it is, the psychological effects of introducing a computer may injure the morale of people who actually will not be otherwise affected by the machine.

When rumors begin to spread to the effect that management is considering using a "giant brain" in the office, there is likely to be an accompanying fear among clerical workers concerning job security. In addition, there is a natural tendency to resent and fear any changes that may occur in the job itself (quite apart from the fear of actual unemployment). People do not like to change, especially when they are faced with the possibility of changes caused by something as mysterious and unknown as the "giant brain."

One of the most critical factors affecting the success or failure of an electronic data-processing system is the attitude of employees throughout the organization toward the machine. As we have seen, the machines are totally dependent upon humans for the provision of accurate input at the proper time, as well as for the planning and designing of adequate programs. Resentment by employees during the system's design and analysis stage, which might cause them to withhold or falsify information concerning the job to be done, can vastly increase the difficulties involved. After the machine is installed, production schedules can be completely disrupted by tardy data, and the machine procedures can be badly snarled by a relatively low proportion of erroneous or missing data.

As an illustration of the problems that can arise, let us consider the installation of a 705 at Detroit Edison. Although this company established a policy that no employee would be laid off as a result of the computer, this did not completely solve the problem.

Detroit Edison recognized that they would have problems obtaining the co-operation of those employees directly related to the processing that was to be converted to the computer, so they were careful to educate them and encourage their help. This proved quite successful, for this group of people were willing to make personal sacrifices to insure the success of the installation. However, a sizable group of people, primarily concerned with customer relations, were also significantly affected. Because they were only indirectly related to the new system, these people were overlooked and did not fully participate in the employee education and orientation program. During the conversion, serious problems were caused by the attitude of these people and their resentment of the machine and the changes it caused. In the words of Mr. Elliott, Director of Central Data Processing of Detroit Edison:

> This resentment resulted in accusations, the magnification of errors, and frictions between the less oriented employees contacting the customers and the more oriented employees maintaining the accounts. It also

resulted in much challenging of procedures, which had been approved by their own superiors in this indirect area of responsibility.

This became quite serious. People were talking about "this 705 system." Feelings became so intense that top management people began to be quite concerned about the adequacy of the new system. Just after the first of this year, our President decided that the whole matter should be looked into. Consequently, outside consultants were hired to evaluate the system. Of course, it is quite a letdown after you've gone through a change of this magnitude to have it questioned as to adequacy.[8]

In the above case, the consultants reported that the procedures employed were sound and that the conversion itself involved no more than the normally expected number of errors. The installation was ultimately successful, yet the human relations problems almost caused disaster.

Experience so far has indicated that, with proper planning, the employee dislocation and the morale problems can be substantially reduced. This, of course, requires that management be concerned with the effects of the machine upon the employees, and that it devote much thought to the retraining, selection, and communications problems involved. Most of the dislocation problems can be ameliorated if management sincerely believes that the company employees are among its most valuable resources and is therefore actively concerned with employee welfare. Under such conditions, the psychological problems are also minimized and can usually be taken care of by a properly planned and timed employee educational program.

Company policy will, to a large extent, determine the effects that the use of an electronic data-processing machine will have on employees. This company policy toward employees, as well as the overall pattern of labor relations, should be determined long before a computer is installed. When the use of a computer is first seriously considered, and *before* rumors have a chance to start, both the policy and the effects of the machine should be explained to all employees who may be affected.

Mr. Wesley S. Bagby describes a seemingly successful program in this area:

At Pacific Mutual we established a comprehensive program to orient our employees on the subject of electronic data processing early in 1953, at the same time that we decided to make a full-scale feasibility survey. A

---

[8] J. D. Elliott, "EDP—Its Impact on Jobs, Procedures and People," *Journal of Industrial Engineering*, Vol. IX, No. 5 (September–October, 1958), pp. 407–10.

member of top management told *all* employees why the study was being made, what we thought it might lead to, and how they would be affected. He emphasized that any jobs eliminated would be the repetitive, monotonous, primarily clerical tasks. He promised that, if the study justified acquiring a machine, each employee would have a chance to qualify for the upgraded jobs which would be created by it. Perhaps most important of all, he assured each employee that even if his or her job were eliminated, the employee would be retained and relocated in suitable work at no reduction in salary.

We kept our staff informed of the progress of our studies and—when a decision was reached—of our reasons for installing a system. We told them of every major step in our long-range plans for converting our ordinary insurance record-keeping activities of manual and punched-card to tape-processing methods. Educational material on electronics was a regular feature in our house organ, and a series of lecture courses was made available for those interested.[9]

It should be noted, however, that those closely associated with electronic data processing have tended to ignore the existence of morale problems, and thus to fail miserably in their solution. For example, in one company on the West Coast where a study was made, the following situation was found:

Many workers have already been transferred, demoted, or dismissed. Interviews with some of the survivors, now in jobs preparing data for a computer, disclosed unanimous discontent with the monotony, routine, and pressure involved. Yet, when asked for his view of employee reaction to the innovations, the EDP Manager asserted in all sincerity that they all "just love" the changes. Moreover, he maintained, they are "thrilled with the challenge of automation."[10]

Organizational Problems

An organization should be designed to meet the requirements of the job to be done. Under manual methods those parts of the organization devoted to data processing are organized in conformance with the capabilities and limitations of people. The tasks to be done are broken down into simple steps so that the processing is accomplished by passing batches of work from one specialized section to another. Because of the poor accuracy of human processing, elaborate systems of control and duplication of efforts are built up to insure accurate

---

[9] Wesley S. Bagby, "The Human Side of Electronics" *Proceedings of the Second Annual AMA Electronics Conference: Pioneering in Electronic Data Processing,* Special Report No. 9 (Published by the American Management Association, February 27–29, 1956).

[10] Reported by Ida Russakoff Hoos, "When the Computer Takes Over the Office," *Harvard Business Review,* Vol. 38, No. 4 (July–August, 1960), pp. 102–12.

results. To a large extent, the organizational structure is dictated by the problems associated with supervising groups of people.

Thus, data processing has traditionally been a decentralized operation. A portion of the work of each department within an organization is concerned with data processing. Certain areas (such as production) may do relatively little data processing, while other areas (such as payroll) are almost exclusively concerned with it.

When an electronic data-processing system is used, a large part of the work must be removed from its previous organizational location and centralized for machine processing. One of the major advantages attained through the use of an electronic data-processing machine is the integration of this work into a single system, thereby avoiding the duplication and wasted effort inherent in a manual system. Therefore, it is often necessary to make widespread organizational changes to use electronic data-processing machines effectively. The work of certain sections of the organization may be completely taken over by the machine, while other sections should be reorganized to parallel the changed functions of the group.

One of the most common complaints concerning the use of electronic data-processing machines is that management has been unable to achieve the savings anticipated. The company has not been able to replace the number of people that it had expected to replace. This condition is partially attributable to the difficulties associated with modifying an organizational structure which evolved through years of experience, in the process becoming so entrenched as to be almost unassailable. Any change in organization involves matters of individual prestige among the management of the affected areas. Some influential managers may violently oppose the trimming of their clerical forces, ignoring the fact that the work no longer exists. Furthermore, each individual worker may perform many different clerical operations, some of which may not be readily accomplished by a machine. For example, at present a computer cannot talk to a customer, answer the telephone, type a letter, or expedite an order. When a relatively small portion of the entire job is taken over by a computer, it is likely that the worker affected may find himself busy eight hours a day doing that part of the job which is left—and be supported in this position by his supervisor.

The more effective the utilization of the electronic data-processing system, the greater the effect is likely to be on the organization as a whole. The machines have not exhibited their full impact on organizational structures because truly integrated data-processing systems have not yet been developed. However, as more powerful machines are produced and as we learn more and more about utilizing their capabilities, the machines will be integrated more thoroughly into the data-processing structure of the organization. They will become operating tools rather than mere record-keeping systems. This thought is expressed by Mr. M. J. Kami as follows:

> We believe that in the long-range future data processing equipment will have to help in the actual operations of the business; that it will be used for direct assistance to the people operating or running the different parts of the company including management at the top who must consider the whole operation. In the system of the future there are certainly going to be people—foremen, credit managers, and salesmen, even vice presidents. Therefore, the system of the future—"integrated data processing system" if you prefer the term—will have on its periphery communicating or talking centers with the various operating departments of the business.
>
> The emphasis will be on the use of the system in operations. For example, the foreman, by putting into the system through his communicating or talking center information about his work in process, or the work which has been completed, will use the central equipment to assist him in deciding what to do next. . . .
>
> To give another example, the credit manager will be able to interrogate the system and get back necessary information about the standing of his customers' accounts to show whether credit should be extended or denied. The salesman will be able to interrogate the system in order to find whether goods are in stock and what delivery dates may be given, and so on.[11]

No one knows what the organizational implications of the data-processing system of the future will be. However, experience indicates that it is absolutely necessary that management understand that organizational problems are involved and that it be willing and able to make the required changes. This is another reason why the use of a computer should be a top-management consideration; without the support of top management, the organizational changes required to effectively utilize a computer cannot be made.

Location of Computer

The position of the data-processing function within the organization is of fundamental importance. In the first place, this position reflects the attitude of management towards the data-processing function. If viewed as a necessary evil or a burdensome overhead,

---

[11] M. J. Kami, "Long Range Data Processing Problems," mimeographed copy of a talk given at an IBM Seminar at Endicott, N.Y., August 6, 1957.

it is almost impossible for data processing to make positive contributions. On the other hand, data processing may be a creative force if viewed, according to the feedback concept, as a necessary and important contributor to the management control process. Data processing may be conceived to be a fragmented, every-man-for-himself operation, or it may be viewed as an over-all system designed to serve the needs of the entire organization. These various viewpoints are reflected in the organizational location of data processing, and in the quality of the personnel assigned to the management of the function.

For it to make its maximum contribution to the management control process, data processing must be approached from the system-wide viewpoint. Thus, the data-processing function must be assigned sufficient authority to enable a system-wide approach to be taken. This is not to imply that the data-processing function must dominate the organization. However, it is not possible to provide an integrated data-processing system on the basis of a "service bureau" operation in which the data-processing function is provided with specified input information and required to produce specified results. It is necessary that the data-processing function have sufficient power within the organization to force the *compromises* necessary to provide an integrated system. Incidentally, the possession of this power to force compromises does not imply that it should be used indiscriminately, for management leadership is frequently more effective in the attainment of the desired result. But the mere existence of the power makes leadership more effective.

Most data-processing centers are located in the finance area under the controller or chief accountant. Among the reasons for this location are: (1) The first interest in using computers in the organization arose among people in this area; (2) this is the traditional location of the punched card data-processing installation; (3) many of the most easily mechanized data-processing applications occur in the accounting area; and (4) the functions of the controller cut across all areas of the organization.

It appears likely that the major potential for the use of computers lies outside the traditional accounting area. Because of the difficulties associated with crossing departmental lines and the natural tendency of employees to be interested primarily in the areas of direct concern to their immediate superior, the location of a data-processing center in the finance area may tend to limit the opportunities to effectively utilize the equipment. If the accounting concept cannot be broadened to include the processing of all types of data, the data-processing center can be organized as a major administrative service function to service the entire organization, avoiding organizational barriers to company-wide integration of data processing.

The organizational location that is required to provide conditions favorable to the development of an integrated data-processing system differs from one company to another, depending upon many factors. In general, it appears desirable to place the manager of the data-processing function near the level of the heads of the organizations that would otherwise dictate the results required.

The proper location of the data-processing center within an organization is not easy to determine, but it may be extremely crucial to the successful use of a computer. Or to put it another way, if a computer is limited by its organizational location to a piecemeal approach to data processing, it is not likely to achieve outstanding results. The internal organization and staffing of an electronic data-processing center are discussed in Chapter 16.

Effects on Decentralized Management

What will be the effect of the computer on the tendency toward decentralized management? One of the major factors motivating decentralized management has been the communication and data-processing bottlenecks that have hindered centralized management in making the required decisions at the proper time. The solution has been to decentralize the decision function to the lowest possible place in the organization. However, the use of the computer, combined with the technique of management by exception, may break the bottleneck of time and information and thus remove some of the basic motivation for decentralization. The use of the electronic data-processing machines may tend to reverse the trend toward decentralization of management by making it less necessary.

The use of a large-scale electronic computer undoubtedly requires a high volume of repetitious processing. Thus, in many organizations, it is necessary to centralize data processing to obtain the volume necessary to make such equipment economically feasible. The question then arises: Can we centralize data processing and still maintain decentralization of management?

In the first place, the importance of this question may be reduced by the use of smaller computers that can process information almost as efficiently as the large machines without requiring such large volume. Equipment exists that makes it possible to decentralize data processing without overwhelming losses in machine efficiency. Second, there are two facets to decentralization. One facet is concerned with geographical decentralization—the location of facilities at widely scattered geographical points. The other aspect is the decentralization of management authority and responsibility, which is independent of actual geographical location. Modern communications advances have significantly reduced the time and distance problems involved in the communication of information. Thus, it is possible to centralize data processing in a geographically decentralized organization, and it should make little difference to a manager whether his data processing is done by a computer in the next room or by a computer thousands of miles away. It should be noted, however, that the cost of the required communications facilities may be an important part of the total cost of data processing.

Indeed, some profess to envision data processing with a centralized computer as a powerful influence for strengthening decentralized management, for the use of a centralized data-processing system to assist top management in the evaluation and control of decentralized management may eliminate one of the major drawbacks of decentralization.

Sylvania Electric Products Corporation has installed a Univac in a specially constructed electronic data-processing center at Camillus, New York. Sylvania is decentralized, both in terms of geographical location and management philosophy, so they have leased a wire communications network which links the data-processing center to Sylvania locations in 61 cities and towns throughout the entire United States. According to Leon C. Guest, Jr., controller:

> It is our plan eventually to have all record-keeping relating to the engineering, manufacturing, and distribution, as well as administrative effort, maintained at the Data Processing Center. The Center will obtain pertinent information from all areas of the company, summarize such information, and present it in the most usable form to the management responsible for each operation.
>
> The Data Processing Center, therefore, will become strictly a service department whose responsibility it is to gather information from the operating divisions, and to transmit that information at the earliest possible moment to the individual who must make the operating decision based on the information so provided in the form most helpful to him.[12]

Serious difficulties may have to be overcome when attempting to centralize the processing of the information that individual decen-

---

[12] Leon C. Guest, Jr., "Centralized Data Processing for Decentralized Management," *Systems Magazine*, Vol. XX, No. 5 (September–October, 1956).

tralized managers are using for decision-making and control purposes. Because of the very great problems of systems analysis and programming, as well as the setup time involved in changing a machine from one application to another, a large-scale data-processing system requires not only high volume but also a considerable amount of uniformity in the procedures employed.

If a manager is given the authority and responsibility to make operating decisions, it is only logical that he be given the authority to determine the information that he will use in his decision-making process and how this information will be processed and presented. Should each manager in a decentralized organization have the right to specify the particular reports he requires without regard to the requirements or desires of others? If each manager were to be furnished his own special reports, the centralized data-processing installation would be faced with almost unsolvable systems analysis, programming, and scheduling problems.

The above problems are illustrated in a company that is geographically centralized but strongly committed to decentralization of management. Under these circumstances, their computer has become a service bureau for 20 separate organizations, with no opportunity for integration. They have over 70 people involved full time in systems analysis and programming, and expect to require over 150 man-years of systems analysis and programming effort before the machine is in full use. Under these circumstances, it is doubtful if they can ever successfully utilize the computer.

Installation and Conversion Problems

The over-all process of deciding to acquire an electronic data-processing machine, preparing for its arrival, and conversion of data-processing operations to the machine involves a tremendous amount of time, money, and planning, as well as a continuous stream of assorted emergencies. In the following section, some of the problems and considerations involved in this process will be outlined.

The Decision to Buy

The first step is that of deciding whether or not a computer should be acquired. Many approaches to this problem have been devised and tested, but, unfortunately, none of them have proved outstandingly successful. They range from the situation where the president of a company orders the machine because it is the popular thing to do, to complete systems studies involving several years and tens of thousands of man-hours.

The approach usually recommended involves the formation of a small *guidance committee* composed of experienced middle-level management men.[13] This committee should be supplemented by a *working committee* composed of representatives from each of the major areas that might be affected by the installation of electronic data-processing equipment. Both of these committees should be composed of the best possible personnel who *must* be released from most of their other responsibilities to conduct the necessary study.

The members of these committees must first learn about the computer and its use. They can do this by going to executive schools provided by the various equipment manufacturers (preferably sampling schools from several different manufacturers), visiting companies that have installed such equipment, and reading the available literature on the subject. This educational phase usually requires a minimum of two months. Then the guidance committee should specify the major areas in which it seems probable that the electronic data-processing machine could be profitably utilized. The working committee should make a thorough study of each of these areas to determine how the job is presently being done, where the input information arises, what files are involved, what results must be obtained, and the present approximate costs, as well as the volumes (both average and maximum) and time factors involved. After obtaining an understanding of what is being done, the committee should attempt to determine what results actually should be accomplished.

The next step, which usually requires from four months to a year, is to tentatively decide upon the types of processing equipment that can be considered, and then to devise procedures for handling the selected applications on each of these types of equipment. Time and cost estimates must then be prepared for each type of equipment. As was discussed at some length in Chapters 8 and 14, at this stage these estimates may be quite inaccurate, yet they must be used, for completely accurate figures may not be available until the applications are actually running successfully on the equipment. Thus, it is desirable to be conservative in estimation and to treat the results with healthy skepticism.

---

[13] Improvements in this approach are suggested in Chapter 16.

Another important consideration, and one that is frequently over-looked, is whether the organization is capable of overcoming the problems associated with the use of computers. Is the management climate sufficiently favorable? Are adequate personnel available? Can the organizational problems be solved? Although these committees tend to spend a lot of time and effort in deciding which equipment to recommend, the above questions are usually of much greater importance in determining whether or not to obtain a computer.

Reputable and experienced consultants can be employed to provide guidance concerning the selection of personnel, the applications that should be considered, the procedures used in evaluation, and so forth. Consultants can contribute a wider experience concerning the pitfalls to be avoided in this process, but they should not be depended upon to make the decision. If an organization does not have the talents required to make such a decision, it is not likely to have the talent necessary to utilize a computer effectively. If a computer is to be installed, the success of the installation must be based upon the experience and knowledge gained in the feasibility study, so company personnel should gain this experience. Furthermore, it is almost impossible for outsiders to learn enough about the organization to adequately analyze its data-processing system.

It should be pointed out that even though the group decides not to acquire a computer, the study usually results in enough improvements to more than repay the organization for the cost of making the survey. Data-processing procedures can become amazingly inefficient; yet, because of the restricted viewpoints of people in the company, no one may realize that this situation exists. In fact, many of the advantages that have been attained through the use of electronic data-processing machines actually may have resulted from procedures simplications that could have been accomplished without the use of the machines at all. When the results of a computer survey are evaluated, care should be taken to discover whether the advantages involved would result from the use of the equipment or from systems changes that could be made without installing additional equipment.

If, as a result of the study, a computer is placed on order, the manufacturer will usually quote a delivery date between one and two years from the date of the order. Although this seems at first glance to be an unreasonably long time to wait, the machine may well arrive before adequate preparations have been completed for its use.

One of the first problems to be faced is that of selecting and training a staff of systems analysts and programmers. This selection and training problem will be considered further in Chapter 16. It is sufficient here to note that most of these highly skilled people must be obtained from *within* the organization and trained in schools conducted by the equipment manufacturer. The word "trained" is used rather loosely here—the manufacturers' schools provide only a kindergarten training. Most of the programmer's competence will be acquired by experience, so it is wise to expect a relatively low-quality product from these people for several months after they are "trained."

Before the machine arrives, a number of programs should be ready for operation so that the machine can be put to productive use as soon as possible. Most computer manufacturers provide facilities for checking out programs on a similar machine before the new machine is installed. This time can also be used to convince your personnel that the machine will actually work, and to familiarize your machine operators with the details of operation of the machine console.

Physical Problems

One of the problems that has caused many headaches has been that of providing the physical environment required by the machines. Although most such machines are transistorized, it is usually necessary to provide a source of well-regulated and disturbance-free power, along with space in which temperature, humidity, and dust are carefully controlled. The floors of the building may have to be strengthened to support the weight of the various units, and channels may be required under the floor in which to run the cables connecting the components together. A machine room layout must be devised which will fit the various equipment components into the area provided in an arrangement that will allow efficient operation of the machine, and which will provide an aesthetically pleasing and intellectually satisfying view of the equipment to visitors (ranging from high school classes and employees' families to delegations of vice presidents), while at the same time not exceeding the restrictions of the machine manufacturer concerning cable lengths.

Thus, substantial modifications to the building may be required to install a computer. Although one might think that these preparations could be easily completed in the one to two years available, it is frequently a nip and tuck battle to complete the physical preparations before the arrival of the machine, and occasionally installations are significantly delayed because remodeling is behind schedule. On the other hand, unforseen difficulties can force the manufacturer to delay the equipment for a few weeks (or months) or the customer may encounter programming delays. When these three factors interact, the resulting uncertainity can be quite nerve racking.

Conversion Problems

Before any major processing can start, it is often necessary to convert large files of information from written or punched card records onto magnetic tape. The difficulties that can be involved in this conversion are almost unbelieveable to the uninitiated. An incredible amount of inaccuracy and nonuniformity can exist in a punched card file. Manual files will be incomplete, inaccurate, inconsistent, and will have unbelievable numbers of unexpected and unexplained deviations from their supposed format. The job of placing these files in a form in which they can be successfully machine processed often involves thousands of man-hours and hundreds of machine-hours for its completion. It is reported that file conversion and "purification" cost a large insurance company around $12 million.[14]

As discussed in Chapter 8, the process of converting an application to the data-processing machine usually involves running the application in parallel; that is, processing in the normal way and through the use of the computer at the same time and comparing the results to detect inaccuracies in the program. The number of processing cycles which must be overlapped ranges from 2 or 3 (if one is lucky) up to 20 or 30. Occasionally, an application will be run in parallel for several processing cycles, converted completely to the electronic data-processing machine, and then, several cycles later, situations will arise that force the application to be taken off the computer and returned to the previous processing method.

During the conversion period, the processing must be performed in two different ways, which may involve originating information in two different forms. Thus, substantial pressure may be placed upon people outside the mechanized data-processing organization

---

[14] "Special Report on Computers," *Business Week*, June 21, 1958, p. 77.

at a time when they aren't too happy with the situation anyway. The difficulties that arise are therefore magnified in importance, and emergencies may become commonplace.

The above discussion may indicate that the process of converting to electronic data processing involves difficult administrative and planning problems. The process extends over a long period of time during which training, systems analysis, programming, debugging, conversion, and production may all be going on simultaneously. As was discussed in Chapter 8, the amount of time required for any of these steps in a specific application is quite difficult to predict, so planning and setting of schedules is complicated. Moreover, considerable time pressure is exerted by the desire to get some use out of the expensive equipment that is available. Effective administration of this process is of extreme importance.

Several approaches that attempt to minimize the conversion problems have been devised and attempted. One of the most popular of these approaches is to take over areas which have already been mechanized by punched cards. This does minimize the conversion difficulties, for punched card mechanization forces the reorganization of procedures and the isolation and standardization of exceptions that are required when converting to a computer. However, for procedures in which punched cards can be efficiently used, most of the benefits of mechanization have already been attained, and it may be difficult for the computer to compete with the cost of punched card processing. In other words, the major potential for the computer lies in areas where it is impossible to efficiently mechanize through the use of punched card equipment.

Another approach which minimizes the disruptions in the organization outside of the data-processing center is that of making the data-processing group a "service bureau" which takes over the data processing without changing the form or content of the input information or the output reports. Then the user is not required to make any adjustments when the computer is installed, and he should not be concerned with whether the processing is actually accomplished by a computer or by other means. This approach is likely to insure mediocrity. Not only may it preclude the efficient utilization of the computer, but it may also prevent the attainment of intangible benefits. In general, it is simply a tacit admission that the data-processing center does not have sufficient support from top management to enable it to be normally successful.

The only realistic approach to minimizing installation and conversion problems seems to be that of providing excellent administrative leadership and allowing sufficient time for thorough preparation *before* the machine arrives, combined with the assignment of sufficient numbers of qualified personnel to the task of studying data-processing problems and developing procedures for using the machine to solve them.

If the organization has not utilized punched cards, it may be advisable to first install punched card machines and use them to gain some of the benefits of (and a great deal of experience in) mechanized processing before considering the installation of an electronic data-processing system. The proper use of punched card data processing is an excellent training ground for the development of systems analysis and procedures personnel, as well as for educating the entire organization concerning the advantages and limitations associated with the mechanization of data processing.

This does not imply that a computer should necessarily be staffed exclusively by people from an existing punched card installation, for one of the most pressing problems associated with punched card installations has been that the people involved did not have the basic ability required to effectively use punched cards.

Pattern of Costs

One of the more interesting and difficult questions to be answered when deciding on an electronic data-processing machine is: What will it cost? If the use of an electronic computer is being seriously considered in an organization, this question should probably be phrased: What will it save? This question is very seldom answered with any degree of accuracy when one is trying to decide whether or not to order a machine. As a matter of fact, it is an extremely difficult question to answer *after* the machine has been successfully installed and is actually making savings—most of the people who are using the machines do not know accurately how much (if anything) they are saving.

In the first place, it is difficult to precisely determine the true costs of data processing under a manual system. Second, during the time in which a data-processing machine is being installed, the job to be accomplished may change radically in terms of the volume involved or the results obtained. Third, it is difficult to place a monetary value on such intangible factors as increased accuracy, more comprehensive information, and faster results. The evaluation of these intangible benefits is of utmost importance, for they often provide the major impetus for introducing electronic data-processing systems.

However, it should again be emphasized that these intangible benefits are not automatically obtained as a by-product of the use of an electronic data-processing machine. They must be deliberately sought through concentrated attention to management's need for higher-quality information and by devoting the best available brain power to the task of devising methods through which the machines can be used to produce the desired information.

Most of the electronic data-processing machines available may be obtained on a rental basis or may be purchased outright from the manufacturer. If the machine is purchased, two additional alternatives arise: Maintenance may be provided by the manufacturer through a maintenance contract, or it may be provided by hiring or training one's own maintenance personnel. Such factors as equipment obsolescence, interest rates and availability of money, the ratio of the purchase price to the rental price, the number of hours per day of planned usage, and the tax position of the organization are involved in deciding whether to rent or buy the equipment. It should be noted that machine obsolescence is not as important as has sometimes been assumed, because the programming cost involved in changing from one machine to another may preclude making such a change even after better equipment becomes available.

Much work has been done on the question of rental versus buying of capital equipment, most of which is applicable when considering electronic data-processing machines. Incidentally, a program for the IBM 650 has been devised that thoroughly analyses many factors and prepares a report showing the rate of return on investment for various useful lives based upon purchase instead of rental.[15] Thus, by estimating the life of the equipment and comparing the corresponding rate of return with that provided by alternate investment opportunities, it is possible to decide whether it is best to rent or to buy the equipment.

Although the absolute magnitude of the costs or savings involved in the use of a computer will vary from installation to installation, and is quite difficult to determine precisely, the over-all cost pattern has been established. For a typical large-scale installation, Figure 15–1 presents a framework in which to view the various components of cost along with their relative magnitudes and their general time

---

[15] See reference *A Rent or Buy Analysis with the IBM 650 Card System* in the supplemental readings.

of occurrence. The horizontal axis of this diagram represents time and is marked in units of one year. Quantities upward on the graph represent costs in thousands of dollars per month, while quantities downward represent similar savings.

The cost of the feasibility study to determine whether or not to order the machine is shown on the first six months of this diagram. After the machine is ordered, the costs of training, systems analysis, and programming gradually rise to a total of around $12,000 per month. The total amount of this type of work before installation may vary from 15 to 30 man-years at an average cost of $10,000 to $12,000 per man-year.

Site preparation costs, which are incurred over a period of approximately one year before the arrival of the machine, range from a minimum of around $50,000 up to a maximum of around $350,-000. The cost of file conversion depends on the type of applications that are being placed on the machine and the previous status of the files involved. Most installations require several hundred reels of magnetic tape at a cost of around $40 per reel.

Since this diagram is based on the assumption that the machine is being rented, when the machine arrives the total monthly cost will immediately jump by the amount of the machine rental, which is assumed to be around $30,000 per month in this illustration. For a period of a few months, very little productive work is accomplished, but from then on, as programs are debugged and parallel operation is suspended, more and more productive work will be assumed by the equipment, and costs will fall until eventually the costs of data processing should return to the level that existed before the machine was considered back at year zero. On the diagram, this break-even point is reached three and one-half years after the start of the feasibility study, or one and one-half years after the machine is delivered.

Total data-processing costs may continue to decrease so that the machine shows a substantial profit. In this case, it is assumed that the machine will produce a profit of $360,000 per year (or $30,000 per month) when it is fully utilized. However, at the break-even point around $780,000 had been invested in systems analysis, programming, physical installation, file conversion, magnetic tapes, and unutilized machine rental. At $30,000 per month, it will take over two years after the break-even point to recover this $780,000. From here on a profit of $30,000 per month is received.

Let us emphasize again that this diagram represents only a conceptual pattern. Both the magnitude of costs and savings and the time factors will vary widely from organization to organization. For example, some organizations have been able to reach the break-even point within a year after the machine was installed, while others have been installed for several years without ever reaching the break-even point—and without showing any indications that they will ever be profitable. The maximum monthly profit attained, which drastically affects the time necessary to recover installation costs, ranges from a loss to around $100,000 per month. On the average, however, the diagram of Figure 15–1 is fairly realistic.

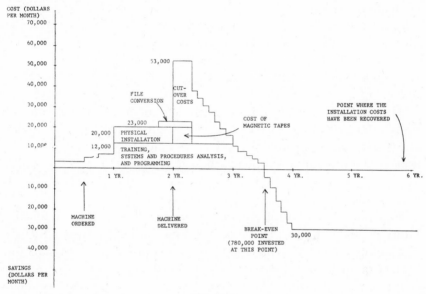

FIG. 15–1.

Nevertheless, it should also be noted that equipment developments are rapidly affecting the costs of mechanized processing. In the first place, a wider range of equipment has been developed so that the volume of processing required to use a computer has been drastically reduced, and machines are available to efficiently satisfy a broad range of data-processing requirements. Secondly, machine developments are continuously lowering the unit cost of processing. For example, in 1956, a typical IBM 705 (Model I) installation rented for about $30,000 per month. In 1960, an IBM 7070, renting for the same $30,000 per month, could do approximately five times the work of the 705 (Model I). Thus, the unit cost of processing was reduced by a factor of five in four years. This progress is typical of what has gone on for several years, and what is likely to continue in the future. Thus, the range of potentially profitable applications of electronic data processing is continuously expanding.

Summary

The introduction of a computer into an organization also introduces significant problems. These problems are usually greater for installations that aspire to the greatest potential benefit, for many of the problems are a result of radical changes in the fundamental information-gathering and processing system of the organization.

Among the most important problems are those involved with people and their reactions to change. These problems can be minimized if they are recognized and taken into consideration from the start of the process. The effectiveness of the use of a computer frequently depends upon the solution of organizational problems which may prevent the use of a systems-wide approach to data processing.

Although most organizations devote a lot of effort to the choice of the specific computer that best serves its needs, the over-all success of the installation is probably much more dependent upon the solution of administrative problems than it is upon equipment details. Management attention must be focused on the problems of administering the over-all process of conversion.

Top-management support and participation is required for the solution of the above problems, for these problems are frequently of a policy nature and affect the entire organization. Although the neglect of such problems does not automatically doom an installation to complete failure, solutions must be found to these problems if the installation is to be more than mediocre.

EXERCISES

15.1 Discuss the effect of the introduction of a computer upon the clerical workers in the organization. Is this effect desirable? If not, how can it be ameliorated?

15.2 What are the relationships between centralization of data processing and management decentralization?

15.3 Discuss the problems that are involved in the process of changing from manual methods to the use of electronic data-processing equipment. If you were in charge of such a conversion what would you do to reduce these problems?

15.4 Prepare a dynamic cost diagram similar to Figure 15–1 for a typical basic 650 installation. How does this differ from the diagram in Figure 15–1?

15.5   Why is top-management participation necessary for the effective utilization of electronic data-processing equipment? Is middle-management participation also required? Why?

15.6   In what respects does the impact of office automation upon the workers differ from the effect of factory automation?

15.7   When deciding between renting and purchasing a computer, it is necessary to estimate the useful life of the machine. What factors influence this useful life?

SUPPLEMENTAL READINGS

A Rent or Buy Analysis with the IBM 650 Card System.   Form No. E20–4040. New York: International Business Machines Corp., 1959.
   Presents a description of the formulas used in the 650 program for using the present value method to determine whether to rent or buy capital equipment.

Automation and Technological Change.   Hearings before the Subcommittee on Economic Stabilization of the Joint Committee on the Economic Report. Congress of the United States, October, 1955. Washington, D.C.: U.S. Government Printing Office, 1955.
   A report of hearings on the general impact of automation upon employment and productivity. These hearings include testimony by John Diebold, Ralph J. Cordiner, James P. Mitchell, Walter P. Reuther, and many others, and contain a wealth of information on the status of automation at that time and its potential impact on the economy.

BAGBY, WESLEY S.   "The Human Side of Electronics," *Proceedings of the Second Annual AMA Electronics Conference: Pioneering in Electronic Data Processing.* Special Report No. 9. Published by the American Management Assoc., February 27–29, 1956.
   An excellent presentation of the human problems involved in the installation of a computer.

BUCKINGHAM, WALTER.   "The Human Side of Automation," *Business Horizons,* Vol. 3, No. 1 (Spring, 1960), pp. 19–28.
   A general discussion of the impact of automation on the worker, much of which is applicable to office automation.

CANNING, RICHARD G.   *Installing Electronic Data Processing Systems.* New York: John Wiley & Sons, Inc., 1957.
   Through use of an illustration involving a single company, this book concentrates on the problems involved in preparing for and installing an electronic data-processing system.

CRAIG, HAROLD F.   *Administering a Conversion to Electronic Accounting.* Boston: Harvard University, Graduate School of Business Administration, 1955.
   This is a detailed case study describing the conversion of an insurance company to punched card accounting. It emphasizes administrative, human, and organizational problems involved in the conversion.

CURRY, ROBERT B. "Facilities for a Large Computer Installation," *Advanced Management*, Vol. 23, No. 1 (January, 1958), pp. 5–11.

Discusses the physical installation problems involved in installing an IBM 705 at the Southern Railway Company, Atlanta, Georgia. Although the use of transistors has reduced some of the problems described, this article gives an excellent presentation of the factors involved in site preparation.

ELLIOTT, J. D. "EDP—Its Impact on Jobs, Procedures and People," *The Journal of Industrial Engineering*, Vol. IX, No. 5 (September–October, 1958), pp. 407–10.

This is an unusually frank discussion of the problems involved in installing a computer by the Director of Central Data Processing of the Detroit Edison Company.

HOOS, IDA R. "When the Computer Takes Over the Office," *Harvard Business Review*, Vol. 38, No. 4 (July–August, 1960), pp. 102–12.

This provocative article presents the author's interpretation of the results of a study of the effects of introducing a computer in 19 West Coast organizations.

LAUBACH, PETER B. *Company Investigations of Automatic Data Processing*. Boston: Harvard University, Graduate School of Business Administration, 1957.

This study is concerned with the problems involved in deciding whether or not to use a computer. One such study is presented in detail, and several others are briefly outlined. Several of the most important considerations involved in such a study are discussed.

SHEA, S. L. "Organizing for Electronics," *Advanced Management*. December, 1957.

This presents a discussion of the process of determining whether or not to acquire a computer. It includes a description of the functions of the advisory and working groups.

SOLO, MYRON B. "Selecting Electronic Data Processing Equipment," *Datamation* (November–December, 1958), pp. 28–32.

This article describes in some detail the approach to equipment selection utilized by the County of Los Angeles. Formulas are developed to relate total costs to annual costs. Then various machines are evaluated according to the costs of processing a "benchmark problem."

"Special Report on Computers," *Business Week* (June 21, 1958), pp. 68–92.

This article discusses many of the problems involved in installing computers, and includes examples of the experiences of a number of users, along with a discussion of the costs involved in a typical large-scale installation.

STARBUCK, WILLIAM H. "Computing Machines: Rent or Buy?" *The Journal of Industrial Engineering*, Vol. IX, No. 4 (July–August, 1958), pp. 254–58.

A rather sophisticated approach is presented to the problem of deciding whether to rent or buy electronic data-processing equipment.

Use of Electronic Data-Processing Equipment. Hearings before the Subcommittee on Census and Government Statistics of the Committee on Post Office and Civil Service, House of Representatives, June 5, 1959. Washington, D.C.: U.S. Government Printing Office, 1959.

This is a report of the use of electronic data-processing equipment in the federal government. It emphasizes the personnel selection, training, and relocation problems involved.

WALLACE, FRANK. *Appraising the Economics of Electronic Computers.* New York: Controllership Foundation, 1956.

This book is concerned with the techniques that can be used to decide whether or not to install electronic data-processing equipment.

WEBER, C. E. "Change in Managerial Manpower with Mechanization of Data-Processing," *Journal of Business,* Vol. 32, No. 2 (April, 1959), pp. 151–63.

Discusses changes in manpower experienced in several instances of the use of computers, with emphasis on shifts in the proportion of management to clerical workers.

CHAPTER 16 · The Data-Processing Organization

A COMBINATION of inadequate administration and organizational problems associated with the data-processing function have been responsible for many of the difficulties that have arisen in the use of electronic data-processing machines. Frequently, data processing is poorly organized and administered without attracting attention, but when a computer enters the picture the resultant centralization of data processing, together with the costs involved, combine to make these inadequacies painfully apparent. In connection with these problems, two closely related questions arise. First, where does the data-processing function fit into the over-all organizational structure? This important question was discussed in Chapter 15. Second, how should the data-processing function itself be organized and administered? This question, and others associated with it, will be discussed in this chapter.

The following discussion will be based on the assumption that our major concern is the establishment of an effective data-processing system for management control of the entire organization. The number of people and type of equipment involved depend upon the size of the organization and its data-processing problems, but the basic tasks to be accomplished and the difficulties to be overcome are essentially the same whether the organization is large or small.

Organization of the Data-Processing Function

A variety of approaches may be taken when organizing the data-processing function. Figure 16–1 shows one possible organization, and while it is by no means the only effective possibility, it includes most of the functions that must be performed and thus can serve as a framework for further discussion. When appropriate, the characteristics desirable in those who fill these jobs will be described.

362

Manager of Data Processing

The importance of placing the right man in the position of manager of data processing cannot be overemphasized, for the success or failure of the entire mechanization effort is as dependent upon his managerial ability as upon any other single factor. The introduction of a computer or a punched card system entails a myriad of administrative problems, some within the data-processing organization itself and others involved with the consequent changes in other parts of the organization.

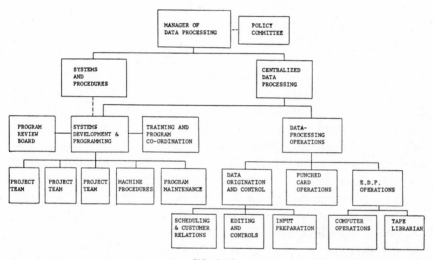

FIG. 16–1.

The function of the manager of data processing is to plan and administer the operation of the data-processing system. He has responsibility for the design and implementation of a data-processing system that will provide the information required for adequate management control of the organization. Although he is directly responsible only for the centralized portion of the data-processing work, he is responsible for the planning necessary to achieve an integrated data-processing system.

This position is difficult to fill, for the manager of data processing must possess a variety of capabilities. In the first place, he must operate on a relatively high level within the organization, and, to be effective, he must have the confidence and respect of the entire organization. He must possess a depth of vision capable of comprehending the data-processing requirements of the entire organization, and must have the ability to lead the various components of the organization to accept an integrated data-processing system. In addition to having a natural ability to sell ideas, he should be a master of the strategies involved in getting things done, for he must know who must be sold, when to attack, and when and how to retreat. He should be an excellent administrator, for he will be responsible for planning and administering a complex process of change extending over a period of several years during which a succession of interrelated steps affecting the entire organization must be scheduled and accomplished. Finally, while not primarily concerned with technical details, he must be capable of assimilating enough of the technology of data processing to be able to interpret its significance for the data-processing function and the entire organization.

Many of the difficulties that have plagued organizations which have ordered computers have resulted because the responsibilities of the manager of data processing have been placed upon the shoulders of men who were technically qualified, but who did not have the administrative ability nor the reputation within the organization to successfully perform the required functions. The assignment of the proper man to this position can be accomplished only if management is committed to the proposition that the data-processing function is of importance, for such men are scarce and of great value.

The first question asked, of course, is: Where can we find a man with those qualifications? There is a temptation to search outside the organization for some experienced electronic data-processing man to fill this position. However, this man must come from within the organization, for his success or failure will depend upon his knowledge of the organization and managers with whom he will be working, his reputation within the company, and his administrative ability. Such men can be found in most successful organizations. The major problem is that they cannot be spared. Any man that can be spared for this job probably should be automatically disqualified.

If the organization is planning ahead, rather than attempting to institute a crash program, it is possible to bring in a good man from outside and allow him to serve in an advisory capacity for a year or two. Then, if he shapes up well, he can be given line responsibility for the data-processing function.

This brings up the question of timing: When should this position be created? A qualified man should be placed in this position before the decision is made to acquire a computer, for the most effective way to decide whether or not to get a computer (and if so which one) is to develop and use portions of the organization shown in Figure 16–1 for this purpose. There is little to be gained from excessive haste in acquiring a computer. Most organizations are far from ready to use one when it arrives. In contrast to a crash program, it is highly desirable to take the time required to find the proper man, acquire and train the people required, thoroughly study the data-processing system, and decide upon the data-processing tools that should be used.

If, by this process, it is decided that a computer is not required, it will be because a better way to achieve the data-processing objectives of the organization has been devised.

The Data-Processing Policy Committee

As discussed in Chapter 15, a common practice is to establish an electronic data-processing policy committee, composed of the heads of the areas which may be affected by the mechanization, to investigate whether or not to acquire a computer and to make the basic policy decisions involved in the conversion process. It should be emphasized that the establishment of such a committee is no substitute for obtaining a manager of data processing with the capabilities outlined above. Also, many of the decisions that have been made haphazardly by such a committee should be made on the basis of an analysis by a competent systems and procedures group. Rather than establish such a policy committee to make a quick decision whether or not to acquire a computer, most organizations should spend some time developing an adequate systems and procedures group. However, even with a well-qualified manager of data processing and a competent systems and procedures group, a functioning policy committee is still required to establish fundamental objectives, and can also perform a valuable service by assuring the co-operation of the entire organization in the development and installation of an integrated data-processing system.

Systems and Procedures

One of the most important groups reporting to the manager of data processing should be concerned with systems and procedures planning for the entire organization. The fact that in many organizations the only such group is referred to as *office methods* or *office procedures* and is primarily concerned with the details of paper work and forms design is a reflection of the fact that this important function is frequently neglected.

As was emphasized in Chapters 2 and 14, the basic problem associated with data processing is that of determining what information is necessary to allow proper management control. A second problem is how such information can most efficiently be provided. These two problems are interrelated, of course, for the desirability of information is at least partially determined by the cost of providing it. The major function of the systems and procedures group should be the solution of problems such as these. This group should be concerned with designing the over-all data-processing system and with devising the over-all procedures involved. Since they are responsible for the design of an integrated system that may involve manual steps, semimechanized steps, punched card processes, and the use of an electronic computer, the members of this group must have an understanding of the capabilities and limitations of all data-processing tools. And since this group is responsible for expressing the over-all system objectives, those who compose it must thoroughly understand the objectives and policies of management.

Such an organization is not created instantly, but must be developed over a period of years. The development of such a group should precede the acquiring of a computer, for this decision should be made on the basis of systems requirements specified by the systems and procedures group. If a competent systems and procedures group does not exist in an organization, its development is of infinitely greater importance than the acquisition of a computer or of any other data-processing tools, for without proper over-all objectives and a satisfactorily designed data-processing system, tools alone are not likely to provide a solution to data-processing problems.

Manager of Centralized Data Processing

The manager of centralized data processing is frequently titled "manager of mechanized data processing" or "manager of electronic data processing." He is in charge of both the development and the operation of mechanized systems. During the installation of a mechanized data-processing system he has the responsibility of developing a technical staff, programming and installing the computer, and converting the data processing to the mechanized system. Obviously, this is also a key position in the organization.

Besides being a man of proven administrative ability, the manager of centralized data processing also needs to be something of a salesman, for the attitude of the personnel outside of the data-processing organization toward mechanization of data processing may be favorably or unfavorably affected by his personality. Although he does not need to be a professional machine programmer, he will be called upon to make decisions involving technical questions, so he should have a certain amount of technical ability. Again, it is desirable that this man come from within the organization, rather than being hired as an expert from outside.

In many companies, the positions of manager of data processing and manager of centralized data processing are combined, and this can be satisfactory. However, the distinction expressed here between the two positions is that the top position is primarily concerned with the over-all data-processing policies and objectives of the organization, while the manager of centralized data processing is more concerned with the means through which these objectives may be attained and the administration of the internal operation of the centralized processing organization. Either of these jobs is neglected at grave peril to the successful utilization of electronic data-processing equipment.

Two basic tasks are involved in a data-processing center. As was discussed in Chapter 15, the period between the ordering of a computer and its installation must be devoted to systems development and programming. After the computer arrives, it is gradually put to productive use in routine data-processing operations, but the development of new systems and the improvement of old programs continues at a high level for a long, long time. Since routine operation and the development of new systems are dissimilar activities, they are performed by separate portions of the organization.

Systems Development and Programming

The actual development of mechanized procedures and the writing and debugging of machine programs are the responsibility of the systems development and programming group. As shown by the dotted line in Figure 16–1, there must be close co-ordination between this group and the systems and procedures group to insure that decisions concerning what data-processing areas to mechanize are properly influenced by technical consideration. In organizations in which the manager of centralized data processing and the manager of data processing are the same, these two systems groups are usually also combined. Again, the two groups represent the separate viewpoints of the two managerial positions, and, if they are combined, it is necessary to make sure that adequate consideration is given to the planning of both the over-all data-processing system and the mechanized portions of the system. In particular, with a single group there is a tendency to concentrate exclusively on the mechanized aspects to the exclusion of the less glamorous manual and semimechanized techniques.

The program review committee, composed of the best systems analysts and programmers in the organization, has the function of reviewing proposed procedures to determine whether they are likely to result in efficient computer programs and of monitoring development of programs to see that an efficient and integrated system is produced. Proper use of a committee such as this can prevent many of the mistakes which tend to plague new organizations composed of inexperienced men.

The training and program co-ordination function associated with systems development and programming has the responsibility for the development of a uniform philosophy for flow diagramming, block diagramming, and programming, including the development and modification of suitable automatic programming systems for the organization. Such standard procedures and philosophies will substantially reduce the communication difficulties within the organization, as well as the problems involved in debugging and the future modification of programs and procedures. This group is also charged with keeping the entire organization educated concerning the latest technical developments in programming and equipment and is responsible for the training of new personnel. If the electronic data-processing group is to function efficiently, the above functions must be effectively performed. Those performing these functions must be expert technicians, and, if they do not already exist in the organization, it is acceptable to hire experienced men from outside.

Organization of Systems Development and Programming

The systems development and programming group may be organized in a variety of ways. For example, it may be organized in terms of the functions of procedures development, block diagramming, and programming, with a separate group performing each of these functions for all applications. As was discussed in Chapter 8, because of the interrelationships between the steps in the over-all process of converting to computer processing, it is better to organize this group in terms of teams, each of which is responsible for the systems analysis, block diagramming, programming, debugging, and conversion of an entire application. Usually, a team consists of from two to five people headed by a senior systems analyst.

Personnel for systems analysis and programming usually come from within the organization and are trained in computer techniques by the machine manufacturer or by the training and program co-ordination group. It is said that it is easier to teach the machine to someone who knows the data-processing problem than it is to teach the problem to someone who knows the machine. Thus, these people are frequently drawn from the areas of the organization that are to be mechanized, although people possessing a wide variety of backgrounds (including accountants, engineers, mathematicians, industrial engineers, and trainees just out of college) have been used. Aptitude tests are available which can be used to screen out people who probably do not have the logical and abstract reasoning ability to perform these functions.

The saying that it is easier to teach programming to someone who knows the job than it is to teach the job to someone who knows programming has likely led some organizations into the trap of minimizing the importance of experience and technical ability in this area. It is highly desirable that a nucleus of competent, experienced people be brought into the organization at the start (perhaps from outside the company) around which a technically competent group can be developed, while at the same time providing the experience that prevents the group from having to learn everything by repeating the common mistakes.

In some organizations, the systems development and programming functions are entirely performed within the sections of the organization for which the data processing is to be done, with the people involved being drawn from these areas and trained by the electronic data-processing organization, but never actually leaving their own areas and becoming a part of the electronic data-processing group. This approach is not likely to lead to the development of an integrated system. In other organizations, these people are attached to the electronic data-processing organization while the systems development and programming is being done, and returned to their parental organizations at the completion of the project. Frequently, the teams are made up of one or two people from the central data-processing organization and one or two people from the customer area; in other organizations the entire job is done by professional systems analysts and programmers permanently attached to the electronic data-processing organization.

Because skill and experience in systems development and programming are highly desirable to produce efficient results, it appears desirable to have professional members of the data-processing organization on each team. On the other hand, because of their knowledge of the application to be mechanized and because of their established relationships with the people working in these areas, it is desirable to include on the team one or more people from the area to be mechanized. Thus, teams made up of both types of people may have the advantages of both without the limitations of either.

Program Maintenance

After a machine program has been written and debugged, and the conversion made to computer processing, the systems analysis and programming job has not been completed. A data-processing system must be dynamic rather than static. The programs must be kept up-to-date and revised whenever changes are made in the input, output, processing, or the equipment used. This is the function of the program maintenance group, and a surprising amount of this type of work needs to be done in an operating data-processing organization.

The program maintenance group is usually divided into teams, each of which maintains a group of related programs. Thus, each group is always familiar with the programs for which it is responsible, so that when changes are necessary they can be made without undue confusion. Upon completion of a major project in the systems development and programming group, one or more members of the development team are frequently transferred to the program maintenance section to maintain these programs.

Machine Procedures

Since, for many data-processing applications, punched card equipment is superior to computers, and for other areas a combination of punched card equipment and computers is desirable, most organizations that have computers also use a substantial amount of punched card equipment. The machine procedures group develops punched card procedures and wires the more complicated control panels for the punched card machines. With the installation of a glamorous computer, there is a tendency to neglect this area, but the quality of the systems analysis and programming of punched card equipment may be crucial in determining the efficiency of the entire system.

Data-Processing Operations

The production work of mechanized data processing takes place in this section. In a large-scale installation, over a hundred people may be employed in the preparation of input material and the operation of punched card machines, auxiliary equipment, and the computer. Supervision of production may be complicated by the fact that partial or complete second- or third-shift operations are common.

Data Origination and Control

Whenever a mechanized data-processing facility becomes loaded to the point where the machines are being efficiently utilized, scheduling and priority questions begin to arise. When expensive equipment is involved, it is particularly important that the gathering of input data, key punching, auxiliary equipment operations, electronic data-processing runs, and report preparation mesh together smoothly so that deadlines can be met and costs can be minimized. This problem is further complicated because the data-processing load fluctuates in terms of the volume of transactions, report deadlines tend to be concentrated at the end of accounting periods, and special one-time reports are frequently required.

If the equipment is to be operated efficiently and the output reports are to be prepared on time, each operation must be precisely scheduled so that the machines are not idle while waiting for input information, yet enough flexibility must be allowed so that occasional machine breakdowns do not cause report deadlines to be violated. The responsibility for such scheduling may be placed in the hands of the manager of data-processing operations, but because of the importance of timely input data, it is often grouped with the input and customer relations area under data origination and control.

Because of the importance of the attitude of the rest of the organization toward centralized data processing, it is desirable to give special attention to the customer relations function. All contacts with these customers, including scheduling of the input and of report deadlines, should be handled by a group that is talented in human relations and interested in providing good service to the organization. If this is not done, both programmers and machine operators are likely to be plagued by complaining customers, to the detriment of the proper performance of their primary functions. Since some of the best technical people may be less than expert in human relations, the relationships between the customer and the data-processing organization may deteriorate.

As was discussed in Chapter 8, the control of accuracy is an important consideration in the design and operation of mechanized data-processing systems. Since most of the accuracy problems are associated with the correctness of the input information, and since the establishment of proper controls originates with the input, the functions of editing and control are grouped together with the preparation of input and contact with customers. This function must also be co-ordinated with the internal and external auditors of the organization.

Input Preparation

The efficiency of a mechanized data-processing system is especially sensitive to the effectiveness with which input information is prepared for machine processing. Ideally, the information should be recorded in processable form with a minimum of manual processing and as near to the source of the information as possible. Input may be placed in machine-processable form by automatic recording in punched cards or paper tape, by mark sensing, prepunching, key punching, and so forth.

Key punching and other input preparation functions are similar to normal clerical functions, such as typing, and are usually performed by women. Since a substantial number of key punch operators may be involved (from 30 to 60 in a large organization), there is no reason why it should not be supervised as a separate section of the organization.

Occasionally, the function of data preparation will be decentralized to the location in which the data arises. In these situations, several key punches may be located in and supervised by the user organizations. This has the advantage of pinpointing the responsibility for the accuracy of input data and can be a satisfactory method of organization if it does not represent a symptom of a function-oriented rather than an integrated data-processing system.

Punched Card Operations

As was mentioned previously, a substantial amount of punched card equipment may be used in an organization that has a computer. Relatively large numbers of machine operators may be involved in the operation of this equipment. These jobs do not require creative ability, but they do require some manual dexterity and an ability to accurately follow predetermined procedures.

The supervision and scheduling of a punched card installation is a complex job, so the supervisor of these activities requires skills similar to those required of a job-shop foreman. Under the organization chart shown in Figure 15-1, the creative functions of punched card procedure design and control-panel wiring are performed under systems development and programming.

Computer Operations

It would appear that the operation of a computer is strictly a button-pushing job, and theoretically this should be true. However, the effectiveness of operation of the computer is heavily dependent upon the skill of the console operator. In the first place, the computer console is composed of a complex set of switches and buttons which must be pressed in a specified sequence. Mistakes in operating these switches can completely foul up the computer processing. Moreover, emergencies due to incomplete or erroneous input information, machine malfunctioning, or inadequately written or debugged programs occur with discouraging frequency. Since the equipment involved may cost several hundred dollars per hour, it is desirable that the console operator be capable of handling such emergencies expeditiously. Thus, a considerable analytical ability and coolness under pressure, combined with manual dexterity, are required of a good console operator. Console operators should have programming training, and are frequently obtained by transferring the less outstanding programmers to this work when the machine arrives.

In addition to the operation of the console, magnetic tape reels must be placed on and removed from the tape units in the proper sequence. This function is usually performed by assistants, who may also operate card-to-tape, tape-to-card, and tape printer equipment.

Detailed records of the emergencies that occur and the steps taken to correct them must be maintained for adequate control of accuracy, otherwise it may be impossible to determine whether mistakes in console operation have introduced errors. Also, detailed records of production time, idle time, machine downtime, and so forth must be maintained for analysis purposes so that realistic schedules can be established and proper performance maintained. Some machines have been equipped with a real-time clock which may be interrogated by the program so that the machine can automatically gather usage statistics.

Tape Librarian

To assure that the correct programs and the proper input and output tapes are used at all times, most installations include a tape librarian who maintains records concerning the tape files and controls and issues the required tapes. It is her responsibility to see that tapes are not released for reuse until the information they contain is no longer required, and that worn-out tapes are retired from use when they begin to cause excessive machine errors.

Cost Accounting

How to charge the costs of data processing within the organization is an important question, for it is an important influence on the relationship between the data-processing center and the rest of the organization. There are two major methods of charging costs, each of which has certain advantages and disadvantages.

It is possible to consider the data-processing department as an overhead cost to be distributed to other departments in the same way as other general overhead. This type of a system might be desirable when developing an integrated data-processing system, for it permits mechanization of data-processing areas without regard to their individual efficiency in order to promote the efficiency of the entire system. On the other hand, this type of costing may lead to the mechanization of areas of data processing that should never be mechanized, because a manager can thereby transfer his data-processing costs into overhead for the entire organization.

The usual method of assigning data-processing costs is by distributing all or part of the cost of the data-processing department according to the machine-hours used on the various applications. This method of costing tends to insure that the areas are efficiently mechanized, for the managers involved can directly compare the cost of the mechanized system with the cost of the system currently used to decide whether or not to change. On the other hand, it may be more difficult to achieve an integrated system under this costing method, for, to increase the efficiency of the entire system, it is frequently desirable to mechanize areas which, considered by themselves, are inefficient.

Salary Ranges

For the position of manager of data processing, it is nonsensical to specify a salary range, for each firm must locate a man who is capable of filling this position and promote him into this job. Thus, his salary must depend upon his previous salary and company policy.

In 1960, the salaries of administrators (other than the top man) within the data-processing organization ranged between $7,000 and $15,000 per year.[2] Senior systems analysts, capable of leading a project team, received between $7,000 and $13,000, and the salaries of systems analysts and programmers ranged from $6,000 to about $10,000. Newly hired trainees in programming and systems analysis were paid between $4,000 and $6,500.

EXERCISES

16.1　What are the abilities required in a good manager of data processing? Why is each of these qualities important? Where can such a man be obtained?

16.2　What are the abilities required in a good systems analyst?

16.3　Why are data-processing operations separated from systems development and programming?

16.4　What is the function of program co-ordination, and why is it important?

16.5　What is the best way to decide whether or not to acquire a computer?

16.6　What changes would be desirable in Figure 16–1 if only punched card equipment were used?

16.7　What changes would be desirable in Figure 16–1 if only small-scale electronic data-processing machines were to be used in connection with punched cards?

16.8　It is possible to decentralize systems analysis and programming to the user organizations. What problems might arise if this were done? What advantages might be obtained through this approach?

SUPPLEMENTAL READINGS

Aptitude Test for EDPM Programmers. Form Number 19–6762. New York: International Business Machines Corp., 1955.

This aptitude test, developed by the Psychological Corporation, has

---

[2] These and the following estimates are based upon figures in *Data Processing Survey* and *Use of Electronic Data-Processing Equipment* (see the supplemental readings).

been widely used in the selection of trainees for systems analysis and programming work.

CANNING, RICHARD G. *Installing Electronic Data Processing Systems.* New York: John Wiley & Sons, Inc., 1957.

This little book, based on the presentation of a case study, discusses the process of installing and using a large-scale electronic data-processing system. Chapters 2 and 3 include discussions of the organizational changes involved and of the personnel required. Appendix 2 presents the characteristics desirable in people filling various jobs in the data-processing organization.

CHAPIN, NED. *An Introduction to Automatic Computers.* Princeton, N.J.: D. Van Nostrand Co., Inc., 1957.

Chapter 2 discusses considerations involved in the efficient operation of electronic data-processing equipment.

Data Processing Manning Survey. Published by the Systems and Procedures Association. Also reprinted in *Datamation,* Vol. 4, No. 2 (March–April, 1958), pp. 31–33.

Presents the results of a survey concerning data-processing job descriptions, titles, and pay ranges in the New York City area.

Supervision of an Electronic Data Processing Machine Installation, 702–705 Customer Assistance Bulletin 2, New York: International Business Machines Corp., March, 1957.

Discusses organization of a data-processing center, staffing, and duties that must be performed for efficient use of the equipment.

Use of Electronic Data-Processing Equipment. Hearing before the Subcommittee on Census and Government Statistics of the Committee on Post Office and Civil Service (House of Representatives, 86th Cong.). Washington, D.C.: U.S. Government Printing Office, June 5, 1959.

This includes reports on the government requirements for data-processing specialists, salary scales, and the selection and training of people. Pages 100 through 120 include interesting comments on selection and training, including opinions concerning the use of aptitude tests.

CHAPTER **17** · Management Responsibility toward Information Technology

TO ANYONE who has had the experience of observing a large number of electronic data-processing installations, it is obvious that we are a long way from realizing the full potential of this powerful, new tool. It is by no means unusual to find comments such as the following:

> Out of a welter of exaggerated claims in the earlier years, there has been growing a more recent chorus of complaint. Costs were higher than had been estimated. Results fell far short of expectations. In a recent survey, a solid 40% of computer users talked of "disappointment."[1]

Most computer installations have turned out to be successful, but considerably less than spectacularly successful, and for each outstanding success, there is probably a miserable failure to provide a contrast. As an example, I visited a large-scale installation in which the basic justification for the computer lay in the area of inventory management. Yet the computer was being used merely to maintain inventory records about three weeks after the fact, management was thoroughly disillusioned, and the situation had deteriorated to the point where no attempt was being made to improve the admittedly unsatisfactory system.

Despite their rather spotty record of success, to my knowledge only one or two companies have reconverted from computer data processing to the previous system and returned the computer. In fact, computers continue to be installed at an ever-increasing rate. Their potential benefits are so obvious and portend such revolutionary possibilities for improved management control that almost everyone is convinced that the problems associated with their use must be overcome.

---

[1] "Special Report on Computers," *Business Week*, June 21, 1958, p. 70.

Thus, in this chapter we are concerned with two important questions: (1) What have been the major causes of failure in the use of electronic data processing? (2) How will the potential of the computer ultimately be realized?

In the first place, the failures have not generally been caused by poor machine performance. According to M. E. Salveson:

> Typically, the failures have not been due to inadequate or defective equipment. Rather they have been from inadequate preparation, insufficient understanding, or lack of participation by *all* levels of management.[2]

It is safe to say that no computer available today will assure success, or is there likely to be such a machine in the future. On the other hand, under the proper circumstances almost any machine obtainable from a reputable manufacturer can be utilized successfully.

As was discussed in Chapter 15, a number of problems must be solved to effectively utilize a computer. Usually, both human relations and organizational problems must be faced, and administrative ability may be taxed to the utmost by the over-all complexity of the changes necessary.

Piecemeal Approach

It is readily apparent that one does not often achieve spectacular improvements by merely inserting a powerful computer in the place of less powerful machines and humans without revising the over-all system. What is relatively efficient in a manual system may be quite difficult to produce with computers, while very desirable information that is too costly to produce through a manual system may be efficiently produced by a computer. Moreover, because of the characteristics of humans, it is difficult to centralize manual processing, thus manual systems are not likely to be well integrated. Unfortunately, most manual systems have just grown, they were not designed. Processing on a computer must be centralized, but the benefits of the potential efficiency are not achieved unless the system is redesigned so that it becomes truly integrated. To build an integrated system, it is necessary to make changes in input, processing, and output, and to reassess the fundamental information requirements of the organization.

One characteristic of most of the disappointing electronic data-

---

[2] M. E. Salveson, "Electronic Computers in Business," *The Journal of Industrial Engineering*, March–April, 1958, p. 104.

processing installations is the lack of a systems approach. Actually, this is probably a symptom rather than the fundamental problem, for usually no one sets out to create a fractured system. A piecemeal approach usually results from not specifying as an objective the achievement of an integrated system, from organizational problems, or from a lack of sufficient management participation in the planning and installation.

Also, a careful distinction must be made between objectives and tactics. In view of the immense problems involved in merely converting to computer processing, it may not be desirable to attempt to completely redesign the data-processing structure of the organization when the computer is installed. Thus, it may be rational to adopt the tactic of achieving an integrated system through a two-stage process: First, install the computer with only the system changes that are necessary and convenient; then, when the conversion has been accomplished, redesign the system, utilizing the knowledge obtained in the first step.

This tactic does not necessarily insure success, nor does it always lead to failure. But, in many of the failures, it is obvious that step one was attempted without realizing that step two would be necessary. The most depressing characteristic of these failures is the realization that management has given up the struggle to attain an effective system.

Lack of Objectives

One of the most apparent characteristics of the failures is that many of them have suffered from a lack of objectives from their very inception. The futility of such situations is expressed in *Alice in Wonderland* in the well-known conversation between Alice and the Cheshire Cat.

"Cheshire-Puss," she began, rather timidly—"Would you tell me which way I ought to go from here?"
"That depends a good deal on where you want to get to," said the cat.
"I don't much care where. . . ." said Alice.
"Then it doesn't matter which way you go," said the cat.[3]

A computer is a challenging and extremely glamorous piece of equipment, and, in a number of cases, one has been obtained primarily because someone wanted a computer. In other words, the major objective has been to obtain an electronic computer. This is a

---

[3] Lewis Carrol. *Alice's Adventures in Wonderland.*

relatively easy objective, but it does not necessarily lead to the attainment of anything else worthwhile, and, in the absence of more rational objectives, it may well lead to considerable unpleasantness.

Although one would think that a mistake of this nature would seldom occur, the indications are that even today there is still a strong tendency in this direction. For example, an extremely high percentage of feasibility studies result in the ordering of a computer. It is not difficult to justify the use of a computer if the persons preparing the justification want one, for rough estimates of present and future costs can easily be manipulated to prove almost anything. Frequently, the persons preparing the estimates have emotional, prestige, and financial interests in obtaining a computer.

As was mentioned previously, a lack of objectives almost inevitably results in a piecemeal approach to the mechanization of data processing, for to approach the use of a computer on a system-wide basis it is necessary to have the improvement of the entire data-processing system as a major objective.

It was emphasized in Chapter 15 that both organizational and human relations problems can lead to failure in the use of electronic data processing. Perhaps the major blame for the widespread adoption of the piecemeal approach must be placed upon these problems, for in very few organizations is it possible to take a systems approach, because of organizational problems and personal empires.

Quality of People Required

As has been repeatedly pointed out in the preceding material, the computer is merely a tool that must be used creatively to provide valuable results. Consider the most spectacular triumphs of the computer described in Chapter 1. Whether it be in science, engineering, automatic control, management science, or data processing, it is apparent that each achievement of a computer should actually be credited to someone who analyzed a problem that did not at first appear to be suitable for solution by use of a computer and devised a way to use the capabilities of the computer to solve that problem. Very seldom does a routine, straightforward approach lead to spectacular results. Perhaps one of the major advantages of the use of the computer is that the analysis of exceptionally creative people can be substituted for the performance of the average clerk.

Not only does the use of a computer provide the opportunity for spectacular success, but it also presents the possibility of equally spectacular failure. Thus, in the use of the computer there is no place for the person with mediocre capabilities. When we talk about the need for people, we do not mean bodies. It is much better to have 5 excellent people than 50 average people. And this is true of everyone involved, including the manager of the installation, the systems analyst, the programmer, and even the console operators.

Management Participation

In Chapters 15 and 16, the administrative problems involved in the installation and use of a computer have been discussed. If not solved, these problems can easily lead to failure in the use of the equipment. It is often said that it is impossible to successfully install a computer without the support of top management. This statement is obviously true. However, it is likely that this statement has frequently been misinterpreted. It does not merely mean that top management must want a computer—it is easy to want a computer, and it is equally easy to not want a computer later on when the problems involved begin to arise. Top management must understand the implications involved in the use of the computer before the word "support" has its proper meaning in the above statement.

In this text a number of problem areas have been pointed out, any one or a combination of which can lead to failure. These problems have not been highlighted to provide guideposts by which one can achieve failure with a minimum of delay—there is no need for such assistance. The concern is with making effective use of electronic data processing, and such success is not likely to occur unless management has been forewarned concerning these problems before a computer is installed.

Thus, one ingredient of success appears to be an understanding on the part of management of the role of data processing in the organization and of the capabilities and limitations of the computer as a tool for data processing. Another important factor in success must be a widespread participation by all levels of management in the design of the data-processing system. A systems analyst, no matter how competent, cannot set the objectives of the entire organization or of its separate parts. This is the job of management. No systems analyst can be trusted to redesign the organization to conform to a computer. A systems analyst cannot set policy—he must incorporate management policy into the system. And no systems analyst can specify what information is to be used to make specified decisions—management must participate in the specification of systems requirements.

All of the above requires widespread concern by management. Either the information system of an organization is of importance to the success of the organization or it is not. If it is not important, there is not likely to be sufficient reason to seriously consider a computer. If data processing is vitally important to effective management control, then the concern and attention of management in the design of the system is imperative, whether a computer is used or not.

Of course, even with the active participation of management it is not easy to design an effective data-processing system for an organization. It is remarkable how little is actually known about organizations and how they work. The fundamental question concerning what information is required for best management control is most difficult to answer at the present. To indicate how long-run progress in this direction may be made, a topic that is closely related to the use of computers will be considered next.

Operations Research

The words "operations research" refer to the use of the scientific method and advanced mathematical and statistical techniques in the solution of management decision problems. Frequently referred to as "management science," "operations analysis," or "quantitative analysis," operations research and the concepts and techniques associated with it are becoming of increasing importance to management. It is possible to trace the history of the use of the scientific method to solve management decision problems back through Frederick W. Taylor and Thomas A. Edison to ancient Greece and the contributions of Archimedes to the defense of Syracuse. However, not until World War II, when teams of scientists were formed into operations research groups to study the problems associated with the use of new weapons systems, did the idea that the scientific method could be applied to the complex problems associated with the management of organizations began to achieve widespread acceptance.[4] Thus, the development of the use of operations research parallels that of the electronic computer, and the two are closely interrelated.

---

[4] For a history of these developments, see F. N. Trefethen, "A History of Operations Research," *Operations Research for Management,* J. F. McCloskey and F. N. Trefethen (eds.) (Baltimore: Johns Hopkins Press, 1954).

Decision Problems

Decision problems have the characteristics shown in Figure 17–1.[5] First, there must be a decision maker. This decision maker may be an individual, or it may be a small or large group. The decision maker must have one or more objectives, such as profits, employee good will, or community service, which he wishes to attain in as large a measure as possible by means of the decision. For a decision problem to exist, there must be at least two, usually many, courses of action which may be chosen by the decision maker. The fundamental characteristic that distinguishes one decision problem from another is the environment or the situation involved. Finally, although it is conceded that certain courses of action will be more effective in attaining the decision maker's objectives than others, there must be some uncertainty concerning which of the courses of action should be chosen.

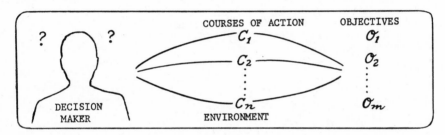

FIG. 17–1.

Basically, the scientific method consists of three steps: (1) observation, (2) formulation of a hypothesis explaining the result observed, and (3) testing of the hypothesis to determine whether or not it adequately explains the situation observed. These three steps are repeated over and over as long as flaws can be found. It should be noted that the testing is of fundamental importance, for much of the progress of science is motivated by the discovery that the presently accepted law or theory is inadequate.

Mathematical Models

In most complex situations, the hypotheses of science are expressed in the language of mathematics. Thus, one of the basic concepts associated with operations research is that of the mathe-

[5] See C. W. Churchman, R. L. Ackoff, and E. L. Arnoff, *Introduction to Operations Research* (New York: John Wiley & Sons, Inc., 1957), pp. 107–14.

matical model—a system of equations which represents an abstraction of the situation being studied. A mathematical model expresses in numeric form the relationship between the courses of action and the attainment of the objectives. In this process, each course of action frequently is represented by the assignment of a specific set of values (over which the decision maker has control) to the variables involved in the mathematical model.

Once the mathematical model expressing the relationships between the variables and the objectives is developed, it can be solved for the values of the variables which best attain the decision maker's objectives. It should be noted that the mathematical model is an abstraction of reality, not reality itself. It includes only the essential and excludes the trivial. As can be seen in Figure 17–2, a solution to the mathematical model is derived and is applied to the situation in the real world. The extent to which this solution to the mathe-

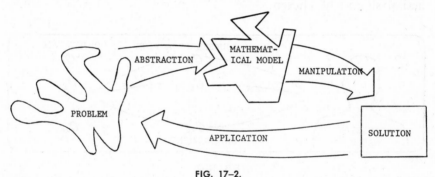

FIG. 17–2.

matical problem is also a solution to the real problem depends upon the model builder's success in achieving a faithful representation of the real world situation through his mathematical model.

In terms of the scientific method, the mathematical model represents the hypothesis. Mathematical models are not good merely because they are mathematical models per se; they are useful only if they adequately represent the situation involved. Thus, the third step of the scientific method, that of testing the hypothesis (mathematical model) to determine whether or not it adequately represents reality, is an essential part of the concept of quantitative analysis.

One of the most interesting consequences of the use of mathematical models is the surprising revelation that problems which appear to bear no resemblance to one another are essentially quite similar. For example, a problem of combining various grains to form an animal feed with a specified analysis may be quite similar to the problem of deciding upon the most profitable product mix to manufacture under known demand and under various capacity restrictions. And the problem of deciding whether or not to hire another machine repairman is, mathematically speaking, similar to the problem of determining how many check-out lanes should be provided in a supermarket.

One of the factors explaining the recent explosive growth of the use of quantitative analysis has been that in recent years several powerful mathematical models have been developed which have been found to be applicable to complex management decision problems. Incidentally, contrary to the popular conception, a mathematician (to another mathematician) is not one who is skillful at manipulating figures and solving problems which exist in textbooks. The mathematician is one who can create new mathematics,[6] and this is his main interest. Mathematics is a rapidly growing and expanding field, for during the past 50 years more mathematics has been created than the total that existed prior to that time, and the creation of some of this new mathematics has been motivated by attempts to analyze management decision problems. Some of this new mathematics is not yet taught in typical college mathematics courses, even on the graduate level, so workers in this area have to be capable of learning it on their own.

Among these new mathematical areas that have been important in quantitative analysis have been linear programming, dynamic programming, the theory of games, queueing theory, statistical decision theory, information theory, and servomechanism theory. Also, such older areas of mathematics as calculus, calculus of variations, set theory, matrix theory, differential equations, difference equations, and the theory of probability have been of great importance.

Simulation

One of the most powerful of the newly developed techniques is called *simulation*. Through simulation the performance of an organization (or some part of an organization) can be represented over an extended period of time. This is accomplished by devising mathematical models to represent each component part of the organization, while linking these models together to account for the interrelationships between these various components. An electronic

---

[6] For an interesting introduction to mathematics as it is viewed by the mathematician, see G. A. W. Boehm, "The New Mathematics," *Fortune*, June, 1958.

computer may be used to progress step by step through short intervals of time, pausing at the end of each interval to compute the interactions between components. Thus, it is possible to obtain a history of the performance of the organization under specified conditions. By repeating the same process under other conditions, it is possible to compare results and decide which alternative is most desirable. Thus, we are able to experiment with changes in the organization or with various decision rules without actually affecting the day-to-day operations of the organization being studied. For the first time organizations can be studied in the laboratory under controlled conditions where changes can be made and alternatives tested at relatively small cost.

One of the most interesting uses of simulation is in the study of job-shop operations.[7] Two major problems in this area have received a great deal of attention from management scientists, operations researchers, and industrial engineers.

The first of these problems is associated with the common situation in which many operations on different jobs must be performed on a number of machines that are at least partially interchangeable, but with the cost varying with the particular type of machine used. If each job were assigned to the most efficient machine for that job, some machines would be overloaded and others idle. Thus, it is usually impossible to assign each operation to the most efficient machine, and the problem becomes one of deciding which operations to assign to each of the machines in order to minimize the total cost of doing all the work. Good results have been obtained by applying the mathematical technique of linear programming to this problem.

The second problem is in scheduling. In a situation where the various jobs involve separate operations on different machines in a fixed sequence, the difficulty is in deciding when to perform each operation to most effectively use equipment to meet the completion schedules for the individual jobs. This is a complex problem because as soon as the shop load approaches a substantial percentage of theoretical capacity, conflicts arise in which two or more jobs are waiting for a single machine while other machines are idle. Although it appears that a simple enumeration of the possible schedules should suffice to solve this problem, the number of possible combinations is so astronomically large that the fastest electronic

---

[7] This illustration is reprinted from E. W. Martin, "Simulation in Organizational Research," *Business Horizons*, Fall, 1959.

computer in existence could not evaluate them all within the time available. Further, no mathematical model that produces a practical short cut has yet been devised for deciding on an optimal schedule.

In the language of operations research, this problem may be considered as a complex queueing or waiting line problem involving both series and parallel service facilities. The queues consist of jobs that are waiting for an operation to be performed on a particular machine. These queueing problems have been studied by use of a simulation technique to test proposed decision rules for deciding which of the waiting jobs to perform next on each machine.[8] If such rules can be devised to operate a shop more efficiently than it is currently being operated, then the rules may be applied by a computer in an automatic production control system.

A job-shop simulation usually involves the use of an electronic computer with an input of a sequence of jobs, each of which is to be released to the shop at a certain time. Each job is represented by certain information, such as the job number, the sequence of operations to be performed, the standard machine time for each operation, the due date for completion of the job, the value of the job, and any other information that is to be used in the decision rules being tested.

Associated with each machine group in the simulated shop is a waiting line of jobs to be processed. By progressing step by step through short intervals of simulated time and examining the status of each job and machine group at the end of each interval, the computer is able to apply the decision rules to be tested in each situation where an operation is completed or a new job enters the shop. During this process, the computer can gather statistics on machine utilization, idle time, overtime used, average length of the waiting line, number of late jobs, or any other criteria that can be used to evaluate the various alternatives being tested.

Associated with each machine group is a "clock" that indicates the simulated time at which that machine will be free. Figure 17–3 shows a simplified sequence of steps that the computer goes through to simulate each time cycle. For simplicity, this block diagram omits the considerations involved in entering new jobs into the shop.

In block 1, the clock showing the earliest time of completion is

---

[8] Much of the pioneering work in this area has been done by Allen J. Rowe of the General Electric Company. See his article, "Computer Simulation Applied to Job Shop Scheduling," in the *Report of the System Simulation Symposium* held in New York City on May 16–17, 1957, published by the American Institute of Industrial Engineers.

selected, indicating that the machine associated with that clock is the next one to complete an operation. If this is the last operation on the job, a card is punched with statistics concerning that job. If

Computer Simulation of Time Cycles

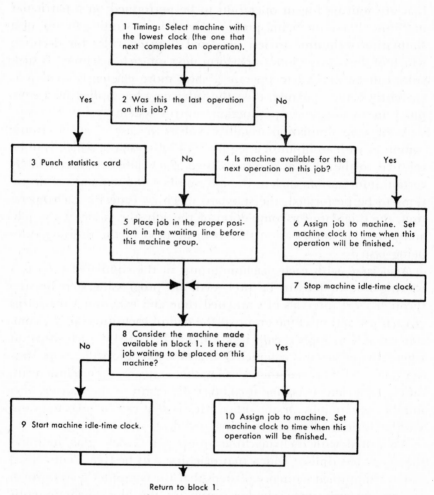

Return to block 1

SOURCE: A simplified version of the block diagram on page 8 of R. W. Conway, B. M. Johnson, and W. L. Maxwell, "The Cornell Research Simulator," mimeographed research report of the Department of Industrial and Engineering Administration, Cornell University, October 1, 1958.

FIG. 17–3.

other operations are to be performed on the job, blocks 4, 5, and 6 assign the job to the required machine if it is available or place the job in its proper position in the queue of jobs waiting for the required machine group. The processing for the particular time period on that job is then completed, so through blocks 8, 9, and 10 the computer can assign a job to the machine that was made available by the original completion of an operation in block 1. The process is repeated by selecting the next lowest clock, indicating the next event of importance, and so on.

The major interest in this process may be focused on block 5, for in the process of assigning a job to a place in line any priority rule or procedure devised may be used. Thus, many such rules may be tested to discover one that provides highest efficiency in the operation of the shop. Furthermore, by altering the number and types of machines available as well as the rules for releasing jobs to the shop and for assigning due dates, the results obtained by various combinations of circumstances may be investigated.

The major limitations on the complexity of the shop that may be handled are the size of the memory of the computer and the ability of the person designing the simulation to characterize the factors involved. Indeed, it is possible that progress in understanding such organizations may consist of a sequence of ever more accurate simulation representations of the situation. In other words, the simulation itself, rather than a word description or a mathematical model, may become the representation of understanding.

Incidentally, this is one of the very few computer simulations in which there is an available computer program that may be used by separate organizations to study entirely different situations. Generalized job-shop simulators, designed to be readily specialized to the particular situation being investigated, have been written for the IBM 704 and the IBM 650 electronic computers and may be used by anyone who has the ability to use either of these machines.[9]

Monte Carlo Technique

Random variations are characteristic of many organizational situations. For example, although the average time between breakdowns may be known, machines require emergency maintenance at unpredictable intervals. Customer orders and deliveries, the weather, results from advertising and research and development, absenteeism, and the occurrence of coronary occlusions all exhibit

---

[9] For the IBM 650 simulation, see the source of Figure 17–3. For the IBM 704 simulation, see "Job Shop Simulation Application," distributed in mimeographed form by the IBM Math and Applications Department, Data Processing Division, White Plains, New York.

unpredictable random variation. In many situations, not only are random fluctuations characteristic of the process but also this unpredictable randomness is so essential that the common simplifying technique of using average values simply "assumes away" the problem, for without the randomness, there is no problem. Whenever uncertainty is an essential consideration in a simulation, the Monte Carlo technique may be utilized.

In the job-shop scheduling problem, the standard operation time used for planning purposes is only an average time, whereas the actual operation may take significantly more or less time than the standard. In a real shop, the standard time can be used for plan-

Time Distribution

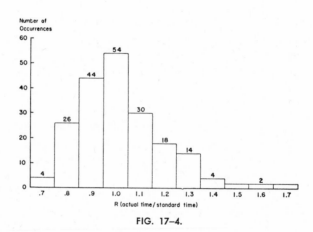

FIG. 17–4.

ning purposes, but the actual time consumed by an operation is not known until after the operation is completed. Thus, in blocks 6 and 10 of Figure 17–3, it is necessary to involve random variations in the determination of how long it will take to complete a particular operation on the machine involved.

Consider how this problem in the simulation might be handled by use of the Monte Carlo technique. Each time an operation is scheduled on a machine, we wish to determine an actual operation time based on the standard time but involving the realistic variation that occurs in actual practice. If R represents the ratio of actual time to standard time, then actual time can be found by multiplying standard time, which is known, by R. Thus, to utilize the Monte Carlo technique in handling this variation from standard time, a statistical distribution of R is used. In the absence of theoretical considerations, it is possible to approximate this distribution by analyzing past experience. Assuming that there are 200 observations of scheduled time and actual time, a histogram of the number of occurrences of each ratio (Figure 17–4) may be plotted.

The histogram may be transferred into a frequency distribution by dividing each of the graphed values by the number of observations (200, in this case) and converting to a percentage to obtain the experimental probability of each ratio (Figure 17–5).

Frequency Distribution

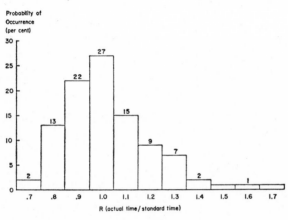

FIG. 17–5.

Table 17–1 may then be constructed from this information, so that the table intervals corresponding to each value of R are equal to the percentage probability associated with that value of R. For example, from Figure 17–5, the percentage probability that R equals 1.0 is 27, while the interval 37 to 63 includes 27 numbers.

To use the Monte Carlo technique to simulate random fluctuations, it is necessary only to have access to a random sequence of two-digit numbers (Table 17–2), each of which may be used with Table 17–1 to determine a specific ratio of actual time to scheduled time.

For example, starting with column 2, Table 17–2, and reading down, the first number is 73. Referring to Table 17–1 gives R as 1.1, so the actual time would be 1.1 times the standard time. The next number is 20; R is 0.9, so the actual time would be 0.9 times the standard time.

By continuing to draw random numbers for use with Table 17–1 to determine the corresponding value of *R*, a pseudo history can be accumulated that in the long run will have the same statistical char-

Time Distribution

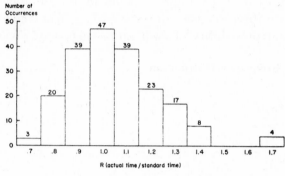

R (actual time / standard time)

FIG. 17–6.

acteristics as the sample from which Figure 17–4 was derived, while the individual occurrences that comprise this pseudo experience are

Monte Carlo Technique

Random Number	Ratio
0-1	0.7
2-14	0.8
15-36	0.9
37-63	1.0
64-78	1.1
79-87	1.2
88-94	1.3
95-96	1.4
97	1.5
98	1.6
99	1.7

TABLE 17–1.

characteristically random. An example of pseudo experience derived in this way from the use of Table 17–1 and a sequence of 200 random numbers is graphed in Figure 17–6. Although there is a marked similarity in appearance between Figures 17–4 and 17–6, they are by no means identical. This should not be surprising, for the distribution of any other sample of 200 actual observations should not be expected to be identical to the first sample.

When a machine time is required in the job-shop simulation of blocks 6 or 10 of Figure 17–3, the next number in Table 17–2 would be used with Table 17–1 to determine a value of *R* that would be multiplied by the standard time to obtain the actual time required.[10]

---

[10] Random digits may be obtained from some chance device, such as spinning a perfectly balanced wheel with equally spaced digits or by reference to published tables of

In any situation in which random variations are of importance, the Monte Carlo technique is utilized in the simulation to provide suitable random occurrences. This technique is frequently used in several places in a single simulation.

Random Numbers

36	73	18	13	03	15	36	19
42	20	51	14	94	53	12	79
98	49	11	59	16	27	09	37
50	84	01	16	74	33	90	85
71	73	94	89	29	95	58	63
55	42	81	98	35	37	28	07
28	51	33	52	23	54	75	05
01	12	42	27	48	49	91	72
26	38	86	34	16	96	84	68
36	00	04	38	92	89	06	26

SOURCE: *Produced by the author by a squaring method.*

TABLE 17–2.

Advantages of Quantitative Approach

One of the major advantages associated with the quantitative approach is that we are forced to explicitly consider the objectives to be obtained, the various factors under the control of the decision maker, and the interrelationships between these factors and the attainment of the objectives. In situations involving many factors and several objectives (which are frequently in partial conflict with one another) an intuitive solution arrived at under the pressure of other day-to-day management problems may be considerably less effective than the solution arrived at through quantitative analysis. Although the intuition of a manager is frequently remarkably powerful, the intuitive solution has often been proved to be extremely poor.

On the other hand, the understanding of the structure of the problem and the factors relevant to its solution, rather than the actual solution itself, frequently provides the greatest benefit obtained through operations research. Thus, once a thorough understanding of the factors and relationships involved in the problem is obtained, an intuitive solution based upon this understanding may be quite satisfactory.

---

random digits, which are also available in punched card form. Alternatively, suitable random digits may be generated by the computer itself by using one of several mathematical techniques that produce sequences of digits that satisfy all tests of randomness.

Limitations of Operations Research

There are, of course, many practical difficulties involved in the use of quantitative analysis to solve problems of the complexity of those facing management. For example, quantification, the process of assigning numbers to intangibles such as employee or customer good will, or of assigning a dollar cost to an item being out of inventory for a certain period of time, frequently requires great ingenuity. The people using these techniques must be intelligent, possess good judgment, and have a broad knowledge of the capabilities and limitations of the various mathematical techniques, along with a high degree of ingenuity and creativity. Furthermore, they must be able to communicate with management in both directions, for not only must they understand the problem as expressed by the decision makers, but they must also be able to explain the solution and how it was obtained, for the decision maker retains the responsibility for the decision itself. People with these capabilities are hard to find, especially since few educational institutions offer extensive training in this area.

Furthermore, it should be emphasized that the use of the scientific method implies that research is the paramount consideration. Thus, obtaining understanding is the objective of the process, and the management problem which may be solved through use of this understanding is only the motivation, although admittedly it is of great importance because it pays for the process. Thus, the technique is not suitable for fighting fires, for effective research takes time, and it cannot be overly hurried and still be good research. Also, this implies that the decision maker himself (or the manager) cannot perform the basic analysis of the problem even though he may be skilled in the use of the techniques involved, for he is neither able to take the time required nor to view the problem in a purely objective manner. But he does have a responsibility for communication with the specialist, and he should have enough knowledge of management science to understand the basic potentials and the limitations of the quantitative approach.

The Computer's Contributions to Operations Research

The electronic computer is a powerful tool for operations research. Indeed, a computer is frequently indispensable, for several of the large mathematical models are to all practical purposes unsolvable unless a computer is available. For example, it has been necessary to simplify many linear programming problems by eliminating or combining some of the variables to bring the problem down to a size that could be solved with the most powerful electronic computer available. Were it not for the computer, the technique of simulation would be of relatively minor interest, rather than the most powerful approach that has been developed in the past decade.

The existence of a computer makes it economically feasible to perform the voluminous computations involved in deriving solutions from complex mathematical models. As an illustration of the change that has taken place, consider the cost of performing one million multiplications. A million multiplications, performed by a human using a desk calculator, would take about 5 years and cost about $25,-000. On an early scientific computer, a million multiplications required 8 minutes and cost (exclusive of programming) about $10. On the LARC, one million multiplications require 8 seconds and cost about 50 cents.[11]

On the other hand, one should not imply that the presence of a big computer is a necessity if the techniques of operations research are to be used, for many of the most fruitful studies have not utilized a computer. In fact, the most aesthetically satisfying results are those which reduce the solution of seemingly complex problems to the use of rather simple and straightforward decision rules. Furthermore, in the over-all course of the study of a problem, the part in which a computer might be required comprises but a relatively small portion of the total time and effort. And since the problems tend to be of a one-of-a-kind nature, rather than repetitive like a payroll, it is usually satisfactory to utilize computing service bureau facilities when the need arises.

Large amounts of data processing, however, are frequently involved in a quantitative analysis study when historical information must be analyzed to formulate the relationships involved in the mathematical model and to determine the values to be substituted into the formulas obtained. This data-gathering phase of the study is frequently time consuming and expensive, and is considerably simplified if the required information is recorded in a form in which it may be processed by a mechanized system. Unfortunately, however, this is almost never true, even if the company involved utilized punched cards or electronic computers, for the information required is seldom available from the data routinely processed.

---

[11] This illustration is presented by A. S. Householder in "Solving Problems with Digital Computers," *Computers and Automation*, July, 1956.

However, the presence of a computer frequently is a powerful motivating factor in the use of the techniques of operations research in an organization, for not only does it attract into the organization men who have an interest in quantitative techniques, but it also interests management in the mathematical approach. Management is likely to reason thusly: We have this extremely powerful computer; let's use it to solve some of our difficult problems.

Contributions of Operations Research to Data Processing

The contributions that operations research may make to data processing are not quite so obvious as the above, but are likely to be of even greater importance in the long run. As discussed earlier in this chapter, the basic question involved in data processing (and the one for which it is most difficult to obtain a satisfactory answer) is: What information should we process to control a complex organization? Actually, operations research in a particular problem area frequently results in an answer to this question. To construct a mathematical model, it is necessary to specify the variables involved and the relationships between them. Numbers must then be substituted for the variables, and the data-processing system must produce these numbers.

The information desired after quantitative analysis is frequently quite different from that provided by traditional data-processing systems. It is not unusual for such a study to demonstrate that the data usually processed are not adequate for proper decisions or control. For example, Forrester[12] has indicated that, under certain conditions, factory warehouse inventory and shipment information may be quite inadequate for planning production, and many inventory control studies have demonstrated that various overhead costs must be accounted for by individual item to provide a true picture of the situation.

Furthermore, it appears that operations research might be applied directly to the study of the information problems of the organization, as a more sophisticated approach to systems analysis. Thus, the techniques of quantitative analysis would be focussed upon the information-processing (or control) problems of the entire organization. Actually, many operations research studies that started with other specific problems have ended by studying the information flow within the organization, for information flows are the sinews that tie the components of the organization together.

---

[12] See J. W. Forrester, "Industrial Dynamics—a Major Breakthrough for Decision Makers." *Harvard Business Review*, July–August, 1958.

This is not intended to imply that quantitative analysis provides an automatic answer to the fundamental question of what information to process, but it appears to be one of the most promising approaches yet devised. It is unfortunate that operations research has not been applied in this area more frequently, for some of the money spent to acquire computers probably could have been more effectively used to analyze the basic problems of the organization. Computers have likely been obtained to solve problems that do not require them for their solution, or that will not be solved by use of a computer until someone gets around to analyzing the problems to determine how they may be solved.

Thus, the combination of electronic computers and quantitative analysis may prove to be more powerful than either of them alone. Expressed in the phrase "information technology," this combination may well lead to gradual improvements in the efficiency with which organizations can be managed, and thus over a period of time exert a significant influence upon our concepts of management, the structure of our organizations, and the economy itself.

Incidentally, the increasing importance of information technology may well increase the difficulties facing small firms in their competition with large ones. This is not merely a problem of the volumes of information necessary to justify the use of a computer, for computers are being reduced in size and costs to the point where they can be utilized with relatively modest volumes. Rather the difficulty is that the information technology problems of the small business may be as complex as those of the larger, but the small organization may not be able to support the staff research effort necessary to solve these problems.

Effect on Management

Perhaps the most important management question concerning the use of a computer in an organization is: What will be the effect of electronic data processing upon me? Of course, the answer to this question depends upon many circumstances. Obviously, managers that are directly associated with the computer will be significantly influenced by the challenges involved in the use of this equipment. They will become more important if the installation is a success, and they may be adversely influenced by failure.

But what about those managers who are not directly associated with the equipment? Assuming that the installation is successful, what are the management qualities whose importance will be emphasized as a result of utilizing a computer?

The utilization of an electronic data-processing machine is likely to emphasize the importance of the ability to formulate plans. To utilize a computer, it is necessary to decide beforehand what information is required. Moreover, this "planned" information must be adequate for the use for which it is intended. Furthermore, management by exception requires the development of comprehensive criteria by means of which the exceptions can be isolated for management attention. The success of the management by exception principle depends in large measure on the effectiveness of the planned criteria in isolating those (and only those) situations in which management action is required.

More emphasis will be placed on the ability of a manager to take effective action to correct the exceptional conditions detected by the machine, since less management time will be devoted to the task of skillfully analyzing large masses of data to determine the conditions that need attention. More emphasis will thus be placed on the ability to determine the proper action to take and to see that this action is effectively carried out.

Speed in making decisions will become more important. According to Don G. Mitchell, Chairman of the Board of Sylvania Electric Products:

Electronic equipment will separate the men from the boys in top management. Heretofore, a person not ready to commit himself has been able to defer decision making on the grounds that he needed more facts. With modern equipment the facts will be available and executives will have to act without excuse for delay. The competitors will have the same facts at the same time; thus decisions will have to be made immediately.[13]

Perhaps the major motivation for installing an electronic computer lies in the area of providing higher-quality information for management to use in controlling the organization. This immediately implies that management must be interested in making decisions on the basis of quantitative factors. If the machine is to be a success, management must desire to have and actually use the results provided by the machine. Conversely, the most successful managers within such an organization are likely to be those that make the most effective use of quantitative information. Furthermore, the presence of an electronic computer is likely to encourage the development of operations research or management science groups within the organization and thus lead to the utilization of some pow-

---

[13] Quoted from Robert M. Smith, "Decentralized Management Not Threatened by Data Processers, AMA Told," *Office Management*, April, 1955, p. 18.

erful and sophisticated mathematical techniques in the area of decision making.

This does not imply that the manager of the future must be an expert mathematician. However, the manager who understands the techniques and limitations of the scientific approach and who can communicate successfully with specialists in these fields will likely be more successful than those who cannot.

The successful use of a computer, and the associated rise in the emphasis on information technology, is likely to increase the importance of staff activities at the expense of middle management. In the long run, information technology may have an important effect upon the structure of management, as expressed in the following significant prediction.[14]

1. Information technology should move the boundary between planning and performance upward. Just as planning was taken from the hourly worker and given to the industrial engineer, we now expect it to be taken from a number of middle managers and given to as yet largely nonexistent specialists: "Operations researchers," perhaps, or "organizational analysts." Jobs at today's middle-management level will become highly structured. Much more of the work will be programmed, i.e., covered by sets of operating rules governing the day-to-day decisions that are made.

2. Correlatively, we predict that large industrial organizations will recentralize, that top managers will take on an even larger proportion of the innovating, planning, and other "creative" functions than they have now.

Finally, it is apparent that the use of an electronic computer is not a panacea to cure poor management. As a matter of fact, it takes excellent management to successfully utilize an electronic computer, and the management attributes emphasized by the computer are already of great importance to management success. Thus, the use of a computer is likely to make good management better and poor management more apparent.

EXERCISES

17.1 What advantages may be achieved through the systems approach to data processing?

17.2 Discuss the reasons why it is difficult to implement the systems approach to data processing.

---

[14] H. J. Leavitt, and T. L. Whisler, "Management in the 1980's," *Harvard Business Review*, November–December, 1958.

17.3   What are the major reasons that contribute to failure in the use of computers?

17.4   Why is the quality of people so important to the success of electronic data processing?

17.5   Why is it necessary to have top-management support to successfully install a computer?

17.6   Why is it necessary to have the participation of all levels of management to effectively utilize electronic data processing?

17.7   What is operations research?

17.8   What is a mathematical model, and what is its relationship to operations research?

17.9   What is a decision problem?

17.10   What are the contributions of the computer to operations research?

17.11   What are the contributions of operations research to the design of a data-processing system?

17.12   What is information technology and what long-range impact is it likely to have upon management?

17.13   What is likely to be the effect upon an individual manager of the installation of a computer in his organization?

SUPPLEMENTAL READINGS

BOEHM, G. A. W.   "The New Mathematics," *Fortune,* June, 1958.
    An excellent and interesting presentation of modern mathematics and of the attitudes and motivations of theoretical mathematicians.

BROSS, IRWIN D. J.   *Design for Decision.* New York: The Macmillan Co., 1957.
    A presentation for the intelligent layman of the major ideas of modern statistical decision theory.

GAUMNITZ, R. K., and BROWNLEE, O. H.   "Mathematics for Decision Makers," *Harvard Business Review,* May–June, 1956.
    Presents the importance of mathematics in decision making and some of the implications for the future.

LEAVITT, H. J., and WHISLER, T. L.   "Management in the 1980's," *Harvard Business Review,* November–December, 1958.
    A very significant article discussing the implications for the future of the growing importance of information technology.

WILLIAMS, J. D.   *The Compleat Strategyst.*   New York: McGraw-Hill Book Co., Inc., 1954.
    An interesting and witty nonmathematical presentation of some of the basic ideas of two-person, zero-sum game theory and its relationships to competitive decision making.

MARTIN, E. W.   "Simulation in Organizational Research," *Business Horizons,* Fall, 1959.

Presents several illustrations of the use of simulation in analysis of organizational problems, and discusses the importance of this method of analysis.

Operations Research for Management. Joseph F. McCloskey and Florence N. Trefethen (eds.), Baltimore: The Johns Hopkins Press, 1954.

This book includes an excellent history of the development of operations research, presentations of several of the important techniques, and several case histories of the early uses of operations research.

RAUNER, R. M. "Laboratory Evaluation of Supply and Procurement Policies (Unclassisfied Version)," R-323. Santa Monica, Calif.: RAND Corp., 1958.

This little book describes a combination man-computer simulation of the Air Force supply system and the results of the simulation runs.

SOLOW, H. "Operations Research in Business," *Fortune,* February, 1956.

An excellent discussion of operations research and its use in decision making. This article includes several illustrations of various uses of operations research and emphasizes its relationship to the role of the manager.

APPENDIX A · Operating the 650

SO THAT some of the exercises included in Chapters 6 and 7 can be debugged and run on the 650, the following discussion presents the rudiments of operation of the 650 read-punch unit and the console. The console allows communication in both directions between the operator and the machine. Thus, the operator can instruct the machine through manipulating the switches and pressing buttons, and through its lights the machine displays the contents of its registers and indicates normal and abnormal conditions that arise.

Each switch and button has its purpose, and they frequently must be used together. Satisfactory results are not obtained by random button pushing—specified sequences of operations must be followed to operate the machine. If the machine stops unexpectedly, the lights should be examined and the contents of the registers written down before the buttons are pushed, for use of the buttons may destroy this important information. The following presents step-by-step procedures which are useful in running and debugging programs. Further information is contained in the 650 manuals, but should difficulties arise that require more than the use of a trace routine or the following procedures, the assistance of an experienced machine operator should be obtained.

Preparing the Read-Punch Unit

In the first place, make sure that the proper control panel has been inserted in the end of the read-punch unit and locked in place by closing the door over it. The power switch on the right end of the read-punch unit must be on. The left-hand lights and buttons on this unit are associated with the read feed and those on the right are associated with the punch feed.

To prepare the read feed, carefully align the cards to be read, place them face down with the 12-edge of the cards toward the machine, and cover them with the plastic weight. If there are four or more cards, press the read-start button, which will cause the first three cards to be fed into the machine and the unlabeled light to go out. If there are less than four cards, simultaneously press the read-start and end-of-file buttons, and the cards will feed into the machine.

To prepare the punch feed, first take out any cards in the feed mechanism, and then hold the punch-start button down for four cycles, so that all cards may be removed from the punch stacker. Then place blank cards in the feed, face down and 12-edge first, cover them with the plastic weight, and depress the punch-start key, which will feed two cards into the machine.

The Console

On the top of the console are located the power control switches (see (1) on Figure A–1). Since it is customary to leave the machine on all day, these buttons should never be manipulated except by those who work in the installation. Below the power controls are the display lights (see (2) on Figure A–1), which display the contents

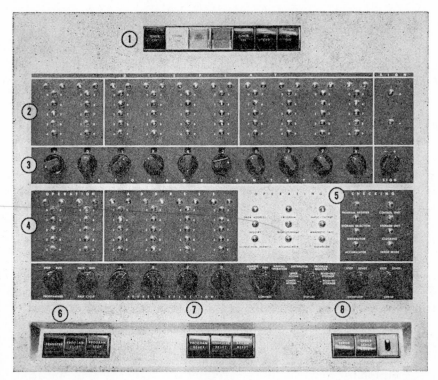

FIG. A–1.

of registers and drum locations under control of the display switch. The storage entry switches (see (3) on Figure A–1), located under the display lights, may be used to enter a ten-digit number and its sign into the machine to be used as data or as an instruction.

The operation and address lights (see (4) on Figure A–1) display the contents of the operation and address registers. The operating and checking lights (see (5) on Figure A–1) indicate the function being performed or the component in which an error has been detected. If the machine stops, these lights indicate why it stopped and what it was doing at the time.

The switches in the next row are used to control the status of the machine. Unless otherwise specified in the following procedures, these switches should be set as follows: programmed switch to stop; half cycle switch to run; address-selection switches as desired; control switch to run; display switch to program register; overflow switch to stop, unless the program uses the *Branch on Overflow* instruction, in which case, it should be set to sense; error switch to stop.

To Label Drum

Some of the most common errors in writing programs result in the machine going for an instruction to a drum location in which the programmer has not placed an instruction. This can occur because of an oversight or because of a clerical error in writing the instruction address. If a previous program was left on the drum, the machine would execute all or part of that program, which might produce confusing results. Thus, it is desirable to clear the drum of old programs before loading a program that is to be debugged.

In addition to removing old programs, it is helpful if the machine can be made to stop whenever it gets off the track as previously discussed. This can be accomplished by a drum-labeling program that inserts in each drum location the number 01 xxxx 9999 −, where xxxx is the location itself. Whenever the machine goes to such a location for an instruction, the machine stops with 01 xxxx 9999 in the program register, thus informing the operator where it was sent by mistake.

Labeling the drum in this way may be accomplished by the following steps:

1. Set the storage entry switches to 70 0004 9999 +.
2. Insert the drum-labeling card in read feed and read it into the machine by simultaneously depressing the read-start and end-of-file button.[1]

---

[1] A single card contains the program to label the drum.

3. Press computer reset (see (7) on Figure A–1).
4. Press program start (see (6) on Figure A–1).

When the machine stops, the drum has been labeled, and the program may then be loaded.

To Load a Program

Each installation has a standard single-word loading routine that uses a specific input block. Let the first word in this block be denoted by xxxx (which must end in 01 or 51). Then the program can be loaded by the following sequence of steps:

1. Place the program deck in the read feed as described in the section on preparing the read-punch unit.
2. Set 70 xxxx 9999 + in the storage entry switches.
3. Push the computer-reset button.
4. Push the program-start button.
5. The machine will stop when out of cards with part of the last card visible in the read feed. Press the end-of-file button. The read-start button may then be depressed to run the last card into the stacker, and the program cards may be removed.

To Start and Run a Program

After preparing the read-punch unit, there are two ways that may be used to tell the machine where to find the first instruction of the program. One of these uses the storage entry switches:

1. Set the storage entry switches to 00 0000 xxxx +, where xxxx is the location of the first instruction of the program.
2. Press the computer reset button. This clears the machine registers and inserts 8000 (the address of the storage entry switches) in the address register.
3. Press the program-start button. This takes the number in the storage entry switches as the first instruction, which merely transfers the machine to the location of the first instruction of the program.

The storage entry switches are frequently used for other purposes. In such cases, the address of the first instruction may be placed in the address register by the following procedure:

1. Set control switch on manual.
2. Set address-selection switches to the location of the first instruction to be executed in the program.
3. Press the computer-reset button.
4. Press the transfer button. This places the contents of the address-selection switches in the address register.
5. Set the control switch to run.
6. Press the program-start button.

When the read feed runs out of cards, the machine will stop with part of the last card visible in the feed. If additional cards are to be processed, place them in the hopper and press the read-start button. If there are no additional cards to process, those still in the machine may be processed by pressing the end-of-file button. To remove the cards from the punch hopper, the blank cards must be removed from the punch feed and the punch-start key must be held down for three or four cycles. Then the cards that have been punched, and one blank card, may be removed from the stacker.

To Stop the Program at Any Point

In debugging, it is frequently desirable to stop the machine at a specific program step so that the results at that point may be examined:

1. Set the control switch to address stop.
2. Insert the address at which the machine is to stop in the address-selection switches.
3. Press the program-start button.

With the control switch in the address-stop position, the machine stops when the address in the address register becomes the same as the contents of the address-selection switches. At this point (before the execution of the instruction designated by the address-selection switches), the registers may be displayed in the display lights by setting the display switch in the desired position. To follow through a few instruction steps, set the half-cycle switch to half. Then each time the program-start button is depressed, the data address or instruction address portion of an instruction is executed. To continue the program, the half-cycle switch should be returned to the run position, the address-selection switches may be set at the next desired location and the program-start button depressed.

To Examine Any Drum Location

With the machine stopped, any drum location may be examined by the following procedure, which destroys the contents of the distributor:

1. Set address-selection switches to the address of the location to be examined.
2. Set control switch on manual operation.
3. Set display switch to read-out storage.
4. Push program-reset button.

5. Push transfer button.
6. Push program-start button.

The contents of the drum location can then be read from the display lights. Before the program can be restarted, the display switch must be set on some position other than read-out or read-in storage.

Those who are familiar with the 650 console will note that the above does not mention manually inserting numbers in memory. Numbers should be inserted by using single-word load cards.

APPENDIX B · Tracing Routines

TRACING routines are used in debugging to reduce the necessity of the slow process of cycling programs through one step at a time by means of the console switches. Trace routines take over control of the program and punch a card for each instruction executed, showing the instruction, its location, and the contents of the machine registers.

A number of trace routines may be used with the 650, and since they differ in the details of their operation, the following does not attempt to present the details of operation of these programs. A detailed write-up of the trace used in each installation is available in the program library or console book of the installation. The purpose of this appendix is to illustrate the ideas and problems involved in trace routines themselves.

First, the trace routine and the program being debugged must be in the machine memory together. Therefore, a sufficiently large block of memory must be available to hold the trace routine. Typical trace routines require blocks of 50, 100, or 150 words, and an installation usually has its trace routine available in versions that can fit into any block starting with 0000, 0100, 0200, 0300, and so forth. The program is loaded first, and then a trace routine is loaded that does not conflict in memory locations with the program.

Before starting the trace routine, it must be informed where the first instruction to be traced is located. In the simple 50-word trace discussed below,[1] this location must be entered by means of the console switches into the tenth word of the trace band. Then the machine is started at the first word of the trace band.

The block diagram of Figure B–1 reveals some of the interesting characteristics of a trace. For example, the trace routine must break the instruction to be traced down into its components and substitute

---

[1] A slight simplification of an early selective trace routine distributed by IBM.

a dummy instruction address so that control is returned to the trace after the program is executed. If the instruction is a branch instruction, a dummy data address must also be substituted or the trace would lose control if the program branched. This breaking down of the instruction must be done in the accumulator, which destroys the contents of the accumulators and the distributor at the end of the previous instruction. Thus, these registers must be restored after the instruction is modified for execution but before it is executed.

Furthermore, the trace routine must create an instruction to obtain the instruction to be traced. This also destroys the contents of the accumulators and distributor. But the 650 can execute instruc-

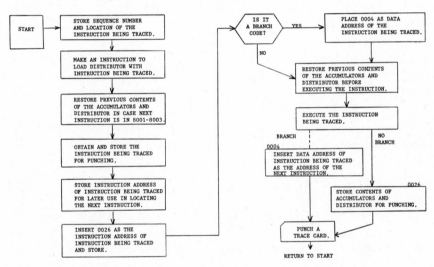

FIG. B-1.

tions from these registers, so they must be restored before the instruction can be obtained.

It should be noted that the trace routine illustrated here does not properly trace load cards, for the read instruction is not treated as a branch instruction. Also, it does not restore the proper sign to the upper accumulator after a division in which the quotient and remainder have different signs. This is why most traces require more than one memory band (50 instructions).

The above tracing routine operates at 100 instructions per minute. For long programs, this routine is intolerably slow. It is usually possible to search efficiently for errors by examining the results of relatively few instructions. "Snapshot" trace routines are available that allow all but these designated instructions to be executed at normal speed. Thus, only the interesting instructions are executed at tracing speed. The snapshot trace routine modifies the program before tracing begins by substituting for each selected instruction one that takes the machine to the designated instruction stored as a part of the trace routine itself. After that instruction is executed and traced, control is again returned to the main program which runs at full speed until the location of another designated instruction is reached.

APPENDIX C · Binary Notation and Arithmetic

TO PROVIDE as fast an arithmetic unit as possible for a given cost, many scientific computers (such as the IBM 704 and the Remington Rand Univac Scientific) operate on numbers expressed in binary notation. The usual notation for writing numbers is called decimal notation, and the value of a digit is based upon the position in which the digit occurs. In the number 957, the 9 does not really represent the number 9, it represents 9 times 100. Likewise, the 5 represents 5 times 10. Thus, 957 is actually $9 \times (10)^2 + 5 \times (10) + 7$. You must know the position in which a digit appears in the number to properly interpret its meaning. Each time we move one position to the left the value of that position is multiplied by 10, thus progressing from the units position to the tens position to the hundreds position to the thousands position, and so forth.

Numbers may be written in several ways. For example, twenty-seven may be written as 27 in decimal notation or as XXVII in Roman numerals. In the usual positional notation discussed above, the number ten is called the *base* of the notation. Ten is used as the base of our notation because we happen to have ten fingers. However, any other number could be used, and in different civilizations both twenty and sixty have been used. Mathematically, it might be more convenient to use twelve instead of ten, for dozens would be easier to express, and fewer fractions would have repeating decimal equivalents (such as $1/3 = .3333. \ . \ . \ .$).

To express numbers in a notation with n as the base, single digits for each number from zero to $n - 1$ are required. Thus, in the decimal system, the digits 0, 1, 2, 3, 4, 5, 6, 7, 8, and 9 are required. If twelve were used as the base, two extra symbols would be required to represent ten and eleven. Thus, we might denote ten by τ and eleven by ϵ, providing the digits 0, 1, 2, 3, 4, 5, 6, 7, 8, 9, τ, ϵ. Then, in base

411

twelve, 10 would represent twelve, 11 would represent thirteen, 1т would represent twenty-two, 1є would represent twenty-three, and 20 would represent twenty-four.

In the binary system of notation the number two is used in place of ten as the base of the positional notation. Since only the digits less than the base number are required, in binary notation we only use the digits 0 and 1, and each number is expressed as a string of zero's and one's. For example, the number five is written in binary notation as 101, $1 \times (2)^2 + 0 \times (2) + 1$, while the number 100 written in binary becomes 1100100, $1 \times (2)^6 + 1 \times (2)^5 + 0 \times (2)^4 + 0 \times (2)^3 + 1 \times (2)^2 + 0 \times (2) + 0$.

Binary to Decimal Conversion

Given any binary number, it is easy to translate it into decimal form by the following process: Start with the rightmost digit. If this is a 1, write it down. Then, working toward the left, the next position represents 2, the next 4, the next 8, and so on doubling each time. Whenever a one is encountered, write down the corresponding positional value. At the conclusion of this process, add them all up. For example, for the binary number 1101001011101 we would have:

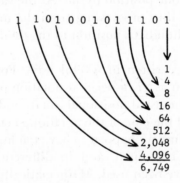

Decimal to Binary Conversion

The process of translating a number from decimal notation into binary is a bit more complicated. One method involves dividing the decimal number by 2 and recording the remainder, then dividing the quotient by 2 and recording the remainder, and continuing this process as illustrated below for the number 6,749 (start at the top and work down):

Remainder

2	6749	
2	3374	1
2	1687	0
2	843	1
2	421	1
2	210	1
2	105	0
2	52	1
2	26	0
2	13	0
2	6	1
2	3	0
2	1	1
	0	1

Then, reading the remainder column from the bottom, in binary notation 6,749 is represented as 1101001011101.

Binary Calculations

If one can forget what he knows of decimal arithmetic binary arithmetic is extremely simple. The addition and multiplication tables, involving only the digits zero and one, are shown below:

Addition	Multiplication
$0 + 0 = 0$	$0 \times 0 = 0$
$0 + 1 = 1$	$0 \times 1 = 0$
$1 + 1 = 10$	$1 \times 1 = 1$

Addition takes place digit by digit, starting from the right. For example, consider eleven plus seven in binary notation:

$$\begin{array}{r} 1011 \\ 111 \\ \hline \end{array}$$

Starting at the right, $1 + 1 = 10$, so we put down the zero and carry 1.

$$\begin{array}{r} 1 \\ 1011 \\ 111 \\ \hline 0 \end{array}$$

Then $1 + 1 = 10$, and $10 + 1 = 11$, so we put down 1 and carry 1.

$$
\begin{array}{r}
1 \\
1011 \\
111 \\
\hline
10
\end{array}
$$

At this point $1 + 0 = 1$, and $1 + 1 = 10$, so we put down zero and carry 1.

$$
\begin{array}{r}
1 \\
1011 \\
111 \\
\hline
010
\end{array}
$$

Finally, $1 + 1 = 10$, so we obtain:

$$
\begin{array}{r}
1011 \\
111 \\
\hline
10010
\end{array}
$$

To check, in decimal notation the binary number 10010 becomes eighteen, which is eleven plus seven.

Suppose we wish to multiply 1011 by 101.

$$
\begin{array}{r}
1011 \\
\times\ 101
\end{array}
$$

The multiplication is easy, since we merely multiply by 0 and 1 to obtain partial products as shown below:

$$
\begin{array}{r}
1011 \\
101 \\
\hline
1011 \\
10110
\end{array}
$$

To complete the multiplication we must add these partial products to obtain 110111. As a check, 1011 is eleven and 101 is five, while 110111 is fifty-five.

Octal Notation

Octal notation, using eight as the base, is convenient for interpreting binary numbers. Since eight is close to ten, it is relatively easy to convert our thinking to the use of octal notation. Also, by dividing the digits into groups of three, binary numbers may be converted to octal notation. Thus, those who use binary machines frequently program in octal notation, and desk calculators which calculate in octal notation are available for their use.

To convert the binary number 1101001011101 (which is 6,749 in decimal notation) to octal, we separate the digits into groups of three, starting at the right: (1) (101) (001) (011) (101). Then interpreting each group as binary representation of a single digit, we produce the octal number 15135. As a check, inserting the powers of eight, this number represents $1(8)^4 + 5(8)^3 + 1(8)^2 + 3(8) + 5$, which is $1(4,096) + 5(512) + 1(64) + 3(8) + 5 = 4,096 + 2,560 + 64 + 24 + 5 = 6,749$.

APPENDIX **D** · Floating Decimal Representation

ANY NUMBER can be placed in a standard form with the decimal point in a specified position and the actual location of the decimal point indicated by multiplying by a suitable power of 10. In this notation, negative exponents (which indicate division by the corresponding power of 10) move the decimal place to the left, while positive exponents move it to the right, as shown below.

$$.0000125 = .125 \times 10^{-4}$$
$$.000125 = .125 \times 10^{-3}$$
$$.00125 = .125 \times 10^{-2}$$
$$.0125 = .125 \times 10^{-1}$$
$$.125 = .125 \times 10^{0}$$
$$1.25 = .125 \times 10^{1}$$
$$12.5 = .125 \times 10^{2}$$
$$125 = .125 \times 10^{3}$$
$$1250 = .125 \times 10^{4}$$
$$12500 = .125 \times 10^{5}$$

Numbers expressed in the above standard form, in which a power of 10 is multiplied by a number with the decimal point to the left of the first nonzero digit, are said to be in floating decimal notation. Arithmetic operations may be performed with floating decimal numbers by using rules that produce the result in floating decimal form.

For multiplication and division, these rules are simple. For example, to multiply $.125 \times 10^4$ by $.200 \times 10^{-2}$ we multiply $.125 \times .200 = .0250$ and $10^4 \times 10^{-2} = 10^2$ to obtain the answer $.025 \times 10^2$. However, because the decimal point is not to the left of the first nonzero digit, we must move it to the right and adjust the exponent to obtain $.25 \times 10^1$. As a check, $.125 \times 10^4 = 1250$, $.200 \times 10^{-2} = .002$, and $.25 \times 10^1 = 2.5$. Since $1250 \times .002 = 2.5$, the results are correct.

The major advantage of floating decimal notation is in division, which can be set up so there is no danger of quotient overflow, since both numbers have the same relative magnitude except for the exponents. As an example of division, consider $.625 \times 10^{-7}$ divided by $.125 \times 10^{6}$ Since $.625 \div .125$ is 5 and $10^{-7} \div 10^{6}$ is 10^{-13}, the result is $5. \times 10^{-13}$, which must be adjusted to obtain $.5 \times 10^{-12}$.

Addition and subtraction are more complicated in floating decimal notation because the decimal points must be lined up (by making their exponents the same) before these operations can be performed. For example, $.625 \times 10^{-3} + .125 \times 10^{-4}$ can be expressed.

$$\begin{array}{r} .6250 \times 10^{-3} \\ .0125 \times 10^{-3} \\ \hline .6375 \times 10^{-3} \end{array}$$

Whenever the exponents are widely different, this adjustment requires a lot of shifting.

Arithmetic units may be constructed to compute directly with numbers in floating decimal form, and automatic programming techniques (floating decimal subroutines or interpretive routines) may be used to compute with these numbers. Computing in floating decimal form makes programming of complex computational problems much easier, for it is not necessary for the programmer to keep track of the decimal point and program the shifts required by the computations. On the other hand, the programmer may have little knowledge of how many figures are significant in results computed by means of floating decimal arithmetic.

Most scientific computers have instructions available (as standard or optional features) that compute with floating point numbers. Because of the shifting involved, floating point addition and subtraction are slower than the corresponding fixed point instructions, but floating point multiplication and division are usually faster than the fixed point operations.

Both the number and the exponent are usually stored in the same word. Since the number itself and the exponent both have signs which may be different, in decimal machines the notation is modified by adding 50 to the exponent so that exponents from -50 to $+49$ may be expressed by the positive numbers 00 through 99. There is no uniformity in floating decimal notation among various computers and automatic programming systems, but one notation places the number (up to 8 digits) in the first 8 positions of the word and the modified exponent in the rightmost 2 positions. In such a machine, the number $-125,000,000,000$ (which is $-.12500000 \times 10^{12}$)

would be stored as 1250000062−, while the number +.0000000125 (which is +.12500000 × 10⁻⁷) would be stored as 1250000043+.

Input and output may be in floating decimal form, or conversion back and forth between fixed and floating notation may be programmed. The programmer must know which locations contain floating point numbers and which contain fixed point numbers, for erroneous results are produced by computing with fixed point numbers by means of floating point instructions or vice versa.

Index

A

Access arm, 281–83
Access time, 87–88, 102
Accounting machine, punched card, 55–58
Accuracy, control of, 45, 194–96, 297–98, 372
Ackoff, R. L., 31, 383
Activity ratio, 270–72
Adder, single-digit, 104, 109
Address, 87, 92
Airlines reservations application, 303–4
Alphabetic sorting, 48
Alpha-numeric code, 222, 225
American Airlines, 303
American Bankers Association, 305
Analog computer, 85
Analog-digital conversion, 8
Andree, R. V., 135
Aptitude tests, programming, 369, 375–76
Argument, 151–53
Arithmetic unit, 89
Arnoff, E. L., 31, 383
Assembly program, 180
Audit trail, 260, 298
Automatic control; *see* Control, automatic
Automatic programming, 180–86
  assembly program, 180
  compiler, 184–86
  generalized sort, 257–58
  interpretive routine, 183–84
  regional, 180
  subroutines, 182–83
  symbolic, 180–82
Auxiliary equipment, 221

B

Bagby, W. S., 341–42, 359
Batch processing, 247–73
Batch totals, 45–46
Bell Laboratories System, 183, 198
Bell, W. D., 98, 310
Bernoulli principle, 282
Binary-coded-decimal representation, 224–25
Binary numbers, 225–26, 301–2, 411–14
Binary search, 152–53
Biquinary notation, 103–4

B (continued in column 2)

Bit, 103, 223–25
Bit structure; *see* Character code
Block diagram, 120–21, 172–78
Block sort, 48
Boehm, G. A. W., 385, 400
Branching, 92–94, 223
Break-even point, 356–57
Bross, I. D. J., 400
Brownlee, O. H., 400
Buckingham, W., 359
Buffer
  magnetic tape, 239–42, 286–87
  punched card, 102–3, 117–20, 278–80
Burroughs Corporation
  Datafile, 288–90
  Datatron 205, 106–7
Business games, 11

C

Calculator, punched card, 61–63
Calling sequence, 183
Canning, R. G., 31, 333, 359, 376
Chaining method, 294–97
Channel search, 278, 295
Chapin, N., 31, 98, 197, 376
Character code, 86
  alpha-numeric, 222, 225
  binary-coded-decimal, 224–25
  biquinary, 103–4
  excess three, 224–25
  self-checking properties of, 103–4, 222–25
  two-out-of-five, 224–25
Checks, processing of, 304–6
Churchman, C. W., 31, 383
Class of total, 57
COBOL, 185
Coding
  of computer programs, 175–80
  of identifications, 27–28
Collation sequence, 222–23
Collator, 53–55
Communication, need for, 17
Compiler, 184–86
Computers
  classification of, 306–9
  decision to acquire, 330–31, 348–51, 364–65

Computers—*Cont.*
  history of, 2
  site preparation for, 351–52
Console operator, 373–74
Control, automatic, 7–10, 18–22, 323–25
Control of computer, 89–90
Control panel, 49–51, 280, 283–84
Control punches, 33–34
Control word, 142
Conversion to computer, 190–92, 352–54
Conversion routine, 161
Cordiner, Ralph J., 1
Costs
  accounting for, 374
  estimation of
    computer applications, 194, 262–66, 349
    punched card procedure, 76–80
  pattern of, 354–58
Counter, 55, 58
Craig. H. F., 359
Creative thinking, 327–28, 380–81
Curry, R. B., 360

D

Data address, 105
Datafile, 288–90
Data processing
  cost of, 328–30, 354, 358
  management of, 363–68
  profit from, 328–30
  purpose of, 19–23
  value of, 328–30
Debugging, 186–90, 404, 408–10
Decentralization, effect of computer on, 346–48
Decimal point, programming for, 124–30
Decision problem, 383
Decision rule, 386–89
Detail printing, 57–58
Detroit Edison, 340
Diebold, John, 359
Digital computer
  definition of, 85
  structure of, 86
Direct access files; *see* Random access files
Dual card, 70

E

Elliott, J. D., 340–41, 360
End-of-file procedures, 234–35, 238
Engineering design, 5–7
Eniac, 2
Equipment, selection of, 330–31
Errors, detection of, 235–37; *see also* Character code *and* Accuracy, control of
Excess-three notation, 224–25

F

Feedback; *see* Control, automatic
Field, definition of, 36
File
  machine processable, 88–89
  maintenance of, 267–69
  random access, 88, 276–98
  reference to, 29, 268–69
  sequential access, 88
  updating of, 29
File Computer, 277–80, 291–93
Floating decimal point, 131, 302, 416–18
Flo-matic, 184
Flow chart; *see* Procedures flow chart
Ford Motor Company, 3
Forms control, 60–61
Forrester, J. W., 22, 396
Fortran, 184–85
Fortransit, 198
Franklin Life Insurance Company, 270
Function, in table, 150–53

G

Gang punching, 52
Gaumnitz, R. K., 400
Generalized sort routine, 257–58
Grad, Burton, 333
Gregory, R. H., 275, 311, 333
Grid chart, 315–17
Group control, 56–57, 138–41
Group printing, 57–58
Gruenberger, F., 190
Guest, L. C., 347
Guetekow, H., 18

H

Heuristic problem solving, 12–13
Hoos, I. R., 342, 360
Hopper, G. M., 197
Householder, A. S., 395
Human problems, 335–42

I

IBM punched card machines, 38–66
IBM *305 RAMAC*, 283–85
IBM *604*, 61–63
IBM *650*
  characteristics of, 99–143
  instructions, 105
    add and subtract, 112–16
    branching, 136–42
    division, 127–30
    input-output, 117–22
    multiplication, 122–24
    shifting, 124–25
    store, 112–13, 117
  operation of, 402–7
  RAM Files on, 285–88

IBM *650—Cont.*
  registers of, 108–10
Identifying information, 27
Index register, 153–55, 302–3
Information, patterns of flow, 24–26
Information, representation of; *see*
  Character code
Information retrieval, 12
Information technology, 397–99
Initialization, 140–57
Input devices, 86–87
  buffering of, 102–3, 117–20, 278–80
  card reader, 102–3
  off-line, 243
  on-line, 243, 304
Instruction, 90–91
  address of, 92
  address within, 91–92
  modification of, 94–95, 143–50
  operation code, 90–91
  single-address, 230
  synthesis of, 147–50
  three-address, 130–31
  two-address, 130
Instruction address, 105
Instructional constant, 148–49
Insurance applications
  fire and casualty, 207–11
  life, 266–70
Integrated data processing, 23–24
Intermediate total, 57
Internal sort, 255
International Business Machines Corporation; *see* IBM
Interpreter, 52–53
Interpretive routine, 183–84
Inventory control application, 258–66,
  290–93
Iterative procedure, 215–19

J

Jewett, G. G., 220
Job shop scheduling, 293–94, 386–92

K

Kami, M. J., 344
Kettering, C., 80
Key punch, 38–40
Key, in sorting, 47–48, 248–50
Key verifier, 43–44
Kircher, P., 31
Kozmetsky, G., 31

L

La Motte, L. H., 338
Language Translation, 11–12
Laubach, P. B., 360
Lear, John, 3
Leavitt, H. J., 399–400

Lee, Tsai-Hwa, 197, 275
Linear equations, solution of, 215–19
Linear programming, 10, 386, 394–95
Listing, 57–58
Load card, 119, 158
Loading program, 157–61, 405
Logic theorist, 12–13
Logical operations
  in computers, 89, 94
  in data processing, 29–30
Looping, 143–47, 154

M

McCracken, D. D., 197, 275
Magnetic core, 88, 226–28
Magnetic disc file, 281–88
Magnetic drum, 88, 100–102, 277–80
Magnetic ink character reading, 305–6
Magnetic tape, 231–39
  blocks on, 232
  labels on, 238
  length of record, 232–33
  processing of, 246–66
  sorting of, 248–58
  start-stop time, 232
Maintenance
  of equipment, 355
  of programs, 370
Major total, 57
Management by exception, 19–20, 259,
  325, 398
Management science, 10–11, 382–97
Management support, need for, 381–82
Manufacturing control application, 293–94
Mark sensing, 40–41, 70
Martin, E. W., Jr. 11, 386, 400
Master card, 52
Matching, 54
Match-merging, 55
Mathematical model, 383–85
Mee, J. F., 333
Memory, 87–88
  access time of, 87–88, 102
  allocation of, 121
  magnetic core, 88, 226–28
  magnetic drum, 88, 100–102
  word, 87
    address of, 87, 92
    contents of, 92
Merging, punched card, 53–54
Microsecond, 226
Middleton, Marshall, Jr., 7
Millisecond, 102
Minor total, 57
Mitchell, D. G., 398
Mitchell, James P., 359
Monte Carlo technique, 389–93
Multiprogramming, 272–73
Murray, Philip, 335

N

Newell, A., 12–13

O

Objectives, 19–20, 379–80
Octal numbers, 414–15
Operation code, 90–91
Operations research, 10–11, 23, 382–97
Optimum programming, 106; *see also* SOAP
Optner, S. L., 333
Order issuance, 20
Organizational considerations, 342–48, 362–75
Organized labor, reaction to computers, 335–36
Output devices, 89
    card, 117–22
    printers, 242, 284–85
Overflow, 141
Overhead cost distribution, 214–19

P

Paper tape, 42, 307
Parallel operation, 190–92, 352
Parallel recording, 101
Parity bit, 225
Payroll
    computer processing of, 3, 167–80
    punched card, 67–80
Planning chart, 110–11
Policy committee, 349, 365
Polya, G., 333
Port-A-Punch, 41
Prepunching, 40, 70
Principia Mathematica, 12
Problem definition, 166–67
Procedures analyst; *see* Systems analyst
Procedures, development of, 167–72
Procedures flow chart
    examples of, 74–75, 169, 318–20
    symbols for, 72, 318
Production recording equipment, 42
Program review committee, 368
Programming, automatic; *see* Automatic programming
Programming
    definition of, 110–11, 175–76
    linear; *see* Linear programming
Pseudo instruction, 183–85
Punched card,
    cost of equipment, 64
    description of, 33–34
    design of format, 35–37, 69–72
    machines, 38–66

Q

Quantitative analysis, 382–97
Quantitative information, 27

Quick-access loop, 106–7
Quotient overflow, 128, 130

R

RAM file, 281–88
RAMAC, 283–85
Randex, 281
Random access files, 88, 276–98
    addressing of, 294–97
    control of accuracy of, 297–98
Random numbers
    as file address, 295–97
    in Monte Carlo method, 391–93
Rauner, R. M., 401
Read-write head, 100–101, 231
Recording, 27–28, 38–47, 328
Redundancy bit, 225
Regional programming, 180
Remington Rand
    File Computer, 277–80, 291–93
    Randex, 281
    Solid State, 106–7
Rent-or-buy decision, 355
Report preparation, 30
Reproducing, 49–51
Requirements application, 200–207, 293
Reservisor, 303–4
Reuther, Walter, 335–36, 359
Reverse-digit sort, 47–48
Roehm, R. M., 267
Rowe, A. J., 387
Rowe, H. T., 9
Russell, B., 12

S

SAGE air defense system, 9–10
Sales analysis, punched card illustration, 80–84
Salveson, M. E., 378
Scheduling
    computers, 371
    punched card machines, 79–80
Scientific computers, 300–303
Scientific method, 383
Selden, L. M., 311
Selection of equipment, 330–31
Selector, 59–61, 142–43, 283–84
Self-checking
    numbers, 45–47
    properties of character codes, 103–4, 222–25
Serial recording, 277
Service bureau
    use for computing, 395
    use for peak loads, 79
Servomechanism; *see* Control, automatic
Shaw, J. C., 12

Shea, S. L., 360
Shonting, D. M., 197
Simon, H. A., 12–13, 18
Simulation, 385–93
Site, preparation of, 351–52, 356
Slater, R. E., 275
SOAP, 180–82
Solo, M. B., 360
Solow, H., 401
Sorter-collator, 257, 278
Sorting, 29
    key, 47–48, 248–50
    magnetic tape, 248–58
    punched card, 47–49
        relationship to accounting machine,
        57
    sequence, 222–23
Special-purpose equipment, 303–6
Sperry Rand Corporation; see Reming-
    ton Rand
Starbuck, William H., 360
Stone, L. D., 197
Stored program, 90–95
    capability of, 96–97
Subroutine, 182–83
Summary punching, 58–59
Switch, 155–57
Sylvania Electric Products Corporation,
    347
Symbolic programming, 180–82
Systems approach, 23–24, 313–15, 378, 379
Systems analysis, 23–26, 193, 312–32
    flow chart, 72–75, 169, 318–20
    grid chart, 315–17
    interviewing, 321–23
    operations research and, 396–97
    organization of, 365–71
Systems analyst
    selection of, 351, 369–70
    training of, 351, 368–69

T

Table look-up, 150–53
Tabulating, 58
Tait, R. C., 335

Tape bin, 288–90
Terry, George, 326
Test data, 188–89
Texaco Polymerization Plant, 8
Time, estimation of
    computer procedures, 262–66
    punched card procedures, 76–79
Toll-road equipment, 42
Tracing, 188–89, 408–10
Transaction, 26–27
Transaction register, 260, 261
Transmission of data, 28–29
Trefethen, F. N., 382
Two-way merge sort, 248–53

U

Unit record, 35
Universal automatic computer, 95–96
Utility billing application, 211–14

V

Van Auken, K. G., Jr., 3, 336
Van Deusen, E.L., 305
Van Horn, R. L., 275, 311, 333
Variable field length, 228–29
Variable word length, 228–29
Verification, 27
    punched card, 42–46
Visual verification, 44
von Neumann, J., 5, 94

W

Wallace, Frank, 361
Webber, Wallace, 336
Weber, C. E., 361
Weiss, Harold, 197, 275
Whisler, T. L., 399, 400
Whitehead, A. N., 12
Williams, J. D., 400
Word, 87
Wrubel, M. H., 198

Z

Zone punch, 33–34

*This book has been set on the Linotype in
11 and 10 point Baskerville, leaded 2 points.
Chapter numbers are in Spartan Heavy and
chapter titles are in Spartan Medium. The
size of the type page is 27 x 46½ picas.*